# Women, Ritual and Liturgy

# Ritual und Liturgie von Frauen

# Femmes, la liturgie et le rituel

*Yearbook of the European Society of Women
in Theological Research*

*Jahrbuch der Europäischen Gesellschaft für
theologische Forschung von Frauen*

*Annuaire de l'Association Européenne des femmes
pour la recherche théologique*

*Volume 9*

**Bibliographical information and books for review
in the Yearbook should be sent to:**
*Dr. Angela Berlis, A. van Nieuwenaarlaan 3A,
NL - 6824 AM Arnhem, The Netherlands*

**Articles for consideration for the Yearbook
should be sent to:**
*Dr. Charlotte Methuen, Ev.-Theol. Fakultät, Ruhr-Universität Bochum,
Universitätsstr. 150, 44780 Bochum, Germany*

# Women, Ritual and Liturgy

# Ritual und Liturgie von Frauen

# Femmes, la liturgie et le rituel

Editors:
*Susan K. Roll, Annette Esser & Brigitte Enzner-Probst*
*with Charlotte Methuen & Angela Berlis*

PEETERS - LEUVEN - STERLING, VIRGINIA

Library of Congress Cataloging-in-Publication Data

Women, ritual and liturgy = Ritual und Liturgie von Frauen / editors, Brigitte
Enzner-Probst ... [et al].
    p. cm. -- (Yearbook of the European Society of Women in Theological
Research; v. 9 – Jahrbuch der Europäischen Gesellschaft für Theologische
Forschung von Frauen)
    English, French, and German
    Includes bibliographical references (p. ).
    ISBN 9042910259
    1. Women and religion. 2. Women in public worship. 3. Ritual. I. Title: Ritual
and Liturgie von Frauen. II. Enzner-Probst, Brigitte, 1949- III. Jahrbuch der
Europäischen Gesellschaft für die Theologische Forschung von Frauen; 9/01.

BL458.W65 2001
291.3'8'082--dc21                                         2001032883

Yearbook of the European Society of Women
in Theological Research, 9

© 2001, Peeters Publishers, Leuven / Belgium
ISBN Peeters 90-429-1025-9
D.2001/0602/47
Cover design by Margret Omlin-Küchler

# INHALT – CONTENTS – TABLE DES MATIÈRES

# Foreword

Women and ritual, women and liturgy, women's celebrations, meditations, prayer services, womeneucharist, Morgenandacht or Abendandacht: each of these names expresses a different nuance, but all of them point to one of the most fascinating and encouraging new signs of development in women's theological research and spiritual praxis. In many different religious traditions a growing number of women are planning and leading public prayer and worship, whether in small groups or large public venues; by the same token women are claiming their own authority to gather a community in rite, song and proclamation. Women of course have always had some limited possibilities to plan and lead some form of group prayer or rite: to lead the praying of the rosary or to mourn and bewail the dead, to light the Sabbath candles or to open their local women's meetings with a short prayer in their own words. What is new and exciting today is the widespread recognition of the fact that being a *subject*, in other words an *agent*, of liturgy marks very clearly the full human dignity of women in the presence of the transcendent/immanent reality which guides and gives meaning to their lives, individually and collectively. When women carry out liturgy, the often sharply forbidding borders between the sacred and the profane which identify women with the profane and the "merely" material are made permeable, enabling both men and women to perceive more clearly the presence and action of the divine being, in whatever way they understand this divine being, in human relationships and in all of creation.

The contributors to this, the ninth Yearbook of the European Society of Women in Theological Research, have used some of these terms almost interchangeably, which may necessitate making some distinctions and describing convergences amongst them. For many English speakers, "liturgy" connotes an official act of a particular religious body, usually codified in books of prayer texts and readings which have the status of official policy for worship. "Ritual" on the other hand, may suggest any of a variety of different meanings: one of these is the technical term for one type of official liturgical book mentioned above, the "Roman Ritual." Another meaning is derived from anthropological or psychological research into human behaviour and its relation to culture and worldview; related to this is the emergence in the 1980s of the academic field known as Ritual Studies.

Still another meaning carries hints of "pagan" or old-religion worship, perhaps with an exotic, primitive or negative sense; and one more nuance is implied in the expression "empty ritual" to describe human or animal behaviour which appears to be habitual, repetitious and not of much practical use.

For speakers of German, the term *Ritual* might carry a more pronounced post-Christian, non-Christian colouration: an anthropological term used in the field of religious studies which thus encompasses a broader range of meaning. As Brigitte Enzner-Probst delineates the terms in her article (p. 79, note 1), the term "liturgical praxis" is used for the ritual Gestalt (the shape or form of ritualising) within Judaeo-Christian tradition, while the term "ritual praxis" is more used outside that tradition, or as one part of the post-Christian ritual movement. However the nuances of *Ritual* and *Liturgie* are fluid and overlap each other.

For some women, particularly if they feel alienated or oppressed by their religious tradition, using the term "liturgy" may feel as if they are cooperating with a strategy which has traditionally excluded and demeaned women; thus they would feel very uncomfortable speaking of what their groups are doing as liturgy. For other women, to speak of women doing liturgy means claiming legitimate authority for women's new worship and prayer forms, rather in the same way that the national and European women's synods have consciously adopted the ancient term "synod" to place their deliberative gathering in a direct line of ancestry with the synods of male religious leaders which have set policy and official teachings down through history. For some women, the term "worship" does not describe what they do, since it suggests self-abnegation before a supreme being constructed out of the presuppositions of patriarchy; for other women "worship" feels perfectly natural. For some women, the word "ritual" feels like a safe, neutral, non-threatening description of their gatherings as well as one which leaves a good deal of room for interpretation and creative structuring, while for others "ritual" is too weird, too off-putting.

A striking feature of the new praxis of women's groups is an increasing self-confidence in their own abilities to create meaningful symbols, enter into symbolic acts, write new texts, compose new music, design the shared worship space, and give voice to the lived experiences of women who too often throughout history have had no voice, or whose voice was not heard. For those whose research is in the field of liturgical studies, this phenomenon neatly contradicts the conventional whine of (mostly male) liturgists in the late 20th century that people are no longer *liturgiefähig*, or to put it another way, that "modern 'man' has forgotten how to celebrate": in other words, that technology, materialism and secularisation have robbed the general population of the ability to understand and deal with the symbolic mindset from which liturgy derives its depth and effectiveness. Instead, since in many cultural and religious contexts women as such have been explicitly excluded from equal participation in worship, including liturgical leadership, the growth and development of the women's liturgical movement shows clearly that women can and do hunger for self-expression in symbols and body involvement, in new texts and music, and in the emergence and correlation of new shared meanings. If there has been a marked decline in the credibility of the official liturgical acts of a number of religious traditions, and a truncation of their power to engage and transform their communities, perhaps part of the reason is that the marginal status of women and women's experience is becoming steadily more apparent, and that women's own experience finds very little echo in official liturgy. This may, at the very least, indicate a trend which must be taken seriously.

Each of the contributors to our Theme section is a scholar, pastoral leader or practitioner of liturgy in her own tradition, some in a situation which merges two or more of the classic (or perhaps newly rediscovered) European religious traditions. The introductory article summarises a dialogue about women and ritual today, carried out among a sampling of invited representatives of religious traditions and trends in Europe: Christian, Jewish, Muslim, and those who blend two or more strands in their life-experience, such as Christian with Hindu, or Jewish with Goddess spirituality. The participants have made an enlightening presentation of insights to each other, and to the extent possible have reacted to and interacted with each other's perspectives. While the range of Christian denominations represented is far less broad than the editors would have wished, nonetheless the dialogue marks a step forward in the incorporation of the Jewish, Muslim and pre-Christian religious traditions of Europe as full dialogue partners in a women-identified context.

In her article, "L'aspiration à une image de la liturgie," Denise J.J. Dijk presents some insights from her study of the Feminist Liturgical Movement in the Netherlands and in the United States, with particular attention to the contribution of the prominent American Protestant feminist liturgist Marjorie

Procter-Smith. Prof. Dijk's doctoral dissertation, which examines these issues in depth, was published in 1999 in the Netherlands as *Een beeld van een liturgie*. Teresa Berger, of German origin, a scholar in liturgical history and ecumenical theology, now Professor at Duke University in North Carolina (USA), explores the implications for women's new liturgical practice of the ancient axiom, *lex orandi, lex credendi* (the law of prayer precedes the law of belief, or more succinctly, liturgy gives form to theology). Nothing less than a new overall concept of what constitutes liturgical tradition is called for, if women are to emerge from invisibility. Brigitte Enzner-Probst shares the key insights from her recent Habilitation thesis concerning the role of the body in worship, a topic which she has presented in guest lectures overseas and at professional liturgy conferences. Drawing upon new women's liturgies in different contexts, Dr. Enzner-Probst distinguishes five ways in which the body is involved in worship, an aspect generally de-emphasized in conventional Christian liturgy in favour of verbal and auditory functions. She draws out the ecclesiological consequences of this body involvement toward a new understanding of Christian community as a "body of Christ." Annette Esser, a German woman completing her doctoral dissertation on women's spirituality in ecumenical perspective at the University of Nijmegen, looks for ways to encourage more dynamic dialogue between women artists and women doing research and praxis in new liturgies and rituals. Ms Esser was co-editor of the first volume of the ESWTR Yearbook (1993). Finally, Gabriella Lettini, an Italian woman completing her doctorate in systematic theology at Union Theological Seminary (New York), contributes an insightful examination of the concept of syncretism. Based upon her work with the World Council of Churches' 1994 study of the relationship between gospel and culture, Ms Lettini unravels the complexities of the relationship of Third World and First World churches and exposes the underlying traces of colonialism and patriarchy in the current discussions on syncretism in worship and rite.

Each of the contributors to our other sections, *Forum, Frauentraditionen* and *Aus den Ländern* brings forward new insights relating to different aspects of women in the rites and religious worldview of a particular denomination or tradition. In the section *Forum* Judith Hartenstein and Silke Petersen, two German Protestant theologians, describe some of the interesting problems in translation and adaptation of the texts of the Gospel of John for the new lectionary of the *Evangelische Kirche in Deutschland*. Caroline Vander Stichele follows this up with a presentation of the most recent discussion in the Netherlands over the Dutch translation of JHWH (HEER/Lord/Herr).

Two articles in the section *Frauentraditionen/Women traditions/Traditions des femmes* trace ancient cultic practices which have continued to influence liturgical practices directly affecting women today. Rosine Lambin presents her doctoral research on the meaning of the veiling of women in the early Christian church, and discovers links with the practice of sacrifice, marriage and cultic virginity in ancient Rome. Bettina Kratz-Ritter describes how ancient Jewish women's rites, rooted in folk religion and intended to protect the newborn child, were truncated in modern ritual practice by a process of cultural assimilation. Contemporary women competent in theology are working toward the renewal and development of rites consistent with a new Jewish women's spirituality.

The presence, broadly understood, of women in contemporary Christian worship is reflected in two articles in the section *Aus den Ländern/From the Countries/Des Pays*. Angela Berlis, theologian and priest in the Old Catholic church of Germany, tracks the evolution of the Old Catholic custom of the "Women's Sunday" service from 1920 to the present. The development of this service illustrates a shift from women as the object of special attention during this particular yearly service, to women as the active subjects organising the service itself, supported by the League of Old Catholic Women in Germany. Finally Charlotte Methuen shares a reflection on issues of power and authority raised by women's presidency at the Eucharist. To whom does the liturgy belong? The priest, the people, the local worshipping community, the global faith community? Women priests are invited to grapple with the challenge of sharing the power of liturgical presidency.

Our yearly section *Büchermarkt/Book market/Foire aux livres* lists a wide range of recently-published works of possible interest to readers of the *Yearbook*. The section *Rezensionen/Book Reviews/Critique des Livres*, among a wealth of significant new books, presents evaluations of several texts which are of particular importance for the field of liturgy and ritual in women-identified perspectives, including the books by Teresa Berger, Rosine Lambin, Rosemary Radford Ruether, Susan A. Ross, and Hanna Strack with Christiane Freking.

The editors of the Theme section wish to thank Charlotte Methuen and Angela Berlis, the ESWTR members responsible for the overall production and publication of the Yearbook; Ninna Edgardh and Denise Dijk who participated in the early stages of planning and offered helpful suggestions; Ruth

Huppert for her extensive assistance in proof reading the German articles; Annick Yaiche and Anneclaude Casse for translating several of the summaries into French.

*Susan K. Roll, Buffalo, NY*

**Susan K. Roll**, born in 1952, is Associate Professor of Liturgy and Systematic Theology at Christ the King Seminary, Buffalo, New York (USA). She completed her Ph.D. in the Faculty of Theology, Catholic University of Louvain (Leuven), Belgium, in 1993. She held the Walter J. Schmitz Chair in Liturgical Studies at the Catholic University of America, Washington D.C. in 1998, and in 2000 was the first Visiting Fellow at Sarum College, Salisbury, England. She is the author of *Toward the Origins of Christmas* (Kok Pharos: Kampen 1995), co-edited *Re-Visioning Our Sources* (Kok Pharos: Kampen 1997), and has published over 35 articles and 50 book reviews.

*Coletta Damm, Thalia Gur-Klein, Katerina Karkala-Zorba,*
*Laime Kiskunaite, Asphodel Long, Caroline Mackenzie and*
*Susan K. Roll*
*edited and commented by Annette Esser*

## A Dialogue on Women, Ritual and Liturgy

### Introduction

Based on 20 years of development in feminist spirituality – since *Woman-spirit Rising*[1] – and more than a decade of discussion about women's spirituality and experience of ritual in the context of the European Society of Women in Theological Research,[2] we regard the interest in and the praxis of women's ritual as one of the most fruitful, yet also most controversial, developments in feminist theology. Therefore, planning this *Yearbook*, we decided to offer an introductory article in the form of a dialogue among different women who represent diverse religious traditions and cultural contexts as well as different feminist (or non-feminist) positions within Europe. By asking them some basic questions, we hope to have shed light on notions, discussions, processes and perspectives of women's ritual and liturgy in Europe today.

Beginning with the ESWTR conference in Helvoirt, The Netherlands, in 1987, where it was not self-evident that women academics / feminist theologians would see themselves as "ritualizing women" or could agree on any kind of mutual ritual or liturgy, we have experienced a long process of growing interest in women's spirituality and participation in conference rituals and liturgies. Yet at the last conferences, in Crete, 1997, and Hofgeismar, 1999, we became aware that many European women theologians did not want to

---

[1]  Carol Christ / Judith Plaskow (eds), *Womanspirit Rising: a Feminist Reader in Religion* (Harper & Row: San Francisco 1992, 1979).

[2]  Annette Esser, "Along the Conferences: European Women Theologians Reflect Upon Spirituality and Celebrate Rituals," in: Annette Esser / Anne Hunt Overzee / Susan Roll (eds), *Re-Visioning Our Sources: Women's Spirituality in European Perspectives* (Kok Pharos: Kampen 1997), 11-33.

identify themselves as feminists, let alone share in the further development of feminist liturgies. The participation of increasing numbers of women from non-"Western" countries and non-"Christian" (or "Post-Christian") backgrounds was challenging for all involved: women theologians from Central and Eastern Europe (especially from the countries emerging from the former Soviet Union) and Greek Orthodox women were encountering these forms of feminist theology and practice as something new, and without having been involved in a long process of feminist-theological deconstruction and reconstruction; they felt at times that their own questions arising from their contexts were not being noticed or taken seriously enough by "Western" theologians from Germany, Britain or Scandinavia. On the other hand, "Western" women theologians were frustrated by the apparently uncritical celebration of an Orthodox liturgy using sexist language which they thought they had already deconstructed in their own gender-studies; they were also at times suspicious about whether Muslim women from Germany presenting their Islamic faith as an alternative to the Judeo-Christian tradition could truly speak out for a religion with an apparently heavy gender-bias and strong contempt for women. Although these conferences found practical solutions for a number of questions – such as the morning and evening celebrations / rituals / liturgies, which were simply made the responsibility of individual women – some questions, including those around women's ritual, were not discussed thoroughly, or, in some cases, really asked at all.

This article attempts to address that lack. Seeking to balance Eastern and Western Europe, younger and older women, and to span a range of inter-religious diversity, we invited women from a number of different cultural and religious backgrounds within Europe who have an interest in and a practice of some form of women's ritual or liturgy to enter into a dialogue with each other. Our contributors are:

*Asphodel Long*, a Jewish woman from Britain, who celebrated some of the first feminist rituals at ESWTR conferences, and may be reckoned one of the mothers of Goddess-spirituality in Britain. *Caroline Mackenzie*, also from Britain, an artist who has participated in many ESWTR conferences and celebrated rituals; her life and work in India transformed her art, making her aware of Hindu symbolism and female imagery. For Caroline, India also marked her initiation to Catholicism, which she interprets in the light of Eastern spirituality. The American theologian *Susan Roll* spent ten years living and studying dogmatics and liturgy in Belgium and now teaches in a Catholic seminary in New York State. She brings to the dialogue the enormous impact of American feminist theological discussion on women's ritual and liturgy. *Laime Kiskunaite* is a visual anthropologist and film-maker from Lithuania; her interest in and development of women's ritual within the context of Lithuanian women's movement is especially moving. *Katerina Karkala-Zorba*, a Greek Orthodox theologian and linguist, now co-president of the Ecumenical Forum of Christian Women, grew up in Germany and studied in France; her insights into Western thinking and her knowledge of and work for Orthodox women's tradition and spirituality make her a most valuable partner for the European discussion. *Coletta Damm* is a German psychologist and therapist who through Sufism found her way to Islam; the trust and support of her Muslim sisters have enabled her to participate in this academic dialogue. *Thalia Gur-Klein* is a Jewish cantor and theologian from The Netherlands whose understanding of Jewish mysticism and the Kabbalah are a most welcome contribution to the inter-religious perspective of this dialogue.

The first two questions we asked these women were:

*(1) What is women's ritual? What does ritual / liturgy mean to me?*

*(2) How do we celebrate it in our context and according to our religious tradition / feminist conviction etc?*

The responses to these first two questions were circulated to all the authors, and they were asked to respond to each other with the help of two further questions:

*(3) What are the similarities and differences between the various perspectives?*

*(4) What is the future development of women's ritual? How do you see it?*

This article brings together the seven authors' reflections on the first two questions. The second part includes excerpts from the further responses in a structured form. We conclude with an editorial evaluation of this dialogue.

### Asphodel Long

*What is women's ritual, what does women's ritual mean for me?*

When I was a child, in an Orthodox Jewish family, I was beset by two contradictory feelings about my religion. On the one hand, sitting in the synagogue gallery with the other women, I bitterly resented our exclusion from the "real service" conducted by the men below. On the other hand, when it came to parts of the service that affected everybody, most particularly the Kaddish for the dead, I, as a motherless girl, became part of the distinctive company of women mourners, who were weeping, passing around and using smelling salts, comforting each other. I had the feeling then that I was a woman among women, that we were connected, that despite my difficult family background, which generally left me feeling alienated, these moments of women mourning together put me in touch with a reality of suffering and hope that transcended every day difficulties. It seemed to make me one, not only with those around me but also with a long tradition of women mourning and comforting and gaining strength from each other. Looking back now, I see that at that time I sensed part of this strength lay in the ritual opportunity of mourning together rather than in individual privacy.

I am also reminded of another similar paradox. In family life and in the Jewish community I resented the primacy given to boys at the expense of girls, and its continuance into adult life. But the lighting of the Sabbath candles was women's – and only women's – business, and these were the most sacred moments of the week. I sensed something of a much stronger power among women than in everyday life, also, a community of women, going back into ages past shielding and sheltering with their blessing hands the sacrality of the Sabbath.

None of this was made explicit in day to day life; the women in my family – my stepmother, her mother and her sister – all apparently acquiesced in, and promoted, the norm of male supremacy in religion and in public life (although their opinion of men in private life fell into a much more critical stance). The rituals that appertained to women, which included keeping a strictly kosher house, obeying all the food laws, and managing the Festival meals, particularly at Passover and the High Holidays, were never portrayed as more than the common practicalities of women's duties.

So, the messages that came to me as a growing girl were mixed: on the one hand, women's interface with the sacred obviously formed the structure of the religion. On the other hand this was apparently deemed massively less important than men's leadership in religion and all other forms of public life. But underlying this paradox were the unuttered relationships of women together performing their sacred tasks, with the community of shared strengths and sufferings that their lives involved.

As a very young adult I left home, joined the world of work and politics and, as I thought, put religion and ritual behind me forever. This meant becoming a "secular Jew", joining the anti-fascist struggles of the 1930s and 1940s and later, through nearly three decades, working for a vision of a just society. This encompassed not only redistribution of wealth between rich and poor, but most particularly a vision of gender equality. Whatever the success or otherwise of the former, the latter was certainly as far away as ever; further, it was noticeable that women were subjected to new forms of exploitation: a position which was passionately addressed at last by the upcoming feminist movement.

At this point, in the early 1970s, the two halves of my life moved together. The unexpressed solidarity of the women's rituals of my childhood was now celebrated openly and nowhere more so than in the newly created "Goddess" circles. These, at first purely political, soon moved to spiritual expressions. "Age-old rituals that we invented last Friday night," as one woman put it, summed up this part of our activity. We built on rituals excavated from folklore, from seasonal cookery calendars, from varying religious traditions, from New Age and Pagan practice and from Jungian psychology. These rituals were simple, built up of a few basic principles: there were women only, they recognized the sacrality of a place or date or event, together with honouring the appropriate female divinity or divinities of such a time or place or circumstance; candles were lit and water poured, both to burn or wash away current pains and burdens and then to affirm the new and positive; the celebration finished with the "feast" and "storytelling".

More complicated rituals could be devised, but the basic, which also usually included women silently washing each others' hands at the start, was as satisfying as any. What do I mean by that? I speak of my own feelings but I know that these were replicated among other women. That reality of suffering and hope, that sense of connectedness, the ability to comfort and support each other and above all, the certainty that what we were doing was in essence what women had done over a very long period, that it indeed represented for us a triumph of women's union and strength over centuries or even millennia of denial was expressed clearly by the ritual. That it was created within a concept of "the Goddess" meant for us an acknowledgement of our spiritual selves. I repeat here what I have often said at a ritual: "In raising Her, we raise ourselves; in raising ourselves, we raise Her."

In so doing, I have found that I have reified the indeterminate perceptions of my childhood. The Jewish women mourning, blessing, cooking and managing festival meals were indeed part of a long and continuous tradition of sacred female activity; here is indeed a connectedness, which becomes outwardly manifest in the modern reclamation of the female in divinity. Further, the latter concept has led me – and others – to search for its historical and hidden presence in Judaism, and an appreciation of the richness of earlier forms of the religion which have been obscured in the interest of a patriarchal agenda. Thus such ritual for women binds together the spiritual with the intellectual, and with the political: it helps create a healing and a wholeness, making a major contribution to our self-empowerment.

## Caroline Mackenzie

*What is women's ritual? What does ritual/liturgy mean for you?*
At the most basic level, ritual/liturgy is a way of channelling energy. I have a picture of the *Yin Yang* symbol where the dark and light parts are in a continuously revolving relationship with one another. The liturgies I grew up with saw the light, masculine *Yang* energy as superior to the dark feminine *Yin* energy. The aim was to overcome the darkness with the light. For me, ritual is a creative relationship between the dark and the light in which both are potentially transformed. Thus I try to balance imagination, creativity, wildness, fearfulness with stillness, chanting, peacefulness, reading from scripture, silence and order. I hope that both women and men can experience themselves as the subject in these rituals.

*How do you celebrate it in your context and according to your religious tradition, feminist convictions etc.?*
The background to my work is formed by the influence of Indian culture, particularly Hindu, on Catholic tradition. I lived for twelve years in India and it is there that my interest in ritual started. Back in Europe, I find myself on the edge of the Church, involved with people inspired by eastern spiritualities and also with the more serious end of the so-called "New Age" movement. I have worked with four main types of ritual.

The most important for me, yet also the most difficult, is to re-work the "great" Christian feasts such as Easter. In 1992-3, Sarah Lionheart and I spent a year preparing an Easter Retreat entitled "The Renewal of the Way". This approximated most closely to my aim of balancing dark and light energies in a creative way. Around the traditional structure of the Easter Triduum there was an interweaving of Indian chants and scriptures. The wild dark side was given a place in a masked performance of "The Green Man" around the Easter fire. This shadowy figure, full of life and energy, represented the renewed vitality of the earth. It was created from my experience of the Hindu deity, Lord Shiva and our Celtic Green Man who is so often found in old churches. Shiva embodies both creative and destructive qualities. The idea behind the appearance of this figure was to suggest that the resurrection includes a new consciousness of the instinctive life-forces. After a vigourous dance, the figure prostrated itself before the Pascal candle. It remained dark and shadowy yet it clearly had a relationship with the light. On the Sunday morning this darkness was balanced by a dance through a labyrinth marked out in ash left from the bonfire. The same performer appeared dressed in yellow. Thus she symbolized the returning sun and gave another dimension to the understanding of the resurrection. All the participants joined in a dance through the labyrinth singing "alleluia" and throwing a golden ball between them.

The second type of ritual concerns the relationship of sacred space and iconography to ritual. At the opening of my exhibitions I create a liturgy which is the main part of the "Private View". In one, the focus was a picture of "The Woman with the Found Coin". In another it was the "Blue Woman Christ" referred to by Anne Hunt Overzee in her article "Shadow Play".[3] I believe these strong female images affect the self understanding of the people participating in the rituals. I try to keep a balance between male and female images. Out of these exhibitions of my personal work, public sacred spaces have grown. The most complete is the chapel of some Cistercian nuns in India.

The third type of ritual is less specifically Christian, although I myself would like it to be more so. These are seasonal festivals that I have developed in my village – the Maypole in spring and *Divali* / All Souls in autumn. The aim here is to experience a relationship between the inner processes and the outer seasonal changes. The people who attend these festivals are rather "alternative". Most of them never attend church.

The fourth type of rituals are very private and personal, created with just one or two friends. Recently, following the death of my father, I did a series of "Grieving" pictures. There I discovered a family "secret" about the death of a brother just before I was born. He had never been mourned. On his death anniversary a woman friend who is an Anglican priest came and celebrated a Eucharist in my meditation room. Just one other friend was present. It was very significant that the celebrant was a woman. She brought a special sensitivity to the situation and the ritual was deeply cathartic and healing.

### Susan K. Roll

*1. What is women's ritual / liturgy? What does ritual / liturgy mean to me?*
For me, as a Roman Catholic woman engaged in feminist theology and academic liturgical studies in both European and North American contexts,

---

[3]  In Esser / Hunt Overzee / Roll (eds), *Re-Visioning Our Sources*, 94-107, here 99.

women's liturgy means an enormous collective burst of creative energy, new self-confidence, an embrace of women's authority and a pro-active stance toward the future. Catholic women have historically been permitted very little place in public worship space except as attendees, and have exerted no direct influence on the symbolic structures of worship and their official interpretations. Words written by women are almost completely absent from official liturgical texts. Where women as such become the focus of liturgy as in Marian devotions, the tone is often sentimental or moralizing, promulgating "appropriate" virtues for women such as humility and self-sacrifice.

Even to speak of women's "liturgies" (because "liturgy" refers to official ecclesial worship), is to create a deliberate, and a delightful, oxymoron. This is even truer of the designation Women's Liturgical Movement. The main characteristics of women's liturgies, in my experience planning, celebrating and teaching women's liturgy, are similar to those already sketched in the literature by Teresa Berger, Mary Collins and Marjorie Procter-Smith, among others. These include the following: (1) In the Women's Liturgical Movement women ourselves act as creators of liturgy, active agents and not merely passive recipients of what the Flemish call "liturgical care of souls." Women's liturgy means (2) mutually shared leadership, (3) a generally circular configuration of worship space with plenty of room for bodily gesture and dance, (4) spoken texts and songs written by women-identified women, (5) often stunningly creative uses of visual, especially natural symbolic elements, (6) attention to colour, drama and thematic unity, (7) new interpretation of traditional ritual forms such as litanies and exorcisms, (8) new rites of passage and of healing, and (9) a new sense of liturgical time as a journey.

## 2. How do we celebrate it in our context and according to our feminist conviction?

A few illustrative examples:

1. At the University Parish in Leuven, Belgium in the early 1990s a local "Vrouw en Geloof" ("Woman and Faith") group was forming with an express interest in liturgy. At the first meeting a number of participants said, "Oh no, we don't want to DO any liturgies, we just want to read and discuss something." So that year we read Herman Wegman's *Geschiedenis van de christelijke eredienst in het West en in het Oost*, chapter by chapter. The following year there was some hesitant openness to trying our own little opening liturgies. I planned and carried out a "demonstrator model" at one point to show what was possible in women's liturgy, and after that the group said to

me, "Bring us some written models we can follow, we don't know how to do this." The following year we spread our wings a bit more, and began each meeting with a modest ritual of some sort, heavily text-based. By the end of that year, the group was soaring with new confidence in their own creativity as liturgists, celebrating with original and highly inventive symbols and ritual actions.

2. When I teach the elective course "Perspectives in Feminist Theology" at the seminary in Buffalo, New York (where seminarians constitute 10% of the student body, and 50% of the total number of students are women), one of the course requirements is for each credit student to plan and organize a short liturgy / prayer service for the class according to the feminist principles of liturgy planning (the main characteristics of feminist liturgy as listed above.) The first class included three men: a Canadian seminarian who had studied in Belgium and taught in Korea, a seminarian from Colombia who had settled in the US, and an African-American Baptist social worker. The "feminist" liturgy that each of these men planned was infused with richness and depth from the individual's own cultural perspective(s) as well as a woman-identified re-reading of his own tradition which showed that "feminist liturgy" is a new way of undertaking liturgy, not merely an identification of the physical gender of the participants. Ultimately women-identified liturgy is a quality of consciousness enacted in patterned public prayer.

3. One aspect of feminist liturgy, which deserves mention precisely because of its profound implications for Roman Catholic women, is that of Womeneucharist, a distinct new genre within the general field of women's liturgy. Womeneucharist takes place when a group of women gathers to share some form of a liturgy of the Word, and to break bread and share wine, explicitly calling it Eucharist. This too is a deliberate oxymoron: according to canon law [in the Roman Catholic church] only an ordained priest can validly and licitly consecrate the bread and wine at Eucharist, and only a baptized male may be ordained a priest. In 1997 a vestment designer named Sheila Durkin Dierks was able to survey members of some 100 regular Womeneucharist groups in the United States, and to publish her findings. For most participants the intent is not so much to protest limitations on women in official liturgical leadership, but simply to survive with some dignity as women linked to their faith community. Many of these women take an enormous risk, particularly if they are employed by the church in any capacity. Interestingly, while the theological content of Eucharist in the Roman Catholic tradition involves both sacrifice and meal, sacrifice as a theological theme is unknown in Womeneucharist.

With the number of priests dropping steadily, almost precipitously in Western Europe and North America, coupled with a trend among the relatively small numbers of seminarians toward a mentality of "entitlement" rather than of identification with the poor, the character of public worship is bound to undergo significant shifts in the foreseeable future. The Liturgical Movement of the 19th and 20th centuries which led to the formal changes in liturgy enacted at the Second Vatican Council in 1963 revolutionized the way Roman Catholics experienced worship. At present, in a sort of second stage of reform, liturgies enacted by Roman Catholic women as part of the Women's Liturgical Movement are providing a laboratory for credible, creative and prophetic liturgies of the future. These experiments, which originally developed almost as ritual play among small local groups of women, have the potential to shift the shape and focus of public worship so as not only to renew liturgical practice in the mainstream, but to assure the authoritative presence of women in the public space of worship.

### Laime Kiskunaite
*1. What is women's ritual / liturgy? What does ritual / liturgy mean to me?*

> A new woman is sitting in the middle of the circle of her friends and elderly women while the leader of the ritual says: "Remember, in your time of sorrow, that you are in the wide women's circle. Remember, being in difficulty, that you can depend upon it. As a sign of our connection we will drink from this goblet of charm."

This is the beginning of the celebration of woman initiation – the first journey of woman's soul through symbols and shapes which enables her to enter into the world of soul-making, the area of the ritual.

In my opinion the ritual is a sacred journey – external as well as internal – while in this action the body and the soul both are active elements with an important task – to break the present barriers of consciousness and create new relations to oneself and to the world. This three-stage process (separation, metamorphosis and reintegration) passing through transitions or life crises is accompanied by symbolic signs. Material: water, milk, honey, clothes, adornments, flowers, food, repetitive gestures or immaterial: songs, dances, prayers, blessings, special words. However, woman needs the ritual energy and safety in the circle of close friends in order to regain a new self perception. The inner power of the circle holds a woman in the highest point of the session and helps to carry a flow of the divine energy.

When I am writing these words I feel that I am myself in the enormous circle with all those women with whom I have ever performed ritual actions, in flats, forests, school sport halls, kindergartens, green fields, deserts, hills, beaches, boats, court-yards, farms, saunas... In such places women perform their rites of the transition into the new life status – womanhood, motherhood; a farewell ritual for an unborn or dead baby; joyful and serious rituals of baptizing (name giving) and blessing of a godmother... According to my personal experience, tears, joy and intense energy are the main elements of all women's rituals.

## A brief characterisation of Lithuanian women's rituals

Women's rituals in Lithuania – new and old – are divided historically by a period of about 50 years. The country women's communities were destroyed during the beginning of the Soviet occupation (1945-1950). The practice of traditional (empirical) midwives was forbidden in the year 1963. Spiritual midwifery and home births again appeared about 1990. Around this phenomenon, a new women's community began to develop, which was based upon a holistic world outlook, spiritual midwifery, feminist spirituality, spirituality of childbirth and motherhood, feminist anthropology and psychology. This system of values, absolutely new because of the disintegration of our inherited convictions and limitations, evokes for many of us younger women the strong desire to create our own authentic life style free from traditional, patriarchal relationships. In this fundamental transition of our lives we inevitably have to remember and creatively re-think old traditions, customs and rites of our grandmothers and create anew whatever it is that we feel is needed at this moment, most often connected with the transition into motherhood.

After ten years it is already possible to state that women's rites are developing in two directions: the creation of new ones and the integration of reconstructed old rituals. The content of new ritual is often based not only on the old rituals and customs of Lithuanian women, but also accepts women's ritual actions from the rest of the world.

## New Rituals
### The sewing of birth shirts

Unexpectedly, the sewing and embroidering of a birth shirt is becoming a very attractive ritual. According to Lithuanian folklore sources, women never used to make any special birth shirts. But the shirt in which the mother had given birth was always regarded as very important. Mothers would lay their baby on this cloth when it was ill or fractious. For this reason, women put off washing the shirt in which they had given birth for as long as possible. Nowadays pregnant women gather together in a small group and make a special birth shirt with protective signs. Pregnant women consciously try to create a safe space. Shirts or little dresses made in this way transfer a spiritual charge to the mother and to the newborn.

### Initiation into childbirth

When a pregnant woman enters her new status and feel separated from her previous, familiar life, she becomes very open to new information, defining her new, as yet unknown, reality. Therefore she is extremely vulnerable but also very strong with her fertility power. When she is not alone she can share that dangerous and sacred way with her chosen friends. Dressed like a newborn, she is welcomed to the ritual feast by women who are already initiated. Having received the gift of physical fertility, here she matures to accept spiritual wisdom.

### Baptising outside the Church

The ending of the birth process and name-giving ritual with blessings for the mother, the father (if he is participating), older sisters and brothers, and a special blessing for the godmother.

### Farewell ritual for an unborn or dead baby

Mourning and meditation after abortion, miscarriage or the death of a baby, which takes place in the supporting and understanding circle of women.

These new rituals need particular safety and women's empathy for each other, for reasons of intimacy and open confessions.

The *Midwife's day* on the first weekend of September has more the character of a mass. The ritual of a small child's *birthday* is celebrated even in some kindergartens. The celebration is performed with a personal story of how this child arrived on this Earth and how she/he has lived up to this birthday, with two circles of children, one representing the stars, sun and moon, the other the earth. The child has to leave the first circle and enter into the next, the circle of the earth.

### Integrated and reshaped old rites

With the collapse of women's community, many old rites, including a social maturity ceremony such as the first bread baking, customs of intercommunication such as the borrowing of fire, the tasting of the sourness of bread, and women's indoor gatherings in the evenings, disappeared from Lithuania in the middle of the 20th century.

For example, in May women would arrange the altar decorated with flowers and wreaths inside the house of a big farm, and throughout the month members of the family and neighbours would gather every evening to chant *mojavos*, special songs and litanies in the honour of the Virgin Mary. At other times of year women would spend evenings singing, praying, telling myths and fairy tales.

Lithuanian saunas were the traditional place for women's rites. In the sauna they would perform a bathing ritual for the bride. In this way she was introduced into the women's community. This action would finish with a ritual meal and drinks.

In eastern Lithuania a woman was called "Bear" immediately after childbirth. "The Bear is coming!" women would shout as she approached the sauna for ritual bathing about five weeks after giving birth. After bathing the new mother would make offerings to the Birth Goddess Laima.

Women could also give birth in saunas while warming themselves and relaxing, surrounded by female company. The rituality was concentrated in the special clothes, herbal drinks and oils which eased the labour. However, there were no particular chants or meditations. In difficult moments women would unbutton the new mother's dress, open doors and windows, and unplait her hair. These were the most important ritual actions during giving birth.

The ritual visiting of new mother has survived almost to our time. Just after birth the neighbouring women would bring food, herb tea for the new mother, clothes for the newborn and give some advice to the new father, especially if he had not looked after his wife properly.

*Celebration of first menstruation*

With the exception of weddings, women's rites at the end of the 19th and the beginning of the 20th centuries were short and simple, performed in the very closed women's community. I suppose the attitudes of Catholicism toward feminine sexuality and woman's body deeply shaped the ritual life of women.

An example of a girl's initiation into womanhood was documented in written form at the end of the 19th century. When the mother noticed that her daughter was bleeding for the first time she showed the blood to her daughter and asked "What do you have here?" and without waiting for an answer slapped her cheek with her palm. From this moment the daughter assumed a higher position in the family and could sit at table with the adult members of the family.

Understanding the importance of woman's initiation, we now mark with girls the day of the ending of her childhood and the birth of a fertile female body. On this day our daughter or another girl is invited into the women's circle where she sits covered by a white cloth in the middle of the singing and dancing circle. Later she is crowned with a wreath of roses and given small fine gifts by her mother and other women. The celebration finishes with a feast, open talking about women's sexuality and fertility, and answering the girl's questions.

Other rituals often performed are the ritual burying of the placenta, and the ritual thanks to the midwife after childbirth. Both parents, or the mother, wash the midwife's hands and present her with the towel and soap.

The rites described above have some common features. All of them are open to every woman and a few for men also. Every action and symbol is carefully deliberated. The choice of symbols and actions depends on a women's ability to accept them and to actively participate in ritual. In every case a woman's ritual journey is performed with deep respect for the level of the woman's self consciousness. A circle is made for every ritual, to ensure a high and strong energetic and spiritual field.

## Katerina Karkala-Zorba

*What is women's ritual? What does ritual / liturgy mean for me?*
*How do we celebrate it in our context and according to our religious tradition / feminist conviction etc?*

"Women's ritual" is not really an expression in the Orthodox Church. We do not distinguish between men's and women's ritual. All rituals are equally for men and women. There are no men's rituals either. On the other hand, there are some prayers or celebrations which are more frequented by women than by men, and those are:

– the prayer-cycle dedicated to the Mother of God before Easter, on five Friday evenings in the Great Lenten season ending on the Friday of the second week before Palm Sunday with the *Acathist Hymn*. Those prayers are called "greetings to the Mother of God" (*Chairetismoi*) and the hymns follow the 24 letters of the Greek alphabet. *Acathist* means the "non-seated song", referring to an eighth-century miracle in Constantinople when the people of God went to the Church of Saint Sophia and sang the hymns to the Mother of God while all standing up together.

– the intercessions (*parakliseis*), when, for two weeks before the Assumption on 15 August, the great and small intercessions are celebrated in the evenings. These are well-known hymns which are also used in every intercession and every prayer request for something specific.

– the song of *Kassiani*: used in the Great Lenten season before Easter, this is the well-known hymn or *troparion* of Kassiani, a woman in Constantinople, who was chosen to become the wife of the Emperor. She was very beautiful and the Emperor, seeing her, said: "Through women evil has come into this world;" by this he meant Eve. Kassiani answered: "But through a woman good has also come into this world;" by this she meant Mary who gave birth to her son, our Lord Jesus Christ. This is understood to be the answer of a very intelligent woman who did not become Queen, yet showed her own will and strength.

Those prayers are not independent of the daily prayer cycle which includes prayers to the Mother of God, as well as to women saints, martyred and glorified with God. What is important is that those prayers are not independent; they are not prayers only for women, but for the whole community.

In Greece today, we can observe that at the prayers before Easter and before the Assumption, more women are present in church, or in some parishes practically only women. But sometimes this is also true for other celebrations and liturgies. Women are present in the church and give their own accent to the celebrations by taking on the wonderful attitude of the women at the tomb of Jesus, the church, the temple of God. The Myrrhophores, the women who brought myrrh to the tomb to anoint the body of Jesus, were the first to witness the resurrection of Jesus Christ. This attitude, and this first evangelisation of humankind, is something very important for women today, too.

For me liturgy does not mean something apart from the community where men and women, old and young, clergy and lay people meet in order to celebrate together. The word "liturgy" comes from the Greek words *laos* = people and *ergon* = work or task. So the liturgy is the task of the people. And as such it is a men's and a women's task.

Within the Orthodox tradition, women are not ordained to the priesthood. But we do recognize the ordination of deaconesses (although this was not in preparation for becoming a priest) from the early church until the 12th century. The deaconesses have disappeared, but some Orthodox churches want to revive this tradition. Still, Orthodox women do not feel excluded from celebration. We are present in the whole liturgical context. We feel that men and women have different tasks to fulfill in order to celebrate the Eucharist, which is the sacrament of sacraments. The priest's task is to administer the sacraments. He does this in a line of succession from Jesus to the Apostles up to today. We continue this tradition because it is still the one in which we are fulfilled as members of the church. This is our conviction. As women we feel that we can express ourselves in other different tasks and ministries (*diakonia*), such as the preparation of the liturgy and of its different parts (bread, candles, the church space etc.), but also by readings, songs, etc. We would perhaps like to have more participation for lay persons in the church, both men and women, but we know that to do that we need more instruction in Byzantine singing. In some Orthodox churches there are good choirs for men and women, or only for women.

I personally think that to a very large extent our faith is transmitted to us through our mothers and foremothers. The liturgical aspect is very important here. Women pay a great deal of attention to the way the liturgy is celebrated. Going to the liturgy feels like we are going to a special feast. This was transmitted to me through my mother. Women feel more free to express themselves bodily in church and during the liturgy; more easily than men, they may make prostrations and kneel down. The whole body takes part, and all the senses are present: I make my cross, I take a candle, I light it, I see the fire, I smell the incense, I feel the icon, I kiss it, etc. I think for women this process is especially important and is transmitted to the children. I still remember a grandmother in a monastery in Greece, who almost forced her little granddaughter to kiss the icon. After the third icon, the child had "learned" and did not want to stop kissing all the icons. Also I remember an old babushka in the Cathedral in Moscow, who turned to me, showing me in which direction I had to look: God is at the Iconostasis, why do I look at the bishop and the priests…? Those women feel themselves to be the guardians of faith, the living tradition-holders. They feel they are the ones who have to transmit what they have received from their mothers to their children, and especially to their daughters. This is perhaps why there is no feeling of exclusion or of being oppressed. The priesthood is just one aspect of the tasks of ministry. But there are so many others.

If I say or hear the word "ritual" I am not sure this is adequate for Orthodox tradition. But there are some habits which are important for Orthodox believers, like making the cross, lighting the candles, or the incense. I would perhaps end by referring to the fact that there is another aspect of life in which women play the most important role and that is the commemoration of the dead. Women go to the graves and light the oil lamps, as they also do at home. They bring flowers and say the prayers at the cemetery. They keep track of the right commemoration days: 3, 6, 9, 40 days; 3, 6, 9 months; and every year after the death of a relative, so that he/she is never forgotten. Women prepare the sweet-wheat cake (*kolyva*) and bring it to the church to be blessed. This is also made visible by their black clothes: they are the women in black. It is very important that dead persons continue to be a part of our community, and this is made possible mainly by the help of women.

## Coletta Damm
*Women's ritual in Islam and Sufism – some impressions*
As a German Muslima and psychologist I was asked to write something about women's ritual in Islam and Sufism. It may be surprising for some Christian women, but for us this is not at all an inferior subject, but an important part of our spirituality. This fact is unfortunately rather unknown in the literature, on the one hand for historical reasons (discussed below), and on the other because many Muslimat (plural of Muslima) seem to believe that those things are not "modern" or not interesting enough for others. I shall try to give some impressions of the background and of my personal experiences, in the hope that better-founded research concerning this topic will be done in the future.

Every pilgrim, woman or man, who walks the ritual way between the hills Safa and Marwa seven times (altogether about 3 km) and drinks from the spring of "Zamzam" is following the example of Hagar, the second wife of the prophet Abraham (as she is seen in Islam), as it has been passed down for centuries. Today the hills Safa and Marwa and the spring "Zamzam" which Hagar found, are part of the Holy Mosque of Mecca. In this way, an important part of the Islamic pilgrim's ritual is attributed to a woman, a "mother bringing up her child alone." Especially for many modern European women, this aspect of the ritual is very meaningful: a woman, standing alone, struggling for survival in the desert, and at last being able to open her heart to the source of all existence, at the turning point, when her human abilities and her human knowledge couldn't help her anymore. At this point she saw the water.

In the Qur'an Allah is called again and again "rahmani rahim", translated as compassionate and all-merciful. In Arabic writing this word is based on the letters "RHM", similar to the Arabic word for uterus. Allah, neither male nor female, the source of everything, is reflected in feminine nature.

For centuries Hagar has been a living symbol of the mysterious connection between effort and grace: the very desperate search for water and at last the opening to the real source. In this way she got the water she needed and we, the pilgrims, expect the same for us. For me the old ritual also has the meaning that it is very important to look for the essence, water, without being satisfied with the "sweet synthetic juices" of modern life, which can never quench spiritual thirst.

Today many Muslimat travel to Mecca and Medina: in our group 2/3 were women. Many of them were married women whose husbands had stayed at home. There is a belief that Hagar is buried just beside the Kaaba, the small nearly quadratic building in the middle of the huge Holy Mosque in Mecca, a simple house, empty on the inside, which is called the House of Allah. In Islam the tradition says that Hagar's son Ismael built the Kaaba together with his father Abraham, who visited them later. The pilgrims have to walk around the Kaaba seven times (this is called "Tawaf"), which for me was also a remarkable experience.

At one time, in the prophet's mosque in Medina (about 1400 years ago), women and men prayed together in one single room. In the early Islamic epoch women also taught in mosques. But in the centuries that followed there came to be a more and more strict separation of women and men. (The reasons for this cannot be discussed here.) Most mosques acquired separate prayer rooms for men and women. The separation in everyday life in parts of South Arabia went so far that there was a unique women's dialect, spoken and understood only by women.

Beside the usual prayer five times a day, in the Islamic world a "separate religious women's culture" developed. Not only in Islamic countries, but also in, for example, Germany, Muslimat (most of whom in Germany are Turkish) meet with friends and neighbours to sing religious songs, pray and recite the Qur'an. No men are allowed to be in the flat during these hours. If he cannot enter through a back door into a separate room inconspicuously, the husband has to visit friends or to spend the time in a tea-room. These meetings always take place 40 days after the death of a relative or on the anniversary of a death; this is a custom also for women who are not very religious. Religious women meet their female friends at least several times a year, and many of them come together every week on a fixed day. In rotation a different member of the circle hosts the group each time. During the ceremony the women wear scarves (even if they do not generally do so in everyday life), and most of the pictures on the walls will be veiled. Sometimes a female Hodsha from the mosque leads the ceremony, or this is done by a woman who "knows how it is done." But often there is no chosen leader, and the women begin to sing or to recite in turn. Not only older women, but also many young women come to such meetings. During this time there is no private talking and everybody is very concentrated. Many songs relate to the prophet Muhammad. A very emotional, loving connection comes into being, sometimes tears are flowing, but at that moment nobody would ask why. The turning towards religious belief is as consoling as the community of the other women. Everyday occurrences or problems are far away from the members of the group; this is another level of understanding. As the psychologists say, rituals function as collection barrels for emotions. During these meetings the women create the opportunity to transcend thinking and feeling. Non-Muslimat, generally friends, may also be invited to join these meetings if they are interested.

After this ceremony (about two hours) the women sit together drinking tea or coffee and eating. The woman who invited the others has prepared something. (During the ceremony normally they only drink a sip of water, if possible water from Mecca, from the spring Zamzam, in memory of Hagar.) Now they like to talk, to have fun and to tell news, to be together.

In Sufism, also called the "Heart of Islam" (millions of Muslims all over the world belong to one of the many Sufi orders), there is a famous, central woman character, Rabi'a al Adawiya (lived ca. 800 CE). Accentuating the love of God, she changed the ascetic tendencies in Sufism at that time; at a later period the famous Ibn Arabi followed this way and many others did too. They also influenced the Christian Spanish mystics. After Rabi'a there were many important women in Sufism, sheikhas, who had female and male disciples. But even in Sufism the separation of sexes became generally accepted, except in the Bektashi Order in Turkey. While in Christian culture women are remembering and rediscovering their "own rituals" or trying to create new ones, many modern (and most western) Sufi women today are still struggling for integration, to have spiritual rituals together with men. For example, in the Ashki Jerrahi Order (New York, Mexico City) the ceremonies are also guided by women and the female members choose whether they want to wear the traditional scarves or headgear like men.

I myself belong to a Sufi order (called Tariqat As-Safinah) of the Andalusian tradition, which is also open to Jews and Christians. Women's rights are a central concern of this order; and this is also a main focus of the work of the German Muslim League in Bonn which is connected with the order. We have been working for integration for many years, and for a long time we always held our ceremonies with women and men together, sitting in a circle, with women on one side, men on the other.

Learning from the oriental women, some of us also found that it is important to have meetings only with women. I asked several women about their experiences with a Dhikr only with women. ("Dhikr" means "remembrance of Allah", which is realised in different ways in different orders, generally with recitation, singing, and sometimes dancing). They described these events as "softer (but without being superficial!), deeper, going deeper into my heart;" others said, "I liked it more than the way the men do it; I wouldn't want to give up these women's meetings, although I appreciate the ceremonies together very much." What is very important is that nowadays we can do both.

In our order we are now exploring the possibility of private meetings – Dhikr – for those of our female members who would like to participate. Some women do not want to join such a private meeting because they are afraid of new tendencies towards separation. But I think there is no danger because nobody in our order would like to restore those traditions, and on the other hand integration in working together in all areas is *a central principle*. (As far as I know, we are the only order with this target in Germany, similar to the Ashki Jerrahi Order in the USA)

When I was growing up, I learned that women alone could not work together, "because they are not capable – there had to be rational men to make things substantial." (My mother – a single mother – also thought this way and I was often angry about it.) So I support the struggle of modern Sufi women for integration, but on the other hand I like to do "substantial things" only with women too. Our difficulty is that most of us do not live together in one town, but insha'allah we will succeed in realising this idea. Writing this article I was more and more confirmed that this would be a very good aim. Therefore many thanks to the initiators of the theme "Women's Rituals"! If somebody would like to see such a ritual, she is invited to join us, because in Sufism it's most important to "taste the hidden things", not only to know about them intellectually.[4]

---

[4] Further literature: Margaret Smith, *Rabi'a the mystic and her Fellow Saints in Islam* (Cambridge University Press: Cambridge 1928; repr. Philo: Amsterdam 1974); Uwe Topper, *Sufis und Heilige im Maghreb* (Diederichs: Munich 1991); Michaela Özelsel, "Die Integration einer kulturspezifischen Sichtweise in therapeutische Rituale," in: *Hypnose und Kognition* 11 (April 1995), 36; dies., *Forty Days* (Rowohlt: Hamburg 1995); Annemarie Schimmel, *Meine Seele ist eine Frau* (Kösel: Munich 1995); Sara Sviri, *The Taste of Hidden Things* (Golden Sufi Center: Inverness, CA 1997); Karimah Stauch, "Ein maghrebinischer Sufi-Schech des 20. Jahrhunderts. Schech Al-Alawi" (essay published on the website of Tariqat As-Safinah: http://members.aol.com/TASafinah/homepage.html); dies., "Die Tariqat As-Safinah und ihr Dialog mit dem Anderen", in: CIBEDO 13/3 (1999), 113-114.

## Thalia Gur-Klein
*To be Holy or not to be Holy: on three forms of Love*

I demonstrate my devotion to Judaism in my research into my Jewish sources, and in my everyday life in singing Hebrew liturgy, story telling and poetry. In all these, I try to find joyful ways to enhance the Jewish-Christian dialogue, for joy is compatible with devotion. I believe that joy opens up people to empathic relationships with the Other; for as people are open to joy, hatred and mutual fear do not persist. I believe that the Self always contains the Other and is contained by the Other, as a woman, as a Jew, and as a human being; and it is to us to experience the Other in empathy or disharmony. To make this belief my own, and to make it communicative to others, I present my belief in a piece of Kabbalistic thought and a poem:

A relatively unknown ecstatic mystic of the 13th century, Abraham Abolaffia, presented a model for man's psyche in the form of two-half-circles. Abolaffia reflected earlier rabbinical writings positing ideal humanity according to the primordial body designed at the Creation; it is an idea in its divinely original intention. The materialisation falls short of its ideal. This arouses the yearning of the Self for harmonious wholeness within an ideal union, in finding its other-half. This perception aroused many interpretations.

The concept of primordial body posits three possibilities of a universal model for the human soul. Philo: The two halves of the circle offer two possibilities. Seen as a vertical circle designed to be divided vertically, the primordial body is perceived as an undifferentiated body, like an embryo which contains the whole of humanity in itself. The two halves of the circle create a vision of a universal soul in which the Other is the other half of the Self. Genesis Rabba 8 explicitly posits the original woman, like the man, as an entity containing the universal soul, on her creation. In this model, one sees the creed of "Love thy neighbor as thyself" (Lev. 19:18), in which the Other is a model for the universally human. The Hebrew verse can be read as "Love the Other as you love yourself" or "Love the Other, who is like yourself". In the first case the Self subjectifies the Other. In the second case the Other and the Self mutually subjectivise each other. Rabbi Hillel's commentary famed him in his saying that the entire Torah stands on this creed, namely that whatever is hateful to the Self, one should not do the Other. All the rest of the Torah is but the interpretation of this one creed. In this, the Self can not find oneself without generating sympathy with the Other, altruistically and reciprocally.

Eros: The other possibility of the vertical model posits the primordial body composed as a heterogeneous union. The primordial body was thus divided into two sexes, and sexual attraction is perceived as a return to a pre-destined union of body and soul (Gen 2.24). Rabbinic literature describes man and woman as originally forming a primordial body, attached to each other back to back, until God cuts them into two halves. The word rib, *tsela*, is translated as an equal side, as the same word appears in other contexts with this meaning, as in Ex 26.20, where it refers to the two sides of the tabernacle. Like the universally human model, this model inscribes man and woman as being contained and containing. This text posits man and woman as equal parts of a whole, the same way that man to man are equal parts of a whole.

Agape: The third model favored by unio-mystics like Abolaffia places the two halves of a circle horizontally. The image of the primordial body becomes a matrix of upper and lower halves. In this model of mankind, the upper part becomes the divine image in humanity. The upper half corresponds to the universal mind. The lower part is the human living soul, which is the Self. The upper part was created after the divine image but can not procreate, and the lower part can procreate but was not created after the divine. As God shared His image with humanity in Gen 1.27, the human is partly divine and partly earthly. Here the yearning to the return to primordial body is materialised in finding the Self in the Other, which is divinity. If the two halves are contradictory, to reach the divine the human must either erase the self, or deny God. On the other hand, if the primordial body contains the divine image as its other half, then it has divinised the other half, the earthly, and humanised the divine. In this the Self yearns to come close to the roots of all that exists through the divine that created it, as it creates sympathy with the divine part within the Self.

Eighteenth-century Hasidic thought saw in this model the divine illumination in human life. They saw the urge to reach harmonious wholeness in finding the divine roots within the Self, which is uniquely personalised in each human being. Human deeds performed with devotion bring each human being closer to the divine roots of the Self. The personalised roots of divinity in the Self are equated with the scattered light of the Sekhina, the divine spirit, perceived as the feminine aspect of God. Finding the personalised divine root in the Self is thus equated with a return to the mystical union of the primordial body containing the divine image and earthly humanity: being one. In this, every phenomenon of life experienced with devotion becomes a manifestation of Grace to rejoice. A human being thus stands in reciprocal sympathy with the immediate environment. This relationship is creative, imposing a task befitting the personalised divine roots of the Self, a task unique only to that

Self. Hassidic thought accords equal worth to all three ideal models of primordial humanity; love of God, sexual love, and human love of the Self to the Other are thus permuted and complementary.

*A Holy Woman*

> *I am a saint*
> *of a miniature statue.*
> *Out of my little side pocket*
> *I jiggle two magic marbles,*
> *with an eye of light;*
> *one with an image of God in man,*
> *the other, with an image of man in God.*
>
> *A card of broken heart*
> *I hide in my right sleeve;*
> *one half with longing for love,*
> *the other with love for another.*
>
> *By the full moon*
> *I duly offer my payment*
> *to the high priests*
> *of water, and electricity.*
>
> *The hungry children*
> *feeding on my generous hand*
> *are my own.*
>
> *The dog too, I would not forget,*
> *and I teach high-school children.*
>
> *For messiah I still long*
> *and thereby hope to find*
> *a new job and/or a lover.*
>
> *I am a saintly woman*
> *of a miniature state.*

## Evaluation of Responses

After their statement to the first two questions had been circulated, the authors reacted to one another, guided by two more questions (*What are the similarities and differences between the various perspectives? What is the future development of women's ritual? How do you see it?*). In their responses, women did not only express what they thought they had in common with each other but also what they regarded as their differences. They also stressed points of special interest in other women's contributions and shared again aspects of their own tradition which they thought important for the mutual discussion and development of feminist ritual / liturgy. In the end, what arose was a vision of what feminist liturgy / ritual in a European context can / will be about.

What follows here are excerpts from their responses discussed under five headings:

(1) Similarities
(2) Differences
(3) Special responses to one another
(4) Contributions to the dialogue from the author's own tradition
(5) Future perspectives

## *1. Similarities*

All participants in the dialogue wished to express what they believed themselves to have in common. Themes that were named included the feeling of being on "a journey – indeed a pilgrimage" as women (*Asphodel*), of "modalities of identification with women's concerns" (*Susan*), of having to struggle with the "perception and object of feminist theology" (*Laime*), of participating in as well as feeling "side-lined" from the mainline of their tradition (*Caroline*), of sharing in "female characteristics and feeling" (*Katerina*) that may open women specifically to an "embodied, incarnate, sensuous perception of liturgy / ritual" (*Caroline*). Here are some of the voices:

### *Asphodel*

It is difficult to respond with any sort of formal analysis of the very varied standpoints described by the seven contributors (of whom I am one). What impacts most strongly for me is the perception that we are all on a journey – indeed a pilgrimage. We start from different backgrounds, countries, languages, beliefs: do we have an actual known destination? I do not think so: it is the journey that matters. The journey itself becomes the homecoming (as Nelle Morton pointed out quite a long time ago).[5] We are women living in the 21st century CE. What is common to most of us is a sense of moving to a sense of our own spirituality and power –

---

[5]  Nelle Morton, *The Journey Is Home* (Beacon Press: Boston, MA 1986).

whether within mixed-gender or women-only groupings – and that this is part of our century's journey.

## Caroline

I think the most striking similarity is the embodied, incarnate, sensuous perception of liturgy / ritual that women share. They all feel side-lined from the mainline structures and each one reacts differently to this.

## Laime

The reading of the contributions to the ESWTR Yearbook reinforced my assumption that the main problem which divides women in theology into "Eastern" and "Western" still remains the problem of perception of the object of feminist theology and of the ability to apply the methods of feminist theology in their own religious tradition. Self-limiting, suspicion toward new ideas, desire to be a part of the prevalent culture and to justify social expectations at any cost are still very strong in women's consciousness. They make a pregnant woman believe that the safest place in the world for her birth-giving is a hospital, women-theologians are assured 'a priori' that feminist theology is a big heresy...

## Katerina

I have learned something myself by writing and reacting on the theme given to us. Women are always present in liturgical contexts. Very often they represent the major part of Church-attendees. But how do they understand their participation? I think we have still a lot of things to share between the different denominations and religions. But let us keep in common what is for sure, i.e. our female characteristics and feelings, our sensitive way of approaching things and matters and our special "motherhood" (bodily or spiritual). My wish is that we can all communicate through the common things which are uniting us, and not through our differences.

## Coletta

All these articles – each in its own specific way – show a wonderful treasure of women's spirituality, different, but similar. In my own life there is always one theme again and again: to accept and to overcome antagonisms... I was very glad to read these stories, to see so many similarities and interesting differences. In all articles I found ideas of separation and unity: partnership with men, but concentration on one's own roots and one's own capabilities.

## 2. Differences

The differences named by several authors relate to two parameters: (1) women's relationhip to their religious and cultural tradition (*Susan, Laime*), and (2) a consciously feminist position of the authors (*Asphodel*). This was formulated as follows:

## Susan

The texts submitted in response to the initial Dialogue article invitation certainly testify to the rich diversity, not only of culture and religious affiliation, but also of modalities of identification of/with women's concerns. Each one is conditioned both by types of participation available to women within one's own tradition/s and by the perceived limitations of those tradition/s. Asphodel, Laime and I [Susan] each describe how involvement in women's ritual provided a deepening of one's identity as a woman within new possibilities for women-identified worship in settings quite apart from the traditions of public worship in Judaism and Catholicism respectively. Katerina and Thalia, on the other hand, identify themselves as women securely within a particular received tradition, and explore instead what that tradition meant to them and where the specific spaces and possibilities for women's participation were located. Coletta describes women's ritualization within the Muslim context but specifically within the Sufi orders, and Caroline merges two vital faith-traditions within a variety of new ritualizing, which is both enacted by women in "free space", as it were, and synthesizing elements of East and West. – While a vast difference appears among the various contributions in the degree to which women see the realities of their own lives and the goodness of their own female bodies reflected in official public worship, each one testifies, one way or another, to a process of grappling with the issues.

## Laime

While contemplating the reflections of a wide variety of women's rituals and liturgy over the world I mainly concentrate on two mainstreams: (1) the remembering and creative re-thinking the tradition of the ritual / "sacred female activity" (Asphodel Long) as well as integrating of "a new consciousness of the instinctive life-forces" (Caroline Mackenzie), and (2) acting within one's own religious tradition (Islam, Catholic, Orthodox, Jewish etc.) "assuring the authoritative presence of women in the public space of worship" (Susan Roll).

## Asphodel

Both Thalia Gur-Klein and Caroline Mackenzie, coming from vastly different background, speak from the realms of the one-ness of mystical experience; Thalia presents hers from Kabbalistic sources, Caroline from Hindu. Both to a large extent are "gender-blind" in that it is the joyful union of Self with Divine, or with Nature, or of Self with the Other that is sought and celebrated. Unlike the feminist path represented by Susan and myself, or the woman-oriented traditions described by Katerina and Coletta, the mystical experience is defined within the journey of the individual.

## 3. Special responses to one another

Authors responded to each other on the basis of their own experience, system of thought, and beliefs. Just as a prism spreads one light into various colours, several women looking at one person and her paper will focus on different aspects according to their own specific perspective. The more voices that can be heard, the more colourful the picture; and yet it is never complete. What we need to remember by reading these responses is always to consider the two sides, the one who perceives as well the one who is perceived. For example, we have here two Jewish women looking at a German Muslim, or an American Catholic Feminist looking at a woman doing ritual in Post-Soviet Lithuania, or a Greek Orthodox woman looking at a British Catholic woman informed by Hinduism. Reading the result is like an invitation to a women's group.

### Reacting to Asphodel
#### Susan

Asphodel's description of her life journey and how it came around in a circle, in a way, has a wonderful depth and wholeness and integration about it: the domestic rituals over which women presided in Orthodox Judaism were echoed, in some sense, in the new/ancient Goddess rites which drew on deep traditional roots of a different sort, discovered, designed and enacted by women.

#### Katerina

The text of Asphodel Long speaks to me and I find a lot of similarities to my own orthodox Christian tradition. We also know the mourning and some rituals reserved to women and men. I think we have a lot in common with Judaism and of course we do, since the Jewish religion and tradition is our precursor. It is very much coherent to Christian understanding and we have common roots. Asphodel has answered in a personal way on the question of women's rituals which I found very easy to relate to. – Still I could not identify with what Asphodel said about Goddess spirituality. It is very difficult for me to understand or to accept any ritual coming from "folklore, seasonal cookery", "from New Age and Pagan practice". In a way and in an Orthodox understanding it is very difficult to "create" in liturgical practice something totally new or something which is a mixture.

#### Coletta

A wonderful message for me from Asphodel Long: Finding one's own way of spirituality – lighting the Sabbath candles in a very deep sense.

## Reacting to Caroline
### Katerina

I have a hard time to understand the text of Caroline Mackenzie as well as that by Coletta Damm. Perhaps it is the fact that there is a "combination" of traditions which makes it so hard. Caroline is coming from a Catholic tradition with Hindu influence. And one can see this when she refers to Easter. I still wonder what there is to be "re-worked", since Easter is referring to something very concrete, which is the Passion and the Resurrection of Jesus Christ. This important event, important also for me as a Christian woman today, can be re-experienced, can be rediscovered, but it cannot be re-worked, in the sense of being changed. And the Resurrection of Christ is present in Eucharist, so this event is very important and is the centre of my liturgical life. And this liturgical life is experienced in the Church (at least in my understanding). So I could not find this dimension in the private Eucharist in her meditation room.

### Coletta

A wonderful message for me from Caroline Mackenzie: The creative relationship of the dark and the light, which together leads us to the essence of life. This reminded me of the 99 names of Allah: The many different aspects of the source of everything, some of them for us seem to be "dark", threatening, others kind and light. We cannot understand this really, but we can try to reach a certain knowledge about it.

## Reacting to Susan
### Asphodel

Susan Roll shows that it is not easy to follow a model of feminist rituals such as that presented by Laime Kiskunaite. Writing of Western Europe, she provides an intense insight, a "lamp of Wisdom" when she says that "many women take an enormous risk": she is referring specifically to those who participate in Womeneucharist, and may be employed by the Roman Catholic church. But all women stepping outside traditional male-directed spiritual conformities take such a risk. It is of becoming an outsider in one's own community, sometimes even in one's family. There are economic as well as emotional and physical consequences. I see in the various contributions to our dialogues some of the different strategies women are devising to enable them to begin and sustain their pilgrimage.

### Caroline

I was particularly struck by Susan Roll's paper because I am working in the same area, that is Roman Catholic liturgy. Inspired by her paper, I want to focus on how women may be able to have a "direct influence on the symbolic structures of worship."

## Katerina

A text that is familiar to me and in which I could slightly see myself is the text of Susan Roll. Coming from a Christian Roman Catholic tradition it is easy to understand what she means when she is saying: "even to speak of women's 'liturgies' is to create a deliberate, and a delightful oxymoron." Although in Orthodox tradition we do not know such renewals, I can understand them, since I have participated in the ecumenical movement in the last ten years and I have come to understand how important it is for traditions where women had no "voice" in the liturgy to get one, to be heard and seen. I also like the new interpretation (e.g. of litanies and exorcisms) which is a very actual and important point for any liturgical renewal. I also found her examples concerning the feminist liturgies and her clear theological and ecclesiastical approach very interesting. I think there a broad field of elaboration is opened up by this.

## Coletta

A wonderful message for me from Susan K. Roll: Being active and no longer passive, but going this way step by step in connection with the growing capabilities of the other women (and such men as she told about!).

## Reacting to Laime
## Asphodel

Laime Kiskunaite's account of women's rituals in today's Lithuania is especially moving. She emphasises that women-only circles enable the participants to "enter into the world of soulmaking"; this includes creating new rituals and renewing old ones. A strong sense of feminist spirituality is engendered not only by the occasion but by the various practical rituals marking different stages of women's life. I find her account particularly interesting as it sits so well with my own experience as a Jewish women in goddess circles; we have to re-invent. Laime and her friends, in a culture that came late both to Christianity and industrialisation, are nearer to folk tradition and memories. It is inspiring that they can integrate these with "holistic world outlook, spiritual midwifery ... feminist anthropology and psychology". My hope is that this provides a model of rituals that more and more women can follow.

*Susan*

When Laime's article arrived, I found it particularly thought-provoking in her sensitive sketch of the support of women for each other in Lithuanian women's rituals.

*Katerina*

Coming to the text of Laime Kiskunaite, I would like to remark that I liked very much her historical approach by referring to Lithuanian history of the last 50 years. I can understand this, since in Lithuania there was a great change in the last years. Then I liked very much the rediscovering of old, earlier rituals which come now to fill the emptiness and which help one to understand one's own tradition (the sewing of birth shirts, etc.). "Creating new rituals and integrating re-constructed old rituals": this is really a good approach. Although I do not know from my own tradition a midwife's day, I think it is appropriate, since she is the one who helps the child to be born. All the rituals concerning the circle of life, (birth shirts, initiation into childbirth, baptizing, etc.) are really interesting (cf. Orthodox tradition) … Then I found interesting in Laime's text the menstruation celebration. I also got a slap from my mother, or rather from my aunt, as she was the first to discover my menstruation. My mother then explained me that she had also been slapped and so on. No-one could really explain why. The red cheek made visible the blood which would come every month, but why? – I would like to reply also to her suggestion: "I suppose the Catholic attitudes towards feminine sexuality … heavily shaped the ritual life of women". This is certainly true and this has something to do with cultural interference and not with religious tradition. Could this perhaps also be the reason why so many women in Western tradition are looking for new rituals today? And since in Orthodox tradition we have maintained a lot of symbolic acts, is this the reason why we do not have to make this step for discovering new ones? This is just an honest reflection which comes into my mind.

*Coletta*

A wonderful message for me from Laime Kiskunaite: To look for old traditions and to create new ones in a very living way, to "create our own authentic life style." Also as a psychologist I like her descriptions of these moving and powerful rituals.

*Reacting to Katerina*
*Asphodel*

I like the story by Katerina Karkala-Zorba of the old woman in the Greek [*sic*] Orthodox church telling the younger one to look for God not at the Bishop and Priests but at the Iconostase. Katerina gives us a moving account of women's religious activities and responsibilities which give them an inner perception of their dignity and power. On the whole she appears to see no need for separation of the genders, but I found it especially interesting that the Greek Orthodox women feel powerful in having their own spiritual tasks and understand themselves to be the guardians of the faith and upholders of community with the dead.

## Coletta

A wonderful message for me from Katerina Karkala-Zorba: " I personally think that to a very large extent our faith is transmitted to us through our mothers and foremothers." Perhaps in all religions women are the guardians of the fire, giving the inner sense of religion to the next generation.

## Reacting to Coletta
### Asphodel

I felt grateful to Coletta Damm for her description of the important part the Muslimat have played historically in Islam and Sufism and how she wants to see more research on this subject which I hope can be widely disseminated. I was struck by her reference to the Arabic word root RHM (basis of description of God as compassionate and all-merciful) meaning uterus; the same of course is true in Hebrew. Phyllis Trible's work on the female nature of God in the Hebrew Bible is based on this fact.[6] Perhaps Muslim and Jewish women walking alongside each other on this pilgrimage, as they have already started to do, sharing what is common to them, can help heal the effects of the atrocious history of the current era.

## Susan

In Coletta's description of the separate women's gatherings, specifically the meeting which takes place forty days after a relative has passed away, I saw a wonderfully cohesive women's ritual community. She also deals with the question of ritual for men and women separate-or-together, as well as the impetus toward greater equality between men and women in the larger Sufi movement.

## Katerina

I do not want to appear to overreact to a Muslim, being myself Orthodox. Of course we have a very painful history in Greece with Muslims – or especially with Turkey – but I really feel that we have to be very honest in our relationship. It is very hard for Christians and Muslims to enter a dialogue just because we interpret some basic notions about justice, freedom, war, peace, love, etc. totally differently. – The text of Coletta Damm, although she is a German Muslim, and so, I suppose, a German woman who became Muslim later in her life, shows a great acceptance and understanding of the Muslim tradition. It is interesting to read about the rituals

---

6   Phyllis Trible, *God and the Rhetoric of Sexuality* (Fortress Press: Philadelphia, PA 1978), 31-59.

in Islam, and also about the meetings with other women, where religious songs and prayers are shared. But I have to struggle not to see in front of me the women in Islam with their black veils, totally covered, where women are equal to any other property of men, where they are just second class human beings. Perhaps it is easy to say that "Women's rights are a central concern of this (Sufi) order," when you live as a German Muslim in Germany, but what about Iraq or some African countries or even in oriental Turkey? – Coletta is speaking of a "separate religious women's culture" developed in Islam. But is this not the case simply because of the fact that women cannot or are not allowed to meet in the same locations as men? Is a separation not therefore implicit to all gatherings? The interesting aspect, which also shows the openness of women, is that women would invite also non-Muslim friends to join the meeting (women, I suppose). Interesting are also the references to Hagar, the second wife of Abraham. This refers directly to the connection with Israel and also with Christianity. I think we can walk together on this path and personally I would welcome an encounter with Muslim women.

### Thalia

I would like to take as my motif the figure of Hagar, whom Coletta Damm has presented as an ideal model for her as a Sufi woman. In Hagar women can see a choice of feminine model – together or alone. Hagar distinguishes herself as a single mother and as such receives God's grace. The biblical Hagar, however, forms a disharmonious feminine pair with Sarah. They fail to collaborate and their competitive relationship becomes ferocious.

### Reacting to Thalia
### Asphodel

From my own background I would say to Thalia that she is blessed in being able to take part in Kabbalistic studies and celebrations, denied to women of my own and earlier generations.

### Katerina

I cannot really see myself in the Kabbalistic thought of Thalia Gur-Klein's text, where she goes through recent Jewish mysticism with a strong symbolism. I just keep from this text the verse which is also important for us Christians "Love your neighbour as yourself," because I think this is common to those two religions. But I do not really know how this fits into the liturgical or ritual context we were asked about.

### Coletta

A wonderful message for me from Thalia Gur-Klein: "I believe that the Self always contains the Other and is contained by the Other…" The model of Abraham

Abolaffia reminds me of the ideas of the Andalusian mystic Ibn Arabi who lived in the same century. I like very much this ideas of separation but unity on many different levels. But most I like the wonderful poem: Being a "saintly woman of a miniature state." That means to me: I try to grow, and while I am trying to grow I try to accept my miniature state...

## 4. Contribution from one's own tradition

Four women responded to other author's contributions by sharing and explaining more of their own traditions. Caroline Mackenzie took one quote by Susan Roll about the symbolic elements and the use of arts in women's liturgy in order to stress the valuable contribution that could be made here from the Eastern Indian tradition, but which has not yet adequately been perceived by women liturgists. Laime Kiskunaite felt a need to explain further to Western women the situation of women in post-Soviet Union. Katerina Karkala-Zorba wanted to share the recent discussions of Orthodox women about the re-interpretation of women's rites as well as liturgies in her Church. And Coletta Damm attempted to evaluate further the problem of separation between men and women in the Islamic community as a question also to other feminists today. This seems to highlight voices that need to be heard for further feminist theological discussion in a European context.

## Caroline

As Roll puts it, women's liturgy can combine "stunningly creative use of visual, especially natural symbolic elements, attention to colour / drama and space for bodily gesture and dance" within a Catholic context. The only other place I have witnessed this combination has been with Catholics in India who are trying to *inculturate* or Indianise their faith. In marked contrast with this, in my context here in Britain I find there is plenty of creative, body-based, imaginative ritual but it will not be found in association with anything Christian. Rather it will be "New Age" or Neo-Pagan. While enjoying this creativity, I often experience a lack of depth because no one can agree who or what is the devotional focus.

I observed in India that deep structural changes have come about through the combination of spiritual / liturgical experiences, theological reflection and political circumstances. This has led to more than fifty new churches and chapels that reflect and *support* a more holistic liturgy. A major problem in my experience of the creative liturgies is that it is so difficult to maintain a sense of continuity and community.

It may be impossible to do things on the scale I achieved in India; however, it is important to pay attention to the iconography and symbols in the space where the ritual is done. The most fruitful commission I undertook in India was for a community of Cistercian nuns. The Hindu architect created a *mandala* style chapel (i.e. circular) and I designed the twelve windows. Since the two sisters I was working for agreed with the idea of *inculturation*, I was given the freedom to develop an iconography that is Biblically based, yet has as many images of women as men. The women are as much the subject of the journey as the men.

This sacred space would be supportive of the rituals described in these articles. It is more cosmic than the average western space. Eastern culture has a language of symbols that fits more easily with a female spirituality than that which has been developed in the West. Perhaps the most salient point is that the combination of eastern symbols with Christian texts is a new development. The problem with so many of the traditional western forms is that they have been created in such a different climate from our own where men have assumed their dominant position without question.

## Laime

I often read in the local press now that at least the aesthetic aspects of our social life (theatre, cinema and art) are undergoing rapid changes: the separation into "East" and "West" is noticeably decreasing and more young people are engaging themselves in these areas. The question is, which people? These optimistic statements raise some suspicion because we almost can not see any courageous and provocative women's works. Even those women artists who dare to show a piece of authentic feminine experience shout ahead that they *aren't* feminists. This situation can be found traditionally in the most active and leading fields of culture. The basic structures of society are much more inert. The Catholic Church of Lithuania still remains the bastion of patriarchy. In such conditions the feminist theories which criticize traditional politics and the fundamental "values" of patriarchy (including theological dogmas) find their way into everyday life of the post-soviet society with great difficulty. – Geographically I come from the post-soviet world – one of those "Eastern European women" – brought up as a resistant Catholic in the time of the Soviet regime. I spent the first 25 years of my life in the secluded and frightened society. There are many other women who were raised in the environment of ideological war, political fanaticism and demagogery, fear, lies and a permanent hypocrisy. For many Eastern European women religious experiences were extremely private and still are. Even today just a few women are open to the spiritual experience in the circle and actively participate in the creation of a new women's liturgy "in the public space of worship" (Susan Roll).

## Katerina

In my own Orthodox Christian way of celebrations and liturgical practices there are a lot of things which wait for me to be rediscovered or reinterpreted. So, I do not need – for myself – to look into other traditions, just because I would not understand fully these other traditions and because my own practice just fulfils me. I also think that in Christianity we have to rediscover some sides of our liturgical or ritual life, sides which perhaps have been hidden so far. In the Orthodox tradition, we have a lot of such practices, like the preparations of the Prosphora (the bread for communion), the preparation of the Epitaphios (the tomb of Jesus on Good Friday), etc. Those practices are done by women. – For example, we have blessings similar to those practised by the women in Lithuania: the blessing of the mother and the child on the 40th day after birth, the name-giving prayer on the 8th day, the prayer after a miscarriage or a still born child. After having given birth and for 40 days, a woman is called "lechona", which means the one who is in bed (from lechos – bed). Of course the blessing prayer after this is not easy to understand as it still has some references to impurity and sin. This comes still from the Jewish tradition. Some other rituals are connecting with liturgy or liturgical ornaments or objects. I already referred to the preparing of the bread. The first dough is prepared out of the water of the flowers of Thursday of the week before Easter (Passion). This is given from mother to daughter. Then the Epitaphios is prepared by women, although now in the big cities flower-shops take the job over. The girls preparing the tomb of Jesus are singing hymns and there are also myrophores at the procession of the Epitaphios on Good Friday. – I would like to end with a short reference to the Report of the Inter-Orthodox Meeting held in May 1997 in Istanbul where I had the chance to participate as a delegate of the Ecumenical Patriarchate. More than 50 women met on the subject "Discerning the Signs of the Times". The second recommendation was on "Liturgical life":

> The perception and interpretation of some of the practices pertaining to liturgical life need to be addressed. We ask for re-evaluation of certain liturgical customs, for example, the presentation of infants and the 40-day rule for childbirth, the prayer for miscarriages, abortions and post-partum mothers, and expectations pertaining to the reception of communion. Some of us feel these practices and prayers do not properly express the theology of the church regarding the dignity of God's creation of women and their redemption in Christ Jesus. We realize that the practices in the various local communities may differ. We recommend the incorporation of the lives of the martyrs, both women and men, and the new experience of the people in this century into the hymnography of the church. While this may be happening in some churches, we recommend a universal incorporation of the new martyrs of this century into the life of our church. Perhaps the best forum for such a recommendation is the upcoming Great and Holy Council.[7]

The meeting of Istanbul was the latest of several inter-Orthodox women's meetings over the last 25 years, including Damascus in 1996 (on the same subject as the Istanbul meeting), Livadia/Greece in 1994, Crete/Greece in 1991, Rhodos/Greece 1988, Agapia/Roumania, 1976. There have been other meetings and of course

---

7   Kyriaki Karidoyanes-FitzGerald (ed), *Orthodox Women Speak: Discerning the "Signs of the Times"* (Holy Cross Press: Brooklyn, MA 1999; WCC Publications: Geneva 2000).

Orthodox women were always invited to and participated at ecumenical and inter-faith meetings, but these were the most important meetings on the role of women in the Orthodox Church and the question of the ordination of women. The liturgical aspect has always played an important role at those meetings. But we have to add that this is the case for men and women. It is also important that at most of those meetings the question has been raised whether the establishment of new ministries for women as well as the creation of a women's association or institution worldwide would be necessary. I have to add that at the biggest clerico-lay Conference of the Ecumenical Patriarchate, held in Constantinople/Istanbul 25 November – 1 December 2000, the two elements which were most discussed were liturgical renewal and women's place in the church. For me it was an honour to introduce the subject "Women in the Parishes", a paper which has caused much discussion; I am still getting reactions to it.

## *Coletta*

In all articles I found these ideas of separation and unity – partnership with men, but concentration on one's own roots and one's own capabilities. The Qur'an says that we are created differently (women and men, people, nations etc.), to become acquainted with each other, to understand each other. I know several women who first left their traditional religious system because they were discontented, and then later they came back or found another form of spirituality. Had I been a man I would have joined Islam when I was about 14 or 15 years old: I was so impressed by the deep mystic reality of Islamic theism, but I couldn't accept the role of women (as far as I knew about at that time). At that age I still belonged to the Roman Catholic Church, where I had the same problems: I wanted to be active and no longer passive, and not sentimental or moralising (as Susan K. Roll wrote). So I joined a meditation group where women and men were accepted in the same way. After this experience I could come closer again to Islam, trying to find my own way beyond those traditions I didn't like, but looking for good traditions like the ones I wrote about.

## 5. Future Perspectives

In our questionnaire we asked women explicitly for their perspectives on the future development of women's ritual. The answers given stressed "different ways" (Asphodel) and the need of "valuing diversity" (Susan), rather than envisioning one mutual ritual for all. It seemed to me that answers were given only with hesitation, because women felt the need to reflect upon their own experiences first, before going a step ahead into the future. Some steps to be taken were named in talking about the rift between body and spirit (Caroline) that needs to be healed, as well as reflection about the positive and negative impact of the experience of difference (Coletta).

## Asphodel

Future development of women's ritual must learn from all different ways; the experiences of the last century exhibit the folly of proclaiming any one course to be the right and only one. This dialogue has shown clearly the resonances that are to be perceived in the effort of women, through ritual, to break through restrictive practice, to retain and maximise collective women's strengths in traditional settings, and to enjoy the freedoms of individual spiritual experience. The pilgrimage rings to the songs, age-old and new, that uplift and heal and give us strength to continue.

## Caroline

Women in Europe have a special role to play in healing the deep rift between body and emotions and spirit in religious culture. This is a theological task but eventually it involves a commitment to create sacred spaces that incarnate the insights in a practical way. It is these spaces that could enable women to have an ongoing "direct influence on the symbolic structures of worship" (Roll).

## Susan

What does this indicate for the future? First off, I see even more that unity is expressed in honoring and valuing diversity. ... Secondly, liturgy is never really just "empty ritual", or hollow words, or in this case a sort of artificially constructed playtime for religiously marginalized adults. In whatever ways, or to whatever degree, women see themselves present and constitutive of communal liturgy, that liturgy does indeed matter. ... I fear that there is a deeper question which underlies the future of women's liturgy, namely: if, in the long term and on a large scale, women continue to form separate groups to do creative liturgy from explicitly women-identified / feminist perspectives, does this reinforce the argument that men and women differ from each other in essence? Or is gender simply one among a range of variations among human persons, whose humanity is held in common? Among Catholics there is an aggressive reactionary right wing promoting the former, "essentialist" argument as a way to keep women "in their place". Does the proliferation of women's liturgies inadvertently give support to this position? Do we want to say instead that eventually, in a world of greater gender justice with sensitivity and acceptance of all human persons as such, liturgical forms should evolve in a more and more inclusive manner to the point that gender injustice is erased? This will take considerable groundwork, since there is a monumental amount of subliminal misogyny present in official public worship (at least from what I can see), and which presents itself uncritically as a universal norm. It looks to me as if the journey toward just and authentic liturgy, in whatever tradition, has barely begun. The good news, however, is that it has indeed begun!

## Laime

Still focusing upon the women's rituals of my country, I begin to feel a lack of a liturgy of the Word. The next very important task which could be achieved through the women's rituals is elaborating new ways, forms of expressing the religious sense and the regular introduction of new people to women-identified liturgy. ... I hope that through my thoughts and words, through the fragments of our spiritual life we will become more familiar and understandable for the women from the rest of the world.

## Coletta

Even today for many people in the traditional religions, "different" means for women and men a specific kind of difference, as Asphodel Long said: men's leadership and a less important role for women, exclusion from the "real service". But on the other hand there are deep connections with the other women and the possibility of transcendence of every day's difficulties. For me one of the main questions is: How can we find (or re-find) and appreciate our own female way of spirituality and how can we live this in our religions / spiritual systems. Should we look for separate ways or should we avoid them, because we could be fixed in a less important role? Women's rituals – this is my conclusion – are as important today as they were in former times and they help us find a better connection to our own roots and the own possibilities. Women should join (and create) them and they should help men to understand and accept their importance.

## Conclusion

The dialogue on women, ritual and liturgy was intended to raise authentic voices of European women from different religious and cultural contexts, rather than presenting an academic discourse in the field of liturgical studies. Thus we are glad to have been able to present not only voices from Christian backgrounds, but also contributions from Jewish and Muslim as well as those with interest in, and knowledge of, Goddess and Hindu spirituality. Our original intention, as incorporated in the four questions, was also to offer a contribution to the feminist theological discussion on women's ritual which arose less out of theory than out of liturgical or ritual praxis within a European context. Having said this, I regret the lack of Protestant and Anglican Christian voices, that is, those Christian traditions in which women are now "blessed in being able to take part" in leading normal worship (as Asphodel said to Thalia, who did not, however, thematise this experience), and in which it is no longer necessarily an oxymoron (however deliberate or delightful: Susan) to speak of women's liturgies.[8] Still the question remains: What has been achieved in this dialogue? And how can we evaluate its results? As editor and silent partner of this dialogue-article, I, Annette Esser, suggest looking at the following feminist theological, liturgical, and sociological aspects:

*Group dynamics*

From a sociometric perspective what arose in this dialogue was a rather interesting group dynamic that may be representative for, or give an image of, similar constellations of women when they discuss or practise rituals, e.g. at ESWTR's conferences. The affinities between and / or rejections of other positions were not always to be expected.

For example I would have expected an affinity between Asphodel Long's Goddess spirituality and women creating new rituals in Lithuania, but found the mutual interest of Asphodel and Katerina Karkala-Zorba in each other's praxis a surprise. Similarly, I wondered how the Muslim voice of Coletta Damm would be adopted by other Jewish and Christian participants and was surprised by the very positive reaction of the two Jewish contributors on the one hand and the very critical Christian Orthodox voice of Katerina on the other hand. To find that the Biblical figure of Hagar, represented at first by Muslim Coletta, was taken up as a new discovery and adopted as a figure of identity by both a Jewish (Thalia) and a Christian woman (Katerina), might also surprise those who are aware of the impact of this figure in African American womanist theology.[9]

Turning to the voices which were more generally accepted or rejected, particularly those of Susan Roll and Caroline Mackenzie, it is revealing to look more closely into women's reasoning and assessment of the other's position. Thus, Caroline's approach to women's ritual as a Catholic woman artist informed by Hinduism was criticised from two different angles: one representing Christian Orthodoxy (Katerina), the other representing a feminist position (Asphodel). What was questioned here was, on the one hand, Caroline's combining of traditions that led her to "re-work" the Easter liturgy, and on the other hand the "gender-blindness" that allowed her to glorify femininity in the Eastern mystical tradition. In responses to Catholic American liturgist Susan

---

[8]  I would like to thank Charlotte Methuen, who in her editorial reading critically remarked the lack of just these voices. This was not intentional; unfortunately, the two Protestant women we had originally invited to participate had to drop out for personal reasons.

[9]  Delores Williams, *Sisters in the Wilderness. The Challenge of Womanist God-Talk* (Orbis: Maryknoll, NY 1993).

Roll, however, these two categories, the relatedness to tradition and to feminism, seemed to have played out in just the other way. Susan was applauded from contrasting sides, e.g. from Orthodox Katerina as well as from Laime Kiskunaite who represents newly constructed women's rituals in Lithuania. Several participants quoted her words explicitly, and Caroline wrote her entire essay as a response to a phrase of Susan's. It seems to me that the way Susan Roll struggles between her own Catholic tradition and her feminism in regards to developing women's ritual and liturgy functions, or can be understood as, a kind of bridge-building between very disparate positions. That Susan, as an American professor of liturgy, is of all our participants the best informed by the academic feminist discussion in the liturgical field, demonstrates also how enriching and constructive this discussion can be in the European context.

*Categories*
Thus said, it is interesting to look more closely at the categories into which women put each other in order to understand or position themselves and the other. Asphodel Long, for instance, uses three categories:
 (1) mystical and gender-blind (Caroline, Thalia)
 (2) feminist (Susan, Asphodel)
 (3) women-oriented (Katerina, Coletta)
But Laime Kiskunaite, whose work seemed so closely connected to Asphodel's, talks about two mainstreams of women's ritual and liturgy around the world:
 (1) the remembering and creative re-thinking the tradition of the ritual / "sacred female activity" (Asphodel) as well as integrating "a new consciousness of the instinctive life-forces" (Caroline), and
 (2) acting within one's own religious tradition (Islam, Catholic, Orthodox, Jewish etc.) "assuring the authoritative presence of women in the public space of worship" (Susan).
In this model, Asphodel is put in the same first category as Caroline, whereas Susan Roll is in a different category from her. The issue at stake seems to be again whether the notion of one's relation to feminism (Asphodel) or to tradition (Laime) counts as the primordial parameter for understanding each other. Therefore it is urgent to look and to communicate more deeply about our respective understanding and definition of feminism and of tradition regarding our ritual / liturgical praxis.
   Concerning the notion of feminism, notice for example that Caroline Mackenzie herself puts her work into a feminist perspective when she identi-

fies women feeling "side-lined from the mainline," and sees a connection between Eastern spirituality and what she perceives as a Western feminist position. It is precisely her intention to contribute to this discussion from the perspective of her practical (and artistic) work in order to influence "the symbolic structures of worship and their official interpretations" (Susan).

With respect to tradition, it is important to notice that although all women seem to need a sense of tradition each of these women has a very different understanding of and relationship to her own tradition, depending on how deeply rooted within or disconnected they are from it (e.g. the contrast between Asphodel and Thalia in regard to Judaism) or the extent to which, and with what additional consciousness, they seek to grasp it anew. I would suggest distinguishing between four categories of relationship with tradition:
– a newly chosen tradition (Coletta, Asphodel, Laime)
– a tradition recognised as a root, but no longer as a direct source of faith (Asphodel)
– the awareness of an unbroken tradition that may have to be rediscovered and reformulated (Katerina, Thalia)
– a feminist consciousness of one's own tradition as patriarchal, and thus in need of deconstruction and reconstruction (Susan, Caroline).

*Voices to be heard*
Considering the discussion on feminism and tradition in women's ritual / liturgy as an agenda, it is interesting to see which women feel an urgent need to contribute to this discussion from her own tradition and perspective. I think that it was not just by chance that lengthy statements were given by Caroline Mackenzie on the Eastern Indian tradition, Laime Kiskunaite on the Eastern European praxis of women in the Post-Soviet countries, Katerina Karkala-Zorba on Orthodox women's discussions, and of Coletta Damm on Muslim women's questions of separation versus unity with men. It seems that these contributions represent the voices missing so far in the European feminist theological discussion on women's ritual and liturgy, voices which now wish and need to be taken into account.

*Future Vision*
What vision for the future arises from this? I would affirm Asphodel Long's remark about "the folly of proclaiming any one course to be the right and only one," which would almost inevitably depend on a superficial evaluation of what unites us all. But I also think that before we fall back into individualism

and just let everyone celebrate her own ritual according to her own belief, we should start to dialogue better with each other. Interestingly, it was Katerina Karkala-Zorba, who at times appeared to be the most critical regarding other women's contributions and praxis, who expressed her wish that we should "all communicate through the common things which are uniting us and not through our differences." I think we should indeed consider our commonalities but also talk open-mindedly about our differences, since these constitute our identities. We need to listen to all the voices amongst us, pleasing or not, before we attempt to reconstruct a mutual feminist vision and practice. In theory, it is politically correct to stress difference and to name our identity (such as mine as a white, Catholic, German woman). But it is another step to experience our differences in encounters that may not always be delightful but can be challenging and painful as well.

What we can build up in this way is a mutual connectedness that does not ignore our differences. I hope that one day we will be able to celebrate this in a ritual that does not lack a "devotional focus" (Caroline), but is a "liturgy of the word" (Laime) as well.

Dieser Artikel dokumentiert einen schriftlichen Dialog zwischen sieben Frauen über die Fragen nach Ritual und Liturgie von Frauen. Dabei repräsentierte jede der Teilnehmerinnen eine, manchmal auch zwei, Frauentradition in Europa, sowie einen unterschiedlichen Zugang zu ihrer Tradition. So kommen die Frauen zwar mehrheitlich aus christlicher und jüdischer Glaubenshintergrund, aber islamische und hinduistische Traditionen, sowie Göttinnenspiritualität und die Praxis feministischen Rituals sind ebenfalls unter ihnen gegenwärtig. In dem Dialogprozess schrieb zunächst jede über ihr eigenes Verständnis und ihre eigenen Erfahrungen als Frau mit Liturgie und Ritual. Diese ersten Statements wurden dann untereinander ausgetauscht, so dass in einem zweiten Schritt eine Reaktion darauf erfolgen konnte. Dabei identifizierten sich Frauen manchmal mit einer anderen Frau aus einer ganz anderen Tradition, oder reagierten in einigen Fällen auch sehr kritisch aufeinander. Für die Zukunft feministischen Rituals / Liturgie bedeutet dies, dass verschiedene Stimmen gehört und verschiedene Perspektiven akzeptiert werden, während wir lernen Brücken zwischen Frauen mit unterschiedlicher Spiritualität zu bauen.

Cet article rend compte d'un dialogue écrit entre sept femmes sur les questions de rituel et de liturgie féminine. Chacune des participantes représentait une voire deux traditions féminines en Europe ainsi qu'un rapport différent à leur tradition. Les femmes viennent certes majoritairement de l'arrière-plan religieux judéo-chrétien mais sont parmi elles également représentés les traditions islamique, hindouiste et la spiritualité mettant en exergue les divinités féminine et la pratique du rituel féministe. Dans le processus de dialogue chacune écrit sa propre compréhension et expérience en tant que femme de la liturgie et du rituel. Les premiers témoignages furent échangés au sein du groupe afin de permettre au groupe de réagir lors d'une seconde phase. Ainsi les femmes s'identifièrent parfois avec une femmes d'une toute autre tradition ou réagirent dans certains cas de manière très critique les unes envers les autres. Pour l'avenir des rituels ou de la liturgie féministe, cela signifie que différentes voix doivent être entendues et différentes perspectives acceptées tandis que nous apprenons à construire des ponts entre des femmes de spiritualité différentes.

*Denise J.J. Dijk*

# L'aspiration à une image de la liturgie

La plupart de ceux qui se sentent concernés par les études féministes en sciences de la liturgie souscriraient sans doute de bon cœur à la devise de Herman Wegman, spécialiste en liturgie: "La vérité n'appartient pas seulement au passé". Dans ma thèse: *L'aspiration à une image*,[1] j'explore en cinq analyses ce nouveau champ des études féministes en théologie. Jusqu'ici, cette nouvelle discipline – les études féministes en sciences de la liturgie – s'est surtout implantée aux Etats-Unis. C'est la raison pour laquelle j'accorde tant d'attention d'une part au mouvement qui aux Etats-Unis porte cette nouvelle pousse de la théologie, autrement dit le Mouvement pour une Liturgie Féministe, et d'autre part à l'une des pionnières de ce mouvement, la féministe protestante spécialiste en liturgie Marjorie Procter-Smith. Je propose également une description ainsi qu'une interprétation de ce mouvement et du travail de Procter-Smith parce que je suis convaincue qu'ils sont d'une grande importance pour une réflexion sur la situation en Europe. Dans les lignes qui suivent, je vous fait part d'un certain nombre d'observations qui, à mon avis, sont d'un intérêt majeur.

Aux Etats-Unis et ailleurs, le point de départ du Mouvement pour une Liturgie Féministe se situe dans l'expérience d'un "ce n'est pas cela", un sentiment de malaise aigu envers la liturgie traditionnelle et particulièrement l'androcentrisme du culte dominical actuel et de la liturgie chrétienne traditionnelle, centrés sur l'univers des hommes, sur l'expérience des hommes avec Dieu et les uns avec les autres.[2] Le malaise des femmes est alimenté par leur profond désir d'une liturgie chrétienne et d'une tradition où elles sont "sujet" et qui reconnaissent comme une évidence la tradition liturgique qu'elles sont en train de mettre en place.

---

[1]  Denise J.J. Dijk, *Een beeld van een liturgie. Verkenningen in vrouwenstudies liturgiek, met bijzondere aandacht voor het werk van Marjorie Procter-Smith* (Narratio: Gorinchem 1999).

[2]  Marjorie Procter-Smith, *In Her Own Rite: Constructing Feminist Liturgical Tradition* (Abingdon Press: Nashville 1990).

Une pratique liturgique féministe s'est développée dans de nombreux pays. Le fait que les femmes se manifestent et qu'elles se retrouvent au centre de la liturgie est caractéristique de cette praxis.[3] Ce sont les femmes qui donnent forme à ces liturgies et, dans ces liturgies, elles ont aussi la priorité. Elles assument les changements souhaitables pour les femmes en matière de liturgie. C'est la dignité de la femme qui importe surtout. Du point de vue du contenu, l'univers concret des femmes d'aujourd'hui est au centre de cette liturgie. Le fait qu'elles souffrent de la liturgie est mis au grand jour. Cette praxis insiste aussi sur la façon de célébrer. Il est ici question d'une utilisation consciente de multiples symboles. La formation d'un cercle entraîne une transformation de l'espace liturgique. La direction se fait de façon égalitaire, c'est-à-dire que les femmes en groupes passent avant. On transforme non seulement la façon dont les femmes s'adressent à Dieu mais aussi la façon dont on mentionne et représente les femmes dans la liturgie. La praxis se caractérise en outre par une tension évidente entre tradition et liberté. On introduit un nouveau contenu dans les anciennes formes liturgiques et les concepts théologiques. On donne des contenus nouveaux aux formes traditionnelles en les élargissant ou en ajoutant d'autres éléments, et on crée des célébrations entièrement nouvelles pour les femmes. Les concepts théologiques sont reconsidérés du point de vue de la libération des femmes, par exemple la notion de péché. L'image traditionnelle de Dieu est corrigée au moyen des images féminines présentes dans la Bible et dans la tradition liturgique, au moyen également des images qui naissent dans l'imagination féministe et enfin en utilisant des pronoms émancipateurs pour désigner Dieu. Les pronoms exclusivement masculins utilisés pour désigner Dieu sont absolument rejetés.

C'est à travers cette pratique du changement que les femmes du Mouvement pour une Liturgie Féministe et tout particulièrement les chercheuses des études féministes en sciences de la liturgie remettent en question la praxis liturgique traditionnelle d'aujourd'hui. Elles se demandent par exemple: Quelles sont les personnes concernées par la liturgie traditionnelle? ou encore: Dans la tradition liturgique chrétienne, le cérémoniel et le discours liturgiques représentent les intérêts de qui? Ces questions sont soulevées aux Etats-Unis non seulement dans le domaine de la liturgie mais aussi dans les principales Eglises. Depuis le début des années soixante-dix,

---

[3]   Teresa Berger, "The Women's Movement as a Liturgical Movement," dans: *Studia Liturgica* 20 (1990), 55-64.

les femmes critiquent le langage et les symboles androcentristes que l'on trouve dans la liturgie.[4] Elles ont profondément influencé à différents niveaux la politique liturgique des Eglises. Elles ont beaucoup innové, surtout dans le domaine du "langage inclusif". Aux Etats-Unis, on est de plus en plus conscient des préjugés concernant la race et le sexe qui se manifestent dans le langage de tous les jours – mais également dans la liturgie. Des éditeurs de renom et des organisations d'enseignement se sont donnés pour ligne de conduite de traiter les deux sexes en égaux dans le langage, d'éviter les stéréotypes et d'élaborer des images féminines et raciales positives. Ainsi le pronom anglais "he" est remplacé par "she or he" ou par "one" et le mot "mankind" par "humankind". Conséquence de cette évolution, la langue en Amérique du Nord est devenue de plus en plus sexuellement neutre. Dans la situation actuelle, les pasteurs courent le risque d'être mal compris par les membres des communautés et des paroisses quand ils parlent de "man's salvation" (le salut de l'homme). Les auditeurs et les auditrices penseront que la rédemption et le salut de Dieu ne concernent que les hommes. Dans ce contexte, l'utilisation d'un "langage de Dieu" masculin fait que, bien davantage qu'autrefois, les femmes et les hommes interprètent Dieu comme masculin.[5]

Le terme "langage inclusif" réfère à la remise en cause de tout langage qui exclut une personne – ou un groupe de personnes – en raison de son sexe, de sa race, de son statut social, de son âge, de sa préférence sexuelle ou physique ou de ses capacités mentales, de son appartenance à un groupe ethnique, à une nation ou à un groupement religieux. En faisant usage d'un langage inclusif, les Eglises s'efforcent de remettre en question et de faire apparaître dans la liturgie les noms, les récits et les expériences des femmes. Cette utilisation d'un langage inclusif commence par la reconnaissance du fait que l'androcentrisme dans la liturgie n'est pas compatible avec l'égalité entre les femmes et les hommes. Les femmes comme les hommes ont été créés à l'image et à la ressemblance de Dieu.

En raison de cette évolution, les principales Eglises des Etats-Unis ont introduit une langue liturgique "inclusive" dans les livres des offices et les livres des chants surtout dans les passages où la langue concerne les êtres

---

[4]  Ruth C. Duck, "Inclusive Language," dans: Letty M. Russell and J. Shannon Clarkson (eds.), *Dictionary of Feminist Theologies* (John Knox Press: Louisville 1996), 152-153.

[5]  Gail Ramshaw, *God Beyond Gender: Feminist Christian Doxological Language* (Fortress: Minneapolis 1995), 25-27.

humains.[6] On a aussi transformé la "langue de Dieu" dans la liturgie mais dans une plus faible mesure. Les gens sont plus réticents lorsqu'il s'agit de changer la façon de parler de Dieu et de Jésus. C'est quand même curieux de voir que l'on accepte de représenter Dieu comme un homme noir et Jésus comme un "campesino" mais que l'on n'arrive pas ou très difficilement à accepter l'image d'une femme sur la croix.

Dans les textes liturgiques et les livres de chants des Etats-Unis, le mot "Seigneur" par exemple est devenu "Dieu créateur" ou "Dieu de miséricorde". Dans de nombreux chants, on a remplacé "Père" par "Dieu". On limite le plus possible les pronoms masculins qui réfèrent à Dieu et on les remplace par des références sexuellement neutres. "His grace" est remplacé par exemple par "God's grace". Quand, dans les nouveaux chants, on opte pour des images féminines, Dieu est souvent appelé "mère". Parler de Dieu de manière alternative, cela se réduit à parler de Dieu une fois au féminin et une autre fois au masculin. En se limitant à cela, on ne met pas la communauté suffisamment en état de faire connaissance avec les métaphores féminines de Dieu, comme par exemple celles d'amie ou de sagesse de femme. C'est un inconvénient. Il est préférable en fait de développer une image féminine tout au long du chant. Tout en chantant, l'assemblée a ainsi le temps et le loisir de s'approprier ces nouvelles images et leur signification.[7]

On rectifie pour une grande part l'androcentrisme que manifestent les rédacteurs du calendrier des lectures dans leur choix des textes bibliques. Ceci revient à y inclure un plus grand nombre de récits bibliques présentant des femmes témoins de l'Evangile. Sous les auspices du Conseil des Eglises Américaines, une traduction inclusive des années A, B et C du calendrier des lectures est proposée – à titre expérimental – à ses membres.[8] Par ailleurs, des traductions plus "inclusives" de la Bible sont utilisées comme Bible de chaire.

Selon la chercheuse spécialiste de la liturgie Marjorie Procter-Smith, ces rectifications de la liturgie androcentriste contribuent à l'élaboration d'une

---

[6] Dijk, *Een beeld van een liturgie*, 64-74. Paul. F. Bradshaw / Lawrence A. Hoffman (eds), *The Making of Jewish and Christian Worship* (Two Liturgical Traditions 2; University of Notre Dame Press: Notre Dame 1991), passim.

[7] Ruth C. Duck, conférence non publiée, "Feminist Emancipatory Liturgy: Building Bridges, Sowing Seeds." An Address to the Hymn Society in the United States and Canada and to the Canadian Liturgical Society, Toronto, Canada, 8. juillet 1993.

[8] Division of Education and Ministry, *An Inclusive Language Lectionary: Readings for Year A* (Pilgrim: New York 1986).

liturgie chrétienne et d'une tradition liturgique. Selon elle, les rectifications que je cite ne suffisent pas à "réparer" l'amnésie liturgique dont les Eglises font preuve concernant les femmes.

Comme la mémoire de l'Eglise a été très sélective et qu'en plus l'héritage liturgique des femmes n'a été conservé que de façon minime, une très grande part de cet héritage a été perdue. Et quand la liturgie chrétienne n'a pas trop souffert d'amnésie à l'égard des femmes, l'Eglise a déformé sa mémoire.[9] C'est l'androcentrisme qui en est la cause. Lorsque l' "ego" masculin collectif occupe la place centrale, les autres "ego" sont définis comme autres et inférieurs à cet "ego" masculin. Ils n'existent qu'en relation avec le "je" masculin. On ne reconnaît pas à l'autre – c'est-à-dire aux femmes – le statut de sujet en soi. Les femmes n'existent que dans les déformations et les stéréotypes à quoi le je masculin les réduit.[10] Dans les dix commandements, les femmes n'apparaissent que comme étant la propriété du prochain masculin: "Tu ne désireras pas la femme de ton prochain, ni ses…". L'androcentrisme fait de l'autre un objet sur lequel "on", c'est-à-dire l'homme, peut agir. Si les femmes ne sont pas sujets dans les 10 commandements, elles ne le sont pas non plus dans bien d'autres textes. Par exemple dans le passage où Dieu conclut un pacte avec son peuple sur le Horeb.[11] L'androcentrisme de ces textes bibliques est repris sans problème dans la liturgie chrétienne, même dans les textes récents. N'est-il pas vrai que ces textes englobent tout le monde dans une culture qui considère cette manière de penser comme évidente?

Quand le sexe est bien spécifié dans les textes liturgiques, on transforme ces textes de façon à ce que les hommes y occupent une place centrale. La parabole des 5 vierges sages et des 5 vierges folles devient un cantique sur un serviteur fidèle. La parabole du berger qui possède 100 brebis et en perd une est un récit essentiel pour se faire une image de Jésus et de la mission pastorale. La parabole qui lui succède, dans l'Evangile de Luc (15) raconte l'histoire de la femme qui possède 10 drachmes et en perd une. Une fois la drachme retrouvée, elle organise une fête avec ses amies et voisines. Cette parabole ne se retrouve pas dans le Livre des Cantiques des Eglises. L'exégèse "normale" marginalise les expériences de cette femme. De plus, sa

---

[9] Procter-Smith, *In Her Own Rite*, 36-54.
[10] Margrit Eichler, *Nonsexist Research Methods. A Practical Guide* (Allen & Unwin: Boston 1988), 19-20.
[11] Judith Plaskow, *Standing Again at Sinai: Judaism from a Feminist Perspective* (Harper & Row: San Francisco 1990), 25-26.

manière de faire est stéréotypée. Elle aurait été très dépensière. En fait, ce texte est un véritable trésor. La façon de faire d'une femme qui se réjouit avec ses amies parce que ce qui a été perdu est à nouveau retrouvé, correspond à la façon de faire et la joie de Dieu pour tout pécheur qui se convertit.

La célébration liturgique ne répond pas à l'attente et manque d'objectivité quand l'assemblée réunie introduit l'histoire du salut – tellement essentielle pour l'identité du christianisme –, comme étant uniquement l'histoire du salut de Dieu avec les hommes. Selon Procter-Smith, nous devons compléter la célébration chrétienne avec la célébration juive qui est dialogique de nature. Il ne s'agit pas seulement ici de célébrer les actes sacrés de Dieu mais aussi de Dieu qui se souvient des femmes, comme Anne et Agar. Cette rectification amène l'élaboration d'une tradition liturgique qui donne à l'héritage liturgique des femmes la place qui lui revient. Cela signifie que, dans la pratique dominicale et quotidienne, on désigne nommément et respectueusement les femmes de la Bible et les femmes d'aujourd'hui ainsi que les actes qui sont les leurs.

Pour finir je donne deux exemples frappants de la manière dont Procter-Smith travaille à la construction d'une tradition liturgique féministe.

Elle évoque en premier lieu une péricope dans Marc (14: 3-9). Selon Marc, Jésus reçoit l'onction d'une femme disciple anonyme. Jésus loue cette femme pour son acte – celui de l'oindre avec une huile coûteuse – par ces mots: "En vérité je vous le dis, partout où sera proclamé l'Evangile, dans le monde entier, on redira aussi, à sa mémoire, ce qu'elle vient de faire." Selon Procter-Smith, on ne retrouve jamais ou pratiquement jamais l'onction de cette femme ni les paroles de Jésus dans les célébrations liturgiques commémorant la Passion de Jésus, ni surtout dans les calendriers des lectures ou les liturgies des onctions. Et quand on retrouve ce récit, il est alors intégré non pas dans la lecture courte mais dans la lecture plus longue du calendrier des lectures. De plus le texte ne se retrouve que dans une seule des années du cycle de trois ans du calendrier des lectures. Si, dans la liturgie, on utilise la "lecture plus courte", on peut laisser tomber la lecture plus longue. Cela veut dire que dans les temples qui utilisent un calendrier des lectures, on ne lit pas publiquement l'histoire de la femme qui oint Jésus. Procter-Smith interprète l'acte de cette femme non seulement comme un acte politique – puisque, comme le prophète Samuel, elle oint le futur roi – mais aussi comme un acte liturgique. Elle pense en effet que l'onction de Jésus par cette femme a eu une signification dans l'acte du baptême au sein des premières communautés chrétiennes. En ne lisant pas ce récit comme appartenant à sa tradition, l'Eglise omet certes de se souvenir des femmes mais elle oublie aussi que les femmes ont été les acteurs d'actes liturgiques. Cette omission de l'Eglise est un paradigme de son amnésie concernant les femmes. L'Eglise ferait bien de se tenir à la promesse de Jésus: partout où l'Evangile sera annoncée, on parlera aussi "à sa mémoire".[12] La commémoration de cet acte liturgique et prophétique amène à une rectification importante qui s'étend jusqu'à la prière eucharistique. Parler et agir "en mémoire de moi" est en effet incomplet si on ne parle pas et si on n'agit pas aussi en mémoire de cette femme.

Le second exemple de rectification est plus radical que le premier. Les récits des femmes disciples sont rares dans les Evangiles. On ne les trouve que de manière marginale. Aussi, dans les assemblées qui se tiennent aux calendriers des lectures et prennent la Bible comme source principale, ces récits sont à peine mentionnés dans le temps de la Passion et à Pâques. Procter-Smith trouve que cela n'est absolument pas justifié car la tradition liturgique reste ainsi enfermée dans un cadre de référence androcentriste. Si l'on veut que cela change, il faut chercher des solutions de manière créative. Selon elle, il est souhaitable de modifier le canon actuel, c'est-à-dire l'usage des textes bibliques dans la liturgie, et d'y ajouter d'autres textes, par exemple des textes écrits par des femmes poètes. Par ailleurs, pour rectifier l'héritage liturgique exclusivement masculin, il faut éveiller et stimuler l'imagination de la communauté afin d'élargir la tradition en ce sens. Car la vérité n'appartient pas seulement au passé. Elle propose un calendrier des lectures chrétien et féministe incluant une page blanche portant simplement en en-tête ces quelques phrases: "La mission des femmes disciples".[13] Comment la communauté remplit-elle cette page vide? Qui sont les appelées? Quels noms de femmes citons-nous? Quels récits du Nouveau Testament sont essentiels en cela et quels récits contemporains? Quels sont les récits de la Bible destructeurs pour les femmes? Peut-on les lire comme un Evangile? Parlent-ils vraiment "en mémoire d'elle"?

Procter-Smith considère que les femmes chrétiennes d'aujourd'hui doivent créer un cadre de référence narratif qui soit communautaire, un cadre pour comprendre ensemble leur vie dans des conditions qui soient les leurs. Un tel cadre est en cours d'élaboration. Il se met en place là où les femmes percent

---

[12] Procter-Smith, *In Her Own Rite*, 39, 175.
[13] Marjorie Procter-Smith, "Beyond the New Common Lectionary: A Constructive Critique," dans: *Quarterly Review* (Summer 1993), 49-58; 55.

les récits qui parlent d'elles dans la Bible: la narration de l'épouse fidèle qui enfante des fils; la narration de la femme qui a "péché" – dans l'ancienne narration, ses péchés sont la plupart du temps d'ordre sexuel –; et la narration pour laquelle les relations entre les femmes n'existent pas ou sont présentées dans une perspective négative.

Pour créer une tradition liturgique qui reconnaît les femmes comme sujets, il est essentiel de raconter ensemble de nouveaux récits; des récits sur ce que sont les femmes et ce qu'elles deviennent. La narration est le pivot autour duquel tourne cette construction féministe. Le processus de la construction d'une tradition liturgique féministe commence par l'expression d'un "non" aux narrations existantes et se poursuit par la mise en mots, dans l'assemblée, de la vérité sur la vie des femmes. C'est à partir de ces récits que de nouveaux dialogues avec Dieu mais aussi les uns avec les autres peuvent se faire. Procter-Smith le formule de manière plus prégnante: "Les récits personnels de vie deviennent aussi des récits de Dieu".[14] Les récits que les femmes racontent dans les célébrations féministes sont des récits de Dieu, des récits sacrés.

The Feminist Liturgical Movement begins from Christian women's experience of discomfort and alienation from the Sunday liturgy and the androcentric presuppositions which support it, together with their desire for a liturgy in which women are the subjects and agents of the liturgy. One serious concern is the introduction of inclusive language in worship by which women become visible and their experience recognized. The conventional language which describes God as "Lord" or "Father" is gradually being supplanted with terms which develop the feminine image of God. An increased use in liturgy of Biblical texts which describe the experience of women is not sufficient to rectify the patriarchal bias written into the texts themselves. Two texts which can contribute to the construction of a feminist liturgical tradition are Mark 14.3-9, the account of the woman who anointed Jesus, whose story was to be retold "in memory of her," and the traces in the gospel accounts of the women disciples of Christ. The stories of women today, together with their willingness to say No to the traditional narratives which exclude or demean women, form the basis for the construction of a feminist liturgical tradition.

Die Frauenliturgiebewegung hat ihren Ursprung in den Entfremdungserfahrungen christlicher Frauen mit sonntäglichen Gottesdiensten und der diesen zugrunde liegenden androzentrischen Voraussetzungen, sowie auch in ihrem Wunsch nach einer Liturgie, in der Frauen Subjekte und Handlungsträger des Ritualisierens sein

---

[14] Marjorie Procter-Smith, *Praying with Our Eyes Open. Engendering Feminist Liturgical Prayer* (Abingdon Press: Nashville 1995), 58-60; Dijk, *Een beeld van een liturgie,* 122-127.

können. Entscheidend wichtig dafür ist, dass in den Liturgien inklusive Sprache eingeführt wird, so dass Frauen sichtbar und ihre Erfahrungen wahrgenommen werden können. Darin wird die konventionelle Gottesdienstsprache, die Gott als "Herr" oder "Vater" bezeichnet, schrittweise durch Begriffe ersetzt, die das weibliche Bild Gottes entfalten. Ein vermehrter liturgischer Gebrauch biblischer Texten, welche die Erfahrung von Frauen beschreiben, genügt allein nicht, um die einseitig patriarchale Ausrichtung dieser Texte zu berichtigen. Zwei biblische Texte werden von der Autorin herbeigezogen, um eine feministische liturgische Tradition zu begründen. Der eine handelt von der Frau, die Jesus salbt, und deren Geschichte "zu ihrem Gedächtnis" erzählt werden soll (Mk 14, 3-9); beim anderen Text geht es um die Spuren, die im Evangelium von den Jüngerinnen Jesu erhalten sind. Die Geschichten der Frauen heute, zusammen mit ihrer Bereitschaft, Nein zu den traditionellen Erzählungen zu sagen, die Frauen ausschließen oder abwerten, bilden die Basis, um eine neue feministische liturgische Tradition zu begründen.

***Denise J.J. Dijk*** (1944) studied theology (Master of Divinity) at the University of Amsterdam, Lexington Theological Seminary, Lexington, KY, USA, and at the American University in Cairo, Egypt, and trained for the ministry of the Netherlands Reformed Church at the University of Amsterdam. She has worked in the field of theological women's studies since 1980, at Erasmus University Rotterdam, at the Theological Faculty of the Free University in Amsterdam (1982-1986), and since 1987 as associate professor at the Theological University in Kampen. She was ordained in the Netherlands Reformed Church in 1998. She holds a PhD in practical theology, focusing on Women's Studies in Liturgy.

*Teresa Berger*

# Prayers and Practices of Women: Lex Orandi Reconfigured

> *God may well operate ... in a particular construct of*
> *textual tradition, but what about the rituals and feasts?*
> *What about the prayers and practices of women?*[1]

## I. Liturgy as a source for theological reflection

In recent years, the liturgy has (re-)emerged as a distinctive source for theological reflection. Theologians from a broad spectrum of positions now claim liturgy as a fundamental site for understanding, interpreting, and configuring the Christian faith. These liturgical theologians often summarize their claim by an oscillating shorthand version of a Patristic axiom, *lex orandi, lex credendi*: the law of praying is the law of believing; worship shapes faith; as you pray, so do you believe. What is striking about this development is the way in which these theologians have occluded the distinct shape of the prayers and practices of women. While emphasizing that God operates not only in textual traditions, but also in "the rituals and feasts", they have clearly not attended to "the prayers and practices of women."[2] The reasons for this inattentiveness are multiple, but three stand out. First, the theological recourse to liturgical tradition is based on a liturgical historiography which is inattentive to the profoundly gendered nature of worship practices in the Christian community. That is, liturgical tradition continues to be constructed as gender-blind or gender-neutral, and our understanding of liturgical history thus continues to be shaped by complex forms of marginalization, of silencing, and of misnaming of women's prayers and practices. Theologians claiming this liturgical tradition for their work cannot but reproduce the androcentrism of the liturgical master narrative. Second, this androcentrism is exacerbated by the nature of the theological arguments made through the

---

[1]  Rebecca S. Chopp, *Saving Work: Feminist Practices of Theological Education* (Westminster John Knox Press: Louisville 1995), 80.

[2]  Ibid.

recourse to liturgical tradition. As Rebecca Lyman notes: "Many theologians have used liturgy or devotion as a conservative weight for theological work or development."[3] An example might be the favour the axiom *lex orandi, lex credendi* has enjoyed in arguments against the use of inclusive language in the liturgy.[4] Reference to liturgical tradition here – and elsewhere – is tantamount to a conservative theological approach. A theological recourse to liturgical tradition has thus (apparently) been capable only of engendering "liturgical erectitude."[5] Third, the claim to liturgy as a theological site has produced its own forms of gendered discourse. For example, discussions of the distinction between *lex orandi* as a form of "primary" theology, and *lex credendi* as a form of "secondary" theology, often point to a "Mrs Murphy" as the one in the pews who engages in primary theology. The secondary theologian is tacitly coded as male.[6] It does not take a feminist theologian to notice that most Mrs Murphy analogies are stereotypically gendered and a caricature of the diversity of (worshipping) women's lives.[7] With these gendered metaphors, however, a seemingly natural alliance comes to be established between, on the one hand, women, *lex orandi*, and non-scholarly liturgical "experience", and, on the other, men, *lex credendi*, and scholarly reflection on liturgy. Like other forms of malestream epistemology,[8] the theological recourse to the liturgy, too, is gendered, with the privileged aspects of knowledge being coded as masculine, while the non-reflective emotions

---

[3] Rebecca Lyman, "Lex orandi: Heresy, Orthodoxy, and Popular Religion," in: Sarah Coakley and David A. Pailin (eds), *The Making and Remaking of Christian Doctrine* (Clarendon Press: Oxford 1993), 131-141, here 138-139.

[4] To name just one example: Richard J. Schuler, "Lex orandi, lex credendi: The Outrage of Inclusive Language," in: *Sacred Music* 121/2 (1994), 6-10.

[5] I borrow the expression from Ronald L. Grimes's wonderfully witty and satirical piece "Liturgical Supinity, Liturgical Erectitude: On The Embodiment of Ritual Authority," in: *Studia Liturgica* 23 (1993), 51-69.

[6] Cf. Aidan Kavanagh, *On Liturgical Theology* (Pueblo: New York 1984), 146-147.

[7] Cf. Paul V. Marshall, "Reconsidering 'Liturgical Theology': Is there a *Lex Orandi* for all Christians?" in: *Studia Liturgica* 25 (1995), 129-151, here 147. Colleen McDannell notes similarly how categories of gender are used to distinguish liturgical art, which is coded as "virile", from liturgical kitsch, which is depicted as "effeminate": see *Material Christianity: Religion and Popular Culture in America* (Yale University Press: New Haven 1995), 163-197.

[8] For more, see Rebecca Chopp, "Eve's Knowing: Feminist Theology's Resistance to Malestream Epistemological Frameworks," in: Elisabeth Schüssler Fiorenza and M. Shawn Copeland (eds), *Feminist Theology in Different Contexts* (Concilium; SCM Press / Orbis Books: London / Maryknoll 1996, 116-123.

and the body (Mrs Murphy is always "in the pew," the male secondary theologian is seemingly location-less) are gendered as feminine.

In light of these problematic constructions of gender in the theological turn to the liturgy, it is not surprising that feminist theologians have only recently begun to give more sustained attention to the themes of liturgical theology in a broader sense.[9] Two examples are Susan A. Ross's *Extravagant Affections: A Feminist Sacramental Theology*, and Elizabeth A. Johnson's *Friends of God and Prophets: A Feminist Theological Reading of the Communion of Saints*. Ross rethinks fundamentals of sacramental theology in light of the liturgical practices of women and of feminist theory. As she rightly asks, if the axiom *lex orandi, lex credendi* suggests that the primary context for theological reflection is worship, what or whose worship are we to privilege?[10] For Ross herself, the answer is clear: both the official worship of the church and women-identified liturgies count as *lex orandi* to which theology has to be attentive. Elizabeth Johnson's book points in a similar direction. She actually begins with an allusion to a feminist liturgical community and focuses her work on "the current resurgence of women's practices of memory."[11] These women's practices of memory are the crucial building-block for Johnson's feminist reading of the communion of saints. Both Ross and Johnson, then, point to the need to reconfigure the *lex orandi* while embracing a theological recourse to liturgical tradition.

Given the fact that theological work as a whole, however, has neither drawn on a gender-attentive narrative of liturgical tradition, nor paid any attention to current liturgical traditioning in women's hands, I see continuing and sustained reflection on a feminist reconfiguring of *lex orandi* as a pressing task. In what follows, I want both to honour the theological turn to the

---

[9] An exception to this is the handful of feminist theologians in liturgical studies. I mention here especially Marjorie Procter-Smith's two books, *In Her Own Rite: Constructing Feminist Liturgical Tradition* (Abingdon Press: Nashville 1990), and *Praying With our Eyes Open: Engendering Feminist Liturgical Prayer* (Abingdon Press: Nashville 1995). See also Denise J.J. Dijk, *Een beeld van een Liturgie: Verkenningen in vrouwenstudies liturgiek, met bijzondere aandacht voor het werk van Marjorie Procter-Smith* (Narratio: Gorinchem 1999).

[10] Susan A. Ross, *Extravagant Affections: A Feminist Sacramental Theology* (Continuum: New York 1998), 30-31, see also 203-204. Cf. also the publication of a collection of essays on the same topic, from the other side of the Atlantic: Regina Ammicht-Quinn and Stefanie Spendel (eds), *Kraftfelder. Sakramente in der Lebenswirklichkeit von Frauen* (Pustet: Regensburg 1998).

[11] Elizabeth A. Johnson, *Friends of God and Prophets: A Feminist Theological Reading of the Communion of Saints* (Continuum: New York 1998), 26.

liturgy, and at the same time to claim women's prayers and practices as a prominent, if largely hidden part of the *lex orandi*. While the historical reconstruction of a liturgical tradition that is gender-attentive will have to await another day,[12] my argument here focuses on the contemporary surge of liturgical practices of women. I contend that these women-identified prayers and practices offer possibilities of challenging, broadening, and reconfiguring established claims to the liturgy as a theological site. I begin by highlighting four recent (and quite divergent) developments which coincide with and substantiate my claim to women's liturgical practices as fundamentally important to theological work. I then offer two small pointers to the material contours of women's *lex orandi*, past and present. I conclude with some thoughts on the nature of a feminist appeal to liturgical tradition.

## 1. Liturgy as a theological site

My argument for women's *lex orandi* as a theological site can draw substantially on well established arguments for the importance of liturgical tradition for theological reflection. Since the publication of Geoffrey Wainwright's *Doxology: The Praise of God in Doctrine, Worship, and Life* two decades ago,[13] a growing number of Protestant theologians have joined the many Orthodox and Catholic theologians who consciously draw on liturgical materials for their work.[14] As a result of this development, *lex orandi* is once again being appreciated as a fundamental part of the Christian tradition and as a crucial source of theological reflection. Although there are distinct differences between theologians as to how *lex orandi* and *lex credendi* are to be related – from claims to the priority of doxology over theology, to the subordination of the liturgy to dogma, to a conviction of worship as theology – all these theological proposals are part of the (re-)turn to the liturgy that so profoundly marked theological work in the second half of the twentieth century.

Because women's faith practices are both an integral and a distinct part of Christian tradition, the fact that the peculiar shape of women's liturgical practices remains invisible constitutes a distinct problem in this theological return

[12] For a beginning, see Teresa Berger, *Women's Ways of Worship: Gender Analysis and Liturgical History* (Liturgical Press: Collegeville, MN 1999).

[13] Geoffrey Wainwright, *Doxology: The Praise of God in Doctrine, Worship and Life* (Oxford University Press: New York 1980).

[14] For an overview of recent developments, see Teresa Berger, *Theology in Hymns? A Study of the Relationship of Doxology and Theology according to "A Collection of Hymns for the use of the People Called Methodist" (1780)* (Abingdon Press: Nashville 1995), 31-57.

to the liturgy. Gender as a fundamental marker of liturgical life is occluded and thus written out of what comes to be constructed as "The Liturgical Tradition". For example, in most theological claims about the importance of the eucharist for the life of the church, there is no acknowledgement of the peculiar ways in which women's gender has shaped, circumscribed, and, last but not least, restricted their engagement with this sacrament.[15] More than half of the church, in its gendered particularity, remains invisible in these claims about the centrality of the eucharist. To put it more humorously, the Roman Catholic girl's response to the priest's question: "How many sacraments are there?" highlights what much liturgical theology has veiled: "Seven for boys, and six for girls."[16] Theologians claiming the liturgical tradition as a profound source for theological reflection have remained satisfied with the first half of the girl's insight. There is no surprise here, since, overwhelmingly, these theologians have belonged to the gender for whom the answer "seven" is quite appropriate.

## 2. Women's ways of worship

Although women's faith practices continue to be written out of the recourse to liturgical tradition, there has been a burgeoning interest in women's ways of worship outside of theology proper. It is startling to realize how much we have learned of women's *lex orandi* from authors other than theologians who profess the crucial importance of worship for theological reflection. I can only highlight a few of these works here, and, indeed, will have to limit myself to more recent studies within the Christian tradition.[17]

---

[15] Glimpses of the importance of gender for eucharistic practices are offered by Caroline Walker Bynum, "Women Mystics and Eucharistic Devotion in the Thirteenth Century," in: *Fragmentation and Redemption: Essays on Gender and the Human Body in Medieval Religion* (Zone Books: New York ³1994), 119-150, and by Miri Rubin, *Corpus Christi: The Eucharist in Late Medieval Culture* (Cambridge University Press: New York 1991), 9, 120-122, 167-173. For other sacramental practices, see, for example, Catherine Vincie, "Gender Analysis and Christian Initiation," in: *Worship* 69 (1995), 505-530, and Ursula Silber, " 'Zwiespalt' und 'Zugzwang'. Katholische Frauen und die Beichte," in: Andrea Günter / Ulrike Wagner (eds), *What does it mean today to be a (Feminist) Theologian?* (ESWTR Yearbook 4; Kok Pharos / Grünewald: Kampen / Mainz 1996), 84-95.

[16] The story is told in Ross, *Extravagant Affections*, 21-22.

[17] For earlier studies, compare especially Marjorie Procter-Smith, *Women in Shaker Community and Worship: A Feminist Analysis of the Uses of Religious Symbolism* (E. Mellen Press: Lewiston, NY 1985), and my own *"Liturgie und Frauenseele". Die Liturgische Bewegung aus der Sicht der Frauenforschung* (Praktische Theologie Heute 10; Kohlhammer Verlag: Stuttgart 1993). A burgeoning interest in women's ways of worship is also evident for religious traditions

Gisela Muschiol's magisterial study *Famula Dei* examines the liturgical life of women's communities in Romano-Merovingian Gaul. Muschiol shows that the center of daily life for these women was a liturgy which the women themselves shaped and celebrated under the liturgical presidency of their abbess, including hearing confession and absolving.[18] These women thus had a considerable measure of control over their own liturgical lives. Robert Orsi, in his study *Thank You, St. Jude*, focuses on the prayers and practices of American Catholic women devoted to St. Jude Thaddeus, the saint of hopeless causes.[19] Orsi uses ethnographic research to read women's prayer practices as ways of negotiating particular cultural shifts in their lives. Marie Griffith's *God's Daughters: Evangelical Women and the Power of Submission* examines the lives and narratives of North American members of the Women's Aglow Fellowship, an international charismatic Christian women's group. Griffith, similarly to Orsi, weaves together in-depth ethnographic research, careful textual analysis, and insights from cultural studies in order to read practices of prayer as a lens through which to view women's strategic ways of negotiating their daily lives.[20] Lesley Northup's *Ritualizing Women* approaches its subject, namely "What women do when they get together to worship?" by drawing broadly on diverse methodological tools, including ritual studies, gender studies, anthropology, and sociology, as well as by attending to diverse faith communities, from Christian feminist groups to Korean women shamans.[21] Northup's study provides an analysis of the distinct patterns and emphases which emerge in women's ritualizing.

What these diverse studies show, whether they are concerned with Romano-Merovingian women's communities, women's devotion to a particular saint, charismatic women's prayer meetings, or feminist ritualizing, is the simple fact that gender shapes *lex orandi* in manifold ways. However, given

other than Christianity. These range from studies of women as ritual experts in Jewish communities, to women's worship of Krishna, to the place of ritual fasts in the religious lives of Hindu women, to women in Korean ritual life.

[18] See Gisela Muschiol, *Famula Dei. Zur Liturgie in merowingischen Frauenklöstern* (Beiträge zur Geschichte des alten Mönchtums und des Benediktinerordens 41; Aschendorff: Münster 1994).

[19] Robert A. Orsi, *Thank You, St. Jude: Women's Devotion to the Patron Saint of Hopeless Causes* (Yale University Press: New Haven 1996).

[20] R. Marie Griffith, *God's Daughters: Evangelical Women and the Power of Submission* (University of California Press: Berkeley, CA 1997).

[21] Lesley A. Northup, *Ritualizing Women: Patterns of Spirituality* (Pilgrim Press: Cleveland 1997), 1.

that none of these studies is explicitly theological, the consequences of the impact of gender on constructions of the *lex orandi* – and the consequences for any claim to liturgy as a theological site – are not explored. Women's faith practices are simply seen as exciting ethnographic, cultural, and historical material. In other words, these studies have not affected theological reflection in any sustained way.

## 3. The theological turn to practice

The recent theological attention to practice, particularly in postliberal narrative theologies with their emphasis on the tradition and practice of the church, also coincides with my argument that women's liturgical practices are fundamentally important to theological reflection. Postliberal theologies understand the church and its canonical texts as a cultural-linguistic universe into which people are initiated and by which they are formed. These theologies consequently turn to traditional ecclesial practices, particularly baptism and eucharist, as shaping Christian identity and as constituting the most foundational source for theological reflection.

I take from this theological turn to the church and its texts and practices the poignant reminder of the importance of what the faith community has actually done through the ages. One of the distinct weaknesses of this approach, however, is the assumption that there is an easily discernible, pristine core of fundamental texts and practices in the tradition of the church, and that these texts and practices are gender-blind and not marred by the pervasive historic marginalization of women. Those texts and practices thus become sheltered from critique and reconfiguration. For most postliberal theologians, a hermeneutic of trust is assumed, and ecclesial practices continue to be drawn on normatively as if they are not also practices of domination and marginalization.

## 4. Privileging ordinary sites

I turn to a fourth development in theology in order to weave it into my claim for women's liturgical practices as of fundamental importance for theological reflection. This fourth development can be described as a turn to ordinary sites of the production of Christian meaning. There are many different forms this particular theological turn to ordinary sites can take, such as attention to local theologies, attention to the marginalized in various liberation theologies (for example, the poor of the base ecclesial communities in Liberation theology, Black slaves and their African American descendants in Black theology, different groups of women in feminist theologies), and attention to popular religiosity, or "theologies of ordinary people,"[22] to name only the most obvious. Rather than privileging official texts and doctrines of the church, these approaches focus on the symbolic and material productions of ordinary Christians. These Christians' discourses and their sites for the production of Christian meaning become fundamental sources for theological reflection. Clearly, this approach is congenial to reading women's liturgical practices as an important source for theological reflection. In actuality, however, little theological work has been done concretely on women's ways of worship as one of those "ordinary" sites which are to inform theological reflection.

Although the four strands highlighted above are rooted in very different theological presuppositions, they each, in some of their argumentative moves, coincide with my claim that women's liturgical practices are of fundamental importance for theological work. From the turn to liturgy as a theological site I derive the claim to women's *lex orandi* as a *locus theologicus* to which theology has to attend. From recent research into a variety of women's devotional practices, I gain the insight of women's ways of worship as distinct forms of *lex orandi*, forged in the crucible of women's lives. From the postliberal turn to the practices of the community of faith, I derive the insistence on women's *lex orandi* as an ecclesial practice, a fundamental part of the life of the church through the ages. With the theological turn to ordinary sites as the source for theological reflection, I lift up women's liturgical practices, often found at the fringes of official worship, as an important site of the theologies of ordinary people. I claim women's *lex orandi* as an ancient ecclesial practice and as an integral yet distinct part of "The Liturgical Tradition". The fundamental problem of this claim is that we have not yet recovered much of women's liturgical history, and, therefore, can only speculate about the impact of gender on constructions of the *lex orandi* and about its consequences for any claim to liturgy as a theological site. In order to show that there is much to (re-)discover about the shape of women's *lex orandi*, past and present, I want to offer two brief pointers to women's ways of worship in the Christian tradition. I will conclude with some thoughts on the nature of a feminist appeal to liturgical tradition.

---

[22] See Kathryn Tanner, "Theology and Popular Culture," in: Dwight N. Hopkins and Sheila Greeve Davaney (eds), *Changing Conversations: Religious Reflection & Cultural Analysis* (Routledge: New York 1996), 101-120.

## II. Women's *lex orandi*, past and present

Women have been liturgical practitioners through the ages, even if often neither in their own right nor in their own rite. Unfortunately, no liturgical history is available to date which goes beyond the problematic add-women-and-stir approach. Liturgical "facts" continue to be constructed as gender-blind or gender-neutral, with little or no recognition that what comes to be counted as "fact" is always theory specific.[23] As feminist research has shown again and again, a theory oblivious to gender as a fundamental marker of reality will: a) present apparently ungendered facts, b) thereby occlude an important shaper of historical practices, and c) therefore offer few guidelines for shaping practices in a world where gender systems are in crisis. For a feminist reconfiguration of *lex orandi* the task is clear, namely to begin to write gender back into the liturgical tradition. Such work is not about discarding the liturgical tradition, but about uncentering malestream constructions by inscribing a gender-attentive narrative in their place. Obviously, this is a colossal task which will demand sustained collaborative effort by diverse women scholars in the future. For the present article, I illustrate the above claims with a brief look at two distinct traditions of women's practices of prayer: biblical accounts, and the recent surge of feminist liturgical practices.

A look at the Scriptures offers a glimpse of the problems related to reconstructing women's ways of worship. As far back as the earlier parts of the Hebrew Scriptures, songs and prayers are put in the mouths of women; however, only about ten of the nearly three hundred instances of recorded prayers or allusions to prayer in the Hebrew Scriptures are clearly those of women.[24] If we look for a biblical *lex orandi*, then, the asymmetrically gendered amount of the evidence is striking. The content of the prayer traditions also speaks to the power of gender in shaping *lex orandi*. The majority of prayers put in women's mouths in the Hebrew Scriptures are related to women's reproductive and maternal roles. There is Hagar's desperate plea in the face of her dying child (Gen 21.16-17); Leah's praise of God at the birth of her son (Gen 29.35); the blessing over Naomi by her women friends on the occasion of

---

[23] I am indebted for this concise formulation to Linda McDowell, *Gender, Identity and Place: Understanding Feminist Geographies* (University of Minnesota: Minneapolis Press 1999), 227.

[24] Cf. Patrick D. Miller, "Things Too Wonderful: Prayers of Women in the Old Testament," in: Georg Braulik et al. (eds), *Biblische Theologie und gesellschaftlicher Wandel* (Herder: Freiburg 1993), 237-251, here 237.

Ruth's marriage to Boaz (Ruth 4.14); and Hannah's agonizing prayer for a son (1 Sam 1.10), followed by her exuberant praise after the prayer is answered (1 Sam 2.1-10). Disproportionally, then, women's *lex orandi* is shaped by women's reproductive and maternal roles (which are, of course, coded differently, namely much more broadly, than today). That these roles exhaust neither women's lives nor women's prayer practices becomes visible in two powerfully prophetic voices of prayer and praise in the Hebrew Scriptures:[25] Miriam's triumphant song after the crossing of the Red Sea (Ex 15.21) which is part of a larger women-centered ritual under Miriam's leadership, and the mighty song of Deborah (Judg 5.1-31) after Jael's killing of Sisera. In the Apocryphal/Deuterocanonical books, indeed, prayer "often undergirds female actions that are courageous, unconventional and subversive."[26]

Looking to the New Testament, we find two prayers put in the mouths of women that became part of the liturgical tradition of the church. Mary's song of praise at her encounter with Elizabeth (Lk 1.46-55), known by its Latin opening word *Magnificat*, has its place in the daily evening prayer of the church. Elizabeth's prophetic blessing of Mary, "Blessed are you among women, and blessed is the fruit of your womb" (Lk 1.42), is part of the prayer known and loved by many Catholics as the *Hail Mary*. These two songs of praise, like their counterparts from the Hebrew Scriptures, are situated within women's reproductive and maternal roles. Both Elizabeth and Mary are pregnant, miraculously so, and their praises emerge out of their encounter with one another as bearers of distinctly God-sent children. Beyond the powerful voices of these two pregnant women, however, the other women described in the New Testament as praying and as praising God remain speechless in the recorded testimony, from the prophet Anna (Lk 2.38), to "certain women" devoting themselves to prayer with the other disciples of Jesus after the Ascension (Acts 1.14), to the four nameless daughters of Philip who prophecy (Acts 21.9). This uneven witness of the Scriptures to the prayers and practices of women continues within the Christian tradition. Two thousand years of women's prayers and practices remain largely hidden; their painstaking

---

[25] Cf. Gail O'Day, "Singing Woman's Song: A Hermeneutic of Liberation," in: *Currents in Theology and Mission* 12 (1985), 203-210.

[26] Toni Craven, "'From Where Will my Help Come?': Women and Prayer in the Apocryphal/ Deuterocanonical Books," in: M. Patrick Graham et al. (eds), *Worship and the Hebrew Bible* (Journal for the Study of the Old Testament. Supplement Series 284; Sheffield Academic Press: Sheffield 1999), 95-109, here 99.

reconstruction has only just begun. Where women's prayers and practices surface, they are often related to women's bodily and reproductive functions.

Given this historical occlusion of women's prayers and practices, the surge of contemporary women-identified prayers and practices is a telling contrast to "The Tradition" (although if we reconfigured this tradition in gender-attentive ways, the contrast would be much less stark). These vibrant songs, prayers, and rituals, I suggest, already allow a glimpse at of the shape of a theological recourse to the liturgy that is gender-attentive. In recent decades, liturgy, indeed, has developed into a crucial site of women's activism within the church, "the symbolic equivalent of the right to vote and receive equal pay," as Catherine Bell has put it.[27] The importance of liturgy as a site of struggle over what shapes Christian women's lives cannot be overemphasized. For the Christian tradition in which liturgical authority seemed to be the prerogative of a male priesthood, or, more recently, a caste of (mostly male) liturgical experts, the fact that women themselves now actively construct and interpret their liturgical world is a primary mode of claiming power.[28] To put it differently, women today have rendered visible the liturgy as a crucial site for what, arguably, it has always been: the negotiation between faith and women's lives. This has involved a recognition both of the regulatory power of the traditional liturgy and of worship as a potential site of alternative liturgical practices.[29]

What shape does *lex orandi* take in this women-identified form of liturgical traditioning? Granted that it is too soon to write a liturgical theology on the basis of women's ways of worship throughout history, it is worth anticipating what it might look like. How would one write a liturgical theology attentive to women's prayers and practices, that is, to the distinct shape of women's *lex orandi*? Taking contemporary women-identified liturgies[30] as an

---

[27] Catherine M. Bell, *Ritual: Perspectives and Dimensions* (Oxford University Press: New York 1997), 238.

[28] Cf. Northup, *Ritualizing Women*, 11, 22.

[29] Christian women-identified prayers and practices are not alone here; there are analogous developments in other faith traditions. Witness for example the long struggle of Jewish religious women to pray publicly at Jerusalem's Western Wall (cf. the documentary film "Women of the Wall," directed and produced by Faye Lederman, 1993).

[30] For a succinct introduction to the North American scene, see Janet R. Walton, *Feminist Liturgy: A Matter of Justice* (American Essays in Liturgy; Liturgical Press: Collegeville, MN 2000). For the European side, see, for example, Ute Knie and Herta Leistner (eds), *Laß hören deine Stimme. Werkstattbuch Feministische Liturgie* (Gütersloher Verlagshaus: Gütersloh 1999).

example, one might say that such a theology would attend to women as subjects of the liturgy who confront the Holy in the crucible of women's lives. In other words, this theology would begin with the presence of women and of women's bodies in worship, rather than being predicated on their absence or on their presence as a problem for the presence of the Holy. This theology, then, foregrounds women's liturgical practices as a primary *locus theologicus*, a site of reflection on God. A women-identified liturgical way of doing theology would also take clues from the careful interplay between liturgical tradition and a reconfiguring of the tradition through women's lives witnessed to in so many of the new liturgies (where a ritual of anointing will be offered to a survivor of rape, an exorcism might be directed at the evils of patriarchy, and a Good Friday liturgy can center on women's suffering). Such a theology would adopt the rich and intense pleasure of symbols readily apparent in women-identified liturgies. It would be a theology not dependent on binarist constructions of the ordinary and the sacred, and able to claim sacred space in all of life, especially in the ordinary of women's lives so often subject to trivialization and marginalization. With the poetic and imaginative language of women-identified liturgies, a feminist liturgical way of doing theology speaks the language of passion and compassion unafraid. From these liturgies' ability to bring women's diverse lives into the presence of the Holy One, such a theology takes clues about presencing women in theological discourse all the while healing and hallowing that presence. Lastly and most importantly, a feminist liturgical way of doing theology will attend to God-talk in ways revelatory of "She Who Is Worshipped" in women-identified liturgies: the Root of Wisdom, the Weaver of the Web of Life, the Divine Midwife and Passionate Sister, Sophia. The wealth of these images in women's liturgies witnesses to the intensity of the search for new and authentic ways of naming and encountering God.

Theology does well to listen to this *lex orandi* of women. Two reasons in particular lead me to stress this claim. First, a theological turn to liturgy, given its own interpretive commitments, can only be enriched by drawing on the centuries-old and ever-new wisdom of women liturgical practitioners. Why impoverish the lex *credendi* by inattentiveness to the prayers and practices of more than half of the Body of Christ? A second reason for my insistence on the importance of a liturgical theology attentive to women's lives is the work this tradition-friendly approach does in reconfiguring what counts as Christian tradition in the first place. I want to conclude with some thoughts on this subject in light of a challenge recently issued by Kathryn Tanner.

## III. Reconfiguring *lex orandi*

In a wise challenge to feminist theologians, Kathryn Tanner has argued that feminist theologians do well to "remain traditional". She writes: "The influence of feminist theology is strengthened to the extent it wrestles constructively with the theological claims that have traditionally been important in Christian theology; the more traditional the material with which it works, the greater the influence of feminist theology."[31] Tanner's starting point for this challenge is a reconceptualization of the task of theology on the basis of marxist and poststructuralist theories of culture. These theories enable her to read theology as a site of struggle over symbolic resources and as an always selective, never stable site of the production of meaning. For Tanner, this reading of theology through the lens of cultural theories means that feminist theology becomes most effective and convincing not in distancing itself as far as possible from the tradition, but in claiming tradition as a site of struggle over meaning today. Thus, the more feminist theology is able to use and realign elements which have been appropriated by patriarchal interests, the greater the feminist claim to theological credibility. Tradition here is quite clearly not understood as a fixed and unified block of material, which is merely received and passed on. Rather, tradition is understood as constructed in the here and now in an ongoing struggle over a diversity of practices and interpretations. As such, what comes to be designated as tradition is firstly, highly selective, but secondly, rather unstable, open to redesignation.[32]

Tanner's argument resonates with my own effort to construct a feminist account of a liturgical way of doing theology. Like Tanner, I am convinced that feminist theology's appeal is strengthened by tradition-friendliness in the sense of claiming as many elements as possible from the tradition, while at the same time reconfiguring what is authorized as "Tradition". The claim to liturgy as a site of theological reflection is a seemingly traditional move, while the reconfiguration of *lex orandi* in the light of women's ways of worship expands the very meaning of liturgical tradition. Tanner's reading of tradition

---

[31] Kathryn Tanner, "Social Theory Concerning the 'New Social Movements' and the Practice of Feminist Theology," in: Rebecca S. Chopp and Sheila Greeve Davaney (eds), *Horizons in Feminist Theology: Identity, Tradition, and Norms* (Fortress: Minneapolis 1997), 179-197, here 192.

[32] For a more detailed account, see Kathryn Tanner, *Theories of Culture: A New Agenda for Theology* (Guides to Theological Inquiry Series; Fortress: Minneapolis 1997), 128-138.

as a struggle over meaning today is also helpful in interpreting the contemporary surge of women-identified liturgical practices. Rather than designating these practices as a decisive break with – indeed, the very undoing of – "The Tradition", women-identified liturgical practices can instead be seen as part and parcel of the continuous construction and reconstruction of *lex orandi* in the life of the church. As Rabbi Sandy Eisenberg claims: "Rather than representing a break with tradition, new ritual and liturgical activity are the very essence of a living tradition."[33]

In reconfiguring the history of the liturgy in gender-attentive ways, we will undoubtedly discover what the contemporary surge of women-identified liturgical practices has made so very clear for our own time: that women engage the liturgy in the crucible of their own lives, including its manifold ways of marginalizing. But we will also discover what Andre Myre has recently put so well with a view to the biblical witness: "There is a word of God to women, spoken millenniums [*sic*] ago [and continuing to be spoken! – TB], a word which has not yet been heard, a word to which the men who wrote the Bible have not really given testimony."[34] Confronting and acknowledging this "word of God to women" will force us to rethink notions of revelation, liturgical tradition, and authority in the church, to name just a few. Confronting and acknowledging this word of God to women will also force a new listening to the word of God which women hear today and to which they witness amidst continuing ways of silencing. The prayers and practices of women are indeed a crucial site of "the word of God to women" becoming flesh today.

Der Beitrag hinterfragt den Rekurs auf die Liturgie als *locus theologicus* im Licht feministisch-theologischer Theoriebildung. Die Autorin argumentiert, daß die traditionelle Diskussion um das Verhältnis zwischen liturgischer Tradition und theologischer Reflexion (*lex orandi, lex credendi*) auf einer Liturgiegeschichtsschreibung aufbaut, die die spezifisch weiblichen gottesdienstlichen Lebenswirklichkeiten unsichtbar läßt. Ein feministischer Rekurs auf *lex orandi* muß von daher das, was als liturgische Tradition zählt, neu konzipieren. Für diese femini-

---

[33] Sandy Eisenberg Sasso, "Introduction," in: Lesley A. Northup (ed.), *Women and Religious Ritual* (Pastoral Press: Washington 1993), IX-XVI, here X.

[34] Andre Myre, "The New Testament in the *Women's Bible Commentary*," in: *Women Also Journeyed with Him: Feminist Perspectives on the Bible* (Liturgical Press: Collegeville, MN 2000), 83-98, here 97.

stisch-theologische Konzeption von *lex orandi* können neuere Kulturtheorien entscheidende Impulse geben.

La contribution remet en question le recours à la liturgie en tant que locus théologicus à la lumière de la théorie théologico-féministe. L'auteur argumente que le discours traditionel sur la relation entre la tradition liturgique et la réflexion théologique (*lex orandi, lex credendi*) construit sur une histoire liturgique, rend opaque les réalités spécifiques de la vie culturelle des femmes. Un recours féministe du lex orandie qui compte comme tradition liturgique, doit donc être reconçu. Pour cette conception théologique féministe du lex orandi, des accents décisifs peuvent être donnés par de nouvelles théories culturelles.

***Teresa Berger***, a native of Germany, is a Roman Catholic theologian and liturgical scholar. She teaches at the Divinity School of Duke University, Durham, North Carolina, USA. Berger is the author and editor of several books, including, most recently, *Women's Ways of Worship: Gender Analysis and Liturgical History* (Liturgical Press: Collegeville, MN 1999), and *"Sei gesegnet, meine Schwester". Frauen feiern Liturgie: geschichtliche Rückfragen, praktische Impulse, theologische Vergewisserungen* (Echter Verlag: Würzburg 1999).

*Brigitte Enzner-Probst*

# Leib Christi und Leib der Frauen
## Überlegungen zur ekklesiologischen Relevanz von Corporealität in der rituellen Praxis von Frauen

### Corporealität und rituell-liturgische Praxis von Frauen[1]

*Zur Geschichte der Frauenliturgiebewegung*
In den letzten zwanzig Jahren hat sich in Amerika und über die Niederlande auch in Europa eine eigenständige Ritual- und Liturgiebewegung von Frauen entwickelt.[2] Frauen, die zum spirituellen Zweig der Neuen Frauenbewegung gehörten, wollten politisches Engagement und religiöse Begründung nicht voneinander trennen. Viele suchten, nachdem sie sich der Enteignung durch androzentrische christliche Tradition bewusst geworden waren, eine matriarchale Kultur, die dieser vorausging. Spirituelle Traditionen, etwa aus der indianischen Kultur, aus anderen Religionen, dem Buddhismus, der neopaganen Szene flossen ebenso ein. Starhawk, amerikanische Psychotherapeutin

---

[1]  Im folgenden verwende ich beide Ausdrücke mit einer spezifischen Nuancierung. Mit liturgischer Praxis bezeichne ich das rituelle Gestalten innerhalb jüdisch-christlicher Tradition, mit ritueller Praxis solches als Teil der postchristlichen Ritualbewegung. Die Übergänge sind jedoch fließend. Charlotte Caron hat in ihrer Beschreibung der Frauenliturgiebewegung vier Typen definiert, die den verschiedenen Standort der engagierten Frauen markieren. Vgl. Charlotte Caron, *To Make and Make Again: Feminist Ritual Thealogy* (Crossroad: New York 1993)

[2]  Vgl. Teresa Berger, *Sei gesegnet meine Schwester, Frauen feiern Liturgie* (Echter: Würzburg 1999), ebenso Veronika Prüller-Jagenteufel, "'Aufrecht pries sie Gott'. Liturgische Feiern von und mit Frauen aus der Sicht feministischer Theologie", in: *Heiliger Dienst* 51/1 (1997), 14–23; dies., *Frauen entdecken ihre Wurzeln und Quellen. Neue Formen von Liturgie als Ausdruck feministischer Spiritualität*, in: jugend und kirche 3 (1990/91), 42-46; vgl. auch Mary Collins, "Principles of Feminist Liturgy", in: Marjorie Procter-Smith / Janet R. Walton (eds), *Women at Worship* (Westminster John Knox: Louisville, KY 1993), 9-26. Im deutschen Bereich sind als erste Zusammenfassungen einer Praxis feministischer Liturgien zu nennen Herta Leistner u.a. (Hgin), *Lass spüren deine Kraft* (Gütersloher Verlagshaus: Gütersloh 1997); dies. u.a. (Hgin), *Lass hören deine Stimme* (Gütersloher Verlagshaus: Gütersloh 1999); Teresa Berger, *Women's Ways of Worship: Gender Analysis and Liturgical History* (Liturgical Press: Collegeville, MN 1999).

und Leiterin eines "Hexen-Covens", Naomi Goldenberg, die ebenfalls Psy-
choanalyse und feministische Rituale zu verbinden sucht,[3] Wendy Hunter
Roberts, die feministische Rituale und Religionskritik miteinander korreliert,[4]
und viele andere haben den Grund für eine rituelle und zugleich reflektierte
Praxis feministischer Spiritualität gelegt.[5] Auch die Frage einer religiösen
Bindung an eine Göttin wurde heftig diskutiert.[6] Rituale im Jahreslauf (Jah-
reszeitenfeste) oder entlang des weiblichen Lebenszusammenhangs wurden
gestaltet. Politisches Engagement und rituelle Praxis verbanden sich in eindrücklichen Demonstrationen gegen Atomkraft und Umweltzerstörung.

Und immer mehr Frauen aus den verschiedensten Kirchen beteiligten sich
daran. In dem Maß, wie sich die Neue Frauenbewegung in den christlichen
Kirchen und Konfessionen ausbreitete, wurden auch die Impulse feministischer
Spiritualität rezipiert und im Rahmen der jüdisch-christlichen Tradition liturgisch gestaltet.[7] Die beträchtliche Anzahl von Publikationen zu Frauenliturgien,

---

[3]   Vgl. Naomi R Goldenberg, "Spiritualität und Theologie", in: Maria Kassel (Hgin), *Femini-
      stische Theologie. Perspektiven zur Orientierung* (Kreuz-Verlag: Stuttgart 1988), 165-189;
      dies., "Anger in the Body: Feminism, Religion and Kleinian Psychoanalytic Theory", in:
      *Journal of Feminist Studies in Religion* 2/2 (Fall 1986), 39-49.

[4]   Wendy Hunter Roberts, "In Her Name: Toward a Feminist Thealogy of Pagan Ritual", in:
      Procter-Smith / Walton (eds), *Women at Worship*, 137-142, bes. 140: "We meet in a circle,
      symbol of the wheel of the year and leveler of hierarchy and difference. There is no face-off
      of clergy and laity here; we are celebrants together." Vgl. auch dies., *Celebrating Her, Femi-
      nist Ritualizing Comes of Age* (Pilgrim Press: Cleveland 1998), 33-49.

[5]   Vgl. Miriam Therese Winter et al. (eds), *Defecting in Place: Women Claiming Responsibility
      for Their Own Spiritual Lives* (Crossroad: New York 1994); Susan Cady / Marian Ronan /
      Hal Taussig, *Sophia: the Future of Feminist Spirituality* (Harper & Row: San Francisco
      1986); für den deutschen Bereich diskutiert dies z.B. Andrea Schulenburg, *Feministische Spi-
      ritualität: Exodus in eine befreiende Kirche?* (Kohlhammer: Stuttgart 1993).

[6]   Vgl. Starhawk, *The Spiral Dance* (Harper & Row: New York 1986); Margot Adler, *Drawing
      Down the Moon* (Beacon Press: Boston, MA 1979; ²1986); Merlin Stone, *When God Was a
      Woman* (Dorset Press: New York 1976).

[7]   Bahnbrechend hat hier neben der liturgischen Sammlungsarbeit von Rosemary Radford
      Ruether besonders auch die Gruppe WATER gewirkt, die von Diann Neu und Mary E. Hunt
      gegründet worden ist. Im Konzept von Women-Church soll Glaube, Ethik und Liturgie aus
      der Sicht von Frauen neu gestaltet werden. Vgl. Diann L. Neu, Women-Church Transforming
      Liturgy, in: Procter-Smith / Walton (eds), *Women at Worship*, 163-178; bes. 175: "Women-
      church feminist liturgies provide a place and a space where women, children, and women-
      identified men can engage in spiritual renewal and social transformation for ourselves, for reli-
      gious traditions, and for social change." Siehe auch dies., "Our Name Is Church: The
      experience of Catholic-Christian Feminist Liturgies", in: Concilium 18 (1982), 135-144;
      Mary E. Hunt, "Defining Women-Church", in: *WATERwheel* 3/2 (Summer 1990), 1-3.
      Teresa Berger interpretiert deshalb die Frauenbewegung in der Kirche u.a. auch als eine Litur-

die in den letzten Jahren allein in Deutschland erschienen ist,[8] zeigt die Relevanz dieser Bewegung für die ritualtheoretische wie liturgietheologische Reflexion, ohne dass dies im Mainstream der Liturgiewissenschaft schon rezipiert worden wäre.[9] Auch ich erhebe im folgenden nicht den Anspruch, die komplexe Geschichte der wechselseitigen Beeinflussung vollständig nachzeichnen zu können und bin mir der begrenzten Darstellung bewusst, wenn ich mich in meinen Überlegungen auf die liturgisch-rituelle Aktivität von Frauen im Kontext christlich-jüdischer Tradition beschränke.[10]

## *Corporealität als signifikantes Medium in liturgischer Praxis von Frauen*

In der Beschreibung liturgischer Praxis von Frauen spielt der *Körper* eine zentrale Rolle. Immer wieder wird davon gesprochen, einen "Gottesdienst mit allen Sinnen" feiern zu wollen.[11] Ebenso fällt die *Priorisierung der sog.*

---

gische Bewegung mit dem Ziel der "Inkulturation" der Liturgie in die Lebenswirklichkeit von Frauen. Vgl. Teresa Berger, "The Women's Movement as a Liturgical Movement: A Form of Inculturation?" in: *Studia Liturgica* 20 (1990), 55-64.

[8]   Aus der Fülle der deutschen Publikationen seien nur einige der älteren und einige der jüngsten Liturgiesammlungen genannt: Elisabeth Aeberli, *Frauengottesdienste* (Rex-Verlag: Luzern 1987); Anneliese Reuschel, *Frauengottesdienste. Gottesdienstfeiern von Frauen für Frauen und die ganze Gemeinde* (Butzon & Bercker / Klens: Kevelaer / Düsseldorf 1989); Leni Altwegg u.a. (Hginnen), *Ich spielte vor Dir auf dem Erdenrund. Frauengottesdienste. Anleitungen und Modelle* (Paulusverlag u.a.: Freiburg / Basel 1990); Christine Hojenski u.a., *Meine Seele sieht das Land der Freiheit* (Ed. Liberación: Münster 1990, ²1992); Hanna Strack (Hgin), *Den Schatz heben* (Kaiser: München 1992); Brigitte Enzner-Probst / Andrea Felsenstein-Rossberg (Hginnen), *Wenn Himmel und Erde sich berühren* (Gütersloher Verl.-Haus: Gütersloh 1993); Roselies Taube u.a., *Frauen in Bibel und Kirche. Ökumenische Gottesdienstmodelle* (Echter: Würzburg 1993); Michaela Ferner, *Du beflügelst meine Schritte. Gottesdienstmodelle – von Frauen gestaltet* (Klens: Düsseldorf / Kevelaer 1993); Barbara Baumann u.a., *Frauenliturgien. Ein Werkbuch* (Kösel: München 1998).

[9]   Ausnahmen bilden hier Hans-Günter Heimbrock, *Gottesdienst: Spielraum des Lebens* (Kok u.a.: Kampen / Weinheim 1993), sowie Michael Meyer-Blanck, *Leben, Leib und Liturgie, Die Praktische Theologie Wilhelm Stählins* (de Gruyter: Berlin / New York 1994), die immerhin Feministische Theologie wahrnehmen. Neuerdings wird die Frauenliturgiebewegung auch erwähnt in der Praktischen Theologie von Steck. Vgl. Wolfgang Steck, *Praktische Theologie,* Bd. 1 (Kohlhammer: Stuttgart 2000), 326-336.

[10]  Die vielfältigen Beziehungen untergründiger Art zwischen postchristlicher Spiritualität, Ritualpraxis und Frauenliturgien im christlichen Kontext können in diesem Rahmen leider nicht genügend gewürdigt werden. Vgl. Mirjam Therese Winter, *Defecting in Place*, die darin diesem Phänomen näher nachgegangen ist. Im deutschsprachigen Raum fehlt m. W. eine solche empirische Untersuchung bisher noch.

[11]  Vgl. Baumann, *Frauenliturgien*, 21-22; siehe auch Berger, *Sei gesegnet, meine Schwester*; Procter-Smith, *In Her Own Rite*.

*Nahsinne* auf.[12] Gegenüber der traditionellen Vormachtstellung des visuellen und auditiven Codes in christlichen Gottesdiensten werden Fühlen und Berühren, wird Hautkontakt und Nähe nicht gescheut, sondern im Gegenteil immer wieder rituell induziert. Die "haptische Hexis", wie sie Duden für die Zeit vor der Aufklärung konstatiert,[13] wird rituell rehabilitiert als ein wesentliches Medium der Verstehens und der Kommunikation. Gesten und Gebärden, *Tanz und Bewegung* spielen eine große Rolle, was für manche, ob nun Frauen oder Männern, fremd, ja manchmal sogar abstoßend wirken mag. Kaum ein Ritual, kaum eine Liturgie, in der nicht in irgendeiner Weise der bewegte Körper der Feiernden zu einem zentralen Medium der Gestaltung, der spirituellen Erfahrung und der religiösen Botschaft wird. Dabei werden Anleihen aus ethnischen Traditionen aller Art gemacht.[14] Der bewegte Körper und der fühlende Körper in Beziehung sind für das Verständnis der rituellen Praxis von Frauen offensichtlich unverzichtbar.

Wie aber kann und soll nun dieser Sachverhalt theologisch angemessen beschrieben und reflektiert werden? Die traditionelle liturgische Rede vom "Leib" bietet sich zunächst an. Ich möchte diesen Begriff jedoch nicht verwenden, weil er in traditioneller Liturgik in der Regel männliche Körpererfahrung generalisiert und überhöht.[15] Aber auch die Rede vom "Körper", etwa bei Elisabeth Moltmann-Wendel, scheint mir kein glücklicher Ersatz dafür zu sein, weil im vorherrschenden technischen Gebrauch dieses Wortes, trotz aller Neuansätze das Phänomen des Belebtseins, ebenso wie das des Personseins und des Bewusstseins außer Acht bleibt.[16] Auch mit dem Begriff "Körperlichkeit" oder "Embodiment", wie er in der amerikanischen "body

---

[12] Im folgenden gebe ich einige Ergebnisse aus meinem wissenschaftlichen Projekt "Die Rolle des Körpers in der liturgischen Praxis von Frauen" wieder, das voraussichtlich Ende 2001 abgeschlossen sein wird.

[13] Vgl. Barbara Duden, *Geschichte unter der Haut* (Klett-Cotta: Stuttgart 1987); dies., "Geschlecht, Biologie, Körpergeschichte", in: *Feministische Studien* 9 (1991), 105-122.

[14] Auf die Dreiteilung der Tanztraditionen in Europa sei hier nur kurz hingewiesen: Volkstanz, höfischer Tanz, Gesellschaftstanz. Vgl. dazu Giovanni Calendoli, *Tanz* (Westermann: Braunschweig 1986).

[15] Vgl. etwa die liturgische Leibphilosophie Stählins, der nur vom "Leib" spricht, aber dabei selbstverständlich den männlichen Leib und dessen Erfahrung meint. Vgl. Wilhelm Stählin, *Vom Sinn des Leibes* (Bahn: Konstanz [4]1968).

[16] Vgl. Elisabeth Moltmann-Wendel, *Wenn Gott und Körper sich begegnen, Feministische Perspektiven zur Leiblichkeit* (Gütersloher Verl.-Haus: Gütersloh 1989).

theology" üblich ist,[17] wäre dieses Wort noch nicht hinreichend erklärt, insofern die "dualistische Erblast" in der Begriffsbildung darin nicht überwunden scheint. Ich möchte deshalb im folgenden von "Corporealität" sprechen. Darunter verstehe ich die umfassende und alles Menschsein fundierende Dimension, die weder rein biologisch noch allein von gesellschaftlichen Einflüssen her zu verstehen ist, vielmehr das Ergebnis eines komplexen wechselseitigen Einflussverhältnisses darstellt.[18] Ich beziehe mich dabei auf den Begriff "Corporeality" des niederländischen Forschungsprogramms "Corporeality, Gender and Religion". Dort wird Corporealität definiert als Schnittpunkt der gesellschaftlichen Einflüsse (Sozialisation), der geschlechtsspezifischen Zuschreibung und der religiös-rituellen Befestigung, aus dem das hervorgeht, was jeweils in einer Epoche, in einer gesellschaftlichen Schicht als "Körper-Bewusstsein" verstanden wird.[19] Dabei spielt die Gender-Kategorie eine wesentliche Rolle. Sie ist kein bloßes Attribut, das als eine spezifische Eigenschaft zur Konstitution von Corporealität noch hinzutreten könnte, sondern sie konstituiert diesen Begriff wesentlich mit. In einer androzentrischen Gesellschaft "funktioniert" die Konstitution von Corporealität durch die Beschreibung von Gender, durch die immer neue In-Kraft-Setzung von Gender. Wenn demnach von Corporealität die Rede ist, dann ist damit die gesamte menschliche Existenz von Frauen und Männern gemeint, jeweils von der unaufgebbaren Perspektive der körperlichen Bedingtheit alles Lebens aus gesehen und gedacht und immer im Kontext der jeweiligen Gender-Definition. Die Herausforderung besteht darin, "vom Körper aus zu denken", ja mehr noch, "den Körper zu denken" in seiner Veränderlichkeit und prozessualen Struktur, der immer nur greifbar ist im Schnittpunkt von Individuum und Gesellschaft. So verstanden ist dieser Neologismus der Versuch, schon im Begriff die dualistische Abspaltung von Leib und Geist, von Natur und Kultur, von Frau und Mann zu überwinden. Ein solch umfassender Gebrauch

---

[17] Zur amerikanischen "body theology" vgl. als eine der bahnbrechenden Arbeiten hierzu James Nelson, *Body Theology* (Westminster John Knox: Louisville, KY 1992).

[18] Auf die heftige Auseinandersetzung zwischen beiden Positionen feministischer Körperphilosophie, die sich mit den Namen Judith Butler und Luce Irigaray verbinden, kann ich nur verweisen. Vgl. Judith Butler, *Das Unbehagen der Geschlechter* (Suhrkamp: Frankfurt 1991); Luce Irigaray, *Zur Geschlechterdifferenz* (Wiener Frauenverlag: Wien 1987).

[19] Jonneke Bekkenkamp / Maaike De Haardt (eds), *Begin with the Body. Corporeality Religion and Gender* (Peeters: Leuven 1998); Maaike De Haardt, "The body as profile, the profile of the body: Women's Studies in the Netherlands", in: Elisabeth Hartlieb / Charlotte Methuen (eds), *Sources and Resources of Feminist Theology* (ESWTR Jahrbuch 5; Kok Pharos / Grünewald: Kampen / Mainz 1995), 181-186.

von Corporealität findet sich nun innerhalb der liturgischen Praxis von Frauen. Dies möchte ich an fünf unterschiedlichen Frauenliturgien[20] deutlich machen.

*Eros-Aspekt: Die Weltgebetstagsliturgie "Gottes zärtliche Berührung"* [21]
Der erste wichtige Aspekt von Corporealität findet sich in Frauenliturgien als zentraler Begriff des „Eros", der Verbundenheit. Thema ist hier die Relationalität von Corporealität, das in menschlicher Existenz gesetzte "Mit-sein" mit anderen. Um diese für alles Menschsein grundlegende Erfahrung kreist etwa die Weltgebetstagsliturgie "Gottes zärtliche Berührung", gestaltet von Frauen aus Venezuela.

Der Weltgebetstag seinerseits ist als eine spirituell-liturgische Frucht der ersten Frauenbewegung im kirchlichen Bereich zu qualifizieren. Mutige Frauen, denen die Not ihrer Mitmenschen nicht gleichgültig war, hatten gegen Ende des 19. Jahrhunderts zu Gebetstreffen der Äußeren und Inneren Mission aufgerufen. In Amerika wurden nationale Gebetstage der angeschlossenen Frauenverbände begangen. Bald vereinigten sich die Initiativen, wurden durch Reisen und Besuche auch in anderen Ländern bekannt. In Deutschland wurde schon 1927 in Berlin durch einige methodistische Frauen der Weltgebetstag gefeiert. Unterbrochen durch das Dritte Reich und den Zweiten Weltkrieg wurde er vor allem durch Antonie Nopitsch, die Leiterin des Bayrischen Mütterdienstes, wieder in Deutschland eingeführt. Seither wächst diese liturgische Bewegung unter Frauen von Jahr zu Jahr.[22] Der Weltgebetstag kann damit als Vorläufer der gegenwärtigen Frauenliturgiebewegung angesehen werden. Unzählige Frauen wurden durch die z.T. sehr einfachen liturgischen Formen ermutigt, selbst zu "liturgical agents"[23] und damit zu Subjekten einer eigenen liturgischen

---

[20] Im folgenden beschränke ich mich im wesentlichen auf die Analyse liturgischer Formulare und verschriftlichter Frauenliturgien.

[21] Weltgebetstag 1999: Gottes zärtliche Berührung. *Titelblatt*: Frauen aller Konfessionen laden ein – Weltgebetstag – Gottes zärtliche Berührung, Freitag, 5. März 1999. Zur Weltgebetstagsliturgie vgl. Ilse Brinkhues, "Ein tiefer Wunsch nach Versöhnung. Zur Geschichte des Weltgebetstages in Deutschland", in: Angelika Schmidt-Biesalski (Hgin), *Ein Freitag im März. Weltgebetstags-Taschenbuch* (Burckhardthaus-Laetare-Verlag: Offenbach/M ²1986), 28-34; vgl. die umfassende Beschreibung der Geschichte des Weltgebetstags bei Helga Hiller, *Ökumene der Frauen. Anfänge und frühe Geschichte der Weltgebetstagsbewegung in den USA, weltweit und in Deutschland* (Klens: Düsseldorf 1999).

[22] 1998 waren es in Deutschland ca.1,3 Millionen Frauen, die den Weltgebetstag feierten.

[23] Vgl. Diann Neu, Vorwort zu Diann L. Neu / Mary E. Hunt, *Women of Fire: A Pentecost Event* (WATERworks: Silver Spring, MD 1990), 16-39.

Tradition zu werden. Die anfänglich eher bescheidene Gebetsstruktur wurde im Lauf der Jahre immer reicher ausgestaltet. Sie ist deshalb zusammenfassend als eine ökumenische, kontextuelle und politische Form von Frauenliturgien zu qualifizieren.[24]

Die Geschichte von der Blutflüssigen Frau (Mk 8) sowie weitere Texte aus Hosea (Hos 11,1-3.4.9) und den Psalmen (Ps 37,4-5) bilden das Gerüst dieser Liturgie. Segenshandlungen, eine doxologische Litanei, verschiedene symbolische Handlungen,[25] Lebens- und Erfahrungsberichte von Frauen und Mädchen aus Venezuela kontextualisieren die biblische Botschaft. Phasen der Stille, eindrückliche Lieder und Gebete, eine Litanei der Klage, die Bitte um Vergebung, ebenso wie die Bewegung hin zur Kerze in der Mitte, die Handfassung mit den Nachbarinnen sind weitere Elemente der liturgischen Gestaltung. Jede Vorbereitungsgruppe ist jedoch frei, hier eigene Akzente zu setzen.

Analysieren wir die vorliegende Frauenliturgie auf Codierungen sinnlicher Wahrnehmung hin, so fällt auf, dass grundsätzlich alle Sinne angesprochen werden. Nicht nur das Hören[26] oder das Sehen[27] ist wichtig, sondern auch das Spüren und Betasten, das Schmecken[28] und das Lachen sind wichtige Medien liturgischer Gestaltung. Die Relationalität von Corporealität kommt u.a. in der Berührung, in Nähe und Hautkontakt sinnlich erfahrbar zum Ausdruck. Durch das Auftreten und Abtreten verschiedener Sprecherinnen bleibt die Liturgie

---

[24] Der Überblick über die bisher gestalteten Themen, zum Teil in unterschiedlichen deutschen, schweizerischen oder österreichischen Ausgaben, macht eine gewisse Verschiebung in der Wahl der Themen deutlich. Aus einer eher traditionell kirchlich geprägten und individualistisch formulierten Gebets-Spiritualität erwächst eine zunehmend politischere Wachheit, sowohl was die Themenwahl als auch die Formulierung der einzelnen liturgischen Sequenzen angeht. Trotz der traditionellen Anbindung an biblische Texte werden die politischen Bezugnahmen allein schon im Weltgebetstags-Thema immer deutlicher (Bitte um Frieden; Ökumene; Ökologie-kosmischer Aspekt). Die programmatische Korrelation von "Beten und Handeln" erscheint immer häufiger auch im Thema der jeweiligen Liturgie, die von Frauen eines bestimmten Landes gestaltet wird. Dies bewahrt die Weltgebetstags-Liturgien davor, sich mit einer rein spirituell-individualistischen Tradition zufriedenzugeben.

[25] In der schweizerischen Übersetzung kommt dies noch deutlicher zum Tragen als in der vom Deutschen Weltgebetstagskomitee autorisierten Übersetzung. In der ersteren wird z.B. eine Zeichenhandlung mit dem Thema "Stricke der Verbundenheit" vorgeschlagen, die in der deutschen Version fehlt.

[26] Etwa durch Singen: Gebete, Lieder, Segensformeln.

[27] An dieser Stelle wird dies durch das Weiterreichen der Kerzen, das Einwickeln mit Bändern deutlich betont.

[28] In manchen Gemeinden findet im Zusammenhang der Weltgebetstagsliturgie ein Begegnungs-Abend statt, in dem Speisen und Getränke aus dem "Liturgie-Land" angeboten werden. Inkulturation wird auf diese Weise "schmackhaft" gemacht.

"in Bewegung". Berührung ist wichtig. Sie vermittelt neben der zwischenmenschlichen Kontaktaufnahme und Kommunikation auch einen Zugang zur Gotteserfahrung. Berührung "offenbart", repräsentiert dabei das Wirken Gottes in dreifacher Form.

Gottes Präsenz zeigt sich zunächst in der Schönheit der Natur, der Schöpfung. Die Freude und das Staunen über diese Wunder wird als eine Weise erfahren, von Gottes Liebe zärtlich berührt zu werden. Aber auch in der innigen Beziehung zwischen Frauen und ihren Kindern, wie überhaupt in ihrer Gemeinschaft, in ihrem Lachen, ihrer Lebensfreude, trotz aller Schwierigkeiten zeigt sich Gottes Nähe. Auch erotische Elemente, die Beziehung von Frau-Mann kann zum Gleichnis der zärtlichen Berührung Gottes werden. Das Evangelium (Lk 8,43-48) will und soll Mut zusprechen, Hoffnung darauf, dass sich die gegenwärtige gewalttätige, unterdrückende Situation verändert durch den Blick auf einen solchen Gott. Jesus selbst hatte sich nicht gescheut, die Berührung einer Frau zuzulassen und positiv zu benennen. Liturgisch-hermeneutisch werden Berührungs-Erfahrungen in die Nähe von Gotteserfahrungen gebracht, jedoch ohne beide zu identifizieren. "Gottes zärtliche Berührung" ist damit eine klassische Metapher für die Art "immanenter Transzendenz", die für Frauenliturgien kennzeichnend ist. Kontiguität als Modus von Wahrnehmung und Beziehung – auch in der Relation zum Göttlichen – genügt. Es ist kein "Wissen über", das hier ausgelegt wird, sondern Gotteserfahrung aufgrund von Berührtsein, von Kontakt und Nähe, von Staunen und Widerstand.

Denn die Erfahrungen liebevoller Gemeinschaft und berührender Gotteserfahrung sind bedroht. Gewalt und Ungerechtigkeit, Korruption und Egoismus zerstören sie. Gottes zärtliche Berührung muss deshalb nicht zuletzt als Widerstand artikuliert werden. Dies wird deutlich in der Zitation von Hosea 11. Der befreiungstheologische Ansatz betont, dass Gottes Option für die Armen und Marginalisierten eindeutig und unwiderruflich ist. Dafür sind die Verheißungen und biblischen Zusagen gegeben.[29]

### *Requiem-Aspekt: Dekadegottesdienst zu Richter 9 "Jeftas Tochter"*[30]
Noch stärker bringt dies eine Liturgie zum Ausdruck, die im Rahmen der ökumenischen Dekade "Kirchen in Solidarität mit den Frauen" gestaltet und

---

[29] Lk 8: die bedürftige Frau wird nicht zurückgestoßen, sondern geheilt. Hos 11: der verlassene Säugling wird nicht dem Verhungern preisgegeben, sondern aufgezogen und genährt.

[30] Diese Liturgie entstand auf Initiative des Frauenreferats der evangelischen Landeskirche in Bayern in Zusammenarbeit mit dem Frauenwerk und wurde exegetisch-liturgisch im Rah-

gefeiert wurde.[31] Besonders der kinästhetische Code sowie die emotionale Expression sind hier liturgisch zentral. "Klagefrauen" treten auf, die sich Masken aufsetzen und mit einer heftigen Bewegung wieder abreißen. Während ihres Rezitativs werfen sie ihre Hände hoch und schreien, mit sich steigernder Lautstärke. Diese ungewohnt expressive Äußerung unterstreicht die Form der Klage. In einem eindrücklichen Wut- und Trauertanz können zudem die Gefühle gemeinschaftlich und körperlich-emotional-expressiv geäußert werden. Bibliodramatische Elemente der Identifikation ermöglichen eine "ganzheitliche" Beschäftigung mit dieser Geschichte. Passende Lieder, ein Psalm aus der Tradition, der die Klage aufnimmt, gehören zu den weiteren Möglichkeiten einer vielstimmigen und mehrperspektivischen Auseinandersetzung mit dem biblischen Text.

Der eigentliche Akzent von Corporealität wird in dieser Liturgie jedoch gesetzt, indem die corporeale Existenz der namenlosen Tochter des Feldherrn Jefta als eine verletzte, vergewaltigte, ausgelieferte so deutlich wie sonst selten in den Mittelpunkt gestellt wird. Der Körper von Frauen wird als Auftreffpunkt von Gewalt,[32] als Definitionsort für unterdrückende Theologie und als Richtplatz einer patriarchalen Gesellschaft und Denkweise interpretiert. Diese Missbrauchserfahrungen von Frauen stellen die traditionelle Kreuzestheologie in Frage, die vom Opfergedanken ausgeht. Die darin begründete Soteriologie und Christologie haben immer wieder gerade religiöse Frauen abgehalten, sich gegen Gewalt und Unrecht aufzulehnen. So wie Christus zu

---

men eines Werkstattwochenendes bearbeitet und gestaltet. In der landeskirchlichen Veröffentlichung sind zwei Fassungen abgedruckt, von denen ich die erstere gewählt habe: *"Versöhnung suchen – Leben gewinnen. Was kommt vor der Versöhnung?"* Gottesdienst zur Ökumenischen Dekade *"Kirche in Solidarität mit den Frauen"* (Landeskirchenamt der Evangelisch-Lutherischen Landeskirche in Bayern, Abt. Ökumene: München 1996).

[31] Die Dekadegottesdienste werden an jede Gemeinde verschickt. Dies motiviert zunehmend liturgische Gruppen in den Gemeinden, sich mit dem liturgisch aufbereiteten Thema zu befassen und es, mit der Vorlage als Grundgerüst, zu gestalten und mit der Gemeinde zu feiern. Mit der in den deutschen evangelischen Kirchen mittlerweile verbreiteten Form der Dekadegottesdienste wird insofern eine neue Weise liturgischer Praxis von Frauen erprobt, als hier sozusagen "von oben", von Seiten der institutionalisierten Frauenverbände bzw. der Kirche solche liturgischen Vorschläge an die Basis gebracht und dort liturgisch gefeiert werden. Die Tatsache, dass mittlerweile auch Männer in diesen Vorbereitungsgruppen mitarbeiten, ist ein Argument für die Wirksamkeit und Breitenwirkung dieser Form der Verbreitung. Sie wirkt einer "Ideologie der Nische" entgegen, die eine neue Exklusivität bedeuten und dem Ziel des Feierns von Liturgie und Gottesdienst im christlichen Bereich widersprechen würde.

[32] Michel Foucault, *Archäologie des Wissens* (Suhrkamp: Frankfurt 1973).

sein, zu leben und zu leiden, wurde vielmehr als höchster Wert eines Christen- und vor allem eines Frauenlebens dargestellt.[33] Nach Procter-Smith ist stattdessen eine Ethik des Widerstands zu begründen und zu lehren, die ihre Kraft und ihre Motivation wesentlich aus den Erfahrungen marginalisierter Frauen bezieht. Gerade die womanistische Theologie und später auch die Theologie der Hispanics[34] haben feministischen Theologinnen die Augen geöffnet für die Begrenztheit ihres eigenen Denkens und die subtil wirkenden Ausschlussverfahren in der Konstitution von Kirche.[35]

### Schalom-Aspekt: Heilungsliturgie für eine vergewaltigte Frau

Wie kann nun aber Heilung und konstruktive Verarbeitung von Verletzungserfahrungen angestrebt und liturgisch gestaltet werden? Als ein Beispiel einer solchen Heilungsliturgie möchte ich kurz ein Ritual beschreiben, das aus dem Zusammenhang der Zürcher Frauenliturgiegruppen stammt.[36] Eine Frau war auf offener Straße von einem Unbekannten ermordet worden. Der Vorfall konnte nicht aufgeklärt werden, der Schock für alle, die diese Frau gekannt hatten, saß tief. Es gab keinen Anlaß, es gab keine Begründung. Die Beerdigung war zu schnell vorbeigewesen, als dass sie diesen Schock hätte auffangen können. Die Freundin der Ermordeten spürte, dass sich an dem Ungeklärten und Grausigen dieser Tat bei ihr depressive Ängste anlagerten. Sie hatte aber auch das Gefühl, ihrer Freundin ein Abschiedsritual schuldig zu sein.

Die Gruppe gestaltete es in einer einfachen, aber symbolisch klaren Weise. An der Stelle, an der der Mord geschehen war, wurde noch einmal an diese Frau erinnert: Wie sie war, wie sie lebte, was sie den einzelnen bedeutete. Die Frauengruppe nahm sich Zeit, zu erzählen, zu weinen, zu danken, was

---

[33] An dieser Stelle bleibt die genannte Frauenliturgie in ihrer theologischen Argumentation hinter ihrem eigenen Anspruch zurück. Dies ist gegenüber einer ganzen Reihe von liturgischen Gestaltungen kritisch anzumerken.

[34] Liturgisch hat sich dies niedergeschlagen in der Gestaltung sog. Mujerista-Liturgien. Vgl. dazu Ada Maria Isasi-Diaz, *Mujerista Theology* (Orbis Books: Maryknoll, NY 1996); Vgl. auch dies., Ada Maria Isasi-Diaz, "On the Birthing Stool: Mujerista Liturgy", in: Procter-Smith / Walton (eds), *Women at Worship*, 191-210.

[35] Vgl. zum womanistischen Ansatz Cheryl Townsend Gilkes, "Mother to the Motherless, Father to the Fatherless: Power, Gender, and Community in an Afrocentric Biblical Tradition", in: *Semeia* 47 (1989), 57-85; William L. Andrews (ed.), *Sisters of the Spirit* (Indiana University Press: Bloomington 1986); Delores S. Williams, "Rituals of Resistance in Womanist Worship", in: Procter-Smith / Walton (eds), *Women at Worship*, 215-223.

[36] Ich selbst kenne es durch Erzählung, m. W. ist es nicht ausführlich dokumentiert worden.

die Freundin ihnen bedeutet hatte. Der Platz an der Straße, an der sie sich versammelten, war schön geschmückt. Im Erzählen legten die Frauen, die sich versammelt hatten, Geschenke und Zeichen ihrer Zuneigung auf den Boden. Als sie sich alles vom Herzen geredet hatten, trat eine lange Zeit des Schweigens ein. Es musste so sein, diese Leere war der Ausdruck ihre Ratlosigkeit und war richtig so. Als das Schweigen zu Ende war, gestalteten die anwesenden Frauen ein Segensritual für die Ermordete. Der plötzliche Abbruch ihres Lebens wurde in den Erzählungen und Segenswünschen symbolisch gestaltet und damit würdevoll zu Ende gebracht. Mit jedem Segenswort wurde den Anwesenden leichter ums Herz. Sie konnten nun die ermordete Freundin loslassen, ihr Schicksal in andere Hände legen, auch wenn deren Ende immer noch unverständlich war. Mehr als zwei Stunden waren vergangen, bevor das Ritual beendet werden konnte. Trotz ihrer Trauer, so berichtete eine der Frauen, hatten sie alle den Eindruck, etwas sehr Wichtiges getan und "erledigt" zu haben. Ihr Leben konnte nun weitergehen, die Erinnerung an das Schicksal ihrer Freundin konnte integriert werden, neue Lebensenergie begann zu fließen.

So und in ähnlicher Weise werden viele Rituale gestaltet, unauffällig, mitten im Alltag, als Zuspruch, als Ermutigung, als Hilfe um loszulassen, als Stärkung, schwierige Entscheidungen fällen zu können. Rituale zeigen: Flucht und Verdrängung ist kein Ausweg, Ängste und Leid können gestaltet und benannt werden.[37] Auch die Liturgie als das gemeinschaftlich gestaltete Ritual im Rahmen der christlichen Tradition sollte diese Chance verstärkt nutzen, um wieder ein Raum zu werden, in dem Gefühle geäußert, in der Heilung

---

[37] Die gesamte christliche Liturgie und Verkündigung wäre auf diesen Aspekt hin einmal kritisch zu analysieren. Es würde auffallen, an wie vielen Stellen eine durch Gewalterfahrung traumatisierte Frau darin eine Rechtfertigung des Täters verstehen müsste, besonders wenn es um die "Erklärung des Unerklärlichen", um die "dunklen Seiten im Gottesbild" geht. Vgl. Sheila Redmond, "Remember the Good, forget the Bad": Denial and Family Violence in a Christian Worship Service", in: Procter-Smith / Walton (eds), *Women at Worship*, 71-82; ebenso Catherine J. Foote, *Survivor Prayers, Talking With God about Childhood Sexual Abuse* (Westminster John Knox: Louisville, KY 1994); Marie M. Fortune, "My God, My God, Why Have You Forsaken Me?" in: dies. (ed.), *Spinning a Sacred Yarn: Women from the Pulpit* (Pilgrim Press: New York 1982), 65-71; James Leehan, *Defiant Hope: Spirituality for Survivors of Family Abuse* (Westminster John Knox: Louisville, KY 1993. Vgl. im deutschen Bereich Carola Moosbach, *Gottflamme Du Schöne, Lob- und Klagegebete* (Gütersloher Verl.-Haus: Gütersloh 1997); vgl. außerdem Ulrike Bail, *Gegen das Schweigen klagen. Eine intertextuelle Studie zu den Klagepsalmen Ps 6 und Ps 55 und der Erzählung von der Vergewaltigung Tamars* (Kaiser: Gütersloh 1998).

erbeten werden kann. In der liturgischen Praxis von Frauen wird "Heilung" in jedem Fall umfassend verstanden, als die ganze Corporealität betreffend. Heilung und Heil lassen sich deshalb nicht grundsätzlich voneinander trennen. Heilung kann in manchen Liturgien auch als *Reinigung* bezeichnet werden. Es geht um das Zurücklassen von alltäglichen Sorgen, von Zerstreuung, von Pflichten. Es bezeichnet den Schritt hinüber in den Raum des Heiligen, des Feierns, des Aufatmens im Bereich des Göttlichen.[38] In anderen Frauenliturgien wiederum können *lösende Erfahrungen* damit beschrieben werden. Spannungen werden abgebaut, abreagiert.[39] Entspannung, Lösung, ja Erlösung können das positive Ergebnis sein. Immer wieder werden aber auch *integrative und transformative Prozesse* beschrieben, die heilsam und heilvoll zugleich wirken. Das Dunkle, gerade wenn es sich mit Corporealität als einer lebenszyklischen Erfahrung verbindet, kann wahrgenommen und innerhalb eines neuen und wertschätzenden Deutungsrahmens integriert werden. Integration des Abgespaltenen gelingt wieder und damit die Transformation ehemals bedrückender Erfahrungen. Aber auch *exorzistische Elemente* sind häufig zu finden. Die Mächte der Gewalt, der Ausbeutung von Frauen, der Spaltung von Geist und Körper, des Ausschlusses von Frauen werden benannt und dann "zum Teufel gejagt".[40]

### *Sakramentaler Aspekt: "Wechsel des Lebens – Reise durch die Menopause"*

Ein vierter Aspekt, der für Corporealität in der liturgischen Praxis von Frauen spezifisch ist, ist die Erfahrung, das Leben selbst als ein Geschenk, als ein verdanktes Leben zu würdigen und zu benennen. Das Leben jeder einzelnen Frau gleicht einer Reise, einer "journey", die von einem Ursprung ausgeht, verschiedene Stationen durchläuft und schließlich, wenn sie gelingt, wieder zum Ursprung zurückkehrt. Nach der "Vollendung des Kreises" ist den

---

[38] So etwa in Brigitte Enzner-Probst / Andrea Felsenstein-Rossberg (Hginnen), *Wenn Himmel und Erde sich berühren, Lieder, Tänze und Anregungen für Frauenliturgien* (Gütersloher Verlags-Haus: Gütersloh 1993).

[39] Vgl. etwa den Stampftanz in der Liturgie zu Ri 9.

[40] Die Liturgie, die die WATER-Frauen bei einer Pfingsttagung auf dem Tiltenberg in den Niederlanden gestaltet haben, ist dafür eindrücklich. Vgl. Diann L. Neu / Mary E. Hunt, Women of Fire: a Pentecost Event, Silver Spring 1990. Aber auch die Frauenprozession zur Mitte der Dekade beim Münchner Kirchentag 1993 enthält solche exorzistischen Elemente. Vgl. Frauenreferat der Evangelisch-Lutherischen Kirche in Bayern (Hgin), *Frauenprozession zur Mitte der Dekade* (Eigendruck Frauenreferat: München 1993).

Frauen eine erneuerte vollmächtige Erfahrung ihrer selbst verheißen. Die Menopause, gesellschaftlich verächtlich gemacht als Altweiber-Krankheit, wird liturgisch als ein wichtiger Schritt auf dem Weg, den Kreis zu vollenden, die Reise zu einem guten Ende zu führen, interpretiert.[41]

Aber auch die Ambivalenz, die sich mit dieser Körpererfahrung verbindet, muss erwähnt werden. Der Zyklus hört auf und damit die Erfahrung von Fruchtbarkeit. Auf der anderen Seite hört auch die Angst vor unerwünschter Schwangerschaft auf. Wichtig ist, beide Seiten dieser körperlichen Erfahrung zu benennen, um einer Idealisierung zu entgehen. Auf der anderen Seite gilt es auch die Trauer um das Abebben von Leidenschaft zu verarbeiten. An die Zeit der "ersten Erfahrungen" wird erinnert: die erste Menstruation, den ersten Orgasmus, das erste Kind. Nur da, wo die Anfänge dankbar erinnert werden, wird es auch gelingen, loszulassen.

In dieser und ähnlichen Liturgien zum Thema Menstruation, Geburt oder Menopause[42] wird das Blut von Frauen grundsätzlich positiv gesehen. Es ist ein zentrales Zeichen ihrer Fruchtbarkeit und ihres Mitschöpferinseins am Werden des Lebens. Es ist mit Würde und Wertschätzung zu interpretieren, nicht mit der exkludierenden Haltung des Ersten Testaments und der institutionalisierten Kirche. Was von der Gesellschaft abgewertet wird, ist in der Sicht der Feiernden Grund zum Danken und Loben. Der doxologische Charakter dieser Frauenliturgie bringt verschiedene Leiberfahrungen von Frauen zur Sprache, die von den Anwesenden bekräftigend aufgenommen werden. Gott ist "Quelle des Lebens" und entspricht damit der Erfahrung des Fließens im Blut der Frauen. Dieses Bild wird noch einmal aufgenommen im Bild von "Ebbe und Flut", die in den Frauen selbst verankert sind. Frauen tragen sozusagen "ihr Wetter" in sich und wissen sich damit eng mit den Rhythmen und Zyklen der Schöpfung verbunden. Ein ungewohntes Bild wird am Schluss gebraucht, indem Gott als die "Gebärmutter des Universums" angesprochen wird. Auch

---

[41] Diann Neu, "Change of Life: Journey through Menopause", *WATERwheel* 9/4 (Winter 1996), 4-5, übersetzt aus dem amerikanischen Englisch von Brigitte Enzner-Probst.

[42] Vgl. dazu Cathleen Rountree (ed.), *On Women Turning 50. Celebrating Mid-Life Discoveries* (Harper & Row: San Francisco 1993); vgl. auch Rosemary Radford Ruether, *Unsere Wunden heilen, unsere Befreiung feiern. Rituale in der Frauenkirche* (Kreuz-Verlag: Stuttgart 1988), engl. *Women-Church. Theology and Practice of Feminist Liturgical Communities* (Harper & Row: San Francisco 1986): Der Gemeinschaftscharakter wird im englischen Titel sehr viel deutlicher. Ruether bringt in ihrer Sammlung die Mikvah, das rituelle Bad nach der Menstruation. Anstelle der üblichen Reinigungsvorstellung wird es nun zu einer Zelebration der natürlichen Rhythmen des Frauenkörpers, ebenso wie das Ritual zu Rosh Hodesh, zum Neumond.

darin drückt sich die Teilhabe an göttlicher Schöpfungskraft aus, die sich in Frauen realisiert. "Frucht" dieser Phase, wenn sie in dieser spirituellen Bedeutung durchlebt wird, ist "Begeisterung", ist Inspiration, eine Leiblichkeit also, die wahrhaft zum "Tempel des Geistes" geworden ist. Im Segen, den sich die Frauen anschließend zusprechen, wird Gott angerufen als die "verbindende Kraft in allem". Durch das "Einander hinaussenden" stärkt die Gemeinschaft jede einzelne Frau, ihre "Reise durch die eigenen Lebensübergänge" nun selbst fortzusetzen. Doch das Bild der Reise enthält noch mehr. Innerhalb der jüdisch-feministischen Liturgiepraxis werden solche neugestalteten Rituale deshalb auch als "Ruheplätze" verstanden, als Zwischenstationen und Rastplätze, auf dem Weg zu einer vollständigen Aneignung der eigenen Tradition durch Frauen.[43] Als Glieder einer Religion des Wortes ist es für jüdische Feministinnen unbedingt notwendig, Rituale zu entwickeln, die die eigene Tradition aneignen, die eigenen Worte festhalten, Platz für Frauen schaffen, selbst zu Wort zu kommen. Als Beispiel erwähnt Elwell die Gestaltung von Rosch Hodesch, den Monatsbeginn, das Fest des Neumondes. Traditionell war dies ein Frauentag. Er wird nun in einer neuen Weise mit dem weiblichen Zyklus gleichgesetzt. Elwell berichtet, dass überall im Land in kleinen Gruppen Rosch Hodesch in dieser neuen Weise gefeiert wird. Dabei versteht sie jüdisch-feministische Liturgien als "half-way houses", also eine Art Pilgerinnenherbergen, in denen sich Frauen "aufwärmen", ermutigen können, stärken für den Weg hinaus "in die Welt der jüdischen Tradition". Wagen sie den Schritt hinaus nicht, bleiben sie abgeschnitten von ihrer Tradition und verkümmern. Außerdem bleibt die jüdische Tradition letztlich vom liturgischen Schaffen der Frauen unberührt. Ohne große Schwierigkeiten lässt das hier Gesagte sich auch in den Kontext christlich-feministischer Liturgien übertragen.

### *Sinn-Aspekt: Frauenliturgie zur "Geschichte von der salbenden Frau"*
Als letzten Aspekt, der im Zusammenhang von Corporealität und Körperkonzepten in Frauenliturgien auftritt, möchte ich den Sinn-Aspekt ansprechen. Als Beispiel wähle ich dafür eine Frauenliturgie zur Perikope von der unbekannten salbenden Frau (Mk 14,3-9). Sie wurde von einer Gruppe der Zürcher Ökumenischen Frauenbewegung gestaltet und veröffentlicht.[44] Für das Entstehen

---

[43] Vgl. Sue Levi Elwell, "Reclaiming Jewish Women's Oral Tradition. An Analysis of Rosh Hodesch", in: Procter-Smith / Walton (eds), *Women at Worship*, 111-126.

[44] Aus der Gottesdienstreihe "Frauen feiern" in Stadt und Kanton Zürich am 29. April 1990 (Helferei; Kirche Oberstrass; Heilig Kreuz; Alte Kirche Schwamendingen; Kirche Dürnten; Christkatholische Kirche Winterthur; Alte reformierte Kirche Schlieren; Reformierte Kirche

der Ökumenischen Frauenbewegung und ihres liturgisch kreativen Zweiges sind zwei Impulse entscheidend geworden. Zum 400. Jahrestag der Reformation in Zürich sollte eine Disputation zur Situation der Kirche stattfinden. Dies nahmen Frauen und Frauengruppen zum Anlass, ihr Unbehagen am Zustand der Kirche, an ihrer Unterrepräsentation zu artikulieren und Mitbestimmung zu fordern. Als eine Möglichkeit, solche Mitbestimmung konkret werden zu lassen, entstanden zahlreiche Frauengruppen, die sich mit kirchen- und gesellschaftspolitischen Fragen beschäftigten. Eine davon hatte es sich zur Aufgabe gemacht, politisches Engagement mit feministischer Spiritualität zu verbinden. Daraus entstand die weit verzweigte Arbeitsgruppe "Frausein – Kirchesein", die bisher mehr als hundert dokumentierte Liturgien vorlegen könnte.[45] Ebenso beeindruckt das reformatorische Engagement um die rechte Schriftauslegung. Frauen machen Männern das Recht streitig, mit Autorität für sie sprechen und die Schrift auslegen zu können. Frauen wollen ihre Auslegung, ihre Sicht der biblischen Schriften, ihre Interpretation selbst formulieren und weitergeben. Diese namenlose Frau hatte schließlich getan, was kein Mann für Jesus getan hatte: sie hatte ihn zum Christus gesalbt und in seinem Auftrag, Gottes befreiende Liebe den Menschen zu bringen, anerkannt und gestärkt. Sie hatte ebenso die Konsequenz dieses Auftrags erkannt, den Konflikt mit den Kräften, die diese Botschaft als bedrohlich und gefährlich eliminieren wollen. Von einzelnen ist die Bedeutung dieser salbenden namenlosen Frau zwar in der Auslegungsgeschichte der Perikope immer wieder genannt worden, sie hat sich aber im Mainstream der Exegeten nicht durchsetzen können.[46] Einer Aufzählung

---

Affoltern; Alte Kirche Wetzwil zum Text Markus 14, 3-9) wird die Liturgie der Gruppe "Frauen feiern in der Helferei" ausgewählt. Sie wurde gestaltet von Hanni Eichenberger, Irene Gysel und Charlotte Treu.

[45] Diese Arbeitsgruppe ist dabei selbst wieder Teil einer übergreifenden Vernetzung verschiedenster thematischer Frauengruppen. Unter dem Namen "Ökumenische Frauenbewegung Zürich" (OeFZ) als Verein konstituiert, verfolgt sie das Ziel, Raum zu schaffen "für frauenspezifische religiöse Anliegen und feministisch-theologisches Denken und Handeln." Die Zürcher Frauenliturgiefrauen beschreiben diesen Raum als "eine theologische, eine spirituelle, eine ekklesiologische und eine politische Dimension. Auch die Gottesdienste bewegen sich in unterschiedlicher Akzentuierung in all diesen Dimensionen." Bisher sind mehr als hundertdreißig solcher Frauenliturgien unter der Bezeichnung "Frauen feiern" gestaltet und gefeiert worden. Sie wurden von Anfang an dokumentiert.

[46] Elisabeth Schüssler Fiorenza, *Zu ihrem Gedächtnis* (Kaiser: München / Mainz 1988). Zur Auseinandersetzung mit exegetischer Literatur siehe Robert Holst, "The Anointing of Jesus. Another Application of the Form-Critical Method", in: *Journal of Biblical Literature* 95 (1976), 435-446. Vgl. auch die Auslegung dieser Perikope von Peter Abälard im 14. Jahrhundert, in der er die Salbung des Christus durch eine Frau als autoritative Handlung würdigt. Zitiert nach Bla-

männlicher Kommentare innerhalb einer Frauen abwertenden Auslegungsgeschichte wird deshalb nun die befreiende, wertschätzende und positive Deutung der Frauengemeinschaft entgegengesetzt. In diesen Kontext ist die im folgenden beschriebene Liturgie einzuordnen.

Wiederum ist es das haptisch-taktile Element, das für deren liturgische Gestaltung charakteristisch ist. Es wird sowohl in seiner historischen Bedeutung erläutert, aber auch mit der Gestalt der namenlosen Frau über bibliodramatisch eingeführte Identifikation verknüpft. Indem dieses Salbritual als Zeichenhandlung vergegenwärtigt wird, verbinden sich die anwesenden Frauen mit der damaligen Geschichte. Ein wechselseitiger Erschließungsprozess findet statt, in der sich über Riechen, Berühren und zeichenhafte Handlung ein spürbarer Kontakt einstellt. Auch die Person Jesu wird dadurch, ohne dass dies großer Worte bedürfte, fühlbar, fassbar. Die Beziehung, die die salbende Frau zu ihm eröffnet, nimmt auch die jetzt Gottesdienst Feiernden in diese Beziehung mit hinein. Begegnung wird möglich, Berührung, Angerührtsein von dem, was Jesus dieser Frau zuspricht: wo das Evangelium verkündigt wird, wird auch dein Name genannt werden! Ausgehend von dieser Zusage Jesu konstatiert die versammelte Frauengemeinschaft jedoch nüchtern, dass dieses Versprechen von der gesamten Kirche bisher noch nicht eingelöst worden ist. Der Anspruch, selbst eine solche mit Autorität sprechende Interpretationsgemeinschaft zu sein, artikuliert sich schließlich in dem Zuspruch an die Schwester vor langer Zeit: "Frau, heute geschieht Evangelium! Heute lösen wir diese Verheißung ein. Wir sind Kirche, weil wir diese Verheißung Jesu als eine freimachende Botschaft endlich realisieren!"

## Ekklesiologische Konsequenzen

Welche Konsequenzen sind nun aus den bisher geschilderten Frauenliturgien für ein Bild von Kirche zu ziehen, die ihrerseits Frauen konstitutiv mit einschließen würde?

### *Die Frauengemeinschaft als Ort der autoritativen Schriftauslegung*[47]

In der Liturgie zur Salbenden Frau wird der Anspruch erhoben, mit Autorität für die gesamte Gemeinschaft der Kirche zu sprechen und in diesem Sprechen gehört zu werden. Was lange in der Vergessensgeschichte der Kirche begra-

---

mires Alcuin, "Paradox in the Medieval Gender Doctrine of Head and Body", in: Peter Biller / Alastair J. Minnis (eds), *Medieval Theology and the Natural Body* (York Medieval Press: York 1997) 13-24. Allerdings hat sich diese Sicht weder damals noch heute durchsetzen können.

[47] Vgl. Elisabeth Schüssler Fiorenza, "Auf dem Weg zu einer biblisch-feminisischen Spiritualität. Die Ekklesia der Frauen", in: *Zu ihrem Gedächtnis*, 408-417.

ben war, kommt nun ans Licht und wird benannt. Das von Jesus Angekündigte ereignet sich jetzt. Evangelium geschieht, indem die Tat dieser Frau erinnert, sie selbst als Teil des Leibes Christi wieder integriert wird. Die Gottesdienst feiernde Frauengemeinschaft versteht sich als Ekklesia und ist damit der Ort neuer Interpretation und heilvoller Restitution einer bislang unvollständigen Verheißungsgeschichte.

## *Die Gemeinschaft der Frauen als Ort erotischer Kommunikation und Verbundenheit*

Darüber hinaus wird deutlich: wirkliche Begegnung mit der Botschaft des Evangeliums, eine heilvolle Begegnung mit Jesus als dem "Christus der Frauen" ist vor allem möglich im Modus der Berührung, der liebenden Beziehung und Bewegung aufeinander zu. Kontiguität ist das Kennzeichen einer solchen christologischen Rede, nicht das "Reden über". Respekt und Hingabe, Vertrauen und Stärkung des anderen auf seinem Weg sind die Kennzeichen, um von dieser Christuswirklichkeit in der rituellen Gestaltung berührt zu werden und Stärkung auch für den eigenen Weg zu erfahren. Zugleich ist damit der Anfang der Kirchwerdung der christlichen Gemeinde angesprochen. Jesus sagt: Wo immer das Evangelium verkündet wird, wird von deinem "guten Werk", von deiner berührenden Zeichenhandlung an mir erzählt werden. Gerade dies aber ist nach reformatorischem Verständnis das Kennzeichen der Kirche: dass in ihr öffentlich und kontinuierlich die Botschaft des Evangeliums (von Christus, dem Gesalbten Gottes) verkündigt wird.[48] Kirche ist da, wo die Gute Nachricht von der befreienden Liebe Gottes erzählt und öffentlich gemacht und dies in Zeichenhandlungen corporeal erfahrbar gefeiert wird.

Aber auch die Verbindung untereinander, die Gemeinschaft der feiernden Frauen, wird in Ritual und Liturgie immer wieder bestärkt und als Quelle erotischer Kommunikation erfahren. Damit eröffnet sie einen Raum, in dem dann auch die "Kommunikation des Evangeliums" in neuer Weise verstanden und aufgenommen werden kann. Die ekklesiologische Dimension besteht im gemeinschaftlichen spirituellen Durcharbeiten von Lebenssituationen. Darin eingeschlossen sind die Erfahrungen von erotischer Bezogenheit, von Lust und Sexualität als Erfahrungsformen, die Spiritualität nicht widersprechen, sondern damit konvergieren.[49]

---

[48] Vgl. *Confessio Augustana*, Art. 7.
[49] Vgl. Elisabeth Moltmann-Wendel, *Wach auf, meine Freundin. Die Wiederkehr der Gottesfreundschaft* (Kreuz-Verlag: Stuttgart 1999).

## Die Ekklesia der Frauen als Heimat der Marginalisierten und als Ort des Widerstandes

Schon Paulus schreibt an die Korinther: Wenn ein Glied leidet, leiden alle mit (1Kor 12). Die Corporealität der Frauen und ihr dadurch begründeter Ausschluss als vollgültige Glieder am "Leib Christi" muss die ganze Kirche angehen. Er ist kein "nichttheologischer Faktor", sondern zentraler Punkt theologischer Auseinandersetzung und Revision.[50] Feministische Ritualtheorie und Liturgik haben deshalb die nicht geringe Aufgabe, das bisher Ausgeschlossene nun ihrerseits als wesentliches Thema in Liturgie und Dogmatik zu etablieren. Die Rehabilitierung von Frauen für die Leitung von Gemeinde und Gottesdienst ist der Anfang vom Ende einer tiefgreifenden strukturellen/ekklesiologischen Sünde christlicher Kirche.

Darüber hinaus ist eine Soteriologie zu entfalten, die die Erfahrungen der Gewalt, und zwar der religiös motivierten Gewalt gegen Frauen ernstnimmt, diese nicht vorschnell harmonisierend entschärft, sondern theologisch adäquat beantwortet. Eine Soteriologie ist zu formulieren, die vom Widerstand und nicht vom Gehorsam ausgeht,[51] dabei nicht im theologisch-religiösen Raum verbleibt, sondern die notwendige Verlängerung in den politisch-gesellschaftlichen Raum hinein aufzeigt. Im Spannungsfeld zwischen Widerstand und Auferstehung können dann auch die notwendigen Schritte versöhnender Veränderung gegangen werden. Eine befreiungstheologische Konzeption von Versöhnung wird die Corporealität von Frauen und die damit verbundenen Gewalt- und Unrechtserfahrungen als grundlegend betrachten. Dabei ist Gewalt in jeder Form wahrzunehmen und zu bearbeiten, nicht zuletzt auch Gewaltverhältnisse unter Frauen und in Frauengemeinschaften.[52] Es ist unbedingt an der Zeit, hier selbstkritisch auch die verdeckten Macht- und Gewaltstrukturen in der Gemeinschaft von Frauen wahrzunehmen und sie in einer solchen Ethik des Widerstandes zu reflektieren.

---

[50] Wie es auf der Vollversammlung des Ökumenischen Rates 1975 in Nairobi formuliert wurde. Vgl. dazu Margot Käßmann, *Die eucharistische Vision* (Kaiser: München / Mainz 1992).

[51] Vgl. Marjorie Procter-Smith, *Praying with Our Eyes Open, Engendering Feminist Liturgical Prayer* (Abingdon Press: Nashville 1995); Irmtraud Fischer, "Geh, und laß dich unterdrücken, Repression gegen Frauen in biblischen Texten", in: *Concilium* 30 (1994), 155-160; Phyllis Trible, *Mein Gott, warum hast du mich vergessen!* (Gütersloher Verlagshaus Mohn: Gütersloh 1984).

[52] Vgl. dazu den längst überfälligen Beitrag von Susanne Andrea Birke, "Kein sicherer Ort – Tabuthema Frauengewalt", in: *FAMA* 16/3 (August 2000), 13-14.

## Die gottesdienstliche Frauengemeinschaft als Gemeinschaft der Geheilten und Heilenden

Die eine Liturgie gestaltende und feiernde Frauengemeinschaft, die "Ekklesia der Frauen", zeigt sich in diesen Liturgien schließlich nicht zuletzt auch als Ort der heilvollen Zuwendung. Darin eingeschlossen sind die Aspekte der Heilung von erlittenen oder imaginierten Ängsten, die aus – und angesprochen werden.

Heilung kann, so haben wir gesehen, in verschiedener Hinsicht erbeten und interpretiert werden. Sie kann Katharsis sein und reinigend wirken. Alte Ängste und Verletzungen können benannt und verabschiedet werden. Sie wirkt lösend, durch Lieder und Gebete, durch Meditation und Stille. Das Wissen darum, nicht allein auf diesem Weg, dieser Lebensreise zu sein, kann helfen, loszulassen und eine neue Lebensphase zu integrieren. Heilung kann sich transformativ zeigen, insofern die physischen Veränderungen, zum Beispiel des Alterns, in einen größeren Kontext von Selbstfindung und Gotteserfahrung hineingestellt werden. Die Kräfte der Spaltung und Abwertung können jedoch im wahrsten Sinn des Wortes auch "zum Teufel gejagt", in exorzistischen Litaneien rituell vertrieben werden.

Kirche zeigt sich in der liturgischen Praxis von Frauen als Ort der Berührung und corporealen Kommunikation, in der das Leben als ein verdanktes und geschenktes akzeptiert und, in allen Grenzen und Behinderungen, wertgeschätzt werden kann. Der kosmologische Bezug, das Wissen darum, dass die eigenen Rhythmen mit größeren abgestimmt und harmonisiert werden können, dass hier Bezüge bestehen, die über das eigene kleine Leben hinausgehen, kann etwas Entlastendes und Befreiendes haben. Der Blick der einzelnen Frau wird geweitet auf ein größeres Ganzes, das mit dem "Projekt Schöpfung" umschrieben werden könnte, an dem sie in ihrem Frausein teilhat, mit dem sie sich verbunden weiß.[53] Das Abschreiten der Pole von Fruchtbarkeit und Menopause, von Fülle und Loslassen ist wichtig, um das Ganze (den Kreis des Lebens) in den Blick zu bekommen, um eine Lebensphase spirituell erschließen zu können. Ohne die Artikulation von Erfahrungen des Verzichts, des Abgebens und Sterbens wäre das ganze Bild schief. Ohne die Erfahrungen von Angst, die sich mit Zyklus und Menstruation verbinden können, würden sich viele Frauen aus einer solchen Liturgie ausgeschlossen fühlen.

---

[53] An dem genauso gut auch Männer teilhaben und Kinder. Allerdings braucht es dazu eine andere Haltung als die der technisch-instrumentellen Vernunft.

Aber auch die Begrenzungen des corporealen Daseins, die durch Krankheit und Behinderungen der verschiedensten Art hervorgerufen werden, sind hier zu nennen. Die gesellschaftliche Ausgrenzung und "Exkommunikation" solcher Menschen ist als eine unheilvolle Abspaltung zu erkennen, die den "Leib Christi" schwächt und der Kirche zu widerstehen hat. In ihrer Communio, die ja gerade an der leiblich–corporeal–materiellen Verfasstheit als "Leib Christi" festhält, ist jede willkommen. Hier kann und muss den Kräften der Exkarnation, des Ausschlusses widersprochen werden, kann sich "Inkarnation jetzt" heilvoll ereignen.[54]

In ihrer liturgischen Praxis suchen Frauen nicht zuletzt die immer wieder sich erneuernde Begegnung mit der Christuswirklichkeit, dem Evangelium. Frauen stellen sich in diese Tradition bewusst hinein, um die "verheißungsvolle Geschichte" Jesu endlich einzulösen.

### *Leib Christi – Leib der Frauen*

Die Corporealität von Frauen und die Rede von Kirche als dem "Leib Christi" miteinander in Verbindung zu bringen, verspricht neue Einsichten in alte theologisch-kirchliche Fragen. Frauen insistieren in ihrer liturgischen Praxis darauf, die Rede vom "Leib Christi" nicht rein metaphorisch zu nehmen, denn dann müsste die gegenwärtige androzentrische Verfasstheit kirchlicher Strukturen und der immer noch andauernde Ausschluss von Frauen nicht thematisiert werden. Sie insistieren vielmehr darauf, dass beides etwas miteinander zu tun hat und dass diese Relation als eine heilvolle und Leben fördernde zu begreifen ist. Solange das Blut Jesu als Zeichen der Hingabe und die Corporealität und das Blut der Frauen als Zeichen ihres Mitschöpferinseins sich jedoch zu widersprechen und dogmatisch auszuschließen scheinen, ist der "Leib Christi", die corporeal verfasste Gemeinschaft der in seinem Namen Versammelten, nicht heil. Das Heil durch die Hingabe des Einen wird wertlos, wenn es auf der unheilvollen Abwertung des Frauenleibes aufbaut. In der Eucharistie werden Brot und Wein gewürdigt als Elemente der Schöpfung und zugleich untrennbar verbunden mit dem heilsamen Prozess von Erlösung und Versöhnung in Christus. Auf den Streit um die rechte Zuordnung von Frauenleib und Christusleib, von Corporealität der Frauen und "Leib Christi" als Festhalten an der Materialität

---

[54] Den Begriff der "Excarnation" verdanke ich einem Gespräch mit Kimberley Willis an der Theologischen Fakultät in Evanston, die zu diesem Thema arbeitet. Sie bezieht sich insbesondere auf Nancy Eiesland, *The Disabled God* (Abingdon Press: Nashville 1994).

und Corporealität dieser Gemeinschaft, gegen alle Spiritualisierungstendenzen, kann hier allerdings nur hingewiesen werden.[55] Ich möchte jedoch einen Schritt vor diese Auseinandersetzung um dogmatische Grundfragen gehen.

Nicht ohne Grund ist die Perikope von der salbenden Frau in vielen Frauenliturgien immer wieder gestaltet worden. Denn mit ihr bewegen sich Frauen zurück, noch vor die eigentlich dogmatische und speziell ekklesiologische Ausformulierung dessen, was sich in der Christusbeziehung ereignet. Sie gehen zurück an den Ursprung tatsächlicher Geschichten, erlebter und erfahrener Beziehungen mit Jesus. Sie entdecken darin eine Wertschätzung ihrer eigenen corporeal- verfassten Existenz als Frauen. Sie können dadurch nachvollziehen, was später systematisch-theologisch auseinandergefaltet wurde in der Dreiheit der Rede vom "Leib Christi", als Bezeichnung der corporealen Existenz Jesu, der eucharistischen Gabe und schließlich der Gemeinschaft der Glaubenden. Wie später in dogmatischer Rekapitulation wird der reale Leib Christi, die corporeal verfasste Person Jesu von Nazareth vor Augen gestellt. In einer Kommunikation der Hingabe, für die erotische Beziehung, Zartgefühl und eine Atmosphäre von Intimität wesentlich ist, wird eine Zeichenhandlung, eine sakramentale Handlung vollzogen. Der tiefere spirituell-theologische "Sinn" liegt in der Zeichenhandlung schon beschlossen, so dass nicht viele Worte gemacht werden müssen, um zu verstehen – oder misszuverstehen. Die Parallele zur Fußwaschung, die im Johannesevangelium an Stelle der Eucharistie steht, sowie zur Taufe als Zeichenhandlung liegt nahe. Damit wird diese Salbhandlung zu einer sakramentalen Zeichenhandlung, die, verbunden mit einem Christuswort, durchaus in den Rang der verbindlichen Sakramente hätte aufgenommen werden können, um einen Auftrag, eine Berufung zu bestätigen. Sie wurde jedoch nicht in den liturgischen Kanon der Kirche integriert, während doch, zumindest in katholischer Tradition, die Salbhandlung als Dienst an Kranken und Sterbenden als sakramentale Hand-

---

[55] Vgl. zur Abendmahlsdiskussion Ute Grümbel, *Abendmahl: "Für euch gegeben"? Erfahrungen und Ansichten von Frauen und Männern. Anfragen an Theologie und Kirche* (Calwer: Stuttgart 1997), sowie die Dokumentation der Evangelischen Frauenarbeit *Wir Frauen und das Herrenmahl*, hg. Frauenarbeit der Evangelischen Kirche in Württemberg (Frauenarbeit der Ev. Landeskirche in Württemberg: Stuttgart 1996). Vor allem der Vortrag von Elisabeth Moltmann-Wendel auf dem Württembergischen Pfarrertag 1995 in Esslingen hat diese Diskussion entscheidend angestoßen. Vgl. Elisabeth Moltmann-Wendel, "Abendmahl aus feministischer Sicht. Abendmahl als Problem", in: *Abendmahl in der Diskussion. Dokumentation*, hg. v. Amt für Information der Evangelischen Landeskirche in Württemberg, 22.3 (1996), 3-9.

lung entfaltet worden ist, obwohl sie sich nur auf eine kurze Erwähnung im Jakobusbrief stützt.[56]

Wenn Frauen von ihren corporealen Erfahrungen und ihrer liturgisch-innovativen Praxis her Kirche beschreiben, dann sehen sie diese als eine lebendige Gemeinschaft, in der die corporeale Existenz *aller* wert geschätzt und als Erfahrungen des realen "Leibes Christi" eingebracht werden können. Sie engagieren sich für eine Kirche, die aus Frauen, Männern und Kindern besteht, sich politisch kraftvoll engagiert, gegen Gewalt in jeder Form aufsteht und für ein geheiltes, versöhntes und beziehungsreiches Leben eintritt. Sie möchten eine Kirche gestalten, die sich als Teil der einen Schöpfung weiß und von der Nähe Gottes und der Inspiration des Geistes lebt.

### Konsequenzen für das Gestalten von Ritual und Liturgie

Dass dies nicht ohne Folgen für das "Liturgieren" und Ritualisieren innerhalb der Kirche bleiben kann, liegt auf der Hand. Was Kirche ist und wie wir Kirche verstehen, zeigt sich nicht zuletzt an der Art und Weise, wie wir Liturgien gestalten und Gottesdienst feiern.

Drei Folgerungen möchte ich zum Schluss knapp benennen.

Am Ausgangspunkt des Körpers, unserer Leiblichkeit kommt kein liturgisches Gestalten und keine liturgietheologische Reflexion mehr vorbei. Mit unserem Leib oder Körper ist der Kontext beschrieben, der unser menschliches Dasein in Zeit und Raum verankert und uns heilvoll begrenzt. Die "Unendlichkeit des Geistes", das Sich- Verflüchtigen aus der konkreten Situation heraus, die Verachtung des Corporealen ist zu verabschieden. Es sind gerade die Grenzen, die uns darin gesetzt werden, an denen wir uns abarbeiten und innerhalb derer wir "Heil" erfahren. In diesem Sinn gestaltet jede Liturgie so etwas wie eine "immanente Transzendenz", zieht sie das "Heil" in ein begrenztes und endliches und gerade darin "heilsames" Geschehen hinein und gestaltet es. Die "Unendlichkeit" liegt im Gewahrwerden der Vielfalt corporeal bedingter Kontexte.

Unsere Leiblichkeit ist niemals solipsistisch. Wir existieren immer schon dialogisch: Sonst hätten wir die Anfangsjahre unseres Lebens nicht überlebt. Unser ganzes Leben ist nach dem russischen Philosophen Bachtin ein

---

[56] Salb- und Segnungshandlungen werden mittlerweile auch in den reformatorischen Kirchen verstärkt rezipiert. Vgl. Christian Grethlein, "Andere Handlungen (Benediktionen und Krankensalbung)", in: Hans-Christoph Schmidt-Lauber / Karl-Heinrich Bieritz (Hg.), *Handbuch der Liturgik, Liturgiewissenschaft in Theologie und Praxis der Kirche* (Ev. Verlagsanstalt: Leipzig / Göttingen ²1995), 959-970.

Gespräch, ist mit Haut und Haaren, mit Leib und Seele, "adressiert".[57] Wir finden unseren Sinn, indem wir uns aussprechen, miteinander kommunizieren, diesen Dialog gestalten. Dies geschieht gleichermaßen in Kultur, Ritual oder Kunst. Die Liturgie der kirchlichen Gemeinschaft weitet dieses Adressiertsein aus und richtet die Adresse unseres Gestaltens auf die essentielle Mitte unserer alltäglichen Wirklichkeit.

Dieses rituelle Gestalten, gemeinschaftlich und dialogisch, ausgerichtet auf eine unergründliche Tiefe unseres Lebens und dieser Welt, ist nie abgeschlossen. Wir verändern uns stündlich, täglich. Noch am ehesten spürbar wird uns die Dynamik unseres Lebens in der Abfolge der Jahre. Das Gestaltete und Gefundene, das in Ritual und Kunst auf vielfältige Weise zur Sprache Gebrachte hat nur zeitweise Gültigkeit. Es wird und muss im Prozess des Miteinanderlebens und des Weitergehens verlassen werden. Der Schmerz des Nicht-Endgültigen ist der Preis, um die Zukunft zu gewinnen. Die Provokation besteht darin, trotz des Fließenden und Veränderlichen unseres gemeinsamen Lebens eben diesem gemeinschaftlich eine Sinn-Gestalt abzuringen. Sie wird ihrerseits durch die Bereitschaft provoziert, das Gefundene immer wieder aufzugeben und auf Neues, noch Unbekanntes zuzugehen. In dieser Spannung zwischen Regression und Progression, der corporealen Dynamik unseres Lebens geschuldet, liegt die Lebendigkeit jeglicher Kunst, alles Ritualisierens und nicht zuletzt auch einer von Frauen mitgestalteten christlichen Liturgie begründet.

The human body and the many dimensions of corporeality play a central role in the feminist liturgical and ritual movement of the past 20 years in North America and Europe. Women's rituals are marked by an emphasis on touch and movement as a medium of perception and of expression, in contrast to the focus on visual and auditory codes (and the underlying dualism) which characterizes traditional Christian liturgy. The author distinguishes five dimensions of the involvement of the body in women's ritual: 1) the *eros* aspect: the relationality mediated by the body, as exemplified in the liturgy for the 1998 World Day of Prayer entitled "God's gentle touch;" 2) the *requiem* aspect: the dance of mourning and grief, for example in the use of the story of Jephthah's daughter in a liturgy marking the WCC Decade for Women in the Bavarian Lutheran Church; 3) the *shalom* aspect: the potential of a women's ritual, for example, to aid in healing the emotional shock and trauma following the senseless murder of a close friend; 4) the *sacramental* aspect, represented by a liturgy marking the journey through menopause; and 5) the aspect of *meaning* expressed in a women's ritual commemorating the woman

---

[57]  Vgl. Michail Bachtin, *Die Ästhetik des Wortes*, hg. v. Rainer Grübel (Suhrkamp: Frankfurt 1989).

who anointed Jesus (Mk 14.3-9). The ecclesiological consequences of these body-dimensions in women's new rituals include women-church as the church which remembers forgotten aspects of its own tradition and which offers a locus of support and relationality, a homeland for the marginalized and a place of resistance, and a community of those who have been healed and made whole. In the Christian women's liturgical movement women are clearly the Body of Christ.

Le corps humain et les nombreuses dimensions du corporel ont joué un rôle-clé en Europe et en Amérique du Nord au cours des deux dernières décennies dans le mouvement pour des rituels et des liturgies féministes. Les rituels féminins se distinguent par ce qu'ils insistent sur le toucher et le mouvement comme moyens de perception et d'expression, et contrastent par-là avec les codes visuels et auditifs (et la dualité les motivant), habituels foyers de la liturgie chrétienne traditionelle. L'auteur distingue cinq dimensions de la participation du corps dans le rituel des femmes: 1) L'*eros*: l'aptitude relationnelle se révélant à travers le corps, exemplifiée dans la liturgie de la Journée Mondiale de pla prière de 1998 intitulée "La caresse de Dieu." 2) Le *requiem*: la danse du deuil et de la douleur, par exemple dans l'histoire de la fille de Jephté utilisée pour une liturgie célébrée dans l'église luthérienne bavaroise au cours de la décennie de la femme du Conseil Œcuménique des Églises (COE). 3) Le *shalom*: montrant le pouvoir d'un rituel féministe pour aider à cicatriser la blessure laissée par un choc émotionnel traumatisant après un meurtre gratuit exercé sur une amie très proche. 4) La dimension *sacramentelle*, représentée par une liturgie relatant l'épopée de la ménopause. 5) La dimension *significative*, exprimée dans un rituel commémorant l'onction de Jésus par la femme à Béthanie (Mc 14,3-9). Les conséquences ecclésiales de ces dimensions du corporel dans les nouveaux rituels féminins incluent l'église des femmes comme une église remettant en mémoire des aspects oubliés de sa propre tradition et offrant un havre d'appui, de soutien et de relations, un foyer pour les marginalisés et un lieu de résistance, la communauté de ceux qui ont guéri. Dans le mouvement liturgique des femmes chrétiennes, les femmes sont nettement Corps du Christ.

***Brigitte Enzner-Probst***, geb. 1949 in Feucht/Nürnberg. Studium der evangelischen Theologie, Philosophie und Soziologie in Erlangen, Tübingen und Rom; Ordination zur Pfarrerin in der Evang.-Luth. Kirche in Bayern; mehrere Jahre Dienst in der Gemeinde, sieben Jahre Frauenbeauftragte in der Kirchenleitung; derzeit Studentenpfarrerin an der Technischen Universität in München. Promotion in Praktischer Theologie mit einem pastoraltheologischen Thema; Fortbildung in Tanztherapie und Meditationsanleitung; verheiratet mit einem Pfarrer; drei Kinder. Veröffentlichung verschiedener Bücher, u.a. *Wenn Himmel und Erde sich berühren. Texte, Lieder und Anregungen für feministische Liturgien* (Gütersloher Verlagshaus: Gütersloh 1993), sowie *Pfarrerin. Als Frau in einem Männerberuf* (Kohlhammer: Stuttgart 1995). Sie arbeitet derzeit an einem wissenschaftlichen Projekt zum Thema "Die Bedeutung des Körpers in der liturgischen Praxis von Frauen".

*Annette Esser*

# Kreation und Performance
# Zur Bedeutung der Kunst für die Gestaltung feministischer Liturgien

*Not only our words but also what we see matters in*
*the performance of feminist liturgies.*[1]

## Zwei Beispiele
### The Durham Quilt
Am 25. Januar 1992 versammelten sich in Durham, England, Frauen zur Feier des "Life of Faith". Kernstück der Feier war die Erstellung des *Durham Quilt*. 72 applizierte und gestickte Tafelbilder, die Frauen vordem in künstlerischer Arbeit erstellt hatten, wurden in einem Patchwork zusammengefügt.[2] Jedes Bild stellte eine Frau dar, die im Glaubensleben oder in der Gotteserfahrungen der einzelnen Frauen eine maßgebliche Rolle spielt, wie u.a. Julian of Norwich, Hildegard von Bingen, Mary Craig, Mary Summer, Evelyn Underhill, Janet Morley und viele andere heilige und auch (außerhalb Englands) unbekanntere Frauen. In dieser Zusammenstellung ist der *Durham Quilt* auch Ausdruck gegen jede Hierarchisierung. Der gesamte Prozess der Erstellung und Zusammenfügung kann als Ritual verstanden werden, in dem ein postmodernes Gottesbildes zum Ausdruck gebracht wird.[3]

### Con moto
Am 27. November 2000 lud das Bildungswerk der Erzdiözese Köln zur "Vernissage mit Jazzperformance" in die Basilika Maria im Kapitol in Köln ein. Einer Eröffnung durch den Leiter des Bildungswerkes und einem Grußwort des

---

[1] Janet R. Walton, *Feminist Liturgy: A Matter of Justice* (Liturgical Press: Collegeville, MN 2000), 36.

[2] Zum Durham Quilt, vgl.: Lavinia Byrne (Hg.), *Christian women together. The Durham Quilt produced by the North East Ecumenical Women's Group* (CCBI Publications: London 1992).

[3] So habe ich es auf einem Podium zum Thema "Gott à la carte", auf dem Katholikentag in Hamburg am 3. Juni 2000, gedeutet.

Stadtdechanten, folgte eine kunsthistorische Einführung in die Ausstellung "con moto". Präsentiert wurden im Kirchenraum Plastiken und Installationen der Künstlerin Maria Lehnen von 1997-2000. Nachdem sich die Besucher vorbei an "Weiblichen Hüllen und Rotspuren", "flying wings" und "burning wings" aus Bandagen, Teer, Polyester... und an "Häutungen", und "Körperschalen" aus Baumwolle, Samt, Eisen... zum hinteren Teil der Kirche bewegt hatten, fand dort eine Performance statt. Neben die "vermummten Stelen", die, so der Katalog, in ihrem "erdhaften Eros die Trauer des Entrückten in sich tragen", und neben die "anthropomorphen Abdrücke" der "Leidenstücher" aus Baumwolle oder Samt, die als Mahnmale für Tod, aber auch für Erinnerung dastehen, waren hier in schwarzes Plastik verhüllte Körperfiguren gestellt, die sich nun langsam aus dem Zustand des Still-Standes in die Welt der Töne befreiten.

> Man sieht die Mauer der Paravents und man sieht und hört gleichzeitig, wie sich das Leben aus dem Schattendasein und der Verpuppung befreit. Man erahnt, wie sich die Musik gleich Lazarus aus den Bandagen des Mumiendaseins befreit, wie eine Melodie die andere hervorlockt und das Solo zu Duett, Trio und Quartett anschwillt. Ein Baß, zwei Saxophone, eine Trompete erlösen die plastischen Filmstills aus ihrem zeitlosen Verharren. Nicht dass sich damit die Skulpturen auflösen. Die ausdrucksstarke Form des künstlerischen Bildes und des Torsos bestehen weiter fort, aber sie verwandeln sich, weil sich ihre Umgebung wandelt – con moto.[4]

Mit der Beschreibung dieser Aktionen, die eigentlich noch sehr oberflächlich ist und weiterer, eingehenderer Betrachtung bedarf, soll hier zunächst nur illustriert werden, welche Rolle einerseits Kunst oder künstlerische Aktivität von Frauen – teilweise in bewußt feministischer Perspektive – in den von ihnen selbst gestalteten Feiern, Liturgien oder Ritualen mitunter spielt, und andererseits, wie sich heute eine Künstlerin im Kirchenraum präsentiert, deren Arbeiten sich jenseits religiöser Kunst im vormodernen Sinne, aber auch jenseits der durch die Religionskritik geprägten Kunst der Moderne bewegen, d.h. postmodern genannt werden können.[5]

---

[4]   Veit Loers, "Maria Lehnens Metamorphosen", in: *Maria Lehnen: Arbeiten 1997 bis 2000,* Ausstellungskatalog hg. vom Bildungswerk der Erzdiözese Köln, 2000, unnummerierte Seiten 8-9, hier 9. Die Ausstellung mit Performance, die als Beispiel postmoderner Kunst im Kirchenraum gelten kann, findet bis März 2002 noch in acht weiteren Kirchen statt.

[5]   Ein Einstieg in den Begriff der Postmoderne gibt A. Wellmer, *Zur Dialektik von Moderne und Postmoderne* (Suhrkamp: Frankfurt 1985), sowie der Band von Linda Nicholson (Hg.), *Feminism / Postmodernism* (Routledge: New York / London 1990).

Die Nebeneinanderstellung dieser beiden Beispiele lässt mich mehrere Thesen aufstellen, die weiter diskutiert werden müssen. Einmal können Parallelen und Gemeinsamkeiten zwischen dem kreativen bzw. künstlerischen Tun religiös motivierter Frauen und den Arbeiten einer Künstlerin, die religiöse Themen reflektiert, gesehen werden; konkret handelt es sich beide Male um Textilarbeiten, und beide Male werden religiöse Motive und Fragen des Mensch-/Frauseins thematisiert. Zum anderen kann der Vergleich zwischen der religiösen Feier von Frauen und der Installationen und Performance einer Frau im Kirchenraum den Gedanken nahe legen, dass beide "Events" nun auf den gemeinsamen Begriff eines feministischen Rituals gebracht werden könnten. Schließlich entsteht vielleicht durch meine Verwendung des Begriffs "postmodern" der Eindruck eines gemeinsamen Grundanliegens, das mit Erfahrungsbezogenheit und post-avantgardistischer Themen- und Formgebung umschrieben werden kann.

Alle drei Annahmen drängen sich mir für eine Reflexion des Verhältnisses von Religion und Kunst von Frauen als Quelle feministischer Rituale heute geradezu auf. Dennoch müssen sie hinterfragt werden. Sonst wird möglicherweise die Intention der Frauen bzw. Künstlerin missachtet, die selbst gefragt werden müssten, welches Anliegen sie mit ihrer "Feier des Glaubens" oder ihrer "Performance" im Kirchenraum verbinden. Auch ist die Vereinnahmung unter einen bestimmten Begriff, z.B. des Rituals, der Postmoderne oder des Feminismus problematisch. Die Frage nach dem künstlerischen und religiösen Selbstverständnis von Frauen muss ernst genommen und verknüpft werden mit der Frage nach dem Verständnis von Ritual und Liturgie. Im Folgenden verwende ich den Begriff Ritual stärker als religionstypologischen Oberbegriff und spreche von Liturgie, wenn ich mich auf die gottesdienstliche Feier christlicher Frauen beziehe.[6]

Es geht mir in diesem Beitrag *zur Bedeutung der Kunst für die Gestaltung feministischer Liturgien*, über eine erste Begriffsdefinition hinaus, um eine grundlegende Reflexion, die ich für eine dialogische Praxis zwischen Kunst und Kirche für relevant halte. Wenn ich nun von der Beobachtung ausgehe, dass in feministischen Ritualen bzw. Frauenliturgien künstlerische Aktivitäten und kreative Ausdrucksformen der partizipierenden Frauen, und auch Männer

---

6   Hierin folge ich auch Brigitte Enzner-Probst, die die Entstehung feministischer Rituale stark im Kontext der Spiritualitätsbewegung (auch Göttinnenbewegung) von Frauen sieht und unter Liturgien eher Feiern oder auch Rituale christlicher Frauen versteht (vgl. ihr Beitrag in diesem ESWTR-Band).

und Kinder, ein wichtiges Element sind, möchte ich in einem ersten Schritt die Frage nach der kontextuellen Entstehung und dem Selbstverständnis feministischer Rituale stellen. In einem zweiten Schritt werde ich dann einen Blick auf die Entwicklung (postmoderner) Kunstkritik und Kunst von Frauen werfen. Die Kenntnis dieser Diskussion, die etwa parallel zur Entwicklung feministischer Theologie lief, halte ich für wichtig, um als Theologin oder Kirchenfrau in einen fruchtbaren Dialog mit Künstlerinnen zu treten. Erst im Anschluss an diese Betrachtungen halte ich eine vertiefte Reflexion über die Gemeinsamkeiten und Unterschiede künstlerischer Performances und feministischer Rituale / Liturgien für sinnvoll. Meine Grundthese ist, dass gute Kunst immer ein schöpferisch-kreativer Akt ist, und ein gutes Ritual immer auch eine gute Performance ist. Dies sollte jedoch nicht zu einem naiven Bergriff von Kunst und Performance verleiten, sondern eher zu einem fruchtbaren Dialog zwischen Theologinnen und Künstlerinnen führen, einem Dialog, über dessen von Janet R. Walton vorgeschlagene Prinzipien ich abschließend sprechen möchte. Ich hoffe, mit diesem Beitrag einen Impuls für eine Vision der Kreation und Performance feministischer Rituale und Liturgien im Raum christlicher Kirchen zu geben.

## Zum religiösen und kreativen Selbstverständnis feministischer Rituale und Liturgien

> *Feminist liturgies offer a regular opportunity for self-invention*
> *through a particular kind of "knowing". We learn not so much by*
> *way of discussion, but rather by doing our ritualising differently.*
> *We enact another way of relating to ourselves, other, and God.*
> *Our understanding changes our performance.*[7]

Der Ursprung feministischer Rituale und Liturgien, die sich zuerst in den USA und dann seit den 1970er Jahren auch in Europa entwickelt haben, liegt – wie die amerikanische Ordensfrau und Liturgikerin Janet Walton bezeugt – in der Enttäuschung und im Zorn von Frauen beim Erleben herkömmlicher Gottesdienste begründet. Aus der Erkenntnis über den Androzentrismus traditioneller Liturgien, die von Frauen entweder in diskriminierenden Stereotypen (als menschliches Mängelwesen, Verführerin, Hure…) sprechen oder Erfahrungen und auch biblische Zeugnisse von Frauen ganz auslassen, und die

---

[7] Walton, *Feminist Liturgy*, 41.

immer noch vom männlichen Gottesbild ("Allmächtiger Vater") und der männlichen Anrede ("Brüder") auch für Frauen geprägt sind, folgte die Einsicht in die Notwendigkeit der Gestaltung von Gottesdiensten außerhalb der offiziellen Strukturen.[8] Dabei spielte die Frage nach der Wahrheit der Liturgie eine fundamentale Rolle.

> Liturgies typically described as "feminist" began to emerge in the late 1960's when women and some men realized that what they were experiencing in the liturgies of churches and synagogues was not only not "enough", but in fact, was not "true".[9]

Die fundamentale Frage nach der Wahrheit christlicher Liturgie, die den Anspruch erhebt, die Gemeinde in einen wahrhaftigen Dialog mit Gott zu führen, hat Marjorie Procter-Smith so gestellt, dass Wahrheit mehr sein muss als ein rein intellektuelles Glaubenszeugnis. Wenn sie die Frage stellt, was im Blick auf die Liturgie für Frauen wahr ist (*"What is true for us?"*), so fordert sie Frauen dazu auf, eine liturgische Wahrheit zu entwickeln, die sowohl ihr Engagement, als auch ihren Körper, sowie ihre ganz spezifische Lebenssituation zum Ausdruck bringt.

> The claim of encounter with God gives the liturgical event its power and truth. Liturgical "truth", then is not at all an abstract or purely intellectual truth, but an engaged, embodied, and particular truth, a truth that cannot only be talked about, but must be done.[10]

Die Suche nach Selbstausdruck und Wahrheit von Frauen in eigenen Liturgien und Ritualen hat zu neuen Fragestellungen, Akzenten und Formen geführt und zu einer Umgestaltung der ersten Visionen feministischer Liturgien, auch auf der Basis feministisch-theologischer Diskussion und Forschung.

> In the intervening thirty years what we knew at first has been clarified, interpreted, developed, and corrected. Participants in this process have talked regularly and honestly with each other about what works and what does not. Academics have offered historical, biblical, theological, and sociological data to undergird what we only guessed was true. People from secular women's movement and others alienated from any official structures have offered strategies to stretch our traditional

---

[8]  A.a.O., 29.
[9]  A.a.O., 12.
[10] Marjorie Procter-Smith *In Her Own Rite: Constructing Feminist Liturgical Tradition* (Abingdon Press: Nashville 1990), 13.

ways of forming communities. What has emerged is a new liturgical vision. This belief and practise is what we know as feminist liturgy.[11]

Janet Walton hat diese neue Vision feministischer Liturgie mit "Verkörperung der Gerechtigkeit"[12] bzw. der "verkörperten Vision der Beziehungen", die wir untereinander und mit Gott haben, ausgedrückt;[13] sie hat in und mit ihrer Arbeit darauf hingewiesen, dass diese liturgische Vision ein religiöser Selbstausdruck von Frauen ist, den TheologInnen auch besonders im Dialog mit KünstlerInnen weiter gestalten können.[14]

Meine erste Begegnung mit feministischen Ritualen und Liturgien fand im Kontext der Konferenzen der *Europäischen Gesellschaft für theologische Forschung von Frauen* (ESWTR) statt. Als katholische Theologin ergriff ich die Chance, meine Kreativität in diesem rituellen und liturgischen Bereich wahrzunehmen und zu entfalten. So brachte mich die Begegnung mit der Engländerin Janet Morley, die 1987 die "Subject Group: Spirituality" in Helvoirt leitete, dazu, die Übersetzung ihrer liturgischen Texte in inklusiver Sprache zu unternehmen; dazu gehören bspw. Glaubensbekenntnis, Schuldbekenntnis und Hochgebetstexte.[15] Seit dieser Konferenz machte ich kontinuierlich selbst Erfahrungen mit der Vorbereitung und Gestaltung von unterschiedlich als "Worship", "Celebration", "Liturgie", "Andacht" oder auch "Ritual" bezeichneten religiösen Morgen- oder Abendfeiern.[16] Ich erinnere mich dabei besonders an unsere ersten liturgischen Versuche. So folgten in Helvoirt (1987) Theologinnen nur zögernd der Aufforderung, sich mit einem Licht in der Hand und in freier Geste in die Mitte des Raumes zu bewegen. In einer sog. "Abendandacht" in Arnoldshain (1989) forderten wir die Frauen auf, ihre eigenen Gottesbilder zu malen; etwas, was ich im Nachhinein als eine

---

[11] Walton, *Feminist Liturgy*, 29-30.

[12] A.a.O., 32.

[13] A.a.O., 47.

[14] Siehe Janet R. Walton, *Art and Worship: A Vital Connection* (The Liturgical Press: Collegeville, MN 1988). Auf dieses Buch werde ich am Ende des Artikels noch ausführlicher zu sprechen kommen.

[15] Janet Morley, *All Desires Known* (MOW: London 1988; 2. erweiterte Ausgabe SPCK: London 1991); deutsche Übers. der ersten Ausgabe von Cornelia Amecke- Mönnighoff und Annette Esser: *Preisen will ich Gott, meine Geliebte. Psalmen und Gebete* (Herder-Verlag: Freiburg 1989).

[16] Annette Esser, "Along the Conferences: European Women Theologians Reflect upon Spirituality and Celebrate Rituals", in: Annette Esser / Anne Hunt Overzee / Susan Roll (Hg.), *Re-Visioning Our Sources: Women's Spirituality in European Perspectives* (Kok Pharos: Kampen 1997), 11-33.

Sprengung des liturgischen Rahmens in Richtung eines therapeutisch-selbster-fahrungsbezogenen Tuns empfinde. Beispiel eines gelungen Rituals bleibt für mich das "Labyrinth-Ritual", das ich zusammen mit der britischen Künstlerin Caroline Mackenzie auf der ESWTR-Konferenz in Bristol (1991) gestaltet habe. Ich bin Caroline dort zum ersten Mal begegnet. Unabhängig voneinander hatten wir beide ein Labyrinth-Bild mitgebracht, mit dem wir nun ein gemeinsames "Ritual", wie es damals zum ersten Mal offiziell hieß, gestalten wollten; ich hatte das Bild aus Chartres mitgebracht, Caroline aus Indien. Für das Ritual bemalten wir nachts den Boden der vieleckigen Kapelle mit einem einfachen indianischen Labyrinth. In dessen Mitte legten wir mit Blättern und Blüten ein Mandala. Das Ritual am Morgen begann damit, dass wir im Kreis um das Bild saßen und uns auf uns selbst besannen,[17] bevor wir dieses (weibliche) Ursymbol und seine Tradition erklärten. Daraufhin luden wir die Frauen dazu ein, mit uns das Bodenlabyrinth in einem alten Prozessionsschritt zu durchschreiten – zwei Schritte vor, ein Schritt zurück – und dabei einen Schöpfungspsalm von Janet Morley zu sprechen,[18] um dann in der Mitte in einer eigenen Geste unsere Haltung der Achtung vor der Schöpfung zum Ausdruck zu bringen. Der Prozess des Durchschreitens des Labyrinthes weckte tatsächlich das Bedürfnis nach dem Ausdruck einer solch achtungsvollen Geste. Sitzend konnte ich voller Staunen wahrnehmen, mit welcher Liebe Frauen ihre Achtung vor der Schöpfung am Mandala zum Ausdruck brachten. Der schweigenden Betrachtung folgte dann ein Lied ("Shalom Chaverim") und ein Segen.

Dieses Ritual, sowie viele andere Rituale und Liturgien im Kontext der ESWTR und auch in anderen Kontexten, z.B. der Frauensynode, des Weltgebetstages der Frauen oder ökumenischer Frauengottesdienste und Rituale einer regionalen Frauengruppe, erschienen mir als ein gelungener und ehrlicher Ausdruck unserer "Wahrheit" oder "unserer Beziehungen" und sind mir teils noch sehr bildhaft in Erinnerung. Dies betrifft besonders die Orte der Feier (z.B. am Grab einer jung verstorbenen Frau, 1993; oder an der Meeresküste von Kreta, 1997) und die liturgischen Aktionen (Gesang, freies Gebet, meditativer Tanz,

---

[17] Durch Sprechen des "Schuldbekenntnisses" von Morley, *Preisen will ich Gott, meine Geliebte*, 69.

[18] A.a.O., 87-88: Benedicte Omnia Opera: "Alle Werke Gottes, jauchzt eurem Schöpfer, rühmt Sie und preist Sie in Ewigkeit…"

Drama, Clownerie, Folklore…). Darüber hinaus hatte ich die besondere Chance, während meines Studiums am Union Theological Seminary in New York (1994-1998), die dortige (feministisch) liturgische Arbeit durch Teilnahme und Mitgestaltung der täglichen "Worship Services" in James Chapel kennen zu lernen, die jeweils von unterschiedlichen Interessengruppen des Seminars vorbereitet wurden (z.B. Black Caucus, Women of Color Caucus, Queer Caucus, Catholic Women Caucus u.a.). Die vielfältigen kontextuellen und ökumenischen Perspektiven dieser Feiern, Rituale, Predigten oder / und symbolischen Handlungen haben mir die Androzentrik traditioneller Gottesdienste und die Exklusivität ihrer liturgischen Sprache immer bewusster gemacht und meinen Leidensdruck als Frau in der katholischen Kirche erhöht. Die Sehnsucht nach weiblicher Symbolik und inklusiver Sprache, welche auch meine Erfahrungen als Frau körperlich und kreativ zum Ausdruck bringt, hat allerdings nicht zu einem radikalen Bruch mit meiner Kirche geführt. D.h. ich habe mich nicht dafür entschieden, herkömmliche Gottesdienstbesuche, Gebete und Gesänge, durch feministisch-rituelle Praxis zu ersetzen, und dann als Frau den Verlust meiner Tradition zu beklagen, denn der Bruch mit meiner Tradition stellt sich mir nicht als Alternative oder als Lösung des Problems dar.[19] Man/frau könnte auch sagen, ich habe die Wahrheitsfrage an traditionelle christliche Liturgien ("Are they true for us?") nicht radikal, sondern eher kontextuell beantwortet, d.h. im Sinne der feministisch-theologischen Einsicht um die Bedeutung des Kontextes und der Konstruktion jedweder Tradition. Dies Verständnis lässt mich sowohl feministische Rituale, als auch traditionelle christliche Liturgien in ihrem jeweiligen Kontext sehen; darüber hinaus lässt es mich aber nach kreativen und realistischen Möglichkeiten suchen, Gottesdien-

---

[19] Walton, *Feminist Liturgy*, 40: "We lament our losses of all kinds: familiar forms of liturgy, songs we sing by heart, work we do in our churches and synagogues, and relationships that offer a particular kind of security. While we miss the collective power of large numbers of people, the beauty of hearty songs, the inspiration of well-done ceremonies, and the stimulation of lofty architecture, we recognize that too often these good things often came packaged with expressions of dominance, diminishment and exclusion." Vgl. auch a.a.O., 42: "The process of naming God requires similar correction: letting go, lamenting, trying something new, adjusting, and trying again. We mourn familiar terms or names that have been comforting to us, e.g. for some of us, the word 'Father' for God. But we have discovered that comfort can be deceiving as well… But the work of correction is not without consequences. Collins wisely warns 'If we are willing to take up a self-critical stance…, we are in danger of being left speechless in our liturgical assemblies-stumbling over our words as Jeremiah and many other mystics have done: Ah… I do not know how to speak (Jer 1:6).' Maybe this fear is the one we dread most, the not knowing, the waiting in silence."

ste in meinem deutschen und katholischen Kontext, z.B. in der Leitung von "Wortgottesdiensten",[20] frauengerecht zu gestalten.

Wenn ich nun wichtige Aspekte feministischer Rituale oder frauengerechter Liturgien benennen möchte, dann tue ich es auch im Blick auf die zukünftige Gestaltung von Gottesdiensten im christlichen Kontext. Denn die Reflexion dieser, in der liturgischen "main-stream-Literatur" immer noch kaum rezipierten Praxis von Frauen, kann sowohl als kritisches Korrektiv herkömmlicher Liturgien (im Sinne einer Dekonstruktion) dienen, als auch Impulse für die kreative Gestaltung alternativer feministischer oder frauengerechter Liturgien (im Sinne einer Re-Konstruktion) bieten.

Folgende drei Aspekte scheinen mir wichtig:

1. Ausgangspunkt feministischer Rituale und Liturgien sind die Erfahrungen und spirituellen Bedürfnisse von Frauen, die bisher in der kyriarchal-hierarchisch strukturierten Kirche kaum wahrgenommen oder gar negiert worden sind. Daher geht es hier – nach der Kritik patriarchaler Strukturen, Bilder und Sprache – um die (positive) Konstruktion von Liturgien, die "Beziehungen ritualisieren, welche Frauen emanzipieren und ermächtigen."[21] Obwohl diese Liturgien primär *von Frauen für Frauen* gestaltet werden, sind sie doch inklusiv auch im Blick auf Männer und Kinder intendiert, und werden zunehmend bewusst auch im Blick auf und von anderen marginalisierten Gruppen praktiziert.[22] Ein wichtiges Grundprinzip ist dabei,

---

[20] Einer "*Instruktion*" des Apostolischen Stuhls vom 15. August 1997 "zu einigen Fragen über die Mitarbeit der Laien am Dienst der Priester" folgend, haben die deutschen Bischöfe am 8. Januar 1999 eine "Rahmenordnung für die Zusammenarbeit von Priestern, DiakonInnen und LaiInnen im Bereich der Liturgie" mit dem Titel *Zum gemeinsamen Dienst berufen – Die Leitung Gottesdienstlicher Feiern* herausgegeben. Auf der Basis dieser Rahmenordnung haben die einzelnen Bistümer besondere "Ausführungsbestimmungen" erlassen, die sich auf die jeweilige Notsituation (keine Gewährleistung bestimmter Gottesdienste aufgrund von Priestermangel) beziehen. Ich selbst habe so, in einer ersten Schulung des Erzbistums Köln, am 12. Januar 2001 eine "Beauftragung zur Leitung von Schulgottesdiensten" erhalten.

[21] Mary Collins, "Principles of Feminist Liturgy", in: Marjorie Procter-Smith / Janet Walton, *Women at Worship: Interpretations of North American Diversity*, (Westminster John Knox: Louisville, KY 1993), 11.

[22] Walton, *Feminist Liturgy*, 12; 31-32: "Feminist liturgy is not esoteric, not weird nor only for women. On the contrary it is ordinary, organic and for everyone... Though feminist liturgy got its momentum in large part from the women's movement and though it initially addressed much of what women noticed was not true for them in institutional liturgies, feminist liturgy is ultimately not just for women, but for all people... Our goal...is to 'ritualise relationships that emancipate and empower women,' and subsequently all those marginalized by class, race, differing abilities, sexual orientations and age."

dass es sich um eine *gemeinschaftliche Praxis* handelt, bei der alle – nicht nur klerikale Eliten – die Verantwortung übernehmen, und im gemeinsamen Prozess Rituale und Liturgien kreieren, die nicht primär text-orientiert, sondern eher (symbolische) Verkörperungen von Beziehungserfahrungen sind.[23] "Feminists ritualise together!"[24] Aus diesem Verständnis folgt der selbstverständlich *ökumenische Charakter*, auch im Sinne einer interreligiösen Öffnung. Daraus folgt auch die *Diversität* feministischer Liturgien, insofern sie von Menschen unterschiedlicher ethnischer, nationaler und sozialer Zugehörigkeit oder sexuellen Orientierung in unterschiedlichen Kontexten geplant und durchgeführt werden.[25]

2. Jede Liturgie, verstanden als eine auf Begegnung ausgerichtete Anrede Gottes (und nicht als bloß theologische Reflexion), drängt dazu, den Namen Gottes zu nennen. In feministischer Liturgie können aber religiöse *Bilder* und ein bestimmtes theologisches Verständnis von *Gott, Mensch und Jesus Christus* nicht selbstverständlich vorausgesetzt werden (etwa in einer Rede vom "allmächtigen Vater" oder in tradierten Bildern von der "Weiblichkeit" der Frau, oder von Christus als "Herr").[26] Diese müssen vielmehr in der rituellen / liturgischen Praxis von den ritualisierenden Frauen selbst neu erschlossen werden. Nach Mary Collins gründet sich eine solche dekonstruktive und rekonstruktive Praxis auf vier Momente feministischer Interpretation der Kultur:

---

[23] Collins, "Principles of Feminist Liturgy", 12.

[24] A.a.O., 15.

[25] Walton, *Feminist Liturgy*, 29: "We came together from specific denominations, across different faith and in some cases, from minimal religious background. Some groups originated in academic settings, others in churches and synagogues. We met in homes, basements, outdoors, and in various community places."; vgl. auch 33: "Since people are different, the naming and cherishing of our differences is essential in our liturgical experiences."

[26] Mary Collins, *Worship: Renewal to Practice* (Pastoral Press: Washington, DC 1987), 228: "An uncritical cherishing of androcentric images of God in public prayer at the end of the 20th century is self-indulgent whether men or women do the cherishing." Walton, *Feminist Liturgy*, 36: "Not even names that we have used for years can possibly convey the total reality of God." Vgl. auch, 42: "The construction of feminist liturgies includes wrestling with many questions about naming and knowing God. Some examples include: What are the boundaries of changes in the Trinitarian formula? When shall we call upon God in female terms, mother, sister, goddess? How do we discover emerging names, constructed from changing experiences of a living God? How do we avoid sanctioning abuse, e.g. the use of 'Father' as the most heard name for God may suggest to victims of sexual abuse wittingly or unwittingly that like an abusing father God cannot be trusted. What must we let go? What shall we add? When is silence the most honest way to identify one who is more than we can imagine?"

*suspicion* in approaching all cultural materials, most especially those considered to be a particular culture's highest achievements, *retrieval* of aspects of women's cultural experience of all kinds of significant relationships, *affirmation* of what has been retrieved both of women's achievements and stories of women's suffering extracted as the price of maintaining patriarchal relationships, and *introducing a future* that affirms the full humanity of women and the value and truth of their achievements.[27]

In diesem Praxisprozess spielt die *feministische Bibelexegese*,[28] die Kreation *inklusiver Gottesdienstsprache*[29] und die Schaffung eines Repertoires an alternativen (d.h. nicht hierarchischen) *symbolischen Formen und Beziehungstrukturen*[30] eine wichtige Rolle, besonders auch in der Erschließung symbolischer *Gottesbilder von Frauen*.[31] Im Versuch eines "wahrhaftigen Erzählens und Verkörperns der Mythen, die unser religiöses Bewusstsein prägen"[32] bemisst sich der Stellenwert biblischer und kirchlicher Tradition nicht

---

[27] Collins, *Worship*, 12-13, verkürzter Text zit. n. Walton, *Feminist Liturgy*, 47.

[28] Nach Walton, *Feminist Liturgy*, 42, 45 sind fehlende Namen und falsch interpretierte Geschichten ein Problem für liturgische Gemeinschaft. Demgegenüber werden Frauen durch das Hören weniger bekannter oder unbekannter Frauengeschichten aus der Bibel an Sonntagen, z.B. über *Maria von Magdala* (Lk 7,36-50), *Jephtas Tochter* (Ri 11,29-40), *die ungenannte Frau* (Ri 19,1-30), *Hagar* (Gen 16,1-16; 21, 9-21), veranlasst, tief und neuartig über eigene Glaubensgeschichten nachzudenken.

[29] Walton, *Feminist Liturgy*, 33: "Verbal language, especially the predominance of male imagery, offered one of the first clues to many of us that something was wrong with our institutional liturgies." Wichtige Literatur zur feministisch-theologischen Diskussion liturgischer Sprache: Walton, *Art and Worship*; Procter-Smith, *In Her Own Rite*; Casey Miller / Kate Swift, *Words and Women. New Language in New Times* (HarperCollins: San Francisco rev. ed. 1991); Procter-Smith / Walton (Hg.), *Women at Worship*; Heather Murray Elkins, *Worshipping Women: Re-Forming God's People For Praise* (Abingdon Press: Nashville 1994); Donate Pahnke / Regina Sommer, *Göttinnen und Priesterinnen. Facetten feministischer Spiritualität*, (Gütersloher Verl.-haus: Gütersloh 1995); Gail Ramshaw, *Liturgical Language: Keeping It Metaphoric, Making It Inclusive* (The Liturgical Press: Collegeville 1996); Teresa Berger, *Sei gesegnet meine Schwester: Frauen feiern Liturgie* (Echter: Würzburg 1999); Walton, *Feminist Liturgy*.

[30] Nach Collins, *Worship*, 14, ist dies ein Prinzip feministischer Liturgien: "to develop a repertoire of alternative forms or relational schemes." Walton, *Feminist Liturgy*, 12, führt dazu aus: "Feminist liturgies began when people got together to *discover how to use symbols, texts and forms that expressed relationships* with God, one another, and our created world more accurately and more authentically. The quest is a matter of justice."

[31] Vgl. Walton, *Feminist Liturgy*, 41-42: "We aim to model beauty differently, making a habit of respecting and loving our bodies and minds. As we discover and accept truer images of ourselves, enevitably we seek truer images of God."

[32] A.a.O., 13.

an ihrer Bedeutung für die dogmatisch-kirchliche Glaubenslehre. Traditionelle Texte werden immer im Blick auf die (auch negativen) Erfahrungen von Frauen (und andere marginalisierte Gruppen), d.h. als Quelle oder Hindernis ihrer Spiritualität, gesehen.[33]

3. Da im Unterschied zu herkömmlichen Gottesdiensten eine möglichst *ganzheitliche Erfahrung* angestrebt wird, spielen neben dem traditionellen Lesen und Hören des Wortes auch *Meditation* und *Imagination* eine besondere Rolle:

> We await one another in feminist liturgies. We have learned that silent time is fertile space, necessary for attentiveness, dreaming and imagining.[34]

Und neben dem traditionellen Selbstausdruck der GottesdienstbesucherInnen in Gesang und Gestik (stehen, sitzen, knien), werden andere *künstlerische Ausdrucksformen* wie Tanz,[35] Musik,[36] Poesie,[37] Bild, Skulptur, Drama[38] und Körperausdruck[39] liturgisch bedeutsam. Besondere Aufmerksamkeit gilt auch

---

[33] A.a.O., 37."We experiment with images of God too. We learn from trying; making new pictures or shapes, using found objects in original arrangements, uncovering nuances in traditional visualizations and most of all, from listening to each other, hearing about images that make connections with what is ultimately holy. Though we certainly cannot contain the essence of God with any real accuracy, we do know we can deepen our own relationships through a never-ending process of imagining."

[34] A.a.O., 40.

[35] Vgl. z.B. die Erfahrungen von Isidora Duncan in: Franklin Rosemont (Hg.), *Isidora Speaks* (City Light Books: San Francisco 1981); und die Reflektionen der am Union Theological Seminary lehrenden Tänzerin Prof. Carolyn Bilderback, *Gathering from a Dancer's Journal* (MagiCircle Press: Weston, CT 1992).

[36] Walton, *Feminist Liturgy*, 38,: "We search for music that has been forgotten,...music of many styles, such as drumming, chanting, wailing, rapping, as well as a variety if instruments, especially percussion. We reject songs with texts or tunes that limit or demean anyone; we rewrite words to familiar, well-loved melodies; and sometimes we commission new songs to meet particular needs."

[37] Walton, *Art and Worship*, 107-108, gibt hier als Beispiel die Lesung von Gedichten in einer Liturgie seitens ihrer Kollegin Dorothee Sölle. Sie bedauert dabei, dass dieser Lesung keine Feier auch im Sakrament gefolgt ist: "What she had given us clearly was a Liturgy of the Word. Now the most natural ritual response would have been the breaking of the bread and the sharing of the cup... But Dorothee Sölle is not ordained."

[38] Hierfür können Inszenierungen, die auf dem von J.L. Moreno begründeten Psychodrama und dem darauf basierenden Bibliodrama eine große Rolle spielen, da sie insgesamt auf religiöser Reflexion basieren.

[39] Während institutionalisierte Liturgien die gottesdienstliche Gestik meist auf Veränderung der Position in der Kirche begrenzen, bemühen sich feministische Liturgien darum, die Körper-

der Gestaltung des liturgischen bzw. sakralen Raumes, wozu auch die Positionierung der Feiernden gehört; diese Verortung sowie das Bewusstsein für die liturgische Zeit, d.h. Tageszeit, Jahreszeit und besondere Zeiten im Leben der feiernden Frauen, findet sich in den besonderen Themen feministischer Liturgien und Rituale wieder.[40]

Bei allen drei Aspekten der Gestaltung feministischer Liturgien ist m.E. Kunst bedeutsam: Erstens muss *Kunst* immer *im Kontext der Erfahrungsbezogenheit* gesehen werden, d.h. als Ausdruck der Erfahrung von Frauen, keinesfalls als museales Objekt oder als liturgischer Überbau, von dem sich die Gottesdienstteilnehmerinnen distanzieren; dies gilt insbesondere auch in Bezug auf die christlichen Symbole und Sakramente. Das Bewusstsein dafür, dass diese nicht nur dogmatisch-theologisch, sondern auch kulturell-kontextuell formuliert wurden, öffnet auch die Tür zur Ausgestaltung alter und zur Kreation neuer Symbole auf der Basis kollektiver und kontextueller Erfahrung. Daher ist zweitens die Sprache der Kunst ganz deutlich in der *Reflexion und Gestaltung religiöser Bilder und Symbole* für Gott, Mensch und Schöpfung gefragt.[41] In christlicher Perspektive geht es dabei auch um die Darstellung der Fragen von und nach Heil / Heilung und Erlösung, sowie um Geburt, Tod und Auferstehung. Die künstlerische Auseinandersetzung mit Perspekti-

---

ressourcen vollständiger, etwa durch "gemeinsames Tanzen, Bewegen, Berühren in Solidarität, Spiel und Segen" und auch durch Prozessionen zu entfalten. Auch wird das Gebet im Stehen und mit offenen Augen betont, d.h. nicht kniend oder gebeugt und mit geschlossenen Augen, wobei auch Gesten des Widerstandes und der geteilten Macht ein Rolle spielen. vgl. Janet Walton, *Feminist Liturgy*, 37-38; und den Beitrag von Brigitte Enzner-Probst in diesem Band.

[40] Auf die besondere Bedeutung von Raum und Zeit bin ich durch die feministisch-liturgische Arbeit von Diann Neu aufmerksam geworden. Diese sensibilisiert für die Bedeutung von Naturräumen und Lebensräumen von Frauen neben bekannten sakralen Räumen (Kirchen, Kapellen...), sowie für die Bedeutung von Frauenfeiern außerhalb der im Kirchenjahr und im Sakramentenverständnis üblichen Feiern (z.B. anlässlich der ersten Menstruation oder einer Fehlgeburt). Material zu diesem Thema bietet aus der Praxis litauischer Frauen auch Laime Kiskunaite in diesem Band. Janet Walton, *Feminist Liturgy*, 36, 37, spricht von Treffen in häuslichen Räumen, die meist von Frauen gestaltet sind. Dabei stellen die visuellen Objekte nur einen Raumaspekt dar, der andere ist das Arrangement der ritualisierenden Frauen selbst.

[41] Für kunstwissenschaftliche Auseinandersetzungen mit dem Symbolbegriff vgl. die Arbeiten von Ernst Cassirer, *Wesen und Wirkung des Symbolbegriffs*, 3. Bde. (Wissenschaftliche Buchgesellschaft: Darmstadt 1923-1929); und ders., *Symbol, Technik, Sprache*, hg. v. J.M. Krois und E.W. Orth (Meiner: Hamburg 1985); vgl. auch Manfred Lurker, *Wörterbuch der Symbolik*, (Alfred Kröner: Stuttgart 1991). Für eine theologische und religionspädagogische Begriffsbestimmung vgl. Paul Tillich, *Symbol und Wirklichkeit* (Vandenhoek: Göttingen ³1986); Manfred Wichelhaus / Alex Stock, *Bildtheologie und Bilddidaktik* (Patmos: Düsseldorf 1981).

ven feministischer Theologie und Spiritualität, z.B. im Blick auf das Gottesbild und weibliche Symbolik (z.B. "Ruach", oder "Barmherzigkeit / Mutter-
schoß", Ursymbole wie die Elemente, das Labyrinth oder die Spirale) oder
auf biblische Frauengestalten, ist dabei noch ein Neuland, das bereits viele
ritualisierende Frauen, aber erst wenige Künstlerinnen betreten haben.[42] Drittens ist die Bedeutung der Kunst für die Gestaltung feministischer Liturgien
besonders deutlich, wenn es um künstlerische Ausdrucksformen geht, die das
traditionelle Repertoire gottesdienstlicher Gestaltung erweitern sollen. Die
Rückbesinnung darauf, dass auch Kunst ihr kreatives Entstehungsmoment in
der Imagination (und möglichen Meditation) hat und nicht ein von außen
Gesetztes oder von oben Vorgegebenes ist, läßt die TeilnehmerInnen einer
feministischen Liturgie am kreativen Prozess partizipieren. Aktive Partizipation drückt sich nicht nur in einzelnen Aspekten, etwa in der Gestaltung des
sakralen Raumes mit Blumen, Kerzen u.a. aus, sondern letztlich in der *gesamten Komposition einer Frauenliturgie oder eines Rituals als Kunstwerk*, dessen einzelne Elemente – etwa Sprache, Bewegung, Gebärde, Tanz, Musik,
Bild u.a. – sich bewusst aufeinander beziehen, sich ergänzen oder auch in
Spannung zueinander stehen können, so dass eine möglichst authentische,
hautnahe und ganzheitliche Erfahrung erreicht wird.

Bevor ich nun aber auf die praktische Bedeutung der Kunst für die Gestaltung feministischer Rituale / Liturgien und die Notwendigkeit eines Dialogs
mit zeitgenössischen KünstlerInnen – MalerInnen, MusikerInnen, TänzerInnen
u.a. – zu sprechen komme, halte ich es für wichtig, den hier zugrunde liegenden Kunstbegriff zu reflektieren. Denn der teilweise unreflektierte Kunstbegriff
auch feministischer Theologinnen (z.B. auch in den stilistischen Darstellungen
der Patchworkbilder) bei gleichzeitig postmoderner Praxis von Frauen (z.B. im

---

[42] Bekannt sind mir die Arbeiten der amerikanischen Künstlerin und ehemaligen Ordensfrau
Meinrad Chraighead und die Arbeiten der indisch-christlichen Künstlerin Lucy da Souza,
wobei ich insbesondere an ihre beiden Hungertücher zum "weiblichen Antlitz Gottes" und zu
"biblischen Frauengestalten" denke. Vgl. Meinrad Craighead, *The Mother's Songs* (Paulist
Press: New York 1986); Anne Bancroft, *Wo Weisheit wächst: Frauen öffnen sich dem Gött-
lichen* (Walter Verlag: Olten / Freiburg i.Br. 1992, 27-41. Für Lucy da Souza vgl.: *Das Mise-
reor Hungertuch: Biblische Frauengestalten – Wegweiser zum Reich Gottes* (Bischöfliches
Hilfswerk Misereor e.V.: Aachen 1990); *Das weibliche Antlitz Gottes: Ein Gemälde von
Lucy D'Souza*, (Missio: München 1991); Gudrun Löwner, "Interrelations: The Christian
Indian Feminist Lucy D'Souza and der Art in German Churches: A Story of Conflict and
Acceptance", in: Andrea Günther / Ulrike Wagner (Hg.), *Was bedeutet es heute feministische
Theologin zu sein?* (ESWTR Jahrbuch 4; Mainz / Kampen: Grünewald / Kok Pharos 1996),
103-115.

Ritual als Performance) lassen mir eine solche Begriffsklärung und eine Vergewisserung über heutige kunsttheoretische und feministische Diskussion im Zuge der Postmoderne als wichtig erscheinen. Dabei möchte ich grundsätzlich danach fragen,

– ob und inwiefern der moderne oder postmoderne Kunstbegriff für die kreative und rituelle Praxis von Frauen verwendbar ist (kurz gesagt: ich denke ja!);

– ob sich der Performance-Begriff feministischer Rituale mit dem der heutiger Kunstszene deckt, bzw. ob wir beide Aktionen überhaupt in begriffliche und inhaltliche Nähe bringen wollen, und dabei etwa auch behaupten wollen, dass "ritualisierende Frauen" per se Künstlerinnen sind (kurz gesagt: ich denke bedingt!);

– ob es so etwas wie eine feministische Diskussion unter Künstlerinnen gibt, und welche Rolle dabei auch religiöse Themen und evt. feministische Rituale spielen (kurz gesagt: ja, es gibt eine solche Diskussion, aber sie ist anders!).

Die Beantwortung dieser Fragen kann letztlich dazu führen, so etwas wie die Vision eines gemeinsamen Weges von religiösen Frauen und Künstlerinnen – auch im Blick auf die Kreation feministischer Rituale und Liturgien – zu imaginieren. Ich möchte beginnen mit einer kurzen Reflexion der feministisch-kunsthistorischen Diskussion, die vielen feministischen Theologinnen eher unvertraut ist.

## Zur feministischen Diskussion in der Kunstgeschichte / Kunstwissenschaft und zum kreativen und religiösen Selbstverständnis von Künstlerinnen

> *Even those women artists who dare to show a piece of authentic feminine experience shout ahead that they aren't feminists.*[43]

Wie auch die feministische Theologie, versteht sich die feministische Kunstgeschichte als Teil der in den frühen siebziger Jahren einsetzenden Frauenbewegung. Diese formulierte zum ersten Mal die Fragen, warum Frauen als Künstlerinnen aus der Kunstgeschichte nahezu ausgeschlossen wurden, und

---

[43] Zitat aus dem Beitrag von Laime Kiskunaite in diesem Band, S. 42.

wie es zu verstehen ist, dass dieser Ausschluss immer noch funktioniere.[44]
Nach Ellen Spiekernagel gehörte es zu den ersten Zielen dieses feministischen Ansatzes,

> die bisher unterdrückte weibliche Kunst und Kreativität wieder in ihr Recht zu set-
> zen, indem sie: (1) Werk, Lebens- und Schaffensbedingungen von künstlerisch
> tätigen Frauen recherchiert und analysiert; (2) das Problem zu klären versucht, ob
> Frauen aufgrund ihrer von Männern unterschiedenen sozialen Rolle einen eigenen
> Zugang zum schöpferischen Vermögen, eine weibliche Ästhetik, entwickelt haben;
> (3) die Darstellung der Frau in der Kunst kritisch untersucht.[45]

Dies schloss eine Kritik der bisher von männlichen Interessen geleiteten Disziplin der Kunstgeschichte mit ein, deren Defizit an Kenntnissen weiblicher
Kunst Frauen nun aufzuarbeiten suchten. Ein zentraler Ausgangspunkt dieser
ersten Studien, für die amerikanische Wissenschaftlerinnen wegbereitend
waren, lag im Versuch einer Geschichtsschreibung verdrängter Künstlerinnen, mit der Absicht, die Kunstgeschichte zu erweitern und umzuschreiben,
wobei einige Teilerfolge erzielt werden konnten.[46] Auch gibt es seitdem mehr
und mehr Dokumentationen, Interviews mit und Erfahrungsberichte von

---

[44] Vgl. Linda Nochlin, "Why Have There Been No Great Women Artists!" in: *Art News* 69
(1971), 22-39, 67-71.

[45] Spickernagel, Ellen, "Geschichte und Geschlecht: Der feministische Ansatz", in: Hans Bel-
ting / Heinrich Dilly / Wolfgang Kemp u.a., *Kunstgeschichte: Eine Einführung* (Dietrich Rei-
mer: Berlin 1986), 264.

[46] Vgl. die Arbeiten von Eleanor Tuft, *Our Hidden Heritage: Five centuries of Women Artists*
(Paddingtom Press: New York 1974); Ann Sutherland Harris/ Linda Nochlin, *Katalog der
Ausstellung: Women Artists 1550-1959* (Los Angeles 1976); Neue Gesellschaft für Bildende
Kunst (Hg.), *Künstlerinnen International: Katalog der Ausstellung* (Berlin 1977); Germaine
Greer, *The Obstacle Race: The Fortune of Women Pianters and Their Work* (Secker & War-
burg: London 1979), dt.: *Das unterdrückte Talent: Die Rolle der Frauen in der bildenden
Kunst* (Ullstein: Berlin / Frankfurt/M. / Wien 1980); Gislind Nabakowski / Helke Sander /
Peter Gorsen, *Frauen in der Kunst*, 2 Bände (Suhrkamp: Frankfurt a.M. 1980); Lea Vergine,
*L'Altra Meta dell'Avanguardia*, (Mazzota: Mailand 1980); Roszika Parker / Griselda Pollock,
*Old Mistresses: Women, Art and Ideology* (Routledge & Kegan: London 1981); Norma Bro-
ude / Mary D. Garrard (Hg.), *Feminism and Art History: Questioning the Litany* (Harper &
Row: New York 1982); Cordula Bischoff / B. Dinger / I. Ewinkel, U. Merle (Hg.), *Frauen-
kunstgeschichte: Zur Korrektur des herrschenden Blicks* (Anabas Verl.: Giessen 1984); Edith
Krull, *Kunst von Frauen: Das Berufsbild der bildenden Künstlerin in vier Jahrhunderten*
(Weidlich: Frankfurt a.M. 1984); Jutta Held / Francis Pohl, "Feministische Kunst und Kunstgeschichte in den USA", in: *Kritische Berichte* 12 (4/1984), 5-25; *Feministische Bibliogra-
phie zur Frauenforschung in der Kunstgeschichte*, hg. v. FrauenKunstGeschichte. For-
schungsgruppe Marburg (Centaurus Verlag: Pfaffenweiler 1993).

Künstlerinnen, die in die Diskussion eingebracht werden können.[47] Im kunstpädagogischen Bereich wurde die Frage nach weibliche Kunst und Kreativität unter dem Begriff der Mädchenästhetik reflektiert.[48]

Stärker feministisch-theoretisch wurde der Androzentrismus der Kunstgeschichte dann seit den achtziger Jahren auf der Basis der postmodernen Philosophie und der Studien Foucaults, Lyotards und Roland Barthes diskutiert, wobei das Geschlechterverhältnis und ihre Konstruktion zum bestimmenden Thema kunsthistorischer Frauenforschung und ästhetischer Theorie wurde.[49] So hat zum Beispiel die historische Quellenforschung gezeigt, "dass zu verschiedenen Zeiten immer wieder Frauen als Künstlerinnen bekannt geworden waren, die heute weder in Museen ausgestellt, noch in historischen Darstellungen aufgeführt werden." Denn, so Sigrid Schade und Silke Wenk,

> Die Frage danach, ob Frauen sich trotz oder wegen der Differenz zu "männlicher" Künstlerschaft durchsetzen konnten, eröffnete einen Blick auf die Konstruktion der Geschlechterverhältnisse innerhalb der Kunstgeschichte, sowie auf ihre Konsequenzen. Der Befund, dass erst seit der Institutionalisierung der Kunstgeschichte als universitärer Disziplin, etwa zwischen 1850 und 1912, Künstlerinnen aus dem Katalog einer universalen Kunstgeschichte eliminiert und dann in separaten "Kunstgeschichten der Frau" als Sonderfälle zusammengefasst worden waren, ließ sich nicht mit schlichten Ein- und Ausschlusshypothesen erklären. Die Darstellung der Künstlerinnen in diesen Kunstgeschichten diente dazu, die Regel zu bestätigen, dass wirkliche Kunst doch nur von Männern erbracht werden könne.[50]

---

[47] Vgl. z.B.: Judith Chicago, *Durch die Blume: Meine Kämpfe als Künstlerin* (Rowohlt: Reinbeck b. Hamburg 1984); Silvia Eiblmayr u.a., *Kunst mit Eigen-Sinn: Aktuelle Kunst von Frauen. Texte und Dokumentation* (Löcker: Wien / München 1985).

[48] Vgl. Helmut Hartwig, "Mädchenästhetik und Frauenkultur: Erfahrungen, die jeder hat und die es doch nicht gibt", in: *Kunst und Unterricht* 80 (1983), 6-14; Irene Below, "Auf die Seele kommt es an", in: *Kunst und Unterricht* 80 (1983), 50-57; dies., "'Frauen, die malen, drücken sich vor der Arbeit': Geschlechtsspezifische Arbeitsteilung und ästhetische Produktivität von Frauen", in: Adelheid Staudte (Hg.), *FrauenKunstPädagogik* (Helmer: Frankfurt a.M. 1991), 129-150; dies., "'Die Utopie der neuen Frau setzt die Archäologie der alten voraus': Frauenforschung in kunstwissenschaftlichen und künstlerischen Disziplinen", in: Anne Schülter / Ingeborg Stahr (Hg.), *Wohin geht die Frauenforschung?* (Böhlau: Köln 1990), 101-126.

[49] Sigrid Schade / Silke Wenk, "Inszenierungen des Sehens: Kunst, Geschichte und Geschlechterdifferenz", in: Hadumod Bußmann / Renate Hof (Hg.), *Genus: Zur Geschlechterdifferenz in den Kulturwissenschaften* (Alfred Körner Verlag: Stuttgart 1995), 241.

[50] A.a.O., 350.

Für dieses heute immer noch weit verbreitete Verständnis und Vorurteil, spielte – seit Vasari[51] – die Konstruktion des Bildes vom männlichen Künstler als mythischem Meister eine prägende Rolle, demgegenüber die Frau in die Rolle des Objekts geriet, z.b. als Aktmodell oder als Projektionsfläche für ein dualistisches Bild der Eva/Maria.[52] Keineswegs gehörte es zu ihren Aufgaben zu malen, denn "Frauen, die malen, drücken sich vor der Arbeit."[53] Der künstlerische Aktionsdrang von Frauen wurde vielmehr in den häuslichen Bereich verlagert (z.b. Näharbeiten und Stickereien), oder zumindest auf einen bestimmten künstlerischen Bereich beschränkt; so werden immer noch bestimmte Genres, Themen, Formate und Materialien herangezogen um zwischen "männlicher" und "weiblicher" Kunst zu unterscheiden:

> Der Konnotation bestimmter Ausdrucksformen wie Miniatur, Stilleben als "weibliche" Künste entspricht die Konnotation etwa der Bildhauerei als "männlicher" Kunst. Dilettantismus und Kitsch sind Begriffe deren Verwendung in abwertender Funktion sich aus der Geschichte der Zuschreibungen bestimmter Genres als "weiblicher" Künste erklären lassen.[54]

Auf dem Hintergrund dieser abwertenden Zuschreibungen ist es verständlich, dass sich Kunsttheoretikerinnen gegen jedweden Versuch einer Ontologisierung der Kunst von Frauen auch in einer "weiblichen" Kunstgeschichte aus feministischer Sicht gewehrt haben. Sie haben demgegenüber jede Unterscheidung zwischen "präsentativer" Kunst und "diskursiver" Betrachtung dekonstruiert und den Zusammenhang zwischen Text und Bild, zwischen betrachtendem Subjekt und betrachtetem Objekt rekonsturiert (vgl. auch die Präsentationen von Catherine David auf der Dokumenta X). Auf diesem Hintergrund wehren sich Künstlerinnen ebenfalls vehement dagegen, auf bestimmte "weibliche" Techniken und Formate festgelegt zu werden, bzw. davon abgehalten oder entmutigt zu werden, bestimmte Techniken (z.B. Bildhauerei oder Architektur) zu praktizieren, die vordem Männern vorbehalten waren. Vielmehr veranlasste

---

[51] Die 1550 zuerst erschienenen Künstlerviten von Vasari gelten als erster tradierter Textkorpus einer Kunstgeschichte. Nach Schade / Wenk, "Inszenierungen des Sehens", 352, spiegelt sich in ihnen "das Interesse einer neuen Sammlerschicht an der singulären Künstlerpersönlichkeit, deren Rang den Wert des Kunstwerks bestimmen soll."

[52] Vgl. hierzu z.B. die Arbeit der Theologin und Kunsthistorikerin Monika Leisch-Kiesl, *Eva als Andere: Eine exemplarische Untersuchung zu Frühchristentum und Mittelalter* (Böhlau: Köln 1992).

[53] So der Titel eines Beitrages von Irene Below (s. Anm. 48).

[54] Schade / Wenk, "Inszenierungen des Sehens", 357-358.

die "Besetztheit" der traditionellen Kunstgattungen und Genres durch die Frauen-
und Männermythen unserer Kultur viele Künstlerinnen seit den 70er Jahren, nach
neuen Techniken zu suchen und mit neuen Medien zu arbeiten, in der Hoffnung,
sie könnten den Zuschreibungen entgehen. Auffällig war jedenfalls zu Beginn der
neuen Frauenbewegung, dass gerade Fotographie, Performance, Videokunst und
Film zu bevorzugten Gestaltungsmedien von Künstlerinnen wurden, in denen sie
traditionelle Blickverhältnisse befragten. Mittlerweile sind Videokunst und Performance, will man den Ausstellungen und Katalogen glauben, wieder zu Männer-
domänen geworden.[55]

Diese Entwicklung in der Kunst von Frauen und in der Kunstszene überhaupt kann auch unter den Begriff der Postmoderne gebracht werden. Nach
Andreas Hyssen beginnt diese da, wo der inhaltliche und stilistische Dogma-
tismus und die Defizite der bis in die 50er Jahre herrschenden Kunst der
Moderne zur Sprache gebracht und nach neuen Formen gesucht wurde. So
wurden "Fragen des Ornaments und der Metapher in der Architektur, der
Figuration und des Realismus in der Malerei, der erzählerischen Darstellung
in der Literatur, sowie des Körpers in Musik und Theater" neu aufgeworfen
und bearbeitet.[56] Zur Kritik an der Moderne, die in Deutschland vor allem im
Zuge der alternativen Bewegungen (Frauen-, Friedens- und Umweltbewe-
gung) der 80er Jahre zum Zuge kam,[57] gehörte auch eine Rückbesinnung auf
Themen, die diese rationalistisch verdrängt oder abgelehnt hatte, wie weibliche Erfahrungen und Gefühle, Körpererfahrung, Intuition, Imagination oder
Religiosität.

Eine Auseinandersetzung mit religiösen Themen und Motiven findet sich
zwar nicht einfach durchgängig bei allen Künstlerinnen, aber sie ist auch kein
"Nachgedanke". Vielmehr wird sie als Teil eines existentiellen künstlerischen Prozesses empfunden, der das zum Ausdruck bringt, was in diskursiver
Sprache nicht ausgesprochen werden kann. Hierzu Susanne Langer:

---

[55]  A.a.O., 360.

[56]  Andreas Hyssen, "Mapping the Postmodern", in: Linda J. Nicholson (Hg.), *Feminism / Postmodernism* (Routledge: New York / London 1990), 240.

[57]  Der amerikanische Germanist Andreas Hyssen hat den Ursprung der Postmoderne seit den
60er Jahren aufgezeigt: "Pop in the broadest sense was the context in which a notion of the
postmodern first took shape, and from beginning until today, the most significant trends within postmodernism have challenged modernism's hostility to mass culture… The very notion
of postmodernism has emerged in Germany only in the late 1970s and then not in relation to
the culture of the 1960s, but narrowly in relation to recent architectural developments and,
perhaps more importantly, in the context of the new social movements and their radical critique of modernity" ("Mapping the Postmodern", 240-241, 245).

What art does to us is to formulate our conceptions of feeling and our conceptions of visual, factual and audible reality together. It gives us forms of imagination and forms of feeling, inseparably;… it clarifies and organizes intuition itself.[58]

Die Künstlerin Mechthild Lohmanns äußerte sich in einem Gespräch mit mir direkt zu religiösen Aspekten der Kunst bzw. des "KünstlerIn"-seins:

Mit Sicherheit ist die Fähigkeit sich künstlerisch auszudrücken ein Geschenk… Ich glaube, umso weiter man in die aktuelle Kunstszene reinkommt, umso mehr wird es zu einer Lebensäußerung und dadurch auch zu einer religiösen Geschichte. Selbst wenn du Atheist bist, wird es immer wesentlicher und immer essentieller… Wenn es essentieller wird, dann spielt deine Lebenssicht und Lebenserfahrung mit da rein. Jeder Schritt, den du machst, wenn du von Religion oder Religiosität sprichst, ist für mich schon wieder Interpretation oder dogmatische Festlegung. Aber die Seele hängt für mich immer mit Transzendenz zusammen und du als Theologin würdest sagen, damit ist es religiös, aber ich bin keine Theologin. Ich würde nicht sagen, damit ist es religiös… Für mich ist Kunst eine Möglichkeit mein Erdendasein dingbar zu machen, deswegen gehe ich wieder in realistische Geschichten rein.[59]

Mit den "realistischen Geschichten" sprach Mechthild Lohmanns m.E. ihre graphischen und bildhauerischen Arbeiten an, die figürlich sind und sich mit der sichtbaren Natur befassen, was bis heute oft abwertend als "traditionell" oder "altmodisch" bezeichnet wird; demgegenüber beschreibt sie ihre früheren Arbeiten als "nicht gegenständlich" aber auch "nicht abstrakt", sondern als "emotionale Bilder, die eine Form von subjektiver Wirklichkeit ausdrücken wollen."

Eine andere Art der künstlerischen und existentiellen Auseinandersetzung mit ihrer "Realität" führt die Künstlerin Sieglinde Kallnbach. Auf dem Hinterhof ihrer Mietwohnung in Köln-Ehrenfeld sammelte sie zwei Monate lang Ausgaben ihrer Tageszeitung, die sie dann gemeinsam mit eigenen Notizen und Manuskripten aus der Vergangenheit im Kachelofen in ihrem Atelier verbrannte. In diesem "Feuer-Ritual" ging sie fast zeremoniell vor.

Ihre alten Zeichnungen und Ideen warf sie einzeln in die Flammen und sinnierte über die Vergangenheit. "Die Manuskripte beinhalten ein Stück Seele von mir. Als ich sie verbrannte, zeigte ich mir damit selbst, dass die Zeit nicht still steht und das Leben weitergeht…Wen interessieren schon die Nachrichten von gestern? Ich

---

[58] Susanne Langer, *Feeling and Form* (Charles Scribner's Sons: New York 1953), 297; zit. n. Janet Walton, *Art and Worship*, 28.

[59] Das Gespräch mit Mechthild Lohmanns führte ich am 15.12.2000 in Köln.

habe gemerkt, wie vergänglich alles ist." Die entstandene Asche füllte sie dann in die beiden knapp ein Meter hohen Kunststoffkörper. "Wie Phoenix aus der Asche. Dabei entsteht etwas ganz Neues", erklärt Kallnbach. "Eben Kunst."... Zwei durchsichtige Kunststofftorsi, jeder gefüllt mit Asche. An die Wand gelehnt daneben ein Bild von Menschen, die die Sonnenfinsternis im vorigen Jahr betrachten. Auf den ersten Blick ist nicht zu verstehen, was die beiden Dinge miteinander zu tun haben, auf den zweiten Blick auch nicht. "Feuer ist das Element, welches uns alle verbindet. Feuer zerstört und schafft auch wieder Neues."[60]

Als Theologin sehe ich hier religiöse Themen im existentiellen Sinne angesprochen und nicht nur "schöpferisch", sondern auch "inkarnatorisch" zum Ausdruck gebracht. Obwohl diese christlichen Bezüge vielen KünstlerInnen als zu "dogmatische" Kategorien erscheinen, haben doch einige auch den direkt christlichen Bezug ihrer Arbeiten zur Sprache gebracht. So äußerte die Performancekünstlerin Maria Lehnen, die bekennt, "in einem ursprünglichen Sinne" religiös zu sein:

> Das Universelle, Existentielle steht in meiner Arbeit im Vordergrund. Da, wo vom christlichen Standpunkt aus existentielle Fragen aufgegriffen werden, sehe ich eine Kongruenz. Die ist ja auch meine persönliche Geschichte und die eines jeden, der im christlichen Abendland und dieser Tradition aufgewachsen ist. Auch ein Atheist kommt am Christlichen oder der Frage nach dem Göttlichen nicht vorbei. Es ist immer ein Beziehen darauf.[61]

Von daher ist auch für sie – wie für viele andere – der christliche "Kirchenraum etwas sehr Besonderes", der sie auch "emotional berührt":

> Mein Versuch der Annäherung an Schöpfung, der sich ja in den Arbeiten manifestiert, spiegelt sich wieder in meinen Kontaktbemühungen zu einem Gotteshaus. Die Arbeiten sind dann "ver-rückt" im wahrsten Sinne des Wortes: also weggerückt aus dem Alltäglichen hinaus an einen spirituellen Ort. Es entsteht fast so etwas wie eine heile Situation im Sinne von "Heil sein", "Ganz sein". Hier können die Arbeiten viel intensiver das sein, was sie sind: die besondere Atmosphäre an einem Ort des Göttlichen, die Stille, die Besinnung potenziert das besondere energetische Feld der Arbeiten. Es ist etwas ganz anderes hier angenommen zu sein oder die Arbeiten hier angenommen zu sehen als im Hinblick auf Verkaufsausstellungen.[62]

---

[60] Vgl. Artikel "Die Asche meiner Zeitung" im *Kölner Stadtanzeiger* vom 16.10.2000. Die Ausstellung "Feuer-Ritual" von Sieglinde Kallnbach war vom 16.-29.10.2000 in der Kunst- und Ausstellungshalle der Bundesrepublik Deutschland in Bonn zu sehen.

[61] Interview von Renate Goretzki mit Maria Lehnen in: *Maria Lehnen: Arbeiten 1997 bis 2000*, Ausstellungskatalog, hg. vom Bildungswerk der Erzdiözese Köln (Köln 2000), unnummerierte Seiten 16-18, hier 18.

[62] A.a.O, 17-18.

Solche und ähnliche Aussagen zum religiösen Selbstverständnis von Künstlerinnen und zur Bedeutung, die der sakrale Raum für sie hat, könnten noch aus vielen anderen Zeugnissen bestätigt und weiter reflektiert werden. An dieser Stelle soll es nun jedoch speziell um die Frage eines Dialogs zwischen künstlerischer Aktivitäten und feministischen Ritualen / Liturgien gehen.

## Kunst und feministische Liturgie als Steine des Anstoßes

> *Alles, was man mit ganzer Geschlossenheit und mit Bezug zur*
> *Schöpfung hin macht, ist ein Kunstwerk.*
> *So habe ich Beuys verstanden.*[63]

Bereits zu Beginn meines Beitrags habe ich Parallelen zwischen künstlerischen Performances und feministischen Ritualen oder Liturgien ins Auge gefasst. Tatsächlich scheint sowohl das Verständnis feministischer Rituale als Kunstwerk und als Ort, in dem Frauen ihren Glauben ganzheitlich-kreativ zum Ausdruck bringen, als auch das Interesse von Künstlerinnen an religiösen Fragen diesen Blick auf die Gemeinsamkeiten zu bestätigen. Diese Gemeinsamkeiten zwischen Performances und Ritualen von Künstlerinnen und feministischen Ritualen halte ich für frappierend. Beide basieren nicht primär auf einem vorgegebenen Religions- oder Kunstbegriff, sondern wollen die Erfahrungen als Frau neu reflektieren und symbolisieren. Beide greifen in diesem Zusammenhang religiöse Themen und Motive auf (Vergänglichkeit, Schöpfung, Reich des Todes...), wobei allerdings traditionelle Ausdrucksweisen der christlichen Kultur in Sprache oder Bild transformiert bzw. neu konstruiert werden. Und schließlich intendieren beide eine Inszenierung / Performance weiblicher (religiöser) Praxis als Kunstwerk im Kontext von Raum und Zeit, das jenseits rein musealer Beschaulichkeit oder veräußerlichter liturgischer Feier auch Besinnung und Imagination einschließt.

Dennoch ist es bisher, soweit mir bekannt,[64] in der konkreten Gestaltung feministischer Liturgien kaum zu einer Zusammenarbeit zwischen Theologinnen und Künstlerinnen gekommen. Im Gegenteil klagen Künstlerinnen, die

---

[63] Zitat aus meinem Interview mit Mechthild Lohmanns, s. Anm. 59.

[64] Ich beziehe mich hier auf meine Kenntnis im katholischen Raum. Im evangelischen Bereich ist die Rede vom Gottesdienst als "Kunstwerk" und vom "performativen" Charakter feministischer Liturgie möglicherweise schon weiter fortgeschritten und es gibt auch bereits wissenschaftliche Arbeiten wie die von Susanne Natrup, die ich hier leider nicht mehr einsehen konnte.

sich mit ritueller Arbeit im Sakralraum beschäftigen, wie etwa die britische Künstlerin Caroline Mackenzie, dass sich "mehr Männer als Frauen für diese Arbeit interessieren."[65] Und obwohl das Thema Kunst und Kirche ein Standartthema ist, das fast "schon abgegriffen" ist[66] und auch speziell viele Künstlerinnen im Kirchenraum ausstellen konnten,[67] gibt es fast keine Literatur zum Thema feministischer Liturgie und Kunst. Die Gründe dafür liegen m.E. weniger in der Frage nach Gemeinsamkeiten und Verschiedenheiten, als im Mangel an tatsächlichem Dialog, sowie in gewissen "Steinen des Anstoßes", die beide Seiten aneinander nehmen. Diese können im Grunde am gegenseitigen (oft mangelnden) Verständnis von Liturgie und Kunst festgemacht werden.

Aus der Sicht von Künstlerinnen besteht zunächst einmal die *Frage nach* der, für sie meist unbekannten Praxisform *feministischer Liturgie* überhaupt. Die meisten Künstlerinnen, die ich kenne, haben die nun bereits 30jährige Tradition feministischer Theologie kaum wahrgenommen, geschweige denn die Diskussion und Praxis feministischer Liturgien. Mir scheint, dass bei vielen gerade eine kritische Distanz zur Kirche, die aus eigener religiösen Sozialisation oder säkularem Zeitgeist erwachsen sein mag, eher zu einem Festhalten und Konservieren von (wenn auch negativ, ablehnender) Vorstellungen von Kirche und dogmatischer Lehre geführt hat, als zum Interesse an neueren Diskussionen und Praktiken feministischer Theologie. Vor diesem kritischen Hintergrund ist auch die mögliche Anfrage von Künstlerinnen an feministische Liturgien, als Frage nach deren christlichem und kirchlichen Charakter zu verstehen, der sich feministische Theologinnen selbstbewusst stellen sollten.

Mir ist es in diesem Zusammenhang wichtig, herauszustellen, dass eine feministisch-christliche Liturgie, auch im Unterschied zu Ritual und Performance, eine dialogische Grundstruktur hat. D.h. es geht um eine dialogische Gemeinschaft untereinander und mit dem/mit der, den/die wir Gott nennen. Menschen wenden sich einander zu und reagieren auf Erfahrungen / Selbst-

---

[65] Äußerung in einer Weihnachtskarte 2000 an mich.

[66] Äußerung einer Kunsterzieherin. Vgl. hierzu auch die Zeitschrift *Kunst und Kirche,* die jährlich vier Themenbände herausgibt.

[67] Z.B. in der Kunststation St. Peter, die in Köln von P. Prof. Friedhelm Mennekes ins Leben gerufen wurde und deren Modell sich viele andere – auch evangelische – PfarrerInnen zum Vorbild genommen haben, fanden bisher Ausstellungen von Cindy Sherman, Gloria Friedmann, Ingrid Hartlieb, Hildegard Weber, Regina Schmeken, Marina Makowski, Mercedes Barros und vielen anderen Künstlerinnen statt.

ausdrücke anderer durch Zuhören, Sprache, Gestik; und sie wenden sich Gott zu in Gebet, Lob, Klage, Bitte und anderen Ausdrucksweisen ihres Empfindens, Denkens und Glaubens, um dann Gott "in Wort und Sakrament" zu begegnen. In dieser Frage geht es nicht bloß um eine mögliche (künstlerische) Erweiterung des Repertoires an Selbstausdruck und anderen sprachlichen und symbolischen Zeichen für die göttliche Präsenz, es geht tatsächlich um die Intention der Veranstaltung, d.h. darum, ob Liturgie als Begegnung miteinander und mit Gott im Zentrum angestrebt und gewollt ist. Wenn es hier Anfragen von künstlerischer Seite gibt, so halte ich dies eher für den Beginn eines Dialogs, als für einen Grund, eine künstlerische Beteiligung am Gottesdienst abzulehnen; es bleibt jedoch eine Frage für die Planung und Feier einer feministischen Liturgie, welchen Ort künstlerisch-existentieller Ausdruck darin haben soll, und ob auch teilnehmende Frauen darin den Raum finden, dialogisch auf künstlerische Äußerungen zu reagieren, etwa im Gespräch, in Gesang, in Gestik oder im Gebet.

Genau an dieser Stelle sehe ich aus der Sicht feministischer Rituals / Liturgie einen möglichen "Stein des Anstoßes" in der *Anfrage nach dem Status der Künstlerin* als allein schaffender, kreativer Persönlichkeit, die sich hier produzieren möchte, aber die anderen TeilnehmerInnen einer solchen Performance in die Position einer/s passiven und möglicherweise auch unverständigen BetrachterIn verbannt. Die Betonung des kollektiven Charakters in der Planung und Durchführung feministischer Rituale / Liturgien steht dem kritisch gegenüber. Allerdings müsste sich auch ein solches Verständnis kritisch fragen lassen, wie demnach denn die vielen feministischen Rituale begründet werden müssten, bei denen ebenfalls die Erfahrung *einer* Frau im Mittelpunkt steht und evtl. auch zum Ausgangspunkt einer gemeinschaftlichen Liturgie gemacht werden kann (wie z.B. ein Ritual für eine vergewaltigte Frau, oder ein ritueller Tanz zweier Frauen[68]). Außerdem müssen feministische Theologinnen, die den kollektiven Charakter der liturgischen Feier ideologisch vertreten, gefragt werden, wie sie in ihrer eigenen Praxis mit der Frage der Leitung von Gottesdiensten umgehen. Mit anderen Worten, hier stellt sich die Frage nach dem adäquaten Umgang mit der Intention und Thematik eines Rituals, einer Performance oder Liturgie seitens seiner PlanerInnen, LeiterInnen und TeilnehmerInnen. Feministische TheologInnen können hier

---

[68] Ich möchte hier auf das Ritual von Anne Hunt Overzee und Caroline Mackenzie verweisen. Vgl. Anne Hunt Overzee, "Shadow Play" und Caroline Mackenzie, "Fire and Water Woman: Background to the Images", in: Annette Esser / Anne Hunt Overzee / Susan Roll (Hg.), *Re-Visioning Our Sources: Women's Spirituality in European Perspective* (Kok Pharos: Kampen 1997), 94-107; 108-111.

den erweiterten Kunstbegriff von Josef Beuys, wonach jeder Mensch ein Künstler ist, auf derselben Ebene reflektieren, auf der auch jede Frau eine Theologin ist. Dann wird vielleicht deutlicher, dass der Unterschied zwischen ritualisierenden Frauen und Künstlerinnen nicht prinzipieller Natur ist, sondern vielmehr auf professioneller Erfahrungspraxis basiert, die auf ihrem Feld zu haben auch Theologinnen für sich in Anspruch nehmen wollen. Die Frage an Theologinnen ist es, inwieweit sie diese (andere) Erfahrungspraxis endlich wahrnehmen und in Dialog treten wollen, so dass aus anstößiger Kunst ein wirklicher Anstoß für die Liturgie von Frauen werden kann.

## Erfahrungen und Prinzipien im Dialog

Stelle ich mir nun einen fiktiven Dialog zwischen Kirchenfrauen / feministischen Theologinnen und Künstlerinnen im Blick auf die gemeinsame Gestaltung einer feministischen Liturgie vor, dann vermute ich Anfragen nicht nur im Blick auf die Intention der Liturgie und deren Spiritualität, sowie auf das künstlerische und kreative Selbstverständnis religiöser Feiern, sondern ich sehe auch das Gespräch zweier, eher benachteiligter Randgruppen in ihrem jeweiligen Kontext, wobei gerade Künstlerinnen oft (aber nicht immer!) mit noch größeren finanziellen Nöten zu tun haben als Theologinnen (zumal solche mit Festanstellung). Ob dann aus diesem Gespräch ein fruchtbarer Dialog wird, dem eine gemeinsame Stärke erwächst oder, ob auch er an materiellen "Umständen" von vornherein verhindert wird, z.B. weil "wir uns eine Künstlerin nicht leisten können", steht leider noch dahin. Es wäre jedoch spannend, Erfahrungen anderer mit einem solchen Dialog zu reflektieren.

Ich kenne keine anderen Arbeiten als die der britischen Künstlerin Caroline Mackenzie und die meiner New Yorker Lehrerin Janet Walton, die sich authentisch und engagiert um den Dialog zwischen Kunst und feministischer Liturgie verdient gemacht haben. Caroline Mackenzie hat dabei nicht nur zahlreiche Rituale, Meditationen und Liturgien mitgestaltet, sondern sich auch professionell mit der Frage der *Gestaltung liturgischen Raumes* beschäftigt, wobei sie einige ganz konkrete Arbeitsprojekte vorweisen kann.[69] Ihre

---

[69] Caroline Mackenzie, "Your Bondage Makes Me Aware of Mine: Reflections on Designing an Indian Christian Temple in South India", in: *Journal of the Interfaith Forum on Religion, Art & Architecture* 26 (1993), 18-21; "Cosmic Awareness and Sacred Space: The Integration of Feminine Symbolism in Indian Christian Art and Architecture" in: Elisabeth Green / Mary Grey (Hg.), *Ökofeminismus und Theologie* (ESWTR Jahrbuch 2; Grünewald / Kok Pharos: Mainz / Kampen 1994), 20-31; "The Cave and the Mountain: Reflections on Designing a Trappistine Chapel in South India", in: *Church Building Magazine* 36 (1995), 4-6.

Beschäftigung mit der Frage, wie die symbolischen Strukturen des Sakralraumes und der Liturgie bewusst frauengerecht gestaltet und verändert werden können, halte ich für relevant, und ihre Klage darüber, dass sich mehr Männer für diese Arbeit interessieren als Frauen, hat mich aufhorchen lassen. Nach meinem Wissen wird auch in Deutschland die Frage der Gestaltung des kirchlichen Sakralraumes erneut ernsthaft in kirchlichen Kreisen reflektiert. So wurden in einer liturgischen Schulung des Erzbistums Kölns[70] alternative Gestaltungsformen für Gottesdienste in Kirchen, Kapellen und Schulräumen diskutiert. Dabei kamen wir neben der Anordnung in Kreisform, die in Frauengottesdiensten oft favorisiert wird, auf Formen des Halbkreises und des Ovals zu sprechen. Es ging um die Frage, wie nicht nur dem Bewusstsein von "Gemeinschaft der Gläubigen" Rechnung getragen werden kann, sondern auch, welchen Ort im Raum die Leitung des Gottesdienstes, die Lesung des Wortes (Pult) und die Feier des Sakramentes (Altar) haben soll. Das in der Schulungsdiskussion favorisierte Oval bietet zwei Brennpunkte, die Orte für Wort und Sakrament sein können. Hiernach sind bereits erste Kirchenräume umgestaltet worden.[71]

Ähnliche Überlegungen zur symbolischen Ordnung des Gottesdienstraumes und zur darauf basierenden liturgischen Praxis habe ich vordem in meiner dreijährigen Zeit am Union Theological Seminary – einem Seminar des liberalen Protestantismus – erlebt, besonders in den täglichen *Worship Services* in James Chapel. Dieser große Kapellenraum im neugotischen Stil wurde 1979 komplett umgestaltet. Bänke und Predigerpult wurden herausgenommen und die dunklen Wände weiß gestrichen, so dass ein heller großer Gottesdienstraum entstand, der von nun an täglich neu gestaltet werden kann. Da Stühle, Pult, Altar, sowie andere Utensilien wie Tücher, Blumen, symbolische Gegenstände je nach gottesdienstlicher Planung ausgesucht werden können und müssen, bietet sich dieser Gottesdienstraum geradezu an, neue liturgische Formen, die die SeminaristInnen als Teil ihrer Ausbildung begreifen, zu erproben. Als katholische Ordensfrau und als Professorin für Liturgiewissenschaft am Seminar hat Janet Walton dieses Programm erneuerter Gottesdienste begründet. Dabei bildete ihr eigener musikwissenschaftlicher Zugang und ihre Erfahrung *feministischen Ritualisierens* einen wichtigen Hintergrund auch für die Zusammenarbeit mit KünstlerInnen, die sich immer wieder unter den Studierenden und auch außerhalb finden.

---

[70] Siehe Anm. 18.
[71] Kirche St. Franzikus in Bonn, Kapelle im Haus Venusberg, Bonn.

Um nun einige Beispiele zu nennen, habe ich während meiner Zeit am Union (1994-1998) – nicht nur im Kontext von Gottesdiensten ("Worship Services") – im Kapellenraum James Chapel erlebt: Bildausstellungen von Studierenden und MitarbeiterInnen aus verschiedenen Kontexten (African American, Marokko...); Modern Dance einer schwarzen Tänzerin und Studentin; expressiven Tanz in der Darstellung der Lebensgeschichte Teresa von Avilas und Hildegard von Bingens durch eine lateinamerikanische Tänzerin; Percussion und Trommel Musik; Gospel; klassische Chormusik; Opernsänger; eine Vodoo-Tänzerin mit Trommler; Lesung eigener Gedichte, meditativer oder politischer Texte; Theater und Drama-Darbietungen; sowie immer wieder die Verwendung und erneute Kreation von Symbolen und symbolischen Handlungen (Patchwork, Prozession, erneuertes Austeilen der Asche und Heilungsgesten...) und die rege Beteiligung aller am Gottesdienst durch Gesang, frei gesprochenes Gebet und Ausführen eigener Gebetsgesten.

Die liturgische Arbeit von Janet Walton, die auch von ihren SchülerInnen und KollegInnen, u.a. Dorothee Sölle, Susan Blain und Chung Hyun Kyung, fortgesetzt wurde, hat im amerikanischen Kontext, wo sie u.a. zeitweise Präsidentin der *North American Academy of Liturgy* war, große Anerkennung erfahren, ist aber in Deutschland wohl noch fast unbekannt. Dabei ist gerade ihr Beitrag zum notwendigen Dialog zwischen Kunst und Liturgie, den sie als promovierte Musikwissenschaftlerin mit besonderem Bewusstsein führen konnte, einmalig. In *Art and Worship: A Vital Connection*[72] stellt sie die ersten Ergebnisse dieses Dialogs vor, die ich kurz referieren möchte.

Ausgangspunkt ihrer Betrachtung ist die Besinnung auf die traditionelle Bedeutung der Kunst für die Kirche. In der Reflektion der historischen Beispiele der Kirchen von *Dura Europos* (232-256 n.Chr.) und *Saint-Denis* (erste Kirche 475 n.Chr; Rekonstruktion der Abteikirche 1135), zeigt sie, wie kontrastreich Kunst in der Liturgie sowohl Ausdruck gemeinschaftlichen Gefühls gewesen ist ("liturgy as an intentional corporate activity rather than as a private, individual exercise"), als auch zur Unterstützung und Erhöhung einer hierarchisch-patriarchalen Kirche diente, wobei historisch gesehen, Saint-Denis der Sieger gewesen ist. Für Janet Walton ist es wichtig aus diesen Beispielen zu lernen:

> Given the pivotal role of history in their artistic choices, our search for an adequate framework to utilize art within worship more fully in this century will begin with an analysis of the needs of the church today.[73]

---

[72] Walton, *Art and Worship*.
[73] A.a.O., 45.

Es folgt eine Analyse dessen, was die Kirche heute braucht, um Verantwortung für die Situation in der heutigen Gesellschaft zu übernehmen. Janet Walton benennt hier die Notwendigkeit zeitgenössischer Kirche zu kritischem Denken, konstruktiven Ideen, Modellen der Zusammenarbeit, Mitleid und Mut.[74] All dies muss sich dann auch in der liturgischen Feier wiederfinden lassen. Dementsprechend benennt sie als die liturgischen Bedürfnisse in der heutigen Kirche die Bedürfnisse nach Transzendenz (Gotteserfahrung), Beziehung (Miteinander), Schönheit, Bestätigung (eigenen Lebens) und Glauben (Unterstützung).[75] Liturgie ist für sie der zentrale Ort, an dem Antwort auf diese Bedürfnisse möglich wird. Jedoch ist der Ausdruck dieser grundlegenden, menschlichen Bedürfnisse komplex und schwierig. Und gerade hierin, nämlich in der Artikulation menschlicher Wirklichkeit, liegt die historische Bedeutung der Kunst.

> Historically artists have been most successful in articulating human realities. They have been able to penetrate beyond superficial interpretations to the heart of human concerns. The contemporary church needs the help of artists to provide expressions of truth.[76]

Was Kunst zu bieten hat, bringt Janet Walton dann auf die Begriffe von Partikularität, Sinn, Offenbarung, Illusion, Emotion, Gewahrwerden / Konversion, Erinnerung und Werten.[77] Schlüssel zum Verständnis ihres Ansatzes ist, dass KünstlerInnen es verstehen, Beziehungen untereinander, zu unseren Gefühlen und auch zur Dimension der Transzendenz herzustellen, woran es der kirchlichen Liturgie leider oft mangelt:

> The key to the problem, I believe is that artists understand how to make connections... New hymnals, renovated church spaces, more communal participation by way of praying or reading together, better trained leaders, all these are not enough. What we need are connections: expressions of the need to love and to be loved, or the fear and reluctance to die, that are connected to the faith of the particular religious tradition... We need to link joy with God and one another.[78]

---

[74] A.a.O., 47: "When churches assume responsibility for the situations that exist in society, such awareness will affect their celebrations. They require critical thinking, constructive ideas, collobarative models, compassion and courage."

[75] Transcendence, Connection, Beauty, Affirmation, Faithfulness.

[76] Walton, *Art and Worship*, 67.

[77] Particularity, Meaning, Revelation, Illusion, Emotion, Awareness / Conversion, Memory, Values.

[78] Walton, *Art and Worship*, 14-15.

Wozu Janet Walton mit ihren Reflexionen über die Bedürfnisse und Angebote von Kirche und Kunst schließlich einladen möchte, ist eine Partnerschaft beider, in der die Bedingungen und der Gewinn gegenseitig sind. D.h. sie fordert einen Dialog, in dem Kirche (Kirchenfrauen) und KünstlerInnen eine gemeinsame Aufgabe erkennen, an der sie zusammen arbeiten können. Aus ihren langjährigen Erfahrungen im Dialog mit KünstlerInnen zur gemeinsamen Gestaltung von Liturgien, schlägt sie folgende *Prinzipien* vor, die als Richtlinien für diesen *Dialogprozess* dienen sollen:[79]

1. Beginnen Sie mit einem Gespräch, in dem beide Seiten, KünstlerIn und KirchenpartnerIn, die Ziele zum Ausdruck bringen, die sie jeweils zu erreichen suchen. Dann suchen Sie nach dem, was beiden gemeinsam ist.
2. Sichern Sie gegenseitigen Respekt dadurch, dass Sie klare Grenzen zum Ausdruck bringen: Was kann erwartet werden und was nicht?
3. Machen Sie deutlich, dass sich beide Seiten auf Erfahrung berufen, und, dass die Erfahrung der einen Seite nicht "besser" ist als die der anderen.
4. Bestehen Sie auf Integration, so dass eine klare Harmonie und Balance deutlich macht, dass kein Teil der Liturgie ein "Waisenkind" oder ein Nachgedanke ist.
5. Zeigen Sie auf, dass Disziplin eigene Früchte trägt, die durch Verkürzungen nicht errungen werden können.
6. Üben Sie eine angemessene Leitung aus.
7. Schaffen Sie eine vertrauensvolle Umgebung.
8. Bewahren Sie eine Haltung der Offenheit.
9. Seien Sie geduldig: Wachstum braucht seine Zeit.
10. Verlangen Sie den höchsten Level an Kompetenz. Gute Intentionen und bloße Fähigkeiten sind nicht genug.
11. Gute Kunst kostet etwas.
12. Diese neue Kreation verlangt Beharrlichkeit: Geben Sie nicht auf!

Janet Walton hat diese Prinzipien noch näher ausgeführt und es lohnt sich, diese einmal im Original zu lesen.[80] Worauf es mir ankommt, ist zu sagen, dass hier bereits ein dialogisches Modell (zwischen feministischer Liturgiewissenschaft und KünstlerInnen) vorliegt, das sich als Alternative zu bereits in Deutschland praktizierten Modellen von Kunst / Performance im Kirchenraum anbietet und eine große Bereicherung für feministische Liturgien wäre.

---

[79] A.a.O., 111-112.
[80] A.a.O., 111-119.

**Zur praktischen Arbeit an der Kreation und Performance (feministi-scher) Liturgien**

Das Modell von Janet Walton konkret durchzuführen, ist vielleicht nur Kir-chenmitarbeiterInnen, PfarrerInnen und TheologInnen mit institutionellem Hintergrund und entsprechenden finanziellen Ressourcen möglich. Da aber bereits in vielen Kirchen im deutschen und europäischen Kontext Kunstpro-jekte durchgeführt werden,[81] ist es die Frage, ob diese nicht auch stärker in den liturgischen Zusammenhang eingebunden und reflektiert werden könnten. Dass nämlich weiterhin interessante Performances in Kirchenräumen angebo-ten werden, zu denen GottesdienstbesucherInnen keinen Bezug haben oder denen sie nur mit musealer Haltung ("Das ist also jetzt Kunst!") begegnen, halte ich mindestens für schade. Der Intention der KünstlerInnen jedenfalls, aufzurütteln, zu bewegen und neue Sichtweisen zu eröffnen, ist damit nicht Genüge getan, und die Chance, (post)moderne oder zeitgenössische Kunst im Kirchenraum nicht nur zu sehen, sondern sich auch in einer gemeinsamen liturgischen Praxis davon bewegen zu lassen, wird vertan. Daher halte ich es für eine Herausforderung für TheologInnen, über Liturgie auch im Sinne einer künstlerischen Gestaltung, und über künstlerische Kreationen und Per-formances auch im Sinne ihrer Integration in christliche und feministische Liturgien nachzudenken.

In der Grundthese dieses Beitrages, dass gute Kunst immer ein schöpferisch-kreativer Akt ist, und ein gutes Ritual immer auch eine gute Performance ist, ging es tatsächlich nicht nur um eine theologische Reflexion künstlerischer Per-formances, sondern auch um die Frage des kreativen Potentials, das uns Theo-logInnen für die Gestaltung von Gottesdiensten und Ritualen zur Verfügung steht. Dabei besteht die Differenz zwischen religiösen Frauen und Künstlerin-nen m.E. nicht so sehr im grundsätzlichen Willen zur kreativen Gestaltung, etwa eines Rituals oder einer Performance, wohl aber im Mut, in der Kraft und in der Erfahrung, solch eine Gestaltung ganzheitlich-körperlich, raumbewusst-besitzergreifend und auch im Blick auf einen kreativen Umgang mit dem Mate-rial und den materiellen Ressourcen vorzunehmen. Das bedeutet dann nicht nur, bereits bekannte "KünstlerInnen" bzw. Persönlichkeiten, die von gehobe-ner Stelle empfohlen werden, für eine Ausstellung in der jeweiligen Kirche vor Ort zu bewegen. Es liegt darüber hinaus in der Verantwortung der Gemeinde (TheologInnen, PfarrerInnen, Gemeindemitglieder...), *künstlerisches Potential*

---

[81] Beispiele: Kunststation St. Peter in Köln (siehe Anm. 62); Pax-Christi Gemeinde Krefeld, Steine des Anstosses: Zeitgenössische Kunst in Pax Christi Krefeld, Krefeld, 1987.

*in den eigenen Reihen* zu entdecken und zu fördern und einen *eigenen Kunst-verstand* zu entwickeln, den Mut, Kunst (postmoderne ebenso wie traditio-nelle) nicht nur "von oben anzunehmen", im Sinne einer musealen Haltung oder eines (feministisch dekonstruierten) Glaubens an den "Künstler als mythischem Meister", sondern selbst in einen kreativen Dialog zu treten. Nach meinem Wissen und meiner Erfahrung aus Gesprächen mit mehreren KünstlerInnen mangelt es an solch einem Dialog. Trotz langer Tradition der Zusammenarbeit von Kunst und Kirche seit der Antike, berichten KünstlerIn-nen immer wieder davon, dass PfarrerInnen vor Ort, denen sie ihre Arbeiten zur Ausstellung anbieten wollen, wenig damit anfangen können, wortkarg bleiben oder diese ablehnen. Und umgekehrt fühlen sich TheologInnen im Dialog mit KünstlerInnen oft sehr unsicher und folgen eher alten Bild-schablonen oder trauen unreflektierten Bewertungen des Zeitgeistes darüber, was nun als Kirchenkunst gerade im Trend ist mehr, als dem eigenen Urteil.

Wenn TheologInnen ihre Naivität und Unreflektiertheit im Umgang mit stilistischen Formen und herkömmlichen Materialien aus der religionspädagogi-schen "Trickkiste" oder aus der "Mottenkiste" unserer Vorväter- und Mütter überwinden wollen, bzw. ihren Kunstverstand nicht einfach dem Zeitgeist unterordnen wollen, dann müssen sie sich fragen, wie sie dies tun wollen. Neben einer evtl. kunsttherapeutischen Selbstreflexion, die dazu dienen kann, alte konservierte Bildvorstellungen zu überwinden, kraftvolle Bilder aus dem eigenen Unbewussten hervorzuholen und damit zu arbeiten,[82] ist es m.E. Auf-gabe von PfarrerInnen und TheologInnen, den Dialog mit KünstlerInnen vor Ort aktiv zu suchen, und auch das künstlerische Potential von Gemeindemit-gliedern zu entdecken und aufzugreifen um es dann evt. in der gemeinsamen Gestaltung einer Liturgie für die ganze Gemeinde fruchtbar machen zu können.

Hier steht ein Lernprozess an, in dem endlich auch aus Fehlern gelernt wer-den muss, wie denen, dass bspw. Künstler mit theologischem Vokabular vor den Kopf gestoßen wurden, oder dass Angebote aus den eigenen Reihen zu tanzen, zu singen, Gedichte vorzutragen oder Bilder vorzustellen ignoriert oder als Anhängsel der "eigentlichen" Liturgie behandelt wurden. Zu begrei-fen, dass im Umgang mit Kunst nicht nur eine sekundäre Fähigkeit verlangt

---

[82] Vgl. Joanna Field, *On Not Being Able to Paint. Foreword by Anna Freud* (Jeremy P. Tarcher / Putnam: New York 1957); Ingrid Riedel, *Farben in Religion, Gesellschaft, Kunst und Psy-chotherapie* (Kreuz: Stuttgart 1983); dies., *Bilder in Therapie, Kunst und Religion. Wege zur Interpretation* (Kreuz Verlag: Stuttgart ⁴1998); dies., *Formen. Kreis, Dreieck, Quadrat, Spi-rale* (Kreuz Verlag: Stuttgart ⁷1995); Susan Hogan, *Feminist Approaches to Art Therapy* (Routledge: London / New York 1997).

ist, sondern dass im eigentlichen Sinne auch die Kompetenz als TheologIn gefragt ist, eben nicht nur vorgefertigte Antworten zu geben, sondern auf existentielle Fragen zu hören und kreative Ausdrucksformen wahrzunehmen, ist schon ein Schritt. Darüber hinaus verdient die dialogische Zusammenarbeit mit KünstlerInnen in einer möglichen gemeinsamen Gestaltung (feministischer) Liturgie mehr Aufmerksamkeit. Was TheologInnen hier selbst einbringen müssen, sind nicht nur evtl. ihre eigenen (unbewussten) Bilder, sondern auch ihr Bewusstsein für den Kontext, die dialogische Struktur und die Zielrichtung eines Gottesdienstes, sowie auch ihre eigene "Kunst", die einzelnen Elemente zu einem harmonischen Zusammenspiel zu bringen und zu integrieren.

In diesem künstlerisch-liturgischen Prozess (der in feministischer Liturgie intendiert wird), ginge es zutiefst sowohl um die Darstellung der Fragen menschlicher Existenz, als auch um die Präsentation der Antworten aus der göttlichen Transzendenz. Dies jedenfalls würde ich als eine zugleich materielle und geistige Darstellung oder Mimesis einer Theologie der Schöpfung / Kreation und der Inkarnation im sakralen Raum verstehen. Und daran zu arbeiten und dies anzustreben ist m.E. eine Vision für die Kirche der Zukunft.

The author examines two examples, one of women's ritual and the other of a woman artist's performance in church, in order to find comparisons and differences between them. In order to go beyond superficial common factors, she first reflects on the impact of art upon feminist ritual / liturgy, and secondly on the impact of religion upon postmodern art / performances by women, with the aim of bringing feminist ritual and art into dialogue. To this end she affirms the conceptual guidelines of Janet R. Walton on the principle of partnership between artists and church women. Her intention is to show that good art is always a process of creation, and that good liturgy / ritual is always a creative piece of artistic performance; both together can contribute to a theology and praxis of creation and incarnation.

L'auteur examine les rituels et l'art féminins religieux, afin d'en dégager les similitudes et les différences. Soucieuse de dépasser des lieux communs par trop superficiels, elle étudie d'une part l'influence de l'art sur les rituels et la liturgie féministes, d'autre part le pouvoir de la religion sur le postmoderne, l'art des femmes et de la célébration de leurs rituels. Son but est d'établir un dialogue entre les rituels et l'art féminins. Elle reprend à cette fin, en les étayant, les idées maîtresses de Janet R. Walton sur le principe de la collaboration entre artistes et femmes d'église. Elle montre que l'art est toujours un processus de création de même que la liturgie et le rituel sont toujours la part créatrice d'un acte artistique. Tous deux contribuent à une théologie et à une pratique de la création et de l'incarnation.

**Annette Esser**, geb. 1957 in Köln. Studium der katholischen Theologie, Kunst und Geographie in Köln, Münster (1976-1986) und am Union Theological Seminary in New York (1994-1998). Fortbildung in Kunsttherapie, Bibliodrama und Psychodrama. Tätigkeit als Religions- und Kunstlehrerin und als Referentin in der Erwachsenenbildung. Mitherausgeberin von *Feministische Theologie im europäischen Kontext* (= ESWTR Jahrbuch 1 [1993]) und von *Re-Visioning Our Sources: Women's Spiritualities in European Perspectives* (Kok Pharos: Kampen 1997). Derzeit Promotion über ökumenische Perspektiven weiblicher / feministischer Spiritualität.

*Gabriella Lettini*

# Hic Sunt Leones?
# A contribution to the Ecumenical Discussion on Rituals and Syncretism

## Introduction

My interest in the debate surrounding rituals and syncretism is deeply rooted in the reality of my own life. In my own experience, the term syncretism has been used first of all as a way to protect my identity, then as a way to deny it. I grew up in the Waldensian church in Italy, the surviving heir of a medieval "heretical" movement that later adhered to the Protestant Reformation. As part of a religious minority with a long history of persecution and of on-going discrimination, I learned very early to counteract oppressive situations by try- ing to nurture and cherish a strong sense of my own diversity. Therefore, I remember the shame I felt when a public school teacher forced me to attend an Ash Wednesday Mass in the local Roman Catholic Church, dragging me in front of the altar so that I could receive ashes on my forehead. Walden- sians did not celebrate Ash Wednesday, since its origins were certainly not Biblical. I thought I had been brought to a sort of pagan cult. I felt abused, humiliated, and guilty for having taken part in something I felt was not Christian. Both at home and within my congregation I was told that Roman Catholics integrated pagan rituals with Christian beliefs: their faith was therefore "syncretic." One of the tenets of our Protestant faith was instead that we had to abide by Biblical teachings: therefore, our worship style and our personal spirituality dismissed traditions that were "merely cultural" or, even worse, were drawn straight from pre-Christian pagan cults. We liked to say that we did not attend "rituals," but worship services, strictly focused on the preaching of the Word of God. All of this certainly took a lot of fun out of my life and often made me feel alienated from Italian culture, but if it was the price for not being pagan I was ready to pay it. When my friends dressed up for Carnival and I couldn't, at least I had the consolation of knowing that they were being very "syncretistic," not many steps away from paganism.

I began to look at syncretism with different eyes only many years later, during my Seminary studies in Rome. Dissatisfied with the Patriarchal and European-centered focus of my studies, I started almost randomly to read materials coming from other perspectives. Once I came across a beautiful poem by an African theologian.[1] It spoke of his painful struggle to be Christian while keeping the faith of his ancestors. Since I had to organize a worship service in the Seminary chapel shortly after that, I decided to read the poem after the Scripture reading and to meditate on it. And so I did. But as soon as I finished reading the poem, one of the professors present at chapel, visibly shaken, stopped me and said something like: "Dear Gabriella, if that man wants to continue to be pagan and worship his ancestors, so be it. Enough of this syncretic nonsense! Let us recite the Lord's prayer." That was the end of that service, and the end of my going to chapel for the rest of my program. This experience marked me profoundly, and kept coming back into my thoughts. In a few minutes I learned a lot about the word syncretism, and how it is used. The power dynamics were exemplary: a European Christian used it to negate the faith of an African brother without even listening to him; a middle-aged man publicly silenced a young woman and took away her leadership; a theology professor – a "specialist" – corrected an erring neophyte.

My involvement within the ecumenical movement, feminist groups and my studies at Union Theological Seminary in New York City also helped me to gain a wider perspective on what constitutes a ritual, realizing that my word-centered Waldensian worship tradition was no less a ritual than Voodoo dancing or sharing milk and honey as a form of communion. I came to realize that rituals are symbolic actions that carry the values and aspirations of the communities or individuals that perform them, within or without a religious context. Within Christianity itself, people worship following a variety of ritual patterns, developed according to the way that different communities have understood – and understand – their faith within their own historical and cultural context. This diversity has been at times a source of enrichment, but often also the cause for much strife and even violence. Today, feminist and Third World rituals are often seen as controversial, and described as syncretic and pagan, and the issue of syncretism in relation to rituals and theology has become a fundamental point of contention both within the ecumenical movement and within individual denominations and local churches. Typical exam-

---

[1]  Unfortunately I have lost my copy of this poem and cannot remember the name of its author.

ples are the public outcry after the Re-imagining conference in 1993,[2] and the heated debate surrounding the WCC's Assembly in Canberra, in 1991.

Different realities have drawn forth this special focus. Certainly there is the anxiety and the questioning around the loss of status experienced by Christianity in many Western countries, which – despite a growing minority of people who are fascinated by forms of non Western spirituality, or try to go back to their pre-Christian roots – are becoming more and more secularized. Furthermore, within Christian churches women are challenging the patriarchal nature of the Western Christian tradition, claiming the right to think and worship "in their own rite."[3] But I think that the propelling force behind this discussion has to be found in the fact that today the majority of Christians no longer lives in the Northern-Western hemisphere. The new Christian majority is raising increasingly radical questions, not only about the way Christianity was brought to them along with colonialism and genocide, but also about the canons of "orthodox" Christianity brought by Western missionaries. At the same time, many of these Christians have also started to re-evaluate the validity of their pre-Christian beliefs and rituals, and strongly affirm the importance of incorporating them in their spirituality and theology. I shall argue here that the discussion of rituals and syncretism needs to be contextualized in this multifaceted process of shifting power, and I will attempt to show how these dynamics are at work by analyzing the historical development of the discussion within the ecumenical movement.

In this paper I will focus on the Canberra controversy, its outcome and significance. The Canberra controversy is particularly interesting because it

---

[2]   The Re-Imagining Conference was held in Minneapolis in 1993 (Nov. 4-6). It was an international theological event organized in response to the World Council of Churches' Ecumenical Decade: Churches in Solidarity with Women (1988-1998). The conference was attended and supported by leadership and members of several mainline denominations, and drew over 2000 participants from 27 countries. The organizers' purpose was to re-imagine God, faith and community from a Christian feminist perspective. The conference received sensationalistic and misinformed media coverage, and caused great controversy within mainline denominations and strong condemnation from the Christian right. Many of the theological addresses and feminist rituals were labeled as "heretic," "pagan," "pantheistic." This controversy resulted in severe backlash against conference organizers and participants. For a closer look at the Re-imagining Conference see: "Re-imagining…God…Community…The Church: From the Ecumenical Decade Conference November 1993," in: *Church and Society* 84/5 (May/June 1994; whole issue).

[3]   See Marjorie Procter-Smith's challenging book, *In Her Own Rite: Constructing Feminist Liturgical Tradition* (Abingdon Press: Nashville 1990).

encompasses a broad range of issues close to the hearts of feminists of all colors and to Third World liberation theologians, and it shows the interconnections between the struggles against the patriarchal, racist and colonial nature of Western Christianity. I will address three closely interrelated questions. First, what do we mean with the term syncretism? Then: What is really at stake when we use this term? Finally: Is syncretism a subject worthy of theological discussion in a world torn apart by violence and oppression? What does this issue have to do with the plight of women and other oppressed?

## The Problem of Definition/s

> *It's often said that life is strange. Oh yes, but compared to what?*[4]

The first problem that is encountered when approaching a discussion on syncretism is that people understand the word in a number of different ways without acknowledging it. In fact, over the centuries, the use of the term has undergone a number of changes in meaning. Further, people working in different fields, such as anthropologists and theologians, have not always given the term the same meaning. I have witnessed the way this confusion of meaning can generate a sort of Tower of Babel experience for people who come together to discuss this theme. Therefore, a brief overview of the history of the interpretation of the word "syncretism" can be extremely helpful in understanding the present controversy.[5]

Plutarch seems to be the first to use the word in *De Fraterno Amore*. For him it meant "to act like the Cretans," referring to a particular moment where the need to fight a common enemy brought unity to the divided peoples of Crete. Much later, during the Reformation, Erasmus used the term to define the unifying of the Protestant Reformers with the humanists, therefore coming back to the concept of a somehow positive and creative union

---

[4] This quotation is attributed to Steve Forbert in: Andrea De Carlo, *Macno* (Bompiani: Milan 1989), 5.

[5] For a detailed history of the use of the term see the following publications: Jerald D. Gort / Hendrik M. Vroom / Rein Fernhout / Anton Wessels (eds), *Dialogue and Syncretism: An Interdisciplinary Approach* (Eerdmans: Grand Rapids, MI 1989); Charles Stewart / Rosalind Shaw (eds), *Syncretism/Anti-Syncretism: The Politics of Religious Synthesis* (Routledge: New York 1994); Nicholas Lossky et al. (eds), *Dictionary of the Ecumenical Movement* (Eerdmans: Grand Rapids, MI 1991); Ans Joachim Van der Bent (ed.), *Historical Dictionary of Ecumenical Christianity* (Scarecrow Press: Metuchen, NJ 1994).

of apparently different points of view. In the seventeenth century the word was derived from the Greek "synkerannumy," a verb meaning "to mix" or "to harmonize", and it was used in reference to the harmonization of different doctrines or philosophies. Very soon the term stopped being positive or neutral and assumed a very negative meaning. Thus, it was used as a polemical term to define heresy in contrast with "true" religion. For instance, in 17th century Europe "syncretism" was understood to be the illegitimate reconciliation of opposing views. In the second half of the 19th century religious historians tried to "objectify" the use of the term, defining early Christianity as syncretic. However, the use of the term "syncretic" still retained a negative meaning, denoting a deviation from original purity. Belief in a pristine form of Christianity is still quite popular today, and strongly informs the discussion about syncretism. According to this position, at its very beginning, the Christian church held an uncontaminated belief system which was then syncretized with Hellenistic beliefs. This view was deeply influenced by the writings of Adolph von Harnack who, in the words of Alister McGrath, saw the hellenization of the gospel as a sort of "chronic degenerative illness."[6]

Today anthropologists tend to give the term syncretism a neutral connotation, understood to describe any mixing of religions, while from a religious perspective the use of the word often includes either a positive or a negative evaluation. As cultural anthropologist André Droogers has pointed out:

> Syncretism is a tricky term. Its main difficulty is that it is used with both an objective and a subjective meaning. The basic objective meaning refers neutrally and descriptively to the mixing of religions. The subjective meaning includes an evaluation of such intermingling from the point of view of one of the religions involved. As a rule, the mixing of religions is condemned in this evaluation as violating the essence of the belief system. Yet ... a positive subjective definition also belongs to the possibilities.[7]

Droogers points out that there is no use in trying to abolish the term, since too many people will continue to use it anyway. He suggests that scholars need to analyze and discuss it, finding the links between its different meanings and analyzing the power relations of the people who use it.

---

[6]  Alister E. McGrath, *Christian Theology: An Introduction* (Blackwell: Cambridge, MA 1994), 342.

[7]  André Droogers, "Syncretism: The Problem of Definition, the Definition of the Problem," in: Gort / Vroom / Fernhout / Wessels (eds), *Dialogue and Syncretism*, 7-25, here 7.

## The discussion within the ecumenical movement

When speaking about the ecumenical movement, I think it is important to remember that it originated from the efforts of Western Protestant churches to maximize their missionary endeavors. Wesley Ariarajah has pointed out that in the early ecumenical mission conferences very little discussion took place on the specific issue of gospel and culture.[8] There was a lack of awareness on the part of Western churches of the fact that in their missionary efforts they were also exporting Western cultures and values as an inherent part of the gospel. In fact, mission organizations and missionaries most often carried with them and disseminated a secular heritage of Western ideological supremacy and colonialism. With a few rare exceptions, the encounter with non-Western cultures was marked by ignorance, misunderstanding, insensitivity, racism, or paternalism in the "best" cases. Non-Western cultures were regarded as being "primitive," "pagan," "heathen," or "savage."[9] After the so-called Second World War, a paradigm shift began to take place as the leadership in Asian, African and Latin American churches became increasingly local. Political nationalism also had a strong impact on religious traditions, and indigenous religions came to be newly valued and celebrated.

Although the ecumenical reflection on syncretism, strictly connected to issues of missiology and gospel and culture, had been developing for decades, many were totally unprepared for the way it erupted into the forefront at the WCC's seventh assembly in Canberra in 1991. The agenda of the conference did not formally allocate space to a discussion on gospel and culture and syncretism. However, for the very first time the focus of the conference was not christological but pneumatological: the theme of Canberra was "Come, Holy Spirit – Renew the Whole Creation."

Two particular events brought the issue of syncretism into the center of the discussions, and they should be remembered as turning points in the history of the ecumenical movement. The conference started with a traditional Aboriginal ceremony to give permission to the assembly to meet on their land. In order to enter the tent where the ceremony and the opening worship were to be held, participants were invited to pass through smoke as a sign of purification. This opening ceremony also involved Aboriginal people dancing in tra-

---

[8]  S. Wesley Ariarajah, *Gospel and Culture: An Ongoing Discussion Within the Ecumenical Movement* (WCC Publications: Geneva 1994), 2.

[9]  Ibid., 3.

ditional costume around the altar. Not all the four thousand people present found this ceremony to be acceptable practice in a Christian assembly.

The second presentation was the controversial keynote address by Korean theologian Chung Hyun Kyung. Invoking the presence of the Holy Spirit, Chung amplified Western traditional understanding of it as she invited the participants to hear the cries of the Spirit for all people and creatures that had been victims of injustice. She called the spirit of Hagar, "Egyptian, black slave woman exploited and abandoned by Abraham and Sarah," the spirit of Joan of Arc, the spirit of "the indigenous people of the earth, victims of genocide during the time of colonialism and the period of the great Christian mission to the pagan world," the spirit of Vietnamese people killed by napalm, the spirit of the many who fought and died for freedom, from Mahatma Gandhi to Malcolm X. Chung recognized that the Spirit of God groans in pain also for the abuse and rape of all creation, as she invoked the Spirit of the Amazon rain forest, and the "spirit of earth, air and water, raped, tortured and exploited by human greed for money."[10] In this invocation of the Spirit to a Christian audience, Chung made clear that her own Korean traditional understanding of the han-ridden spirits could help her to achieve a better understanding of the Spirit of God. She saw these spirits as God's agents, as the vehicles of God's compassion and wisdom for life. Challenging her audience to let the Spirit break free and to be open to a broader understanding of the Spirit, Chung boldly stated:

> Without hearing the cries of these spirits we can not hear the voice of the Holy Spirit. I hope the presence of all our ancestors' spirits here with us shall not make you uncomfortable. For us they are icons of the Holy Spirit who became tangible and visible to us. Because of them we can feel, touch and taste the concrete bodily historical presence of the Holy Spirit in our midst.[11]

Many participants at the conference accused these two presentations of syncretism. The strongest response came from representatives of the Orthodox Church:

> ...it is with alarm that the Orthodox have heard some presentations on the theme of this assembly... they observe that some people tend to affirm with very great ease the presence of the Holy Spirit in many movements and development without

---

[10] Chung Hyun Kyung, "Come Holy Spirit – Renew the Whole Creation," in: Michael Kinnamon (ed.), *Signs of the Spirit: World Council of Churches Official Report, Seventh Assembly* (WCC Publications: Geneva 1991), 37-47, here 38-39.

[11] Ibid., 39.

discernment. The Orthodox wish to stress the factor of sin and error which exist in every human action, and separate the Holy Spirit from these. We must guard against a tendency to substitute a "private" spirit, the spirit of the world or other spirits for the Holy Spirit who proceeds from the Father and rests in the Son. Our tradition is rich in respect for local and national cultures, but we find it impossible to invoke the spirits of "earth, air, water and sea creatures." Pneumatology is inseparable from Christology or from the doctrine of the Holy Trinity confessed from Christology or from the doctrine of the Holy Trinity confessed by the church on the basis of divine revelation.[12]

The issues of discerning the spirits and of the necessity of keeping a strong christological focus were at the center of the many other criticisms that the opening presentations received during and after the assembly. The heated debate generated by Canberra moved the World Council of Churches to deal with renewed energy with the issue of gospel and culture. The WCC started a thorough international study process in preparation for the next conference on world mission and evangelism, to be held in Salvador, Brazil, in 1996, with the title: "Called to One Hope: the Gospel in Diverse Cultures." The process aimed to involve mission agencies, local congregations and church leadership as equal partners to offer a broader framework within which syncretism could be studied and discussed.

The preparatory guide for the Salvador conference presented syncretism as a term with a long history of negative connotations, but which was now being re-evaluated and understood also in positive terms. It said that at times in the syncretic process the integrity of the gospel might be lost, but that in many other cases this very process might help people to have a richer and more authentic understanding of it. The study guide also made a reference to the issue of the use of power, naming the history of Western missionary colonialism:

> At times, vested interests have been legitimized in the name of the authority of the church. Through the use of power or position within the church, sexism and racism have been condoned. Those in power have often been quick to pronounce expressions of the gospel by and among the poor as heresy and syncretism. Hence the question regarding the nature of the teaching authority of the church is raised: when there is a conflict between two interpretations of a biblical text or a doctrine, who decides? Because power in intercultural encounter is often misused to dominate, oppress and humiliate, the ground must be cleared before communication can take place.[13]

---

[12] "Reflections of Orthodox Participants," in: Kinnamon (ed.), *Signs of the Spirit*, 279-282.

[13] *Preparatory Papers for Section Work Conference on World Mission and Evangelism, Salvador, Bahia, Brazil 1996* (WCC Publications: Geneva 1996), 72.

In the beginning of 1994 I started working on the WCC gospel and culture study process for Church World Service and Witness-NCC in New York City. I thus had the experience of becoming familiar not only with the "official discussion," but also with what could be defined as the "subtext" of the process: all the thoughts and positions that, for different reasons, never made it into the official documents of the study. I came to consider this raw knowledge to be as important as the information I could cull from papers and official statements.

At the Salvador conference, there was strong criticism of the attention that the ecumenical movement was paying to the issue. Very interestingly, this criticism came from opposite quarters. Western church delegates were worried that the WCC was "glamorizing" syncretism, which, they felt, should instead be considered the greatest perennial threat to Christianity. On the other hand, many Third World delegates informally expressed their concern that the focus on syncretism was a way not to struggle with much more important and controversial issues like social justice, North-South relationships and racism. Indigenous delegates often protested against what they saw as a patronizing attitude of Western Christianity in considering their traditional faiths as "seeds of revelation" instead of fully grown trees in their own right. Spanish-speaking delegates felt cut off from the discussion because they were not offered an adequate translation system. They walked out in protest from my subgroup on syncretism because the documents to be discussed had not been translated into Spanish: an apparently minor organizational detail with serious political implications. The discussion within my own subgroup strongly polarized Europeans and White North-Americans and Third World representatives. German representatives often referred to the example of Nazi Germany to illustrate the dangers of syncretism. Eastern European Orthodox representatives were extremely vocal in their condemnation of syncretism and on the necessity to distinguish the Holy Spirit from the spirits of the world, often breaking into lectures about the history of dogmatic controversies. Third World representatives and indigenous minorities felt so patronized and disillusioned by the debate that they stopped talking at all. In my discussion group, I eventually stood out as the only white person advocating an understanding of syncretism as natural and pointing out the power relationships that are played out in the definition of syncretism itself. Several people thanked me for it, but also expressed a profound disappointment for the present and the future of the debate. Our final report then went through such a radical process of "revision" in the hands of some Conference organizers that at the end we could barely recognize it.

This experience highlights an important problem in the study processes of the WCC: what can be read in the final reports of a conference is not necessarily the best representation of what the discussions and the power struggles were really about. For instance, the final Conference Message included the following statements:

> We have recognized the caution of Christians in Germany about being too ready to see God's spirit in all human cultures, growing out of their painful memories of how the churches risked becoming captive to Nazi ideology in a previous generation. We have heard how the churches, against the post-modern culture influencing much of Western Europe, are studying the phenomenon of secularism and engaging those turning from traditional faith and seemingly seeking a private "pick and mix" spirituality.[14]

These statements are certainly representative of the concerns of some of the Western participants at the conference. The problem is they represent only a small group and that that other voices and perspectives are not presented. Furthermore, they misrepresent the situation: German churches did not "risk becoming captive to Nazi ideology;" they had indeed become captive. While I agree that this example illustrates a type of this kind of "death-giving" syncretism, I think that Europeans tend to present it to people from other continents in a way that shows both their paternalism and their narrow understanding of other people's faiths and cultures. The use of this example also witnesses to a certain lack of self-awareness within Western Christianity: it is so worried about preventing other sisters and brothers from committing fatal mistakes, but is in fact itself extremely prone to syncretize with life-denying beliefs, as its heritage so clearly demonstrates.

The report on the Gospel and Culture Study Process (Hearing on Unit II) offered at the Harare 8th ecumenical conference in the month of December 1998 stated:

> Among its contributions to the development of mission thinking and practice were that the conference "moved forward" in its understanding of culture and in viewing religion as integral to it. While affirming the necessity of a positive approach to culture, the conference spoke repeatedly of the ambiguity of each culture. Culture can and must be challenged, particularly in relation to its life-denying elements.[15]

[14] "The Conference Message," in: *International Review of Mission* 86/340-341 (January/April 1997), 7-11, here 9-10.
[15] "Gospel and Culture: Hearing On Unit II," in: *Assembly Workbook: Harare 1998* (WCC Publications: Geneva 1998), 46-49, here 49.

On the one hand, one might applaud the fact that the ecumenical movement has finally broadened its horizons in respect to the issue of gospel and culture. On the other, the report continues with a reference to syncretism that I find quite ambiguous and disturbing:

> There was equally strong affirmation of the need and right to live out and celebrate the faith according to each culture, and a tacit recognition that any inculturation is to some extent syncretistic. Salvador discussed criteria for discerning the work of God's Spirit in cultures and appealed for the elimination of aggressive practices against indigenous spiritualities.[16]

First of all, the term syncretism is used once again in opposition to inculturation, an understanding that was strongly challenged during the whole study process. In fact, this statement seems in a way to represent a step backwards from Salvador, and not forwards. Secondly, I find the expression "to some extent" quite troubling: it once again implies that there might be a sort of "hierarchy of syncretism," where some expressions of faith are less "syncretic" and thus more pure than others. The use of the expression "tacit recognition" is also problematic, as it implies that an agreement can be made without deliberation, in virtual silence. Finally, the Harare report statement does not make any reference to the power dimension that characterizes the whole controversy on syncretism, which was a major point of discussion at Salvador. In fact, the report does not address power dynamics at all in its affirmation of the need to discern some criteria to define the work of the Spirit; thus it fails to acknowledge one of the major learnings of the study process and of the Salvador Conference.

At the eighth ecumenical assembly, held in Harare in December of 1998, the debate over syncretism did not have an official slot, but it was interwoven with many aspects of the event.[17] Some representatives at the conference were allegedly offended by the presence of Korean theologian Chung Hyun Kyung, whose keynote address in Canberra had caused such scandal in parts of the ecumenical movement. Chung was a visitor at the Harare assembly, and participated in the Decade Festival, held immediately before the Assembly, which was organized to mark the conclusion of the Ecumenical Decade of Churches in Solidarity with Women. At the Decade Festival, Chung led a healing service drawing on indigenous Korean spiritual traditions during a

---

[16] Ibid., 49.
[17] The theme of the conference was "Turn to God – Rejoice in Hope."

hearing about violence against women. In an interview with ENI during the assembly, Chung addressed the "syncretism" controversy:

> The Orthodox Church talks about my presentation as syncretism, but when I look at them and the German theologians who criticized me, they are as syncretistic as I am, only our ingredients are different... I made it very clear, I said: "Yes, I am a syncretist, I know where I am coming from." I think that any Christianity which is meaningful, which is incarnated in a specific people's history, is sure to be syncretistic... Christianity has to be relevant, otherwise it becomes a museum piece. Who wants to see a museum piece? If we want to see something alive today, it should be incarnated in a real context.[18]

In the same interview Chung also said that humanity was called to defy "5000 years of patriarchy," linking the question of who has the right to define Christianity to the question of who has the right to define women's realities. I think these two questions should always be posed at the same time. For instance, this twofold question could have been posed to the different sides involved in a controversial debate at the Harare conference. I will use this example as a case study to conclude this section on the discussion over the ecumenical movement, pointing out the importance of naming the power dimension of each theological debate.

At the Harare assembly, eight churches were to be evaluated for WCC membership. All applications were accepted except the one by the Celestial Church of Christ: its membership was denied for the time being and the discussion postponed.[19] The Celestial Church of Christ is an indigenous African church established in Nigeria after the Second World War; until 1986, it admitted polygamous clergy, in that it allowed clergy who lived in polygamous unions before that date to continue to do so, because the church did not condone divorce. According to Densen Mafinyani, general secretary of the Zimbabwe Council of Churches (ZCC) – who urged the World Council of Churches to accept Celestial Church of Christ as a member of the WCC – polygamy was not a problem for local churches in Africa, and many church leaders are polygamous:

> This is not a problem for the local churches. These leaders are accepted in their churches, their followers accept the cultural dimension where the tribal headman

---

[18] Stephen Brown, "Korea's controversial feminist theologian has 'no regrets'," ENI-98-0560, Harare, 7 December 1998.

[19] Noel Bruyns, "Accept polygamy as an African tradition," ENI-98-0580, Harare, 12 December 1998.

had more than one wife. The local churches see nothing wrong with this… Can the WCC please open a door where the African spirituality can be rediscovered? We don't want our Christian faith to be limited by the mindset of Europe, where it came from, a theology too narrow to accommodate what God has done with Africans long before the missionaries came – those missionaries who threw out our ancient religious experiences and sacred beliefs as pagan.[20]

This example well illustrates the complexity of the debate. In a world still shaped by Western supremacy and imperialism, who decides what faithful Christianity is? Where do the criteria come from? On the other hand, in a world characterized by "5000 years of patriarchy," who are the ones who determine culture and gender roles?[21] In the example of the Celestial Church of Christ, issues of Western supremacy and sexism seem to me to be strictly intertwined. In my view, both the WCC and the Celestial Church of Christ positions need to be viewed with critical eyes. Furthermore, the voices of women within the Celestial Church of Christ need to be listened to. What is the "good news" for them?[22] To be "freed" from a traditional, sexist custom,

---

[20]  Ibid.

[21]  The WCC, an organization formed and strongly shaped by Western Protestant liberals, refused to accept the membership of this church as part of its ethical stand in regard to marriage. The WCC's position could be explained as part of a strong concern for women's rights. However, I detect a certain level of inconsistency in this discussion. I am certainly suspicious and critical of a society that allows polygamy but not polyandry, thus granting a particular status to its male members. However, if respect for women's rights and equal status were really a criterion for belonging to the WCC, very few churches, if any, would be members. The WCC must, therefore, really be concerned, not for women, but with cultural norms of marriage. It seems ironical to me that other gross violations of human rights, such as the endorsement of economical structures that produce suffering and oppression, are not being addressed as membership criteria. This decision seems to reflect a Western-oriented understanding of what is "ethically" faithful to the gospel, and a very biased list of priorities.

[22]  For an interesting analysis of the controversy over the African custom of polygamy see Mercy Amba Oduyoye's chapter on "Marriage and Patriarchy" in Mercy Amba Oduyoye (ed.), *Daughters of Anowa: African Women and Patriarchy* (Orbis: Maryknoll, NY 1995), 131-153. Oduyoye states: "The challenge for me lies in the critical assessment of the meaning of marriage, not only in Africa but throughout the world where the institution is in crisis. Both churches and governments are unable to regulate their most intimate yet public of institutions. It is not whether a marriage is polygynous or monogamous that defines the status of women; rather it is the dependence and domination mentalities of the women and men sharing marriage that need transformation. Above all, I feel that real change will come about when women can say – with or without husbands, with or without children – that the most important fact is that women are human and will find fullness in reaching for goals that we set for ourselves" [146-147].

even when this "freedom" entails being left without support and resources when their husband, forced into monogamy, has to decide for one of his wives? Is the Western model of monogamy inherently more liberating for women, and thus more faithful to the gospel, than polygamy? My hope for the future of the ecumenical movement is that it can learn to ask these questions officially, moving away from universalizing answers to an attitude that takes the reality of human suffering as its main concern. As James H. Cone states:

> The particularity of human existence is important when one begins to speak of Christ's relation to culture. For Christ's relation to culture is not defined in cultural generalities but in terms of the concreteness of human pain and suffering.[23]

## Of Myths, Monsters and the Emperor's Clothes

Whose problem is syncretism? Perhaps it is the problem of the White males who invented it. The faith of people from all over the world and from very different religious backgrounds witnesses to the fact that while the very idea of syncretism is completely alien to them, the process of incorporating and harmonizing beliefs flows very naturally from the reality of life itself. In many contexts, as Chung Hyun Kyung powerfully asserts, syncretism is seen not as an issue but simply as a reality:

> In their struggle for survival and liberation in this unjust women-hating world, poor Asian women have approached many different religious sources for sustenance and empowerment. What matters for them is not doctrinal orthodoxy. Male leaders of the institutional church always seem preoccupied with the doctrinal purity of their religions. What matters to Asian women is survival and the liberation of themselves and their communities. What matters for them is not Jesus, Sakyamumi, Mohammed, Confucius, Kwan In, or Ina, but rather the life force which empowers them to claim their humanity.[24]

In many ways, the issue of syncretism is a Western, male created monster, a myth about what constitutes "normativity" that has generated or is related to a multitude of other myths. I see the naming and uncovering of such myths as essential to my vocation as a theologian, for I believe that while people create myths, myths also shape people. This is the reason for my interest in this mythical beast, which does not exist and yet has really harmed innumerable

---

[23] James H. Cone, *God of the Oppressed* (Orbis: Maryknoll, NY 1975, 1997), 82.
[24] Chung Hyun Kyung, *Struggle To Be the Sun Again: Introducing Asian Women's Theology* (Orbis: Maryknoll, 1990), 113.

people. I have already pointed out some of the myths that surround syncretism, such as the existence of an original, "pure," orthodox form of Christianity that has been adulterated by the incorporation of other beliefs. Unfortunately, it does not seem to me that anyone has really been able to define
with any integrity where and when this pristine Christianity existed. Furthermore, this myth idealizes cohesion and purity as normative and superior to
any form of mixing or "bastardization."[25]

Another myth related to syncretism is the Western belief that culture and
religion are totally different entities, and that it is therefore possible to separate gospel and culture. In this framework, religion is understood as a particular aspect or part of human life, and not as a dimension permeating life and
coming out of life itself. This position is constantly challenged by the voices
of Third World and indigenous people. For instance, the Final Statement of
the Fifth EATWOT Conference (New Delhi, August 17-29, 1981) states:

> Culture is the foundation of the creativity and way of life of a people. It is the basis
> and bond of their collective identity. It expresses their worldview, their conception
> of the meaning of human existence and destiny, and their idea of God. It includes
> the historical manifestations of the people's creativity, such as their language, arts,
> social organization, philosophy, religion, and theology itself. Thus religion is cul-
> turally conditioned.[26]

From this perspective, everything human is a source of culture, and nothing
human can exist outside of culture. Therefore, even religion is necessarily
shaped by culture. According to Leonardo Boff, religion is the soul of culture
itself, as it tries to gather, elaborate and ritualize the cultural response to transcendence and the question about ultimate meaning.[27] Along these lines,
Ghanaian theologian Mercy Amba Oduyoye states that: "...religion is the
deepest element in African living culture."[28] Aloysius Pieris points out the
same reality when describing Asian spirituality: "In our context, religion is

---

[25] In Western cultures the term "bastard," used to define someone born outside a traditional
marriage, has a very negative connotation.

[26] "The Irruption of the Third World: Challenge to Theology: Final Statement of the Fifth EAT-
WOT Conference, New Delhi, August 17-29, 1981," in: Virginia Fabella / Sergio Torres
(eds.), *Irruption of the Third World: Challenge to Theology* (Maryknoll, NY: Orbis 1983),
191-206, here 200.

[27] Leonardo Boff, *New Evangelization: Good News to the Poor* (Orbis: Maryknoll, NY 1991),
21.

[28] Mercy Amba Oduyoye, *Hearing and Knowing: Theological reflections on Christianity in
Africa* (Orbis: Maryknoll, NY 1986), 54.

life itself rather than a function of it, being the all-pervasive ethos of human existence. This is even more true of tribal religion, which often overlaps with 'culture'."[29] Pieris also highlights the tendency to squeeze religion out of human existence by way of sacralization and secularization as typical of Western tradition. He criticizes Richard Niebuhr's approach to culture in *Christ and Culture* on the basis that it divides culture from religion, "an academic pastime that has bred confusion into the West."[30] Thinking of culture and religion in these terms helps us to unmask another popular Christian myth, that defines "inculturation" as a faithful embodiment of the gospel and likes to oppose it to syncretism, seen as an illegitimate and superficial process. As Boff notes, if we say that the gospel must be inculturated we presuppose that there is such a thing as a gospel-in-itself, a gospel outside culture:

> This familiar jargon suggests that there is such a thing as a gospel-in-itself, endowed with an intrinsic power to fertilize the various cultures. Actually, this is not the case. The gospel is never naked. It is always culturally clothed. The fact that revelation and the gospel have been codified in Western Jewish and Christian cultures, and that the Bible is the inspired book (it remains to define precisely in what dogmatic sense this should be taken) does not mean that its cultural expression participates in the irreformable essence of the gospel and revelation. We must say that every cultural expression not only assumes the gospel, but it restricts it as well. It concretizes it, but it limits it as well.[31]

Another Western myth is that syncretism is only someone else's problem: the problem of feminist spirituality, of the popular religiosity of "uneducated and superstitious people," or of "ethnic" people, or of Third World Christians. As Mercy Amba Oduyoye points out:

> The word "syncretism" has become a bogey word, used to frighten all who would venture to do theology in the context of other worldview and religions. But is syncretism not in fact a positive and unavoidable process? Christian theology and practice have always interacted with the religious and philosophical presuppositions of the various periods. Practices like the observance of Sunday, distribution of Easter eggs, and the festival of the Nile in the medieval Coptic church are instances of the acculturation of Christianity.[32]

---

[29] Aloysius Pieris, "The Place of Non-Christian Religions and Cultures in the Evolution of Third World Theology," in: Fabella / Torres (eds), *Irruption of the Third World*, 113-139, here 117.

[30] Pieris, "The Place of Non-Christian Religions," 131.

[31] Boff, *New Evangelization*, 31-32.

[32] Mercy Amba Oduyoye, "The Value of African Religious Beliefs and Practices for Christian Theology," in: Kofi Appiah-Kubi / Sergio Torres (eds), *African Theology En Route: Papers*

This attitude of Western theologians reminds me of the Latin phrase "Hic Sunt Leones," which was written on ancient maps just under the coast of Northern Africa. "Hic Sunt Leones" means "Here there are lions." For the ancient Romans, what was unknown to them and was not under their power was just wilderness. It was impossible to imagine that outside boundaries of the Empire and the reach of its ideology culture and knowledge could exist. There could only be beasts, wild and dangerous ones. It seems to me that today Western Christians often do just the same thing. The term "syncretism" is a modern version of "Hic Sunt Leones."

As if we were playing with Russian dolls, as we begin to open up this belief we discover another popular myth: that Western Christianity somehow has a better understanding of what the gospel is about. Therefore, Western Christians have a tendency to feel called to warn what they call the "younger churches" in the Eastern and Southern hemispheres against the threat of syncretism. This patronizing and racist attitude is well depicted by Emmanuel Martey when describing his African context: "Veritably, for the 'parent Church of Europe,' Africa is still an infant which must be spoon-fed theologically."[33] Chung Hyun Kyung wittily underlines Western assumptions regarding Christianity:

> Traditional Western theologians seem to say to us that they have the copyright on Christianity: "All rights reserved – no part of our teaching may be reproduced in any form without our permission."[34]

From a Western feminist perspective, I entirely subscribe to Chung's view, highlighting the patriarchal nature of the Western tradition criticized by liberation theologians.

Another popular Christian myth is that the Bible, namely the Old Testament, very clearly condemns syncretism. As religious historian Anton Wessels points out, Western theologians like to shake a remonstrating finger at their brothers and sisters in Asia and Africa, reminding them of the Old Testament opposition to Canaanite cults. But many of these Western theologians are themselves unaware of their own presuppositions in reading the Bible itself. Thus, according to Wessels, scholars often overlook the fact that the

*from the Pan-African Conference of Third World Theologians, December 17-23, 1977, Accra, Ghana* (Orbis: Maryknoll, NY 1979), 109-116, here 114.

[33] Emmanuel Martey, *African Theology: Inculturation and Liberation* (Orbis: Maryknoll, NY 1996), 66.

[34] Chung, *Struggle To Be the Sun Again*, 113.

cult of Yahweh is dependent on Canaanite culture and religion. Although the prophets Elijah and Hosea radically refuse certain aspects of both El and Baal, they also adopt certain aspects of their cults. The Jewish Scriptures never speak negatively of God when called El. Wessels points out that scholars have widely acknowledged the fact that the Old Testament was shaped also by cultural and literary Canaanitc influences. But he asks: "Is it possible to speak only of literary influence on the Old Testament by the mythology of fertility, without any concomitant influence in the area of 'dogmatics'?"[35] And he goes on to underline the fact that the faith of Israel has a history which crystallized from a long process of mutual interchange with its Canaanite environment. The religion of Israel is thus the result of a process of give and take. Furthermore, I greatly appreciate Wessels' attempt to show the parallels between the formation of the cult of Yahweh and the formation of truly contextualized forms of African and Asian Christianity:

> ...we ought to operate more cautiously than is sometimes the case, in my opinion, when evaluating the contributions of Asian and Africans to theology. One ought not to reject syncretism with a simple appeal to Elijah's example. In the Old Testament Yahwism, there was apparently a place for a "yea-saying attitude" toward Canaanite culture, as well for condemnation, thus providing a place for authentic contextualization.[36]

I have often wondered whether the whole debate about syncretism was not, even on an unconscious level, a means of diverting attention away from other unsettling issues that should occupy churches instead, such as racism, world poverty, militarism, North-South relations, sexism, homophobia. I think that this is certainly the case. But more often that not this debate serves also to impose an issue that is not at all universal. For most Western churches this question is of great importance, since they are generally still more worried about the "orthodoxy" of disembodied beliefs than about the suffering of people around the world. For many churches in the Third World the issue is important because Western missionaries told them so.

This controversy is also related to the concept of the Patriarchal Western "norm." My study on the issue of syncretism as discussed within the ecumenical movement leads me to feel like the child who looks at the pompous

---

[35] Anton Wessels, "Biblical Presuppositions for and Against Syncretism," in: Gort / Vroom / Fernhout / Wessels (eds), *Dialogue and Syncretism*, 52-65, here 53.
[36] Ibid., 64.

king parading in his imaginary garments and exclaims: "The King is naked!" For me, the king is the Western traditional characterization of syncretism as something negative, as a mingling of beliefs and practices which adulterates the purity of faith. In my assessment of the latest phases of the discussion, this approach is all but fully surpassed. To be like the child in the story for me means to put oneself in the position of looking at the king and his followers, and seeing through their hypocrisy, vanity, self-centeredness and pretenses. To be like a child means to unmask the royal power game pointing out its obviousness. It also means to name the sexist and racist nature of the assumptions that undergird the king's mentality. Using another children's story as an example, Elizabeth Kamarck Minnich argues that people in the Western world have come to be like the ducks in Hans Christian Andersen's tale of "The Ugly Duckling":

> …we have come to believe that one "kind" of human (one kind of fowl in Andersen's story) was the generic kind, the inclusive kind, the representative and normative and ideal-setting kind. … Like the ducks, then, some few of our species judged others not just somewhat in some regard different, but "ugly", lesser, odd, deviant… From the perspective of standards set for ducks, a young swan can only be judged "ugly." From the perspective of European "civilization," other civilizations came to be called "cultures" and adjudged "primitive," "irrational," "undeveloped."[37]

It seems to me that the debate surrounding syncretism is really a debate about who has the power to monopolize and define the gospel. It might well be the swan song of a dying Western Patriarchal Christianity struggling against its loss of centrality in the Christian body. Truth claims have always been used as power tools: those who define truth retain power. To prevent people from affirming their own truth is to keep them powerless.

## From Apologetics to Struggle for Life: the Importance of Defining Life-Centered Syncretism

I see the process of creating syncretic rituals and belief systems as being similar to cooking, an act that as a Mediterranean woman I view with the greatest respect since it not only insures survival, but can have a fundamental role in fostering socialization and dialogue. When you cook, you put different

---

[37] Elizabeth Kamarck Minninh, "If You Want Truth, Work for Justice: Some Reflections on Partiality versus Particularity in Relation to Universality," in: David A. Hoekema / Bobby Fong (eds.), *Christianity and Culture in the Crossfire* (Eerdmans: Grand Rapids, MI 1997), 95-112, here 96-97.

ingredients together. They may completely blend together in an all-new creation, or they may keep their different colors, texture and tastes. The final result may be a good dish that nourishes you for the journey ahead. Or you may end up with a wonderful looking dish that poisons you, or that does not give you the essential elements your body needs. Furthermore, one dish can fully nourish one person, and be unappealing and also indigestible to another.

Syncretic processes are always in motion, in every expression of faith. The gospel is always culturally clothed, just as nourishment is not an abstract idea and does not exist apart from fruits, grains and vegetables. Syncretism is not necessarily positive or negative, it just is: it is a process. It can help us to discover what is liberating in each culture, thus enabling us to "taste" the gospel in many new forms and giving us liberation and life in abundance. However, it can also lead us to worship realities that are oppressive and death-giving. If syncretism should not be demonized, it should not be romanticized either. The danger of adopting a mainly apologetic stance when talking about syncretism could lead us to overlook the fact that all cultures and spiritualities need to be "tested" by the liberating message of the gospel, because they all have the potential to be ambiguously life-denying and oppressive. We cannot accept uncritically any culture or belief system. James Cone has taught us to ask about whose culture we are really speaking about when we speak of culture. In his critique of H. Richard Niebuhr's categorizations in *Christ and Culture*, Cone states:

> When the scriptural witness to divine revelation is examined, it cannot be said that Christ has the *same* attitude toward all cultural expressions. Indeed the message of the Exodus, prophets, and Jesus' life and death is the proclamation of God's decisive partiality toward the struggles of the unfree. Therefore, if we are to understand Christ's relation to culture, we had better be clear about whose human strivings we speak of, the oppressed or the oppressors.[38]

Which kind of syncretism would best serve the purpose of proclaiming "good news to the poor"? Indian theologian M.M. Thomas advocated a Christ-centered syncretism, or a "syncretism with a sense of Christian direction."[39] Since I find the definition of "Christ-centered" to be problematic in

---

[38] Cone, *God of the Oppressed*, 83.

[39] M.M. Thomas, "The Absoluteness of Jesus Christ and Christ-centered Syncretism," in: *The Ecumenical Review* 37 (1985), 392. It is a convention not to spell out Indian names. It is the fruit of colonization, I think, but it still a convention. M.M., used by the author himself and all who quote him, stands for Madathilparampil M.

many respects,[40] I prefer Chung's definition of "survival-liberation centered syncretism":[41]

> I want to name my mothers' distinctive spirituality as "survival-liberation-centered syncretism." The heart of their spirituality was the life power that sustained and liberated them. "Life-giving power" is the final criterion by which the validity of any religion is judged.[42]

I would argue for the more user-friendly definition of "life-giving syncretism," taking survival and liberation to be the main characteristics of what life is about. How do we go about defining what life-giving syncretism is? After my severe criticism of the assumptions and power dynamics undergirding the traditional definitions of syncretism, I might find myself at a loss to elaborate any criteria. However, in a world torn apart by violence and oppression, quite often perpetrated in the name of religions or with their consent, I believe that a totally laissez-faire relativism has the potential to be harmful and shameful. As a theologian, I am convinced that self-criticism of the imperialistic tendencies of my Western heritage needs to be held in tension with a call to responsibility for humanity as a whole. As Mercy Amba Oduyoye states, "we are humans because we are jointly responsible with others for what happens to our community."[43]

I therefore claim the importance of formulating some tentative criteria to define life-giving syncretism. I strongly believe in the need to move beyond an apologetic or "romantic" attitude towards syncretism to a creative definition of what life-giving syncretism is, so that we might struggle to implement it in our communities of faith. The tentative criteria that I have developed are offered for further discussion and elaboration, in a continuous process of dialogue. Furthermore, while I recognize that they come from what could be seen as the limited perspective of a White Protestant European, they are not made in isolation. They are my own elaboration of the learning gained by listening to the voices of people coming from different faith perspectives and social and geographical locations. In particular, they are the fruits of learning from the

---

[40] For instance, it can be interpreted as just a new form of Christian imperialism.

[41] Chung, *Struggle To Be the Sun Again*, 113.

[42] Chung Hyun Kyung, "Following Naked Dancing and Long Dreaming," in: Letty M. Russell / Kwok Pui-Lan / Ada Maria Isasi-Diaz / Katie Geneva Cannon (eds.), *Inheriting Our Mothers' Gardens: Feminist Theology in Third World Perspective* (The Westminster Press: Louisville 1988), 54-72, here 67.

[43] Oduyoye, *Hearing and Knowing*, 110.

theological wisdom and struggles of women from Asia and Africa, who point out that no culture or context is yet fully liberated, and whose voices and pleas have profoundly shaped this paper. The witness of Asian and African women speaks clearly to those Christian theologians who still think the spirit of God should be discerned in terms of orthodoxy versus heresy, as they point out the importance of orthopraxis, and of discerning life-giving syncretism by its fruits. Asian and African women use their own lives, their own experience of suffering to discern the godliness of their beliefs and practices: their experience of liberation and healing is the measure by which these are judged. Chung defines this as an "epistemology from the broken body."[44]

As I fully own up to the limitations present in the following and final part of this essay, I claim that any truly liberating elements come from larger and diversified communities. Returning to my metaphor of cooking, I will spell out the ingredients of a life-giving syncretic meal. In my vision, each community will have to find the recipes that best nourish the people in their midst. Each community will also be in touch with others in order to exchange ideas, critical comments and suggestions. Local ingredients will be preferred, as some ideas, like food, might change their flavours and nutritive values when exported. In some cases, appropriation of other people's recipes against their will should be regarded as stealing.[45] In my recommendation, I will speak of "beliefs/practices" instead of "beliefs and practices" to avoid a typical Western split, for, as Mercy Amba Oduyoye points out, many cultures do not make a distinction between religious beliefs and cultural practices. I therefore advocate the use of:
– beliefs/practices that promote the integrity of all bodies, and in particular of the bodies that have been traditionally abused by many world religions: the bodies of women and children;[46]

---

[44] Chung, *Struggle To Be the Sun Again*, 104.

[45] For instance, the Western "pillaging" of Native American spirituality in order to recreate their lost sense of the divine has often been strongly criticized by Native American communities and theologians.

[46] Asian and African women often share another painful reality: the abuse of their bodies, perpetuated in the name of patriarchal traditions and religions, colonialism, capitalistic economy and militaristic culture. The list of the acts of violence perpetuated against women is painfully endless, from clitoridectomy rituals and other forms of genital mutilation, to sex tourism, to torture exercised as an instrument to retain political power, to mass rapes, to the custom of Sati, where Indian widows are forced to die on their husbands' funeral pyres. Even when women are not killed or mutilated, they are quite often the victims of cultures that see their bodies as unholy and polluted, or as mere sexual or reproductive objects. Even when women survive the acts of violence perpetuated against them, their self esteem and self-respect are

- beliefs/practices that empower people to liberate themselves from abuse and oppression, instead of passively accepting it in the name of a higher good or awaiting a better time;
- beliefs/practices that respect and promote the integrity of all creation, in a world where the earth is raped and destroyed every day;
- beliefs/practices that celebrate and promote life, thus assuring that every person has equal access to food, shelter, education, health care, work, decision making processes;
- beliefs/practices that promote and assure equal sharing of resources;
- beliefs/practices that affirm and celebrate the equal dignity and worth of each human being, without regard to gender, race, ethnic group, sexual orientation, age, ableism;
- beliefs/practices that refuse to accept the rights of some to oppress, violate, and exploit others, thus strongly accusing and fighting against any form of injustice;
- beliefs/practices that promote a peaceful and righteous resolution of conflicts;
- beliefs/practices that promote community building locally and globally;
- beliefs/practices that promote a welcoming of the stranger and an appreciation of the "other."

## Conclusion

African theologian Elizabeth Amoah introduced me to an Akan saying: "One person's hand is not enough to stretch across the face of God."[47] In a story that is very familiar to me, a Samaritan woman learns that in order to drink the water of life she does not have to drink from the well of her ancestors. My hope is that as Christians we will learn not to drink the stagnant and often poisoned water of colonialist and patriarchal wells, but to thirst for the water of life, wherever we find it, from whomever offers it to us.

often virtually annihilated. Indian theologian Crescy John defines these different realities as acts of "desacralization of the body." She sees the body as the temple of God's spirit, and denounces any attempt to treat women as something less then temples of God's spirit as contrary to God's will: see her "Women and the Holy Spirit: From an Indian Perspective," in: *Pro Mundi Vita Dossiers*, 39 (1986), 11-16. I myself would say that whenever women's bodies are desacralized, God and life themselves are profaned.

[47] Elizabeth Amoah, "A Living Spirituality Today," in: Kururilla Chrukava Abraham / Bernadette Mbuy-Beya (eds.), *Spirituality of the Third World: A Cry for Life. Papers and Reflections from the Third General Assembly of the Ecumenical Association of Third World Theologians, January, 1992, Nairobi, Kenya* (Orbis: Maryknoll, NY 1994), 50-54, here 53.

L'auteur examine la question du syncrétisme comme point de controverse dans le mouvement œcuménique ainsi que dans quelques églises particulières. Plusieurs évolutions ont contribué à la discussion actuelle: la fascination que quelques chrétiens éprouvent devant des formes de spiritualité de l'avant-christianisme ou hors-christianisme; les femmes qui s'opposent à la nature patriarcale des traditions chrétiennes et la prise de conscience croissante que la chrétienté a été liée au colonialisme et au génocide au cours de sa propagation dans le nouveau monde. La septième assemblée du COE à Canberra en 1991 a été un tournant concernant la confrontation entre la chrétienté et les aspirations des chrétiens du nouveau monde. Le discours fondamental de la théologienne coréenne Chung Hyun Kyung est l'expression d'une idée unique qui met en relation le saint esprit et les esprits des ancêtres (coréens) assoiffés de justice (*Han*). Quelques participants soutiennent l'idée que l'esprit divin, la troisième personne de la trinité, ne peut être identifié à l'esprit des ancêtres, d'autres demandent une concentration christologique plus intense. Le COE entama en 1994 un processus d'étude sur l'évangile et la culture. Chung adressa au COE la question suivante: "Qui a le droit de définir la chrétienté?" et "Qui a le droit de définir la réalité de la femme?" Pour certains la discussion implique que les églises non-européennes n'étaient pas crédibles sur le plan théologique, tandis que pour d'autres le débat à propos du syncrétisme empêchait le COE d'aboutir à la justice sociale. L'auteur conclut que le syncrétisme est un processus combinatoire de thèmes comme la libération et la survie semblables aux elements qui constituent l'art de cuisiner.

Die Autorin untersucht die Frage des Synkretismus als ein strittiges Problem innerhalb der ökumenischen Bewegung sowie in bestimmten Kirchen. Verschiedene Entwicklungen haben zur gegenwärtigen Diskussion beigetragen: da ist zum einen die Faszination von ChristInnen für vor- und außerchristliche Formen der Spiritualität; da sind Frauen, die den patriarchalen Charakter der christlicher Tradition aufzeigen; nicht zuletzt gibt es ein wachsendes Bewusstsein dafür, wie das Christentum mit Kolonialismus und Völkermord verknüpft war, als es sich außerhalb der westlichen Hemisphäre verbreitete. Die 7. Vollversammlung des Ökumenischen Rates in Canberra 1991 wurde zu einem Wendepunkt in der Auseinandersetzung des westlichen Christentums mit den Erwartungen von ChristInnen in nichtwestlichen Kulturen. Die bahnbrechende Präsentation der koreanischen Theologin Chung Hyung Kyung drückte ihr Verständnis des Heiligen Geistes aus, den sie in den von "Han" erfüllten Geistern ihrer Heimat mit ihrem Schrei nach Gerechtigkeit verkörpert fand. Einige der Teilnehmenden meinten, dass der Heilige Geist als die dritte Person der Trinität nicht mit den Geistern der Vorfahren identifiziert werden könnte, andre wünschten sich einen stärkeren christologischen Bezug. Chungs Rede auf der Vollversammlung des Ökumenischen Rates in Harare 1998 verknüpft die Frage danach, wer das Recht hat, das Christentum richtig zu definieren, mit der Frage, wer sich das Recht nehme, die Lebenswirklichkeit von

Frauen zu bestimmen. Für einige implizierte dies zugleich die Auffassung, dass den außereuropäischen christlichen Kirchen die eigenständige theologische Arbeit nicht zugetraut würde. Andere dagegen sahen darin die Absicht, den Ökumenischen Rat von der Frage nach der sozialen Gerechtigkeit abzulenken. Die Autorin schließt jedoch mit der Überzeugung, dass Synkretismus als ein fortwährender Prozess zu verstehen sei, in dem die lebensdienlichen Elemente einer Kultur, ähnlich wie im Vorgang des Kochens, zu einer spirituellen Kraft des Überlebens und der Befreiung werden können.

*Gabriella Lettini* is a graduate of the Waldensian Theological Seminary in Rome and a minister of the Waldensian Church in Italy. She holds a Master of Philosophy from Union Theological Seminary in New York City, where she is writing her Ph.D. dissertation. Since 1995 she has been an Ecumenical Associate at Jan Hus Presbyterian Church in NYC. She has worked at Church World Service and Witness – NCC USA as a researcher on the Gospel and Culture Study Project of the WCC. She is the author of *Omosessualità* [Homosexuality] (Torino: Claudiana), 1999.

*Judith Hartenstein / Silke Petersen*

# Zur Übersetzung von Texten aus dem Johannesevangelium in "gerechte Sprache"
# Anmerkungen zu einem schwierigen Projekt

## 1. Das Projekt

Die Übersetzung von Texten aus dem Johannesevangelium gehört zu einem Projekt, Texte für Gottesdienste in gerechter Sprache vorzulegen, das von zwei evangelischen PfarrerInnen herausgegeben wird.[1] Nach zwei Bänden mit Gebeten für normale Sonntagsgottesdienste und Kasualien und einem Band mit Psalmübertragungen soll ein letzter Band Lesungs- und Predigttexte in neuer Übersetzung bieten. Enthalten sind die Texte der sechs Perikopenreihen der Evangelischen Kirche in Deutschland (alttestamentliche, Evangeliums- und Epistellesung sowie weitere Predigttexte für die Sonntage im Kirchenjahr), Wochensprüche, Lesungstexte für Kasualien sowie Texte aus zwei neuen Perikopenreihen.

Aufgabe der Übersetzungen ist es, patriarchale Fehlübersetzungen zu beseitigen und in den Texten vorkommende Frauen sichtbar zu machen. Die Lebenswirklichkeit von Frauen und Männern soll deutlich werden, ohne dabei diskriminierende Klischees zu verwenden. Eine einseitig männliche Festlegung des Gottesbildes soll vermieden werden. Auch bei anderen benachteiligten Gruppen und insbesondere im Verhältnis zu Israel und zum Judentum ist eine würdige und gerechte Darstellung anzustreben.

Die Texte sind für die gottesdienstliche Praxis bestimmt, in vielen Fällen für eine Verlesung ohne weitere Erläuterungen. Deshalb sollten sie einerseits sprachlich gut verständlich sein, andererseits müssen exegetische Erkenntnisse schon in der Übersetzung selbst zum Ausdruck kommen. Die Verwendung im Gottesdienst bietet keinen Raum für eine differenzierte Betrachtung der Bibel als historisches Zeugnis, sondern soll die HörerInnen direkt und aktuell ansprechen.

---

[1] *Der gottesdienst. Liturgische Texte in gerechter Sprache*, hg. v. Hanne Köhler / Erhard Domay, 4 Bände (Gütersloher Verlag: Gütersloh 1997-2001).

Für das Übersetzungsprojekt wurden verschiedene ExegetInnen für einzelne Schriften bzw. mitunter auch nur für Abschnitte gewonnen. Wir haben die Texte aus dem Johannesevangelium (knapp zwei Drittel des gesamten Evangeliums) übernommen und dabei zwar die Texte unter uns aufgeteilt, uns aber abgesprochen und zusammengearbeitet. Im Gesamtprojekt fand dagegen relativ wenig Austausch und Absprache statt, eine Einheitlichkeit der Übersetzungsstile ist nicht angestrebt. Unsere Überlegungen gehen deshalb nur vom Johannesevangelium aus, lassen sich aber sicher auch auf andere biblische Schriften übertragen.

## 2. Vorüberlegungen

Die Bibel ist und wirkt an vielen Stellen frauendiskriminierend, in erzählenden ebenso wie in präskriptiven Texten, in Einzelheiten und Nebenaspekten wie in zentralen Aussagen. Außerdem besteht in weiten Teilen kein oder nur ein geringes Interesse an Frauen, ihre Sicht und ihre Lebenswirklichkeit kommen nicht vor. Daneben gibt es aber auch zahlreiche Texte, die – ob sie nun explizit von Frauen handeln oder nicht – Frauen zu allen Zeiten ermutigt und gestärkt haben. Beide Tendenzen lassen sich kaum je klar trennen, weder indem die einen von den anderen Texten, noch indem die "eigentliche" Botschaft von einer kulturell bedingten Einkleidung geschieden wird.

Es ist folglich mehr nötig als eine besonders korrekte oder auch freie Wiedergabe des Textes. Unsere Übertragung ist das Ergebnis eines Dialoges zwischen dem Bibeltext und heutigen, feministischen Frauen[2] sowie zwischen den verschiedenen Tendenzen in der Bibel selbst. Wir gehen mit unserem Interesse an Gerechtigkeit für Frauen – oder auch an Gerechtigkeit im Verhältnis zwischen der Kirche und Israel – an die Texte heran und stellen so bestimmte Aspekte an ihnen in den Vordergrund. Jeder Versuch, den Bibeltext für eine veränderte Zeit zur Sprache zu bringen, tritt in einen solchen Dialog mit ihm. Dabei besteht die Gefahr, die Grenze zum Neudichten zu überschreiten, aber auch die Chance, bisher unterbelichtete Züge neu zu entdecken.

Problematisch bleibt jedoch, dass eine Auseinandersetzung mit dem Text primär auf der sprachlichen Oberfläche stattfindet – möglicherweise werden tiefergehende Probleme so kosmetisch überdeckt. Antijüdische Pauschalisierungen ("die Juden") können vermieden werden, aber der grundlegendere Dualismus zwischen "Wir" und "Ihr" wird damit nicht beseitigt. Die μαθηταί in den

---

[2] Vgl. Claudia A. Camp, "Feminist Theological Hermeneutics: Canon and Christian Identity", in: Elisabeth Schüssler Fiorenza (ed.), *Searching the Scriptures*, Bd. 1: *A Feminist Introduction* (Crossroad: New York 1993), 154-171.

Abschiedsreden können sachlich angemessen als "Jüngerinnen und Jünger" übersetzt werden. Dadurch bekommt jedoch die Tatsache, dass nur Männer mit Namen genannt werden, ein zusätzliches Gewicht. Außerdem kommen im Gespräch vielleicht wirklich keine Anfragen und Anliegen von Frauen vor – dies zu erkennen wird durch die inklusive Übersetzung erschwert.

Zunächst stellt sich die vergleichsweise einfache Aufgabe, bei allen Gruppen zu entscheiden, ob Frauen als beteiligt gedacht sind, und dafür sprachliche Lösungen zu finden. Ein besonderes Problem ist die Bezeichnung "die Juden" (οἱ Ἰουδαῖοι) und die mit dieser Bezeichnung verbundene antijüdische Polemik im Johannesevangelium, die zwar aus der Situation des Evangeliums her erklärbar, aber als heutige gottesdienstliche Lesung ausgesprochen problematisch ist. Eine weitere Aufgabe ist es, für die Anrede, den Titel und die Gottesbezeichnung "Herr" (κύριος) weniger belastete Begriffe zu finden. Die größte Herausforderung einer geschlechtergerechten Übersetzung des Johannesevangeliums stellt schließlich die Metapher "Vater" (πατήρ) als Gottesbezeichnung dar, die extrem häufig und an theologisch zentralen Stellen vorkommt.

## 3. Probleme des Textes und Vorschläge zur Übersetzung

*a) Gruppenbezeichnungen und allgemeine Aussagen*

Im Johannesevangelium werden – wie im Griechischen und auch weithin im Deutschen üblich – Ausdrücke im Maskulinum Plural sowohl zur Bezeichnung von männlichen als auch von gemischt männlich-weiblichen Gruppen benutzt.[3] Oft sind in solchen Bezeichnungen Frauen selbstverständlich eingeschlossen, oft ist jedoch nicht eindeutig, ob auch Frauen gemeint sind, oder ob die jeweiligen AutorInnen sich schlicht keine Gedanken über diese Frage gemacht haben.

Wir haben zur Entscheidungsfindung einerseits den Kontext (die Verwendung der Begrifflichkeit innerhalb des Evangeliums) zu Rate gezogen, andererseits die historische Plausibilität des Vorkommens von Frauen in den jeweiligen Gruppen. Dabei reicht auch eine geringe Wahrscheinlichkeit für die Beteiligung von Frauen aus, um sie zu nennen. Die Beweislast liegt auf Seiten der Nichtbeteiligung von Frauen.[4]

---

[3] Vgl. Luise Pusch, *Das Deutsche als Männersprache. Aufsätze und Glossen zur feministischen Linguistik* (Suhrkamp: Frankfurt a.M. 1984).

[4] Vgl. Luise Schottroff, *Lydias ungeduldige Schwestern, Feministische Sozialgeschichte des frühen Christentums* (Kaiser: Gütersloh 1994), 59.128; Elisabeth Schüssler Fiorenza, *Brot statt Steine. Die Herausforderung einer feministischen Interpretation der Bibel* (Edition Exodus: Freiburg/Schweiz 1988), 52.

Eine rein männliche Gruppe liegt u.E. nur bei den Priestern und den Solda-
ten vor. Historische Belege gibt es für Pharisäerinnen, Prophetinnen, Hirtin-
nen, Fischerinnen, Zöllnerinnen, Königinnen und viele andere.[5] Bei der
Gruppe der JüngerInnen rechnet das Johannesevangelium wohl auch mit
Frauen, denn diese Gruppe ist kein auf die Zwölf begrenzter Kreis, sondern
inhaltlich durch ein bestimmtes Verhältnis zu Jesus definiert, das Frauen wie
Männer zeigen.[6]

Sprachlich haben wir die Einbeziehung von Frauen meist durch die Ver-
doppelung der Bezeichnung (Jüngerinnen und Jünger, Pharisäerinnen und
Pharisäer) deutlich gemacht. Dies ist zwar oft eine umständliche Formulie-
rung, aber die einzige Möglichkeit für Texte, die zum Vorlesen gedacht sind.
Wo es sprachlich möglich war, haben wir generische Ausdrücke verwendet
(Geschwister, jüdische Menschen, samaritanische Bevölkerung des Dorfes).

Diese Sichtbarmachung von Frauen führt zu einigen interessanten Effek-
ten: So wird die Ehebrecherin aus Joh 8 nun von Pharisäerinnen und Pha-
risäern bedroht, sie steht nicht mehr einer Gruppe von Männern gegenüber.
Eine heilsame Verunsicherung von oft als selbstverständlich vorausgesetzten
Fronten! Auch die Sendung von Maria aus Magdala zu den als Geschwistern
bezeichneten JüngerInnen Jesu in 20,17 bedeutet eine inhaltliche Klärung:
Eine weibliche Einzelperson wird den anderen Frauen und Männern gegenü-
berstellt und besonders gewürdigt – sie ist nicht als Frau Männern gegenüber
überlegen. An dieser Stelle untergräbt das konsequente Ernstnehmen von
Frauenbeteiligung auch eine der möglichen feministischen Auslegungen.

Bei allgemeinen Aussagen, die im Singular Maskulinum formuliert sind
("jeder, der...") haben wir stattdessen den Plural gewählt (11,25-26: *Alle, die
an mich glauben, werden leben, auch wenn sie sterben; und alle, die leben
und an mich glauben, werden...*). Dadurch können sich nicht nur Frauen in
den Aussagen wiederfinden, sondern diese werden auch allgemein offener,
das Heil wird umfassender angeboten.

---

[5] Vgl. Schottroff, Schwestern, 127-129; auch Tal Ilan, "Jüdische Frauen in der Spätantike. Ein
Überblick", in: *Kirche und Israel* 15 (2000), 7-15, hier 10-11.

[6] Vgl. Raymond Brown, "Die Rolle der Frau im vierten Evangelium", in: Elisabeth Moltmann-
Wendel (Hg.), *Frauenbefreiung. Biblische und theologische Argumente* (Kaiser: München
²1978), 133-147, hier 147. Aber selbst wenn der Begriff auf eine rein männliche Gruppe
beschränkt wäre, wäre eine Wiedergabe, die Frauen ausdrücklich einschließt, angemessen.
Denn gerade im Begriff der JüngerIn sind nicht nur damalige Personen bezeichnet, sondern
auch die heutige Gemeinde, die GottesdienstbesucherInnen – und das sind überwiegend
Frauen – angesprochen. Gerade weil ein Evangelium nicht nur ein historisches Zeugnis ist,
sondern auch heutige Menschen meint, ist eine verändernde Aktualisierung notwendig.

Allgemeine Beispiele etwa über das Verhältnis von SklavInnen und Herr-Innen, die zur Erläuterung dienen, haben wir durch eine zusätzliche weibliche Wendung verdoppelt (15,15: *Ich nenne euch nicht mehr Sklavinnen und Sklaven, denn eine Sklavin weiß nicht, wie ihre Herrin handelt und ein Sklave kennt das Vorhaben seines Herrn nicht*). Die Beispiele gewinnen dadurch eine zusätzliche Dimension. Aus feministischer Perspektive interessant ist vor allem, dass nun auch eher negative Rollen mit Frauen besetzt werden.

*b) "Die Juden" im Johannesevangelium*

Das Johannesevangelium zeichnet sich unter den neutestamentlichen Texten durch eine besondere Verwendung des Begriffes οἱ Ἰουδαῖοι aus. In konventionellen Übersetzungen ist an den entsprechenden Stellen "die Juden" zu lesen. Diese Übertragung erzeugt problematische Assoziationen bei heutigen Lesenden, und zwar gleich auf mehreren Ebenen. Erstens – hier lässt sich an das im vorherigen Abschnitt Ausgeführte anknüpfen – suggerieren Bezeichnungen wie "die Juden" oder "die Pharisäer" die Abwesenheit von Frauen in diesen Gruppierungen. Auch wenn wohl niemand die Existenz von Jüdinnen in der Spätantike an sich in Zweifel ziehen wird, so ist darüber hinaus zu betonen, dass die Quellenlage durchaus erlaubt, sowohl von Pharisäerinnen als auch von Frauen in unterschiedlichen Leitungsfunktionen innerhalb des Judentums auszugehen.[7]

Die zweite Irreführung, die bei einer Übertragung des johanneischen Begriffs Ἰουδαῖοι in den deutschen Ausdruck "Juden" in Betracht zu ziehen ist, ist die heutzutage in Deutschland weit verbreitete Unkenntnis über Juden und Jüdinnen sowie das oft vorherrschende klischeehafte Bild vom Judentum, das von der Vorstellung des Judentums als einer rigiden Gesetzesreligion gespeist wird und Differenzen innerhalb des antiken und heutigen Judentums nicht wahrnimmt.

Die dritte und entscheidendste Schwierigkeit bei der Übertragung des Begriffs Ἰουδαῖοι resultiert aus den vollkommen unterschiedlichen historischen Kontexten, in denen der antike Text des Johannesevangeliums einerseits

---

[7] Zu den Pharisäerinnen vgl. Schottroff, *Schwestern*, 128, u.a. mit Verweis auf Mischna Sota III 4. Zu Frauen in synagogalen Leitungsfunktionen vgl. die grundlegende Darstellung von Bernadette J. Brooten, *Women Leaders in the Ancient Synagogue. Inscriptional Evidence and Background Issues* (Brown Judaic Studies 36; Scholars Press: Atlanta 1982), sowie dies., "Iael προστάτης in the Jewish Donative Inscriptions of Aphrodisias", in: Birger A. Pearson (ed.), *The Future of Early Christianity, Essays in Honor of Helmut Koester* (Fortress: Minneapolis 1991), 149-162.

und seine heutige Lektüre andererseits stehen: Die Polemik gegen die Ιουδαῖοι, die wir im Johannesevangelium antreffen, steht in Zusammenhang mit der historischen Situation der johanneischen Gemeinde, bei der es sich wohl um eine Gruppe innerhalb des Judentums handelte, die aus der Synagoge ausgeschlossen worden war.[8] Der historische Ort der Polemik ist demnach wahrscheinlich in der Situation einer Minderheiten-Gruppe zu finden, die gegenüber der dominanten Mehrheit der Ιουδαῖοι kaum etwas anderes unternehmen konnte, als polemische Sätze zu formulieren.[9] Diese Situation unterscheidet sich so grundlegend von der heutigen Situation im Deutschland nach der Shoa, dass eine einlinige Übertragung der johanneischen Polemik gegenüber den "Juden" nur als absurd zu bezeichnen ist.[10]

Für die Arbeit an der Übersetzung des Johannesevangeliums bedeutet das bisher Ausgeführte, dass eine deutsche Übertragung anzustreben ist, in der deutlich wird, dass nahezu alle im Text auftretenden Personen Juden bzw. Jüdinnen sind. Die im Johannesevangelium geschilderten Konflikte sind folglich nicht als Konflikte zwischen JüdInnen einerseits und ChristInnen anderseits zu betrachten, sondern als innerjüdische Auseinandersetzungen.[11] Aus diesem Grund haben wir uns dafür entschieden, den Begriff Ιουδαῖοι mit "die anderen jüdischen Menschen" oder "die Menschen aus seinem / ihrem Volk" wiederzugeben, um deutlich werden zu lassen, dass nicht nur etwa die jüdischen Menschen, die 1,19-27 Johannes den Täufer nach seiner Identität befragen, dem Judentum zugehören, sondern selbstverständlich auch Johannes der Täufer selbst. Dasselbe gilt natürlich auch im Hinblick auf Dispute zwischen dem Juden Jesus und anderen Menschen aus dem jüdischen Volk, wie sie z.B. in Joh 8,21-30 zu finden sind.

Diese Übersetzungspraxis lässt sich nicht nur durch den historischen Sachverhalt begründen, sondern auch im Hinblick auf andere Passagen des Johannesevangeliums plausibel machen. So wird z.B. in der Geschichte von Maria

---

[8]  Vgl. die nur im Johannesevangelium gebrauchte Bezeichnung ἀποσυνάγωγος in 9,22; 12,42 sowie in 16,2, wo Jesus seinen AnhängerInnen den Synagogenausschluss voraussagt.

[9]  Zu der hier skizzierten These vgl. Klaus Wengst, *Bedrängte Gemeinde und verherrlichter Christus. Ein Versuch über das Johannesevangelium* (Kaiser: München ³1992).

[10]  Die Verantwortlichen für die derzeit geltende Perikopenordnung scheinen diesem Problem Rechnung getragen zu haben, indem sie den Abschnitt, wo von der Teufelskindschaft der "Juden" die Rede ist (8,44), in keine der Perikopenreihen aufgenommen haben, sowie die bis vor kurzem zum Israelsonntag vorgesehene Tempelreinigungsperikope (2,13-22) anderweitig ersetzt haben.

[11]  Die Bezeichnung ChristInnen (χριστιανοί) gibt es im Johannesevangelium nicht.

und Martha in Joh 11 mit großer Selbstverständlichkeit berichtet, dass die Ἰουδαῖοι sich bei Maria und Martha befinden, um diese zu trösten (11,19), und abschließend konstatiert, dass viele von den Ἰουδαῖοι zum Glauben kamen (11,45). Hier wird deutlich, dass – auch nach eigener Aussage des Johannes – auf beiden Seiten (auf der Seite der Glaubenden ebenso wie auf der Seite der Menschen, die Jesus ablehnten) jüdische Menschen zu denken sind. Noch deutlicher ist die Geschichte von der Begegnung einer Samaritanerin mit Jesus am Brunnen (4,4-42), in deren Verlauf Jesus feststellt, dass die Erlösung ἐκ τῶν Ἰουδαίων komme (4,22). Aus heutiger Perspektive bleibt bedauerlich, dass das Johannesevangelium nur innerhalb einer Geschichte, die Jesus im Gegenüber zu einer Fremden, einer Nicht-Jüdin schildert, eine solche Aussage zu treffen in der Lage ist. Auch dies sollte uns jedoch als Hinweis auf die Verschiedenheit des historischen Kontextes dienen.

Problematisch bleiben bei aller Übertragungsarbeit diejenigen Geschichten, die einen latenten Antijudaismus transportieren, dem mit übersetzerischen Mitteln schwer zu begegnen ist. In der aktuellen Perikopenordnung – die allerdings viele der polemischen Passagen nicht enthält – sind in dieser Hinsicht vor allem zwei Abschnitte zu hinterfragen. Zum einen Joh 5,39-47, wo der johanneische Jesus die Ἰουδαῖοι anklagt, die Schriften des Mose falsch zu verstehen, weil sie nicht an ihn (Jesus) glauben. Dieser Text legt die Vermutung nahe, ausschließlich eine christliche Deutung des Ersten Testaments sei sachgerecht, und gehört damit zu den Texten, deren Wirkungsgeschichte einer Enteignung des Ersten Testamentes vom Judentum durch eine exklusiv christliche Deutung der hebräischen Bibel Vorschub geleistet hat.

Der zweite außerordentlich schwierige Text ist die breit rezipierte, aber eigentlich nicht zum Johannesevangelium gehörende[12] Geschichte von der Ehebrecherin (8,2-11). Dieser Text hat nicht nur eine frauenfeindliche Wirkungsgeschichte,[13] sondern ist auch dazu verwendet worden, antijüdische Klischees zu bedienen: Jesus als der Retter der Frau vor dem jüdischem Legalismus der Pharisäer, die sie steinigen wollen (zieht man in Betracht, dass es auch Pharisäerinnen gewesen sein können, so ändert sich das Gefälle dieser Geschichte nicht unbeträchtlich!).

Bei beiden Perikopen sollte u.E. erwogen werden, statt dieser Texte andere zu lesen; werden die Texte weiter im Gottesdienst verwendet, ist es

---

[12] Der Handschriftenbefund ist hier eindeutig, vgl. die einschlägigen Kommentare.

[13] Zur Wirkungsgeschichte dieses Textes vgl. die Darstellung bei Schottroff, *Schwestern*, 286-288.

als Aufgabe ernstzunehmen, nicht in dieselben klischeehaften antijüdischen Deutungen zu verfallen, die in den Kommentierungen dieser Texte viel zu lange üblich waren.

*c) Der "Herr" und die "Herrlichkeit"*
Das griechische Wort κύριος wird in deutschen Übersetzungen üblicherweise mit "Herr" wiedergegeben. Vorgabe für die Übertragung in "gerechte Sprache" war es, die Bezeichnung "Herr" sowohl für Gott als auch für Jesus zu vermeiden. Alternativen sind schwierig zu finden; einen Ansatzpunkt unserer Überlegungen zu diesem Thema bietet die Unterschiedlichkeit der Verwendung des Begriffs κύριος im Johannesevangelium.

Einige Verwendungen von κύριος finden sich in Zitaten aus dem Ersten Testament.[14] An diesen Stellen geben wir κύριος mit "Gott" wieder.[15] Die weiteren Zusammenhänge, in denen κύριος im Johannesevangelium gebraucht wird, beziehen sich nahezu alle auf Jesus und reichen in ihrem Bedeutungsspektrum von höflicher Anrede einerseits bis zu titularem Gebrauch für den Auferstandenen andererseits. Letzteres begegnet vor allem im Zusammenhang der Erscheinungserzählungen (20,18.20.25.28; 21,7.12), ersteres vorwiegend in Dialogen Jesu mit anderen Personen. Dass die Anrede κύριε nicht immer als textliches Signal für ein Bekenntnis zu Jesus verstanden werden muss, zeigt die Tatsache, dass auch Philippus so angeredet wird (12,21). Neben κύριε wird als Anrede für Jesus im Johannesevangelium auch ῥαββί gebraucht. Dies haben wir uns für die Übersetzung zu Nutze gemacht, und an den Stellen, wo κύριε primär als höfliche Anrede verstanden werden kann, als deutsches Äquivalent "Rabbi" gewählt. Man könnte einwenden, dass damit der Bekenntnischarakter der Anrede κύριε verloren gehe. Allerdings ist dazu zu bemerken, dass an

---

[14] Vgl. die Bezugnahmen auf Jes 40,3 und 53,1 in Joh 1,23 bzw. 12,38.

[15] Dass wir hier nicht – wie für die Übersetzungen des Ersten Testament selbst vorgesehen – Adonaj schreiben, hat mehrere Gründe: Es erscheint problematisch, auf das hebräische Original zurückzugreifen, wenn Johannes selbst der griechischen Übersetzung näher steht. Außerdem würde die Verwendung von Adonaj in einem neutestamentlichen Text, in dem diese Bezeichnung dann nur in zitierten Passagen auftaucht, diese Passagen dem Rest des Textes entfremden. Schließlich wäre es problematisch, jene Bezeichnung, die von JüdInnen beim Lesen des Ersten Testaments als Gottesbezeichnung verwendet wird, in neutestamentlichen Zusammenhängen zu benutzen, in denen sich κύριος auch auf Jesus beziehen lässt (vgl. 1,23) – dies wäre wohl kaum im Sinne jüdischer Überlieferung. Auch aus feministischer Perspektive scheint die Verwendung von Adonaj nicht die glücklichste Lösung zu sein: Bedeutet es doch "mein Herr" und stellt somit nur solange eine Alternative zu "Herr" dar, wie die Lesenden des Hebräischen nicht kundig sind.

vielen Stellen nichts darauf hindeutet, dass die Anrede Jesu mit κύριε tatsächlich ein Bekenntnis der Anredenden darstellen soll. So wird etwa im Laufe von Kapitel 11 Jesus von seinen JüngerInnen erst als ῥαββί (11,8) und dann als κύριε (11,12) angesprochen. Die Aussage, die der Anrede in Vers 12 folgt, enthält ein so deutliches Missverständnis der JüngerInnen, dass es schwer fiele, ihnen hier einen Erkenntnisfortschritt im Hinblick auf das wahre Wesen Jesu zu unterstellen. Ähnliches lässt sich von der Samaritanerin sagen, die Jesus bereits dreimal im Verlaufe des Gespräches mit κύριε angeredet hat,[16] bevor sie auf die Idee kommt, dass der, mit dem sie spricht, ein Prophet sein könnte (4,19) – was ja auch noch nicht die ganze Wahrheit im Sinne dieser Geschichte und des Johannesevangeliums ist (vgl. 4,25f).

Nicht verschwiegen werden soll, dass es auch Stellen gibt, in denen die Anrede κύριε von einer Person gebraucht wird, die sich im folgenden zu Jesus bekennt (vgl. Petrus in 6,68f und Martha in 11,27). Auch diese Stellen haben wir, um zumindest ein Minimum an Einheitlichkeit zu wahren[17] – und in Ermangelung einer besseren Alternative –, κύριε mit Rabbi wiedergegeben.

Neben der Übertragung "Rabbi" für κύριε in der Anrede und "Gott" für κύριος in Zitaten aus dem Ersten Testament, gibt es noch einige Stellen, an denen wir uns entschieden haben, κύριος mit "Messias" oder "Jesus" wiederzugeben. Letzteres betrifft die κύριος-Stellen der Auferstehungsgeschichten, wo ja gerade deutlich gemacht werden soll, dass die JüngerInnen tatsächlich den Jesus sehen, der gestorben ist (vgl. 20,19-29). Um den besonderen Charakter der Aussagen in 20,18 und 20,25 hervorzuheben, haben wir hier mit *"Ich habe (bzw. wir haben) Gott in Jesus gesehen"* übertragen.

Die Wiedergabe von κύριος durch "Messias" schien als eine Möglichkeit in Joh 11,2 einen alternativen Titel zu wählen, der dem Kontext angemessen ist, heißt es hier doch: *"Maria aber war die, die den* κύριος *mit Salböl gesalbt und seine Füße mit ihren Haaren getrocknet hatte"*. Sowohl der Verweis auf die Salbungsgeschichte als auch das Vorkommen des Messias-Titels später in derselben Geschichte lassen es sinnvoll erscheinen, hier κύριος mit Messias zu übertragen.

In mehreren Passagen des Johannesevangeliums wird κύριος als Gegensatz zu δοῦλος und als Herrschaftsbegriff verwendet, der auf den Kontext der

---

[16] Joh 4,11.15.19.
[17] Beide Personen gebrauchen die Anrede κύριε auch dann, wenn sich kein explizites Bekenntnis zu Jesus anschließt, vgl. für Martha 11,21.39 und für Petrus 13,6.9.

spätantiken Sklavenhaltergesellschaft verweist. An diesen Stellen ist es notwendig, bei der Übersetzung das im Begriff κύριος implizierte Statusgefälle zu erhalten und entsprechend "autoritär" zu übersetzen. Notwendig ist dies vor allem deshalb, weil der Kontext deutlich macht, dass der mit den Begriffen gegebene Rangunterschied aufgehoben werden soll: Die JüngerInnen Jesu sind FreundInnen Jesu und nicht SklavInnen (vgl. 15,14f). Und Jesus selbst, den sie διδάσκαλος und κύριος nennen, wäscht ihnen die Füße (vgl. 13,13f). Um auch hier die Übersetzung "Herr" zu vermeiden, haben wir 13,13 mit *"Ihr lernt von mir, ihr verehrt mich und gehorcht mir"* übertragen. Vergleichbares gilt auch für das Thomasbekenntnis in 20,28, das wir mit *"Ich verehre dich und will dir gehorchen, du bist mein Gott!"* wiedergegeben haben, um die im κύριος -Begriff enthaltenen Konnotationen von Verehrung und Gehorsam zu erhalten. Allerdings bleibt es grundsätzlich schwierig, das Bedeutungsspektrum von κύριος aus der antiken in eine moderne Gesellschaft zu übertragen.

Ein spezifisches Problem deutscher Übersetzungen sind die Worte δόξα und δοξάζω,[18] die üblicherweise mit "Herrlichkeit" bzw. "verherrlichen" wiedergeben werden, womit im Text eine Verbindung dieser Begriffe zu "Herr" entsteht,[19] die dem Griechischen in keiner Weise entspricht. Wir haben δόξα je nach Kontext entweder mit "Ehre" (so z.B. 5,44; 7,18) oder mit "Glanz" (so z.B. 1,14; 2,11; 11,40; 12,41; 17,22.24) übersetzt. Die Übertragung durch "Glanz" statt durch "Herrlichkeit" hat den zusätzlichen Effekt, dass Leseerwartungen irritiert werden – was bei so bekannten und abgeschliffenen Texten wie etwa Joh 1,14 durchaus als Vorzug gesehen werden kann, da es eine neue Wahrnehmung und ein erneutes Hören des Textes ermöglicht.

*d) Der "Vater", der "Sohn" und der "Geist"*
πατήρ ist im Johannesevangelium die häufigste Gottesbezeichnung. Mitunter redet Jesus noch genauer von "mein Vater" (πατήρ μου). Dem korrespondiert die Benennung von Jesus als Sohn. Problematisch ist daran die implizierte Männlichkeit Gottes, aber auch der Bezug zu irdischen Vätern: Auf der einen Seite kann Vaterschaft dadurch überhöht werden, auf der anderen Seite ist es für viele Frauen aufgrund der Erfahrungen mit ihren Vätern unmöglich, diese Gottesmetapher zu benutzen.

---

[18] In englischen Übersetzungen wird δόξα mit "glory" übersetzt; hier gibt es dieses Problem nicht.
[19] Herr und herrlich bzw. Herrlichkeit sind tatsächlich sprachlich miteinander verwandt, wenn auch nicht direkt, vgl. Luise F. Pusch, "Sind Herren herrlich und Damen dämlich?" in: dies., *Alle Menschen werden Schwestern. Feministische Sprachkritik* (Suhrkamp: Frankfurt am Main 1990), 209.

Es gibt u.E. keine Möglichkeit, "Vater" durchgehend durch ein anderes Wort zu ersetzen. Denn das Wort ist eine Qualifizierung und Beschreibung Gottes bzw. des Gottesverhältnisses Jesu, für die es kein Äquivalent gibt. Bei der Verwendung der Metapher "Vater" sind im Johannesevangelium Inhalte wie Schöpfermacht, Liebe, Treue und Zugewandtheit Gottes, die den Begriff in vorausgehenden jüdischen Schriften prägen, vorausgesetzt.[20] Der eigene Akzent liegt jedoch vor allem auf der Besonderheit der Gottesbeziehung Jesu; seine Herkunft von, seine Verbundenheit mit und sein Wissen über Gott sind von zentraler Bedeutung im Evangelium.

Allerdings hat die Bezeichnung nicht immer das gleiche Gewicht, weshalb wir an vielen Stellen einfach "Gott" gesetzt haben.[21] An anderen haben wir das u.E. Gemeinte umschrieben, z.B. mit Begriffen wie Quelle (4,23: *Aber es kommt die Stunde und ist schon jetzt, wo die wahren Betenden Gott als ihre Lebensquelle in Geisteskraft und Wahrheit anbeten werden.* 6,57: *So wie mich der lebendige Gott gesandt hat und ich aus dieser Quelle lebe, so werden...*) oder Ursprung (20,17: *Halte mich nicht fest, denn ich bin noch nicht zu Gott, meinem Ursprung, zurückgekehrt. Gehe aber zu meinen Geschwistern und sage ihnen: Ich steige auf zur Quelle von meinem und eurem Leben, zu meinem Gott und eurem Gott.*). Diese Worte entsprechen sachlich zumindest einigen Aspekten der Vatermetapher, auch wenn das Gottesbild dadurch weniger personal wird.

Mitunter bietet der Text Näherbestimmungen für Gott, die sich als Metaphern verwenden lassen (8,26: *Die Wahrheit hat mich gesandt, und das, was ich von ihr gehört habe, dies spreche ich in die Welt hinein.*). Auch sind Formulierungen mit Verben wie "senden" oder "ausgehen" möglich, die auch sonst im Text vorkommen. Schwierig sind dabei jedoch maskuline Relativanschlüsse ("Gott, der mich gesandt..."); wir haben sie vermieden bzw. mit femininen Konstruktionen kombiniert. (16,5: *Jetzt aber gehe ich dahin, woher ich gesandt wurde.* 14,23: *Und sie werden auch von Gott geliebt, von dem ich ausgegangen bin, und wir werden zu dieser Quelle allen Lebens gehen und bei ihr wohnen.*)

---

[20] Vgl. Angelika Strotmann, *"Mein Vater bist du!" (Sir 51,10) Zur Bedeutung der Vaterschaft Gottes in kanonischen und nichtkanonischen frühjüdischen Schriften* (Knecht: Frankfurt a.M. 1991), 360-375.

[21] Dies durchgehend zu tun wäre aber eine Verflachung des Textes. Außerdem scheint an einzelnen Stellen eine unterschiedliche Verwendung der Begriffe vorzuliegen (z.B. 16,2f), obwohl an anderen Stellen beide äquivalent verwendet werden (z.B. 16,27-28).

An einigen Stellen ist der Bezug der Vaterschaft Gottes zu irdischen Vätern bzw. Eltern deutlich; hier haben wir die Terminologie von Elternschaft bzw. Vater/Mutter verwendet (5,19-21: *Das Kind kann nichts von sich aus tun, wenn es nicht die Eltern etwas tun sieht. Was nämlich jene machen, das macht genauso auch das Kind. Denn die Eltern lieben das Kind und zeigen ihm alles... Denn wie Gott als Vater und Mutter Tote auferweckt und lebendig macht, so...*).

Schließlich haben wir auch neue Metaphern für Gott kreiert, wie etwa in 15,1: *Ich bin der wahre Weinstock und Gott ist meine Gärtnerin.*

Solche Formulierungen sind ungewohnt, aber sie bleiben im Rahmen der johanneischen Theologie. Das Neuartige regt an, über die inhaltliche Füllung der Aussagen nachzudenken und die Begriffe sind oft klarer und präziser als die im Gottesdienst schon sehr gewohnte und abgenutzte Metapher Vater. Natürlich könnten auch andere Aspekte in den Vordergrund gestellt und entsprechend andere Ausdrücke gefunden werden. Durch solches Nachdenken wird das Gottesbild variabler und dynamischer – dies entspricht auch dem johanneischen Umgang mit Sprache.

υἱός haben wir durchgehend mit "Kind" übersetzt, auch in Zusammensetzungen wie Kind Gottes oder Menschenkind.[22] Obwohl bei dieser Übersetzung die Gefahr besteht, zuerst an das Jesuskind in der Krippe zu denken und so die Christologie zu verniedlichen, ist der mit dieser Übersetzung verbundene Verfremdungseffekt anregend. Außerdem ist es mitunter korrekter, Kind statt Sohn zu setzen, denn Gott hat ja nicht seinen einzigen Sohn (anstelle seiner drei Töchter) gesandt, sondern wirklich sein einziges Kind (3,16). Dieser Sprachgebrauch führt zu einem Herunterspielen der Männlichkeit Jesu, seine weiblichen Züge haben wir dagegen betont. Damit entsprechen wir der Absicht neutestamentlicher Schriften, in denen kein Gewicht auf der Männlichkeit Jesu liegt. Theologische Relevanz hat sie erst im Laufe der Kirchengeschichte bekommen,[23] so dass heute männliche Bezeichnungen Jesu anders gehört werden als im ursprünglichen Kontext. Gerade im Johannesevangelium werden sowohl weibliche Bilder (7,37f) als auch mit weiblichen Gottheiten verbundene Traditionen (Prolog) auf Jesus

---

[22] Auch wenn sich der Begriff auf andere Personen als Jesus bezieht: Z.B. Simon, Kind des Johannes (1,42; 21,15ff) oder das Kind des königlichen Beamten, das ohnehin in der Geschichte nicht nur als υἱός, sondern auch als παῖς bezeichnet wird (4,46.50.53 und 4,49.51).

[23] Bis hin zur Begründung des Ausschlusses von Frauen vom Priesteramt.

übertragen.[24] Eine Verstärkung der weiblichen Seite ist in verschiedenen Bereichen möglich: So haben wir Logos im Prolog mit Weisheit wiedergegeben, was dem weisheitlich-weiblichen Hintergrund des Hymnus entspricht. In 13,4 bindet Jesus sich eine Schürze um, so wird der soziale Kontext der Szene – Füße waschen als SklavInnen- und Frauenarbeit – auch heute sichtbar.

πνεῦμα haben wir mit "Geisteskraft" übersetzt. Dieser Begriff ist in der Gebetssprache geläufig. Er ist nicht nur feminin, sondern drückt auch mehr Bewegung und Dynamik aus als "Geist". Bei zusammengesetzten Ausdrücken haben wir deshalb auch "Kraft" alleine verwendet ("Kraft der Wahrheit" 14,17). παράκλητος ist durch "tröstende Geisteskraft" wiedergegeben und an einer Stelle auch als "Trösterin" (14,26: *Die Trösterin – nämlich die heilige Geisteskraft –, die Gott...*). D.h. πνεῦμα ist nicht nur als neutral, sondern als weiblich dargestellt. Dadurch bekommt das Gottesbild eine weibliche Note – das sollte uns aber nicht daran hindern, nach weiblichen Metaphern auch für andere göttliche Gestalten zu suchen.

## 4. Abschließende Reflexion

Jede Übersetzung ist ein kreativer Prozess von Bedeutungsvermittlung. Dabei lässt sich prinzipiell unterscheiden zwischen Übersetzungen, die eine möglichst genaue sprachliche Nachzeichnung des Ausgangstextes anstreben, und solchen, die primär auf die Übertragung des Sinns in einen neuen Kontext abzielen.[25] In beiden Fällen stehen ÜbersetzerInnen immer wieder vor dem Problem, Sprachspiele und Feinheiten des Originals nicht wirklich wiedergeben zu können, sowie in exegetischen Zweifelsfällen Entscheidungen treffen zu müssen und damit den Text letztlich zu vereinfachen und zu verflachen.

---

[24] Vgl. Martin Scott, *Sophia and Johannine Jesus* (JSNT Suppl. 71; Sheffield Academic Press: Sheffield 1992).

[25] Vgl. die zitierte Unterscheidung Friedrich Schleiermachers: "Entweder der Uebersetzer läßt den Schriftsteller möglichst in Ruhe, und bewegt den Leser ihm entgegen; oder er läßt den Leser möglichst in Ruhe und bewegt den Schriftsteller ihm entgegen." (Methoden des Übersetzens, wieder abgedruckt in: Hans Joachim Störig [Hg.], *Das Problem des Übersetzens* [Wege der Forschung 8; Wissenschaftliche Buchgesellschaft: Darmstadt 1969 38-70; hier 47]). – Aus der Fülle der Veröffentlichungen zur Übersetzungstheorie sei hier nur exemplarisch hingewiesen auf: Eugene A. Nida / Charles R. Taber, *The Theory and Practice of Translation*, (Helps for Translators 8; Brill: Leiden 1969); Elisabeth A. Castelli, "Les Belles Infidèles / Fidelity or Feminism? The Meanings of Feminist Biblical Translation", in: Schüssler Fiorenza, *Searching the Scriptures*, Bd. 1, 189-204.

Die Kriterien, von denen der Übersetzungsprozess gesteuert wird, können dabei sehr unterschiedliche sein; zu betonen ist jedoch, dass jede Art der Übersetzung Entscheidungen trifft, dass es also so etwas wie eine "wörtliche" Übersetzung der Sache nach gar nicht geben kann.

Im vorliegenden Fall waren die Kriterien des Übersetzens den Beteiligten am Projekt vorgegeben, und es waren Kriterien, die von einer Vorstellung von "gerechter Sprache" ausgehen, wie sie heute sinnvoll und notwendig erscheint, aber zur Zeit der Entstehung biblischer Texte in der Regel nicht denkbar gewesen sein dürfte. Man könnte einwenden, dass damit den Texten eine ihnen selbst fremde Vorstellung aufgezwungen würde. Es wäre aber andererseits auch möglich, diesen Prozess als eine konsequente Fortschreibung der Erkenntnis anderer Übersetzer zu interpretieren. Luther schreibt in seinem "Sendbrief vom Dolmetschen", man müsse beim Übersetzen "die Mutter im Hause, die Kinder auf der Gassen, den gemeinen Mann auf dem Markt drum fragen, und denselbigen auf das Maul sehen, wie sie reden und darnach dolmetschen."[26] Eine deutlichere Aufforderung, sich einer zeitgemäßen Sprache zu bedienen, ist wohl kaum vorstellbar. Zu einer zeitgemäßen Sprache gehört heute auch, die Erkenntnisse der feministischen Linguistik ernstzunehmen. Die Idee, dass eine "konservative" Übersetzung näher am Original bleibt, negiert auch die Tatsache, dass sich das Original selbst ebenfalls ändert, wie Walter Benjamin zu bedenken gibt: "Denn in seinem Fortleben, das so nicht heißen dürfte, wenn es nicht Wandlung und Erneuerung des Lebendigen wäre, ändert sich das Original. Es gibt eine Nachreife auch der festgelegten Worte. Was zur Zeit eines Autors Tendenz seiner dichterischen Sprache gewesen sein mag, kann später erledigt sein, immanente Tendenzen vermögen neu aus dem Geformten sich zu erheben."[27] In diesem Sinne lässt sich das hier skizzierte Übersetzungsprojekt als ein Versuch verstehen, die Veränderungen von Sprache und geschichtlicher Perspektive für eine Übertragung biblischer Texte fruchtbar zu machen.

This article documents the work of its authors in a project which aims to produce a new German translation in "inclusive language" of the lectionary texts of the German Protestant Church. These translations seek to avoid androcentric mistakes in translation, anti-semitic formulations and a one-sidedly masculine image of God. For texts from the Gospel of John problems are posed by the translation of terms referring to groups and of general statements formulated in masculine terms,

---

[26] Wieder abgedruckt in: Störig, *Problem des Übersetzens*, 15-32, hier 21.
[27] "Die Aufgabe des Übersetzers", in: Störig, *Problem des Übersetzens*, 156-169, hier 160.

by the Johannine use of the term "the Jews", by the Greek words generally translated into German as "Herr" ("Lord") and "Herrlichkeit" ("glory"; this latter does not present a problem in most other languages), and the use of masculine terms to refer to the divinity (e.g.: "Father", "Son", "Spirit", "Paraclete"). The authors discuss both linguistic problems and the problems of content which arise, for instance, from the historical changes in the relationship to Judaism. They describe their own suggestions for solutions and offer their ideas for translations: neutral or less loaded formulations; the explicit naming of women and the effects of this for the interpretation of texts; the attempt to make clear the historical situation of the gospel; the search for new ways of speaking about God. The article concludes with a reflection about the function and the boundaries of translation.

L'article documente le travail de ses auteures dans un projet en cours de réalisation dont le but est de présenter une nouvelle traduction du lectionnaire de l'Église Protestante d'Allemagne visant à éliminer les erreurs "androcentriques", à contourner les formules antisémites et à éviter la propagation d'une image de Dieu masculine, et donc de parti-pris. Des solutions sont recherchées pour les termes génériques et collectifs de genre masculin dans l'Évangile selon saint Jean, "les Juifs" par exemple, les mots grecs traduits par "Herr" (Seigneur) et "Herrlichkeit" (gloire, ce mot contenant en allemand la syllabe Herr = Seigneur), ou les désignations masculines "Père", "Fils", "Esprit" et "paraclet" pour les personnes divines. Les auteures exposent le problème linguistique et le problème de fond résultant par exemple des changements historiques dans le rapport au judaïsme. Leurs propositions de traductions pour certains passages préconisent des formules neutres ou moins connotées, la mention explicite des femmes quelles qu'en soient les conséquences pour l'interprétation des textes, la tentative d'expliquer la situation historique de l'Évangile, et de trouver d'autres mots pour désigner Dieu. L'article se termine par une réflexion sur le rôle et les limites de la traduction.

*Silke Petersen* (1965): Studium der evangelischen Theologie in Hamburg;1998 Promotion über Jüngerinnen Jesu in christlich-gnostischen Schriften; 1998/99 Postdoktorandenstipendium im Würzburger Graduiertenkolleg "Wahrnehmung der Geschlechterdifferenz in religiösen Symbolsystemen"; zur Zeit wissenschaftliche Assistentin am Institut für Neues Testament in Hamburg, Arbeit an einer Habilitation über die Ich-bin-Worte des Johannesevangeliums.

*Judith Hartenstein* (1964): Studium der evangelischen Theologie in Bonn und Berlin; 1997 Promotion im Neuen Testament an der Humboldt-Universität zu Berlin; Vikariat in Essen; Pfarrerin z.A. als Assistentin an der Kirchlichen Hochschule Wuppertal; der zeit wissenschaftliche Assistentin im Fach Neues Testament an der Philipps-Universität Marburg; Arbeit an einer Habilitation zum Johannesevangelium.

*Caroline Vander Stichele*

# The Lord Can No Longer Be Taken for Granted
# The Rendering of JHWH in the New Dutch Bible Translation

Since 1993, a new, interconfessional Bible translation for the Netherlands and Flanders has been under preparation. In 1998 a first pre-publication appeared with translations of Esther, Ecclesiastes, Jonah, Judith and Acts and in 2000 a second one with Genesis, 31 Psalms, Zechariah, Mark, 1 Corinthians, Revelation, and Tobit.[1] The translation in question is the *Nieuwe Bijbel Vertaling* [NBV] which is expected to be published in 2004. It is a joint venture of the two Dutch Bible Societies, The Catholic Bible Society (KBS) and the Protestant Dutch Bible Society (NBG), and is supposed to become the standard edition for the first half of the 21st century in the Dutch-speaking world.

Besides the 20 translators working on this translation, some fifty supervisors, representative of the future readership, check each translation and comment on it. To guide their work, a number of translation rules and principles have been developed. One of these principles concerns the use of inclusive language; another one deals with the translation of the name(s) of God. The first principle states that exclusive language should be avoided where possible, and that both the cultural identity of the source text and what sounds natural in Dutch need to be taken into account in the translation.[2] The second principle holds that the Hebrew name of God JHWH (the tetragrammaton) is to be rendered with HEER, always written in four small capital letters.[3] In the first pre-publication, this choice was explained as follows: it is in line with the tradition of both Judaism and Christianity, it guarantees continuity

---

[1] *Werk in uitvoering. Eerste deeluitgaven van de [Nieuwe Bijbelvertaling]: Ester, Prediker, Jona, Judit, Handelingen. Met verantwoording en toelichting* (NBG / KBS: Haarlem / 's-Hertogenbosch 1998); *Werk in uitvoering 2. Deeluitgaven van de [Nieuwe Bijbelvertaling]: Genesis, 31 Psalmen, Zacharia, Tobit, Marcus, 1 Korintiërs, Openbaring. Met verantwoording en toelichting* (NBG / KBS: Haarlem / 's-Hertogenbosch 2000).

[2] *Werk in uitvoering* 1, 241.

[3] *Werk in uitvoering* 1, 243. The Dutch "Heer" corresponds to "Herr" in German, "Lord" in English and "Seigneur" in French translations.

between the Old and New Testament, it is international practice, and alternatives only raise new objections.

In 1997 three supervisors, who considered these arguments to be problematic and in contradiction with the principle of avoiding exclusive language, raised objections against this translation and started a protest action under the slogan: "De HEER? Dat kan niet meer!" ("The Lord? That is no longer possible!").[4] As a result, hundreds of letters and petitions were sent to the secretariat of the NBV and the discussion also attracted the attention of the media.[5] This massive response came as a surprise to the translation steering committee and the promise was made to reconsider the translation of the tetragrammaton, taking into account other available options.[6] Nevertheless, on February 16, 2001 (as this article was going to press) the two Dutch Bible Societies took the final decision to render the tetragrammaton in the NBV with HEER, written in four small capital letters, claiming that no consensus could be reached on any of the alternatives. In response, the three supervisors who started the protest action, together with one member of the steering committee, decided to resign.[7] Despite the decision of the Bible Societies, the public debate and the protest have raised the awareness of the problem at stake. "The Lord" is no longer taken for granted.

In what follows, I will give an overview of the arguments against rendering JHWH with HEER and present those in favour of what seems to me to be the strongest alternative. It should be noted that the discussion here is limited to the representation of the tetragrammaton and that the arguments are only related to this particular issue.[8]

---

[4] The three supervisors in question are Dr. Anneke de Vries, Dr. Manuela Kalski and myself. They were later joined by Prof. Dr. Judith Frishman, a member of the steering committee. The protest action was supported by the IWFT, the Dutch network of feminist theologians.

[5] In total some 2200 persons protested against the rendition of the tetragrammaton with HEER and articles of various lengths (including letters) appeared in newspapers and periodicals. These numbers date from November 1999 and were published in a report issued by the NBV itself. Cf. *De vertaling van de Godsnaam JHWH in de Nieuwe Bijbelvertaling. Rapportage van de discussie gevoerd in de pers en in brieven* (Project [Nieuwe Bijbelvertaling]: Haarlem 1999), i-ii.

[6] In total 113 alternatives were proposed in the protest letters. The three most popular were "Eeuwige" (the Eternal One), JHWH and "Aanwezige" (the Present One). Cf. *De vertaling,* iii.

[7] See note 4.

[8] An earlier version of this part of my article has been published in *Met Andere Woorden* 19/3 (September 2000), 5-9 and in K. Biezeveld et al. (eds), *Proeven van Vrouwenstudies Theologie* 6 (Meinema: Zoetermeer 2000), 213-218.

## 1. HEER as the Exclusive Rendition of the Tetragrammaton

The most important arguments given in favour of the rendition with HEER were that this choice was in line with Jewish and Christian tradition, in that it corresponds with the Septuagint; that it guarantees the continuity between the Old and New Testament; that it is common practice; and that alternatives only raise new objections.[9]

The argument from tradition is not as strong as it may seem. First, the argument itself is limited by the reference to the Septuagint, which itself is a translation of the Hebrew Bible. Second, it raises the question of what should be considered tradition: the fact *that* a substitute for the tetragrammaton is used or the substitute itself? In referring to the Septuagint, the practice itself and the substitute are identified, but this is not necessary. In practice this one name has generally been used as a substitute for the tetragrammaton, because most Masoretic manuscripts of the Hebrew Bible suggest that *adonai* (Lord) be read where the tetragrammaton stands written, since the name of God should not be pronounced.[10] The rendition of the tetragrammaton with HEER (*adonai* in Hebrew or *kurios* in Greek) is relativized by the many names for God in the Bible itself, of which 'Lord' is only one.

The second argument given in favour for HEER is that the continuity between the Hebrew Bible and the New Testament is guaranteed by this rendition of the tetragrammaton. Again, this is only partially so: the continuity in question is primarily a continuity with the Septuagint rather than with the Hebrew Bible. Moreover, a closer inspection of the New Testament shows that not all quotations of the Old Testament come from the Septuagint. Such an inspection also indicates that there is no uniformity in the rendition of the tetragrammaton, since not only *kurios* (Lord) but also *theos* (God), is used to translate it (see for instance John 6.45 / Is 54.13; Gal 3.6 / Gen 15.6). Here again, the fact that a substitute is used can be considered more fundamental than the substitute itself. In addition, the idea that the continuity between the HB and the NT needs to be guaranteed would appear to be a theological and Christological concern rather than being based upon the texts themselves. In the NT, *kurios* is indeed used to refer not only to God, but also to Christ. However, this usage should not be allowed to play a role in the decision about the rendition of the

---

[9] See *Handboek Nieuwe Bijbelvertaling* (January 1998), B7: Vertaling van de Godsnamen, 2.

[10] The reading *Jahweh* is based on what is supposed to be the original vocalisation, while *Jehovah* is based on a misinterpetation of the principle of substitution, in that the consonants of the tetragrammaton are combined with the vowels of *adonai*.

tetragrammaton in the Hebrew Bible, since to do so is to disregard Jewish sen-
sibilities at this point as well as the integrity and autonomy of the Hebrew
Bible *per se*.

The third argument, with its reference to common international practice, is
also only partially valid, since there is no real consensus on this point[11] and
the translation problems involved are often different in different languages.
Even in previous Dutch translations, there was no consensus.[12] More importantly, however, this is a purely formal argument, because no reference is
made to the reason for the choice itself. It is also a conservative argument,
because it supports the *status quo*: nothing can ever change if such arguments
are viewed as justifiable reasons for leaving things as they are.

The fourth argument, that any alternatives will simply give rise to new
objections, can hardly be seen as convincing, because the rendition with HEER
does precisely that as well. There simply no longer exists a rendition that is
totally unproblematic. The question, therefore, is how the different objections
are to be assessed and which rendition is the most justified and thus the most
tenable. It should not be taken for granted that this will be HEER.

This brings us to the question of the arguments that can be raised against the
continuation of HEER as standard rendition of the tetragrammaton in the NBV.
The most important objection is that replacing the tetragrammaton with HEER
makes the biblical image of God even more masculine than it already is. This
choice is in contradiction with the already minimalist principle of avoiding
exclusive language where possible. But there is more. As Helen Schüngel-
Straumann has argued, this rendition is especially problematic because of its
hierarchical overtones, which are absent from the meaning of the Hebraic
JHWH. HEER evokes the distance of a master-slave relationship, rather than
God's presence with his people, as expressed in, for instance, Exodus 3.[13] The
same point is also made by Gail Ramshaw who considers the title Lord to be
"androcentric and archaic. It casts divinity as masculine, and it hearkens back

---

[11] The latest edition of the Bible de Jérusalem (1998) still has the translation "Yahvé".

[12] There are two traditions at this point. The first tradition is to render the tetragrammaton with
(a variant of) Lord, either HEERE (Statenvertaling), HERE (Nederlands Bijbel Genootschap)
or "Heer" (Groot Nieuws Bijbel). The second tradition is to represent the tetragrammaton
with a vocalised version such as "Jahwe" or "Jahweh". This was traditionally done in the
Catholic Willibrord Vertaling, but this practice was abandoned in favour of HEER in the
revised translation of 1995.

[13] Helen Schüngel-Straumann, *Denn Gott bin ich, und kein Mann. Gottesbilder im Ersten Testament – feministisch betrachtet* (Grünewald: Mainz 1996), 97.

to an economic system in which vassals were pawns of the power of the ruling class."[14] It is therefore important to look for a different rendition of the tetragrammaton. Alternatives have already been suggested and are in use as well. The question however remains: which alternative is to be preferred?

## 2. Other options?

Gail Ramshaw suggests that in the decision about a viable alternative four criteria should be taken into account. It has to be a word or phrase

(1) that renders the tetragrammaton; (2) that acclaims Jesus' divinity; (3) that is felicitous in both biblical translation and liturgical texts; and (4) that does not have disadvantages exceeding its advantages.[15]

The radical solution she herself puts forward is "the Living One". This choice is based in the first place on the passage in Exodus about God's self-revelation as "I AM", to Moses. "Today *the Living One* captures more essentially than a title of authority the sparks of the burning bush and may symbolize more effectively the life of God."[16] Ramshaw further defends her choice with the argument that this title can be used for both God and Jesus, especially the risen Christ. However, as has already been mentioned, this christological criterion is highly problematic, because of its exclusive Christian focus. It should therefore be discarded.

Other authors also refer to God's response to Moses in Ex 3.14-15 as an important biblical text in deciding in favour of a particular alternative. Helen Schüngel-Straumann believes that the tetragrammaton does not say anything about God or God's qualities, but expresses how JHWH relates to the people whom Moses has to address. It is the promise that God will be there for them now and in the future, as has been the case in the past.[17] In her discussion of the same text, Anneke de Vries remarks that what can be deduced from the text is that eternal presence is the main characteristic of this God. She therefore suggests the use of "the Present One" or "the Eternal One" as a rendering of the tetragrammaton.[18]

---

[14]  Gail Ramshaw, *God beyond Gender: Feminist Christian God-Language* (Fortress Press: Minneapolis 1995), 52.

[15]  Ibid., 54.

[16]  Ibid., 54-55.

[17]  Schüngel-Straumann, *Denn Gott bin ich, und kein Mann*, 95.

[18]  Anneke de Vries, *Het kleine verschil. Man/vrouw-stereotypen in enkele moderne Nederlandse vertalingen van het Oude Testament* (Kok Pharos: Kampen 1998), 24; Anneke de Vries, "De Heer is niet meer van deze tijd," in: *de Bazuin* 81/11 (1998), 20-21.

Rather than favouring one of these or another alternative, I would like to plead for what I would call a qualified appeal to tradition. In my view, it is important to make a distinction between the principle of substitution itself on the one hand and the term which is precisely being substituted and read on the other. The first is more fundamental than the second and it concerns a practice which has been applied to the Hebrew textual traditions themselves. We are thus dealing with a phenomenon which relates to the source text and which as such precedes every translation. The rendition of the tetragrammaton in a translation of the Hebrew Bible most adequately reflecting this phenomenon is, therefore, the transcription of the Hebrew characters into Latin ones as JHWH and not its "translation" with HEER, which reads something other than what is actually written. Mary-Phil Korsak's English translation of Genesis offers a concrete example of a translation where the tetragrammaton is systematically rendered with JHWH.[19] In what follows I will give linguistic, philosophical and theological arguments to motivate this choice.

With respect to its linguistic character, it can be noted that the tetragrammaton is not just a word, but a name.[20] This name can further be specified as being a proper name, rather than a class-name or noun. A proper name refers to two characteristics of the one who is thus indicated: identity and exclusivity. A proper name therefore does not need to be translated, even if, etymologically speaking, the meaning of the name is known. In the Hebrew Bible the tetragrammaton functions as a proper name for the God of Israel, and thus distinguishes this deity from other gods, who also have proper names, such as Baal, Astarte or Moloch. It can therefore be argued that in order to represent the uniqueness of this god over and against other gods, the rendition of the Hebrew tetragrammaton must keep its character as a proper name and thus remain a tetragrammaton in the strict sense.

There are also philosophical arguments in favour of preserving the tetragrammaton. As Chris Doude van Troostwijk points out, proper names have a deictic aspect, because they refer to something outside language itself.[21] The

[19] Mary Phil Korsak, *At the Start... Genesis made new. A translation of the Hebrew text* (European Series. Louvain Cahiers 124; Leuvense schrijversaktie: Leuven / Sheffield Academic Press: Sheffield 1992).

[20] Lambert Wieringa, "Een eigennaam vertaal je niet," in: *Met Andere Woorden* 18/1 (1999), 21-39. Compare Mary Phil Korsak who understands YHWH as "the personal name of the God of the Hebrews" [Mary Phil Korsak, *At the Start...*, 5, note 4].

[21] Chris Doude van Troostwijk, "Het geschil en de godsnaam. Semiotische en filosofische notities bij de vertaling van het tetragrammaton," in: *Tijdschrift voor Theologie* 39 (1999), 346-357.

meaning of a proper name can therefore never be reduced to its semantic component. A name always remains a reference mark. This also holds true for the tetragrammaton as the indication of God's proper name. Yet, the tetragrammaton is special because it also has the character of a letter combination which can not be translated. It has the qualities of a visual sign and can therefore not be pronounced. It is a "letter image",[22] which resists the reduction of the visible to the audible.

The question, therefore, is whether the meaning of that which resists such a reduction should be defined or whether its meaning should be left open, recognising that it cannot be completely represented in language. In the latter case, the tetragrammaton stimulates interpretation: the giving of names, or, better, nicknames. On the one hand, this can be considered a problem, but on the other it can also be appreciated as a never-ending story, an invitation to be creative. The preservation of the tetragrammaton in the translation of the Hebrew Bible keeps this process open and provides a vivid awareness of its ultimate irreducibility. The tetragrammaton is only an indication of God's proper name, not the name itself. This name is hidden behind the image and is thus represented only indirectly.

The preceding argument can further be supported by a number of theological considerations. First, the use of the tetragrammaton makes visible that no semantic concept can fully represent or describe God; or, as Mary Phil Korsak has put it, "To leave it as it stands is to respect its transcendent character, in keeping with Hebrew tradition."[23] Secondly, the tetragrammaton creates room for a plurality of names, a practice which is in line with what the Bible itself does in bestowing name after name upon its deity. Thirdly, the tetragrammaton can also function as a *locus theologicus*, a place in the text where God can be looked for and found. Both our speaking and thinking are thus kept in motion.

For all these reasons, rather than translating this name, it should simply be represented in the text. The question then becomes how this can be done appropriately.

### 3. An Alternative Practice

Of course, the final issue relates to how this could work in practice. There are several ways to render the tetragrammaton: it can simply be left in Hebrew or

---

[22] Doude van Troostwijk, "Het geschil en de godsnaam," 354.

[23] Mary Phil Korsak, "Genesis: A New Look," in: Athalaya Brenner (ed.), *A Feminist Companion to Genesis* (Sheffield Academic Press: Sheffield 1993), 39-52, here 42.

it may be transcribed as JHWH. According to Chris Doude van Troostwijk, the advantage of keeping the tetragrammaton in Hebrew is that it confronts the readers with the fact that the Bible is in its origin a Jewish book. He also suggests printing the two middle characters in a smaller font and writing in that open space "the name" in a smaller print as an invitation to determine which (nick-)name can be used to name the Unnameable. The use of Hebrew in a translation, however, might meet with too many objections. An alternative could be to apply the same technique to the transcription of the tetragrammaton written as JHwH.

However, this does not solve the practical problems, and an important question remains: how can the tetragrammaton, in Hebrew or transcribed, be read aloud? A major objection often raised is that the tetragrammaton will be pronounced and that this is blasphemous; however, that is not yet a sufficient reason simply to write a different word, as is the case when it is rendered with HEER. In my view it would be far better to look for more creative solutions here. Such solutions already exist, in so far as there are both Jewish and Christian communities where the tetragrammaton is replaced by another name, such as "the Name" or "the Eternal (One)". I do not see why this could not become the practice on a much larger scale. That may require time and consciousness-raising, but should not be considered impossible. Several means could be used to introduce this alternative: the principle can be explained in the introduction to the translation in question; this could be supplemented with a bookmark giving several alternatives already in use. [24] However, whether this more daring solution will at some stage win the day still remains to be seen.

In diesem Artikel stellt die Autorin die neue niederländische Bibelübersetzung [NBV] und die Diskussion über die Übersetzung des hebräischen Tetragrammatons mit HEER (Herr) in der NBV dar. Sie gibt eine Übersicht über die Argumente, die gegen HEER als ausschließliche Wiedergabe des Tetragrammatons angeführt werden können. Nachdem sie auch andere Möglichkeiten erörtert hat, nennt sie die Argumente, die für die ihrer Ansicht nach beste Alternative sprechen, nämlich die Übertragung der hebräischen Buchstaben in die lateinischen Buchstaben JHWH. Der Artikel schließt mit einigen Betrachtungen darüber, wie dies in der Praxis funktionieren könnte.

---

[24] In a note accompanying the first occurrence of the tetragrammaton, Mary Phil Korsak suggests pronouncing it as "Adonai", "Yahweh" or "the Lord" [Mary Phil Korsak, *At the Start...*, 5 note 4].

L'auteur présente dans cet article la nouvelle traduction néerlandaise de la Bible [NBV] et met en perspective le débat autour de la traduction, dans cette nouvelle bible, du tétragramme hébraïque par HEER (Seigneur). Elle expose les arguments pouvant être élevés contre le mot HEER, comme seule interprétation du tétragramme, et présente, après avoir examiné d'autres solutions possibles, les arguments en faveur de la traduction des caractères hébreux par les quatre lettres latines JHWH, qui lui paraît être la plus adéquate. L'article se termine par quelques observations pratiques sur la lecture au quotidien d'un nom qui ne se prononce pas.

***Caroline Vander Stichele*** teaches New Testament at the University of Amsterdam and is currently working on a book, "From Eve to Evil: Wicked Women in the New Testament," which considers the cultural reception of biblical women. She is one of the supervisors of the New Dutch Bible Translation and co-editor of the European electronic journal for feminist exegesis, *lectio difficilior*.

·

*Rosine Lambin*

# Le voile dans le Christianisme et ses racines dans la religion romaine

À la fin du IIIe siècle, l'Église romaine développa un rite particulier qui la distingua de l'Église d'Orient. Les "vierges" (*virgines*) d'Italie et d'Afrique qui se vouaient au service de l'Église, étaient consacrées par le voile. Ce rite, accompli par la *"consecratio capitis"*, prit le nom de *"velatio virginalis"*.[1] En Orient, les femmes, comme au demeurant, les hommes qui optaient pour une vie ascétique étaient consacrés par la prise d'habit. Comparée à cette forme de consécration, la *velatio* en Occident apparut comme une innovation de l'Église. Mais la branche orientale de l'Église chrétienne se méfiait en général beaucoup plus des innovations, si bien que l'imposition du voile ne fut jamais vraiment intégrée dans les rites de consécration des femmes d'Orient. De même que le rite romain du mariage, repris par celui de la consécration des vierges, n'y fut jamais pleinement admis.[2] La discipline des églises orientales reste en la matière très différente de celle des églises occidentales et, malgré quelques percées tardives dans la pratique, le rite de la *velatio* des vierges ne figurera jamais dans les eucologes grecs.[3] Qu'un lien se soit établi entre le port du voile pour les femmes, et la religion, vu notamment la division de l'Islam, puis renforcé en Orient au cours du XXe siècle, est pareillement une nouveauté dans l'histoire.[4]

---

[1]  Jérôme (v. 347-419), *Epistolae*, CXXX/2 (Les Belles Lettres, G. Budé: Paris 1949-1963), vol. 7, 167; CXLVII/6, vol. 8, 126; Sirice (pape) (Pont.: 385-398), *Epistolae*, Patrologia Latina, (Petit Montrouge: Paris 1845) [= MPL], vol. 13, 1183; Ambroise de Milan (v. 330/340-397), *De virginibus*, III/1/1, MPL, vol. 16, 219; Ambroise de Milan (pseudo), *De lapsu virginis*, V, MPL, vol. 16, 372.

[2]  Emilianos Timiadis, *Le monachisme orthodoxe, hier, demain* (Buchet / Chastel: Paris 1981), 200.

[3]  Aimé Georges Martimort, *Les Diaconesses, Essai historique*, Bibliotheca Epemerides Liturgicae subsidia 24, (C. L. V. Edizioni Liturgiche: Rome 1982), 198.

[4]  Rosine A. Lambin, *Le vêtement religieux féminin, les débats dans l'Église au XXe siècle: ses recours aux origines et à la tradition ancienne*, Doctorat "Nouveau Régime", Université Paris IV-Sorbonne (Atelier de Reproduction des Thèses de Lille, Université de Lille III 1992), 216-29, 731-819; *Le voile des femmes* (Studia Religiosa Helvetica: Series Altera 3; Peter Lang: Berne 1999), 89-97.

Comment et pour quelle raison les pères de l'Église latine eurent-ils l'idée de vouloir voiler les vierges pour les consacrer à Dieu? Dans quelles traditions ce rite est-il né? Quels étaient ses objectifs? Autant de questions qui seront exposées au cours de cet article.

## La devotio

Dans une étude historique précédente, j'ai pu constater que le voile de consécration des vierges dans le christianisme occidental plongeait naturellement ses racines dans le paganisme romain.[5] Dans la religion romaine, le voile avait trois fonctions majeures étroitement liées: il signifiait le sacrifice aux dieux, le mariage et la consécration virginale. Son port, dans les rites de sacrifice, d'où provient son sens initial, n'était pas limité aux femmes. Lorsque les romains, hommes et femmes, priaient les dieux ou offraient un sacrifice, ils se recouvraient généralement d'un voile qui exprimait leur retraite pendant la durée de l'acte religieux et manifestait leur consécration momentanée aux dieux (*devotio*). Le voile était un objet de culte très important au coeur des rites romains de sacrifice et de dévotion.[6] Son port pendant l'acte de dévotion spécifiait que ceux qui s'en recouvraient étaient séparés du monde terrestre et isolés, l'espace de cet instant sacré. Dans les rites religieux romains de sacrifice, le voile était porté, soit en signe de dévotion et de respect, par l'officiant qui sacrifiait pour marquer l'importance de l'acte, soit par celui qui était sacrifié, soit encore par qui se vouait à un dieu, en signe de consécration. Se voilait qui venait adorer, s'initier, se consacrer ou se purifier.

---

[5] Lambin, *Le vêtement religieux féminin*, 560-636; "L'entrée du voile des femmes dans les religions monothéistes: la première lettre de Paul aux Corinthiens (11:2-16)", in: *Clio: Femmes, Histoire et Sociétés* 2 (1995), 61-84; *Le voile des femmes*, 63-88.

[6] Sacrifice: Virgile (v. 70-19 v. C.), *Aeneis*, III/403-409 (Les Belles Lettres, G. Budé: Paris 1937-1980), 84; Varron (v. 116-v. 27 v. C.), *De lingua latina*, V/130 (Les Belles Lettres, G. Budé: Paris 1985), 85-7; Macrobe (début V^e s.), *Saturnaliorum libri*, I/8/2 (Garnier: Paris 1953), vol. 1, 71; III/6/17, 337; Plutarque (45-125), *Questiones romanae*, X-XI (David Lopes de Haro: Leyde 1637), 9-11; *Vitae*, Numa, 10/12 (Les Belles Lettres, G. Budé: Paris 1957-1983), vol. 1, 196; Tite Live (64 ou 59-v. 10 v. C.), *Historia romanae*, I/26, Ab urbe condita, libri 45 (Les Belles Lettres, G. Budé: Paris 1940-1984), vol. 1, 43; VIII/9, vol. 8, 22; Cicéron (106-43 v. C.), *Orationes*, IV/13 (Les Belles Lettres, G. Budé: Paris 1960-1973), vol. 9, 142; XLVIII/124, Pro Domo. Flamminica: Aulu-Gelle (v. 115/120-après 158), *Noctes atticae*, X/15/26-30 (Les Belles Lettres, G. Budé: Paris 1967-1978), vol. 2, 168; Pompeius Festus (fin III^e s.), *De verborum significatione*, VI (Panckoucke: Paris 1846), 153; Servius Honoratus (V^e s.), *P.Virgilii Maronis cum veterum omnium commentariis*, XII/602, nova editio (Lyon 1645).

La tradition du *ver sacrum* (printemps sacré), qui remonte à la période italique, permet de mieux comprendre et de souligner l'importance du voile dans la religion romaine. Lorsque les romains étaient menacés par un danger, ils faisaient vœu d'immoler tous les êtres animés qui naîtraient au printemps suivant. Or, les anciens sacrifices humains ayant été jugés trop cruels, ils furent remplacés par le rite de couvrir d'un voile les jeunes filles et les jeunes gens arrivés à l'âge adulte, puis de les chasser complètement voilés hors des frontières.[7] Ce voile manifestait leur sacrifice. De même, les vestales[8] coupables d'avoir failli à leur vœu, étaient, lors de leur châtiment, recouvertes d'un voile par le *Pontifex Maximus* avant d'être livrées à la justice divine, ensevelies vivantes. Seuls les dieux pouvaient ravir la vie à une vestale.[9] Les condamnés à mort étaient voilés en signe de l'holocauste qu'ils évoquaient.[10] Dans les rites de sacrifice proprement dit, le voile conserve un sens similaire. Les femmes se couvrent d'un voile frangé appelé *rica* pour offrir un holocauste.[11]

Le voile romain de sacrifice était, pour ceux qui le portaient, le signe de la consécration temporaire de leur vie au moment du sacrifice. Sacrifiés ou sacrificateurs, leur vie était dédiée au royaume du sacré et aux dieux aussi longtemps qu'ils portaient le voile. Le père de l'Église, Cyprien de Carthage, (déb. IIIᵉ s./258) l'interpréta également ainsi, puisqu'il félicitait, au cours des persécutions des chrétiens de l'empire romain au IIIᵉ siècle, les *confessores* (*viri, foeminae, virgines, pueri*) dont la tête était demeurée dénuée du voile impie des sacrifices pour rester consacrée à la couronne du Seigneur.[12] Lorsque les chrétiens abjuraient leur religion sous les persécutions, ils devaient sacrifier aux dieux romains et se recouvrir d'un voile durant le sacrifice. Sa connaissance des rites païens n'empêcha cependant pas Cyprien de Carthage de reprendre les prescriptions de Tertullien (150-160/222?) quant au port du voile pour les vierges chrétiennes qui, si elles allaient tête nue, étaient

---

[7]  Pompeius Festus, *De verborum significatione*, XIX, ver sacrum, 684.

[8]  Sur les vestales, cf. Hildegard Cancik-Lindemaier, "Die Priesterinnen der Vesta. Eine Fallstudie", in: R. Faber & S. Lanwerd, *Kybelee – Prophetin – Hexe: Religiöse Frauenbilder und Weiblichkeitskonzeptionen* (Königshausen & Neumann: Würzburg 1997), 109-126.

[9]  Plutarque, *Vitae*, Numa, 10/12, vol. 1, 196.

[10]  Tite Live, *Historia romanae*, I/26, Ab urbe condita, libri 45, vol. 1, 43; Cicéron, *Orationes*, IV/13, vol. 9, 142.

[11]  Varron, *De lingua latina*, V/130, 85-7.

[12]  Cyprien de Carthage (début IIIᵉ s./258), *De Lapsis*, MPL, vol. 4, 466. Sur l'utilisation chrétienne des rites païens, cf. Kate Cooper, *The Virgin and the Bride: Idealized Womanhood in Late Antiquity* (Harvard University Press: Cambridge, MA 1996), 76-7, 284.

considérées comme la honte de l'Église.[13] C'est aussi pour se vouer à la divinité qu'un personnage s'est fait représenter, dans le temple de la Fortune Primigenia à Rome, la tête recouverte de toges, qu'il était interdit de soulever.[14] La distinction que concrétise le port du voile conduit à l'idée de *consecratio capitis*, la mise à l'écart de l'objet ou de la personne dédiés aux dieux par la consécration de la tête.[15] Le voile était consacré aux choses à part et sacrées, il était utilisé dans les cérémonies cultuelles, car il avait pour propriété de dissimuler, de créer le mystère, d'isoler du monde les choses destinées au domaine divin, de discriminer le pur et l'impur. Le voile romain aurait donc une fonction similaire à celle du voile distinguant le sacré du profane, que l'on retrouve dans le judaïsme.[16] Sur la grande frise de la Villa des mystères de Pompéi, l'on voit, par exemple, une femme romaine, qui a subi la flagellation, ressusciter entourée de l'orbe de son nouveau vêtement. L'initiée est voilée et habillée comme une jeune épouse.[17] La pureté de son nouveau corps est symbolisée par le voile. La tête est consacrée car elle est le lieu où siège l'esprit, tandis que le corps est le centre des passions. La tête, partie supérieure du corps, représente aussi l'autorité et la suprématie. En portant le voile, les romains se décapitaient symboliquement afin de signifier leur obéissance et leur soumission aux dieux. En se soumettant, ils se purifiaient et entraient dans le monde du divin. À Rome, l'épouse du flamine de Jupiter devait, de même, se recouvrir de la *rica*, qu'elle utilisait comme voile rituel ou comme manteau.[18] Elle se couvrait au quotidien du *flammeum* couleur de flamme de la fiancée; contrairement aux autres femmes, il lui était interdit de divorcer.[19] Il existe un lien entre le port du *flammeum* et l'interdiction de divorcer. L'obligation de demeurer pure rendait le divorce impossible. Dans le christianisme, il fut aussi strictement défendu aux vierges consacrées et voilées de rompre leur vœu d'épouses du Christ, qui était considéré comme un mariage.

---

[13] Lambin, *Le vêtement religieux féminin*, 704-706.

[14] Ovide (43 v. C.-v. 17 n. C.), *Fasti*, IV/569-623 (Les Belles Lettres, G. Budé: Paris 1990), 190-91.

[15] Ovide, *Fasti*, IV/569-623, 190-91.

[16] Lambin, *Le vêtement religieux féminin*, 573-5.

[17] Amedeo Maiuri, *La peinture romaine* (Éditions d'Art Albert Skira: Genève 1953), 52-9.

[18] Pompeius Festus, *De verborum significatione*, VI, 153; XVI, 518-19; Aulu-Gelle, *Noctes atticae*, X/15/27-28, vol. 2, 168; Servius Honoratus, *P.Virgilii Maronis cum veterum omnium commentariis*, XII/602.

[19] Pompeius Festus, *De verborum significatione*, VI, 153.

Pour conclure, la *velatio* des vierges dans le christianisme reprit donc à son compte les aspects centraux de la claustration et de la soumission de la religion romaine. Cette signification du voile prit une ampleur sans pareille chez les femmes à qui l'Église demandait d'offrir leur vie entière en sacrifice et de renoncer au monde. La prise de voile, imposée à partir du IVᵉ siècle aux vierges chrétiennes qui marquaient par là leur consécration définitive et complète, semble avoir en partie conservé le sens religieux du voile romain de sacrifice. Le voile romain de sacrifice et le voile chrétien des vierges ont au moins en commun la consécration à la divinité. Comment le rite chrétien du voilement des vierges aurait-il eu, sinon, le pouvoir d'accomplir une consécration? Que le rite de la *velatio* se soit imposé dans le christianisme latin au IVᵉ siècle plaide en faveur de cette thèse. À cette époque, les Pères n'avaient en effet plus à combattre aussi violemment qu'auparavant le paganisme, affaibli et privé du soutien de l'empereur.[20] Le rite romain de la *devotio*, exprimé par le voile, pouvait être absorbé par la tradition de l'Église sans trop faire de remous. Les Pères limitèrent l'usage de ce rite aux seules femmes. Mais l'idée de sacrifice demeura intacte dans le rite de la consécration des vierges chrétiennes. Seule la vierge pouvait recevoir le voile et subissait l'acte de la cérémonie sous forme d'un sacrifice opérant une consécration et un mariage. Le voile rituel des hommes s'évanouit. Outre ses différentes utilisations dans les rites romains pour la consécration, le voile fut également lié, dans l'Église romaine, à la mort, à la respectabilité, au bien face au mal. Les défuntes représentées sur les monuments mortuaires sont, dans tout l'Occident, généralement voilées.[21] Que dans le christianisme le voile ne soit porté que par les femmes provient d'une part de la tradition paulinienne qui estime qu'une femme convenable doit se couvrir la tête et cacher sa chevelure,[22] réservée à son époux, d'autre part du voile de mariage romain.

### Les rites de mariage

Dans la religion romaine, la tradition d'imposition du voile se limitait aux femmes durant la cérémonie de mariage. Seule la fiancée était couverte, d'un

---

[20] L'édit de Milan, émis en février 313 par Constantin, mettait fin aux persécutions contre l'Église lui permettant ainsi d'évoluer librement.

[21] Rome: Catacombe de Domitille, Rome, via Ardeatina, tombe de Veneranda, arcosolium, lunette, post. 356, *in situ*, en comparaison avec l'Hypogée païen de Vibia, Rome, galerie contiguë au cimetière de Pretestato, IVᵉ s., *in situ*. Afrique: Mosaïque de dalle funéraire de Tabarka, IVᵉ s., Musée du Bardo, Tunis.

[22] Lambin, "L'entrée du voile des femmes dans les religions monothéistes", 61-84; *Le voile des femmes*, 63-72.

voile de fine étoffe presque transparent qui ne lui couvrait pas la face. Il était d'un rouge orange vif ou tirant sur le brun, d'où son nom de *flammeum* suggérant la couleur de la flamme en mémoire du feu sacré de la déesse Vesta.[23] La fiancée se soumettait au rite de la *conferreatio*,[24] consistant, parmi d'autres rites vestimentaires,[25] à se faire poser sur la tête le *flammeum* par le prêtre de Jupiter, le *Flamen Dialis*.[26] Une couronne de marjolaine et de verveine qu'elle-même avait cueillies était placée sous son voile. La couronne de la fiancée romaine fut introduite dans le christianisme et devint, malgré l'aversion qu'avaient eu pour elle certains Pères de l'Église avant la paix de l'Église (313), un élément de la panoplie vestimentaire de la consécration des vierges chrétiennes au Moyen Âge.[27]

Le rituel de vêture de la cérémonie de mariage romaine, consistant à imposer le voile à la fiancée, fut conservé dans l'usage chrétien et repris dans la cérémonie de consécration des vierges.[28] Le mariage romain était aussi une consécration car, à l'origine, pendant la cérémonie la fiancée était initiée au culte domestique de son époux. Nul doute que ce rite du voile de mariage comprenne l'idée de consécration (*devotio*) que nous avons déjà détectée dans l'usage, par la religion romaine, du voile rituel de sacrifice, le voile de la

---

[23] Juvénal (v. 55-v. 140), *Saturae*, II/120-125 (Les Belles Lettres, G. Budé: Paris 1957); VI/224; X/334; Pompeius Festus, *De verborum significatione*, VI, flammeum, 153; cf. O. G. Harrison, "The formulas 'ad Virgines sacras': a Study of the Sources", in: *Ephemerides Liturgicae*, 66 (1952), 252-73, 352-66, ici 256; Maiuri, *La peinture romaine*, 30.

[24] Roger Metz, *La consécration des vierges dans l'Église romaine* (Presses Universitaires de France: Paris 1954), Appendice I, "Le rituel du mariage", 367-8.

[25] Pompeius Festus, *De verborum significatione*, XVI, regillis, 515; cf. John P.V.D. Balsdon, *Roman Women, their History and Habits* (Barnes and Noble: New York 1983), 182-6.

[26] Harrison, "The formulas 'ad Virgines sacras'", 256.

[27] Pompeius Festus, *De verborum significatione*, III, corolla, 107; Pline l'Ancien (24-79), *Naturalis historia*, XXI/3/8 (Les Belles Lettres, G. Budé: Paris 1950-1981), 28; cf. Justin (v. 100-v. 165), *Apologiae*, I/9 (Études Augustiniennes: Paris 1987), 107; Tertullien, *De corona militis*, XIII, Patrologia Latina, vol. 2 (Petit Montrouge: Paris 1844), 95-7; Clément d'Alexandrie (v. 150/v. 215), *Pedagogos*, II, VIII/72/2-4-73/1-2 (Sources Chrétiennes 108; Cerf: Paris 1965), 143-5; Minucius Félix (IIe-IIIe s.), *Octavius*, 12, 38 (Bibliothèque Ecclésiastique: Paris 1837), vol. 2, 17, 54.

[28] R. d'Izarny, "Mariage et consécration virginale au IVe siècle", in: *Supplément de la Vie Spirituelle*, 6 (1953), 99. Cooper, *The Virgin and the Bride*, 101-104, d'après Franca Ela Consolino, "Modelli di comportamento e modi di sanctificazione par l'aristocrazia femminile d'Occidente", in: Andrea Giardina (ed.), *Società romana e impero tardoantico*, I (Laterza: Bari 1986), argumente que Jérôme attaqua le mariage romain idéalisé, pour discréditer la tradition commune au paganisme et au christianisme du mariage idéalisé.

mariée signifiant le nouvel état que la jeune fille s'apprêtait à embrasser pour toujours. Le voile était le témoignage d'une conversion. La jeune fille quittait ses dieux familiaux et passait à l'état de matrone, soumise à son époux et aux dieux domestiques de celui-ci. L'étymologie confirme cette thèse. Le verbe *"nubere"* signifiait à l'origine "se voiler", puis il devint synonyme de "se marier", et de ce mot naquit également le dérivé *"nuptiae"* signifiant "mariage".[29] L'état de mariage et le voile formaient donc une unité. Isidore de Séville (v. 570-636), Père de l'Église espagnol, explique que les *"nuptae"* (mariées) tenaient leur nom de ce qu'elles se voilaient le visage. Ce mot était d'après lui originellement une métaphore pour *"nubes"*, les nuages qui recouvrent (voilent) le ciel, de là proviendrait le mot de *"nuptiae"* (noces), lors desquelles on voilait pour la première fois la tête des jeunes mariées. *"Obnubere"* signifiait en effet recouvrir totalement (*cooperire*) et son contraire *"innuba"*, ou *"innupta"*, désignait la vierge qui ne se voilait pas encore le visage.[30] L'explication étymologique d'Isidore de Séville est vraisemblable malgré son caractère spéculatif. En hébreu, la "nuée" derrière laquelle se trouve Dieu peut aussi se traduire par "voile".[31] La cérémonie de consécration des vierges chrétiennes empruntera au rite du mariage romain sans trop les modifier ces trois principaux éléments: le voile, la couronne et l'anneau.[32] Cette tradition attestée demeure encore vivante dans l'Église romaine au XXIe siècle. Elle se maintient dans les rites conventionnels de mariage et dans les ordres religieux féminins dont certains, notamment celui des cisterciennes, ont conservé le rite de la *velatio*.[33] Mais pourquoi des vierges chrétiennes furent-elles incitées à se recouvrir d'un voile réservé au mariage, recelant l'idée de conversion et de dévotion aux dieux de l'époux? La réponse à cette question réside peut-être dans l'étude du voile des vestales.

---

[29] Pompeius Festus, *De verborum significatione*, XII, nuptiae, 293-4.

[30] Isidore de Séville (v. 570/636), *Ethymologiae*, IX/7/10 (Les Belles Lettres, G. Budé: Paris 1984), vol. 9, 228; cf. Servius Honoratus, *P.Virgilii Maronis cum veterum omnium commentariis*, XI/77, Aeneis.

[31] Exode 19/9; 24/15-18; 34/5; 40/34-35; 1Rois 8/10-11; Ezéchiel 1/4; 10/4; cf. Matthieu 17/5; Marc 9/7; Luc 9/34.

[32] Metz, *La consécration des vierges dans l'Église romaine*, 374-5; cf. Aulu-Gelle, *Noctes atticae*, X/10, vol. 2.

[33] *Prières du Rituel cistercien pour les cérémonies de vêture*, commentaires par S. Gertrude, avec approbation des supérieurs de l'Ordre (Monastère des Cisterciennes de Blagnac 1921); *Prières de la prise d'habit* (Abbaye cistercienne La-Joie-Notre-Dame à Campeneac 1921); *Dictionnaire de droit canonique*, R. Naz (dir.) (Letouzey et Ané: Paris 1935-1965), tome 6, 935; tome 7, 348.

## Les vestales

Les vestales avaient pour fonction d'être les statues vivantes de Vesta (Gr. Hestia) déesse voilée et vierge, comme Junon (Héra) et Cérès (Déméter). Les vestales étaient choisies parmi les jeunes patriciennes sans tares physiques, logées sous un même toit, l'*atrium Vestae*, vouées au culte de la déesse pendant trente ans et soumises au vœu de chasteté. Habillées d'un vêtement distinctif, compromis entre la toilette de la fiancée romaine, celle de la femme patricienne,[34] et une tenue exprimant une certaine fonction religieuse,[35] elles étaient reconnaissables à leur mise. Toute coquetterie était proscrite et sévèrement punie.[36] Pendant toute la durée de leur ministère, les vestales étaient doublement voilées. Elles portaient un voile blanc et rectangulaire, le *suffibulum*,[37] sous la partie supérieure de leur vêtement, la *stola* des matrones, qu'elles rabattaient sur leur tête.[38] Leur voile, un voile de *devotio* continue, était le signe de leur appartenance à une vie consacrée, et leur coiffure évoquait celle des fiancées romaines. Certaines vestales sont aussi représentées portant le *capital*, bandeau que les prêtresses coiffaient lors du sacrifice.[39]

Les Pères de l'Église paraissent avoir voulu perpétuer cette tradition dans l'empire romain bien après sa christianisation. La consécration des vestales de la Rome païenne, exprimée par le port du voile, est comparable à la *velatio* des vierges dans le christianisme romain d'occident. À l'image des vestales, vierges elles aussi consacrées, les vierges chrétiennes vouées à Dieu durent porter le voile en signe de leur consécration et de leur

---

[34] Une longue *stola* et une *palla*: cf. Pline le Jeune (61-v. 114), *Epistolae,* IV/11/9 (Les Belles Lettres, G. Budé: Paris 1928-1955), 104.

[35] Un vêtement de laine blanche et des bandelettes saintes: cf. Ambroise de Milan, *Epistolae*, XVIII/1-12, in: Prudence (348-v. 415), *Psychomania, Contra Symmachum*, II/1055, vol. 3 (Les Belles Lettres, G. Budé: Paris 1948), 123; le *suffibulum*, de couleur blanche, bordé, rectangulaire: cf. Pompeius Festus, *De verborum significatione*, XVII, 627.

[36] Tite Live, *Historia romanae*, IV/44/11, 73.

[37] Pompeius Festus, *De verborum significatione*, XVII, 627, qui donne cette description, précise que les vestales mettent ce voile lorsqu'elles sacrifient et qu'elles l'attachent sur la poitrine avec une agrafe (*fibula*). À Rome, dans l'*atrium* des vestales, on a découvert une seule représentation exacte de ce voile, la plupart des statues étant dépourvues de tête.

[38] Pline le Jeune, *Epistolae*, IV/11/9, 104.

[39] Varron, *De lingua latina*, V/130, 85. Un médaillon à l'effigie de Bellicia Modesta v(irgo) V(estalis) nous montre cette coiffure: *Dictionnaire des Antiquités Grecques et Romaines*, Charles Victor Daremberg / Edmond Saglio (dir.) (Hachette: Paris 1873-1919), tome 1, vol. 2, 897, fig. 1144. Le diadème est de laine, divisé en six cordons (*infula*).

virginité.[40] Cette parenté entre vierges chrétiennes et vestales païennes créa, logiquement, un problème au christianisme. La ressemblance entre les vierges païennes et les vierges chrétiennes était telle que certains Pères de l'Église, dont notamment Ambroise de Milan (v. 330/340-397), se virent contraints de déprécier la chasteté, la mise et le mode de vie des vestales afin de mieux exalter la virginité chrétienne. Mais, à force de dissocier les deux institutions en les comparant, ils en soulignaient du même coup les similarités.[41] Car s'il n'y avait eu aucune analogie, il n'aurait pas été nécessaire de défendre la virginité chrétienne face à l'institution des vestales. Le voile devint, peu à peu, l'élément central de la cérémonie de la *velatio* des vierges chrétiennes, comme il l'était pour les vestales. Le voile des vestales et celui des vierges chrétiennes ont d'ailleurs une symbolique commune que l'on retrouve dans les rites du mariage romain. L'imposition du voile de la couleur du feu de Vesta (*flammeum*) à la fiancée romaine (*obnubilatio capitis*) confirme la parenté entre l'institution des vestales et le rite de la *velatio* des vierges chrétiennes au IVe siècle, voilées pour manifester leur mariage au Christ.

### Le voile dans le christianisme

La *velatio* des vierges chrétiennes s'apparente donc à trois traditions romaines imbriquées les unes dans les autres. Elle comporte, premièrement, des éléments du voile de la *devotio* et du sacrifice, porté par les deux sexes en signe de consécration momentanée lors de l'acte religieux, deuxièmement, des éléments du voile du mariage, signifiant la soumission et l'obéissance de l'épouse à l'époux et à ses dieux domestiques, troisièmement, des éléments du voile des

---

[40] Ines Stahlmann, *Der gefesselte Sexus: Weibliche Keuschheit und Askese im Westen des Römischen Reiches* (Akademie Verlag: Berlin 1997), 121, prétend, en s'appuyant sur l'article de C. Koch, "Vesta", in: *Paulys Realencyclopädie der classischen Altertumswissenschaft*, tome VIII A2, 1717-76, que la différence principale entre les vestales et les vierges chrétiennes se trouve dans la forme de leur ascèse. Les vestales menaient une ascèse pour le salut public de Rome (*salus publica*) alors que les vierges chrétiennes n'auraient eu pour but que leur salut personnel (*salus privata*). C'est oublier que les vierges chrétiennes représentaient aussi l'Église avec pour signe leur voile et leur vêtement, comme le suggèrent de nombreuses sources, telles que, par exemple, Méthode d'Olympe (fin IIIe s.), *Le Banquet*, Sources Chrétiennes 95 (Cerf: Paris 1963), Prélude 5-6, 47-9; Discours VII, II/154-155, 183-5; Hermas (+92), *Le pasteur*, Sources Chrétiennes 53 bis (Cerf: Paris 1968), 293, 319 etc.

[41] Origène (v. 185-v. 254), *Contra Celsum*, VII/48, Sources Chrétiennes 4: 150 (Cerf: Paris 1969), 129-31; Tertullien, *Ad uxorem*, I/VI/3-4, Sources Chrétiennes 273 (Cerf: Paris 1980), 113; Ambroise de Milan, *Epistolae*, I/18/11-12, À l'empereur Valentinien Ier, MPL, vol. 17, 975; Prudence, *Psychomania*, Contra Symmachum, II/1055, vol. 3, 193.

vestales, indiquant la virginité consacrée à la divinité. Il semble que les Pères latins aient fait une synthèse entre le voile nuptial romain, celui de l'oblation, de l'initiation religieuse, des vierges vestales et de la femme mariée. Le rite romain du voile manifestait une double consécration aux dieux et à l'époux. Le rite de l'*obnubilatio capitis* de la Rome païenne, qui signifiait le sacrifice et la soumission de la femme, fut donc incorporé à la liturgie chrétienne. L'ancien rite romain reproduit essentiellement la cérémonie du mariage romain en transformant l'*obnubilatio capitis* en mariage mystique entre la vierge et le Christ; l'*obnubilatio capitis* était l'acte le plus représentatif des cérémonies profanes de mariage, et le terme de *velatio* s'appliquait souvent aux deux cérémonies, mariage et consécration des vierges, qui suivirent parallèlement le même rituel.[42] Non seulement les vierges chrétiennes étaient consacrées par le voile, mais aussi mariées au Christ. Le rituel vestimentaire du mariage romain fut d'abord entièrement conservé dans l'usage chrétien occidental du mariage, puis transposé dans la cérémonie de consécration des vierges.[43] La vierge chrétienne fut appelée "épouse du Christ" dès le IIIe siècle et l'imposition du voile devint l'acte clé sanctificateur du passage de l'état de non-mariée à l'état de mariée (*virgo velata*).[44] Ce mariage virginal étant considéré comme réel, les lois concernant le mariage et l'infidélité furent toutes, par la suite, appliquées à la vierge consacrée.[45] Mais, contrairement à une femme mariée, une vierge voilée faisait vœu de chasteté. La virginité et le mariage étant virtuellement opposés, seules une cérémonie parfaitement similaire[46] et des lois identiques[47]

---

[42] Metz, *La consécration des vierges*, 123.

[43] À partir du IVe s., dans les milieux chrétiens romains, l'imposition du voile devint le premier élément de la liturgie de mariage. À propos de la *velatio conjugalis*: cf. R. d'Izarny, "Mariage et consécration virginale", 92-5; Metz, *La consécration des vierges*, Appendice I, 380-410. La liturgie chrétienne de consécration des vierges retint ce qui lui paraissait être le plus représentatif: l'imposition du voile (*obnubilatio capitis*): Metz, *La consécration des vierges*, 381-3; Lambin, *Le vêtement religieux féminin*, 435-9.

[44] Ambroise de Milan, *Epistolae*, XIX/7, 984; Sirice (pape), *Epistolae*, I/6, 1136-37; Optat de Milève (fin IVe s.), *De schismate donatistarum*, VI/4, MPL, vol. 11, 1074-75.

[45] Concile d'Ancyre (314), canon 19, *Sacrorum conciliorum nova et amplissima collectio*, Joannes Dominicus Mansi (éd.), (Hubert Welter: Paris 1901-1927), vol. 2, 519: les vierges infidèles encourent la peine des bigames; Concile de Vannes (465), canon 4, *Histoire des Conciles*, Carl-Joseph Hefele / Jean Leclercq (éd.), (Letouzey et Ané: Paris 1907-1952), vol. 2, 905; Isidore de Séville, *Canones*, II/VI, MPL, vol. 84, 48 B-C.

[46] Sulpice Sévère (pseudo), *Ad Claudiam sororem de virginitate*, in: Sulpice Sévère, *Epistolae*, MPL, vol. 20, 228.

[47] Concile d'Elvire (300-303), canon 13, *Dictionnaire d'archéologie chrétienne et de liturgie*, vol. 11/2, 1791; Sirice (pape), *Epistolae*, 1182; Ambroise de Milan (pseudo), *De lapsu virginis*,

pouvaient les rapprocher concrètement. C'est probablement pour que l'analogie symbolique entre les deux états devienne réelle que les rites concrets du mariage furent utilisés dans la cérémonie de consécration des vierges. La vierge voilée en public était considérée comme *sacra* ou *sacrata*, elle passait radicalement d'un état à un autre sans possibilité de retour en arrière.[48] La cérémonie de la *velatio* se pratiquait à peu près partout en Occident dans la seconde moitié du IVe siècle. Il existait deux catégories de vierges: celles qui demeuraient dans leurs familles et celles qui vivaient en communauté. Toutes pouvaient recevoir le voile de l'évêque. Les vierges à simple émission de vœu ne recevaient pas le voile (*propositum*) contrairement aux vierges consacrées qui recevaient la sanction de l'Église par la cérémonie du voile (*consecratio* ou *velatio*).[49] Il fut de plus en plus impensable, au sein de l'Église, de laisser des vierges consacrées vivre libres dans le monde, leur mariage avec le Christ devant être hautement protégé. Ainsi, la hiérarchie ecclésiastique développa-t-elle des formes de contrôle, dont le voile, signe tangible et manifeste de la consécration, renforcé par la clôture à partir du Ve siècle.[50]

Il est fort possible que la vierge consacrée ait eu à porter deux voiles différents: le voile de consécration et le voile porté par toutes les femmes dans la vie courante, comme la mariée portait son voile de mariage (*flammeum*) pendant la cérémonie, puis revêtait ses vêtements ordinaires de femme

---

V/20, 372; IIe Concile de Tours (567), canon 20, *Sacrorum conciliorum nova et amplissima collectio*, J. D. Mansi (éd.), vol. 9, 798-800; Innocent Ier (pape) (Pont.: 401-417), *Decreta ex epistolis excerpta*, II/13, MPL, vol. 20, 478-9; Concile romain (402), canon 1-2, *Histoire des Conciles*, vol. 2/1, 136. Cf. E. Le Blant, *Inscriptions chrétiennes de la Gaule antérieures au VIIIe siècle* (Paris: Imprimerie Impériale 1856-1865), Propositum n° 44.

[48] Ambroise de Milan, *De virginibus*, I/11/65, 206; ce passage fait allusion aux trois actes de la consécration: l'imposition des mains, dont il est l'unique témoignage, la prière sacerdotale et la *velatio*.

[49] Sirice (pape), *Epistolae*, Aux évêques de Gaule, 1182-83, oppose les termes *virgo velata* et *mondum velata est*; Innocent Ier, *Epistolae*, II/13-14, À Victrice, MPL, vol. 20, 478-9; Léon Ier (pape) (Pont.: 440/461), *Epistolae*, II/167, À Rusticus évêque de Narbonne, MPL, vol. 54, 1207; Jérôme, *Epistolae*, XLIV/1, À Marcella, vol. 2, 95 (*velatarum virginum*); CXXX/2, À Démétriade, vol. 7, 167 (*flammeum virginale sanctum operuerit caput*); CXLVII/6, Au diacre Sabinianus, vol. 8, 126 (*Christi flammeo consecrata est*); cf. E. Le Blant, *Inscriptions chrétiennes de la Gaule antérieures au VIIIe s.* (voir note 47), Propositum n° 44.

[50] Ve Concile d'Orléans (549), canon 19, *Histoire des Conciles*, vol.3/1, 163; Césaire d'Arles (470/471-543), *Regula ad virgines*, (III), 4/1-3, MPL, vol. 67; Ferréol (+581), *Regula*, 5, MPL, vol. 66, 962.

mariée à son entrée dans la vie quotidienne.[51] Des auteurs chrétiens mentionnent d'ailleurs le port de voiles fantaisistes par les vierges, des voiles élégants, de couleur ou transparents, ce qui exclut, selon eux, le port d'un voile uniformisé.[52] La question de savoir si le voile des vierges consacrées se distinguait de celui des autres femmes à la fin de l'antiquité chrétienne en Occident demeure une question difficile à élucider. Il n'est pas non plus aisé de déterminer la couleur du voile utilisé lors de la consécration, la cérémonie s'appuyant sur deux traditions différentes: les rites romains de mariage et le baptême.[53] Certains textes suggèrent que le voile était rouge ou orange, comme le *flammeum* romain,[54] d'autres évoquent la couleur blanche, celle du voile de baptême.[55] Plus l'Église s'institutionnalisa, plus le voile et la sacralisation des vêtements se ritualisèrent. La puissance de l'Église s'amplifiant, les ascètes indépendantes furent amenées à rejoindre les monastères, où les règles vestimentaires se précisèrent et se différencièrent toujours plus pour les religieuses. Les monastères l'emportant progressivement sur toute autre forme de vie consacrée, l'on aboutit à l'assimilation, lente mais continue, de toutes les femmes consacrées aux vierges voilées. De plus en plus de femmes non vierges entraient en outre au monastère, où l'on ne discriminait pas par le costume les vierges et les autres religieuses.[56]

Avec la fondation des grands monastères du VIIe siècle, les règles devinrent plus sévères et le rite de la *velatio* se compliqua dans les sacramentaires

---

[51] Ambroise de Milan, *Epistolae*, XVIII/1-12, in: Prudence, *Psychomania*, Contra Symmachum, II/1055, vol. 3, 123: les vierges portent un *ignobile velamen usui*.

[52] Augustin (354-430), *De sancta virginitate*, XXXIV, MPL, vol. 40, 415; Aldhelm (v. 650-709), *De laudibus virginitatis*, LVIII, MPL, vol. 89, 157.

[53] En ce sens que le baptême signifie le passage d'un état à un autre, de l'état de péché à l'état de purification, ce que signifie aussi, d'une autre manière, la consécration. La plus ancienne formule prononcée lors de la remise du voile béni est celle du *pallium* (*Accipe, puella, sanctum pallium quod perferas sine macula ante tribunal Dei nostri Jesu Christi*), très proche de la formule prononcée lors de la vêture de la robe baptismale, le mot *velum* ou *velamen* ne remplaçant le mot *pallium* qu'à partir du XIe s.: O. G. Harrison, "The formulas 'ad Virgines sacras'", 358.

[54] Optat de Milève, *De schismate donatistarum*, VI/4, 1072-74; Ambroise de Milan (pseudo), *De lapsu virginis*, II, 369; Ambroise de Milan, *De instructione virginis*, XVII/108-109, MPL, vol. 16, 331-2 (*flammeo nuptiali*); Jérôme, *Epistolae*, CXXX/2, vol. 7, 167 (*flammeum virginale sanctum operuerit caput*); CXLVII/6, vol. 8, 126 (*Christi flammeo consecrata est*).

[55] Ambroise de Milan, *De instructione virginis*, XVII/110, 332; *Exhortatio castitatis*, X, MPL, vol. 16, 355.

[56] Césaire d'Arles, *Regula ad virgines*.

et les décrets pontificaux.[57] Les libertés des religieuses ne cessaient, en même temps de diminuer. À mesure que les couvents prenaient de l'importance, les ascètes, les vierges, les veuves, les diaconesses ou les pénitentes séculières devenaient moins nombreuses.[58] Les femmes ayant fait profession dans un monastère et les veuves avec plusieurs années de vêture à leur actif furent déclarées inaptes au mariage. Ainsi, la plupart des nonnes rentrant dans cette catégorie furent assimilées aux vierges voilées. L'uniformisation de l'apparence extérieure, qui prit forme entre le IVe et le VIIe siècle témoigne du contrôle de plus en plus serré exercé par l'Église sur les femmes consacrées. Ce contrôle fut tout d'abord établi en Occident par la prise de voile, puis, les vierges indépendantes et les ascètes furent forcées de vivre en communauté et enfin soumises, aux Ve et VIe siècles, à la clôture. Les Pères de l'Église des IIIe et IVe siècles ont utilisé le voile de la Rome antique païenne comme tout premier signe de la clôture et de la soumission des vierges consacrées à la hiérarchie de l'Église.

Woher stammt die Verpflichtung für die Ordensschwestern der römischen Kirche, einen Schleier zu tragen? Aus welchem Grund hatte der Schleier eine solche Bedeutung in den ersten Jahrhunderten des Christentums? Eine Untersuchung der römischen religiösen Traditionen über den Schleier läßt auf zahlreiche Bedeutungen und Funktionen schließen. Diese werden in den Riten der im vierten Jahrhundert eingeführten *velatio* der christlichen Jungfrauen sichtbar. In der römischen Religion hatte der Schleier seinen Platz bei drei Ereignissen, die eng miteinander verbunden waren: Er bedeutete das Opfer und die Ergebenheit den Göttern gegenüber, die Heirat und die Ergebenheit der Braut den Hausgöttern des Bräutigams gegenüber und schließlich die jungfräuliche Weihe als Vestalin. Die christlichen Jungfrauen wiederum wurden durch den Schleier Gott geopfert und mit Christus verheiratet, und ihre Unberührtheit wurde geweiht. Diese drei Zustände – Opfergabe, Heirat und Jungfräulichkeit – weisen gewisse Ähnlichkeiten mit den Schleierriten in der römischen Religion auf, die in das Christentum eingegangen sind.

---

[57] Réglementations du *Missale gallicanum vetus*, Cod. Vatic. Palat. lat., 493 (Rerum Ecclesiasticorum Documenta, Fontes 3; L. K. Mohlberg / Herder: Rome, 1958), 7-8, notes 15-16; du *Missale Francorum*, Cod. Vatic. Regin. lat., 257 (Rerum Ecclesiasticorum Documenta, Fontes 2; L. K. Mohlberg / Herder: Rome 1957), 16-17, notes 51-55; du *Sacramentaire gélasien*, Cod. Vatic. Regin. lat., 316 (Rome: L. K. Mohlberg, Herder, Rerum Ecclesiasticorum Documenta, Fontes 4, 1960), 124-6, notes 787-792.

[58] Le Concile de Ver (755) force les vierges qui ont pris le voile à vivre dans un monastère et marque le début du déclin des vierges isolées dans le monde franc; à partir du IXe s., il n'est plus officiellement question de ces vierges indépendantes.

What is the origin of the requirement that the nuns of the Roman Church shouuld wear a veil? Why is the veil of such importance in the first centuries of Christianity? An investigation of Roman religious traditions concerning the veil indicates numerous functions and meanings in the rites surrounding the *velatio*, introduced in the fourth century for Christian virgins. In Roman religion, the veil was used in three important – and related – contexts: to indicate sacrifice and devotion to God, marriage and the submission of the bride to the house gods of her husband, and the consecration of the vestal virgins. By use of the veil, Christian virgins, were offered to God, married to Christ, and showed that their virginity was consecrated. The three states of sacrifice, marriage and virginity demonstrate certain parallels to the rites of the veil in Roman religion, which were thus integrated into Christianity.

***Rosine A. Lambin*** est née à Paris en 1961. De 1980 à 1986, elle étudia la théologie à Montpellier (France) et à Louisville (USA). Puis en 1992, elle obtint son Doctorat en Histoire des Religions et Anthropologie Religieuse à l'université de la Sorbonne, Paris. Elle est chargée de recherches à l'université d'Oldenburg (Allemagne) dans le département théologique où elle travaille sur la tolérance et la liberté religieuses. Ses domaines sont la tolérance et la liberté religieuse en Europe; l'usage des vêtements, la sexualité et les genres dans les religions.

*Bettina Kratz-Ritter*

# Religiöse Rituale rund ums Kinderkriegen:
# Die Wöchnerin in der Synagoge

Wenn eine jüdische Frau, die vor kurzem ein Kind geboren hat, zum ersten Mal wieder das Haus verlässt, führt sie dieser Ausgang in die Synagoge. So will es der Brauch, so war es in traditionellen Gemeinden üblich.

Wie die meisten Synagogenbräuche, so hat auch dieser einen direkten Bezug auf die Zeit des Jerusalemer Tempels, in der der priesterliche Opferkult vollzogen wurde. Hier existierten klare Vorschriften, gemäß denen die Wöchnerin nach Ablauf einer genau festgelegten Frist – übrigens brauchte die Reinigung nach der Entbindung von einem Mädchen mit 66 Tagen doppelt so lang wie nach der von einem Knaben! – sich zu reinigen und den Tempel aufzusuchen hatte. Dort sollte sie ein Reinigungsopfer darbringen, wie es das *"Gesetz für die Wöchnerinnen"* in Leviticus 12 vorsieht:

> Und sie soll daheimbleiben dreiunddreißig Tage im Blut ihrer Reinigung. Kein Heiliges soll sie anrührern, und zum Heiligtum soll sie nicht kommen, bis die Tage ihrer Reinigung um sind. (Gebiert sie aber ein Mädchen, so soll sie... sechsundsechzig Tage daheim bleiben in dem Blut ihrer Reinigung.) Und wenn die Tage ihrer Reinigung... um sind, soll sie dem Priester ein einjähriges Schaf bringen zum Brandopfer und eine Taube oder Turteltaube zum Sündopfer vor die Tür der Stiftshütte. Der soll es opfern vor dem Herrn und sie entsühnen, so wird sie rein von ihrem Blutfluß.

## Das biblische Gebot und seine Auslegung

In späteren Zeiten, nach dem Ende des Tempels und seines Opferdienstes, und zumal in der Zeit nach der jüdischen Aufklärung (Haskala) sollte nicht nur die praktische Umsetzung, sondern auch die theologische und halachische Auslegung dieses Gebotes größte Mühe bereiten. Gerade in einer Zeit, in der die deutschen Juden um ihre rechtliche Emanzipation und Gleichstellung kämpften, waren sie darum bemüht, ihre staatsbürgerliche Treue unter Beweis zu stellen und jeden Verdacht auf zionistische Sonderinteressen zu zerstreuen. Hier galt es, Texte in Bibel, Talmud und Gebetbuch (Siddur), die das Land

Israel, den Zion oder den Jerusalemer Tempel thematisierten, auf die veränderte gesellschaftliche Situation hin auszulegen. So wurde etwa im Gefolge von Samson Raphael Hirsch, einem modern gebildeten, der halachischen Tradition jedoch uneingeschränkt verpflichteten Rabbiner des 19. Jahrhunderts, folgende Neuinterpretation angeboten:

Der Frage, warum einer Frau, die gerade entbunden hatte, neben eher nahe liegenden Gefühlen wie Freude und Dankbarkeit auch solche der Sühnebereitschaft zukommen sollten, wurde mit dem Hinweis auf die überwältigende körperliche Erfahrung einer Geburt begegnet: In diesem Moment extremen Ausgeliefertseins an die Kräfte der Natur sei ihr freier menschlicher Wille zeitweilig ausgeschaltet gewesen, und so sei es angebracht, dass die Frau durch den Gang zur Synagoge, durch Teilnahme an Gebet und Liturgie von der Passivität des Schmerzes zurückfinde in die aktive moralische Energie eines sittlich reifen Menschen.

Offenbar empfand man in der Emanzipationsepoche des deutschen Judentums solche, der aufklärerischen Philosophie und prüden Sittlichkeit des 19. Jahrhunderts verpflichteten Erläuterungen für nötig, um mit dem überlieferten jüdischen Brauchtum adäquat umgehen zu können. Denn dieses stammte ja nicht nur aus biblisch-talmudischen, sondern auch aus regional geprägten folkloristischen Traditionen und bewegte sich gerade beim Thema "Frauen und Kinderkriegen" mitunter sehr im Bereich einer inoffiziellen Frauen-, ja "Gegenreligion" mit klaren Tendenzen zu mystischem bis abergläubischem Brauchtum.

## Rituale der Alltagsreligion

So war es beispielsweise bis in dieses Jahrhundert hinein – im osteuropäischen Judentum sogar bis 1933 – üblich, dass der Wöchnerin biblische Verse ins Ohr geflüstert[1] und sie Tag und Nacht nicht allein gelassen wurde aus Angst vor bösen Geistern bzw. vor der – oft in Gestalt der Lilith[2] vorgestellten – "Kinderfresserin". An sämtlichen Fenstern und Türen der Wochenstube wurden sogenannte "*Kindbettzettel*" angebracht, die mit biblischen Versen, Psalmen oder auch mit Beschwörungen beschriftet waren.[3] Der Hintergrund

---

[1] Vgl. für das Folgende Max Grunwald, Art. Kindbett, in: *Jüdisches Lexikon*, 4 Bde. (Jüdischer Verlag: Berlin 1927-1930; Nachdruck Athäneum: Frankfurt 1987), Bd. 3, 696-697.

[2] Vgl. Pnina Navè Levinson, *Eva und ihre Schwestern. Perspektiven einer jüdisch-feministischen Theologie* (Gütersloher Verlagshaus Mohn: Gütersloh 1992), 67-71: "Lilith – negativer Mythos und positives Bild".

[3] In den letzten Jahren ist das öffentliche Interesse an solchem, vorwiegend im ländlichen Raum verbreiteten jüdischen Brauchtum wieder gewachsen, besonders nachdem im Dachboden süddeutscher Landsynagogen ganze Lager solcher Schriftstücke und Dokumente in Form von

solchen Brauchtums ist deutlich: Ein Volk, das über Jahrhunderte hinweg als verfolgte und unterprivilegierte Minderheit in fremden Ländern in teilweise großer Armut überlebt, kämpft gegen die Kindersterblichkeit und umgibt seinen Nachwuchs mit aufwendigen und hochgradig ritualisierten Schutzmaßnahmen.

Ein weiteres volkstümliches Ritual im Zusammenhang mit Geburt und Kindbett ist das des *"Holekreisch"*,[4] bei dem alle Kinder aus der Nachbarschaft und Verwandtschaft sich kreisförmig um die Wiege des Neugeborenen aufstellen, um diese gemeinsam drei Mal anzuheben und dabei auszurufen: *"Holekreisch, wie soll das Kind heißen?"* Daraufhin wird der Name des Kindes laut ausgesprochen und somit offiziell benannt. Dieser Brauch hat seine Wurzeln vor allem in Frankreich und Süddeutschland und scheint sich im Laufe der Zeit besonders für kleine Mädchen eingebürgert zu haben. Möglicherweise wurde er zunehmend als gerechter Ausgleich für das den kleinen Jungen vorbehaltene kultische Ritual der Beschneidung angesehen. Bei dieser Zweiteilung fällt auf, dass das männliche Ritual im offiziellen und kultischen Rahmen des Synagogengottesdienstes stattfindet, das weibliche hingegen im häuslich-familiären Bereich.

## Jiddische Literatur

Auch wenn es sich bei solcherlei volkstümlichem Brauchtum überwiegend um mündlich tradiertes, von Generation zu Generation weitergegebenes Gut handelt, steht es dennoch auf dem Boden einer reichen schriftlichen Überlieferung: der jiddischen Literatur. Das Jiddische hat im Laufe der Zeit, aus der jeweils aktuellen gesellschaftlichen Situation heraus, die unterschiedlichsten Namen und Bezeichnungen erhalten: "Jüdisch-Deutsch" – politisch einigermaßen korrekt, wenn auch philologisch widersinnig; "Jidisch" bzw. schlechthin: "Taitsch" als eher innerjüdische Bezeichnung für die – in hebräischen Lettern geschriebene – deutsche Sprache der aschkenasischen Juden. Als "Jargon" oder "Judendeutsch" wurde der voraufklärerische Gettodialekt dann in Folge der Aufklärung massiv inkriminiert. Die Bezeichnung *"Waibertaitsch"*

---

Genizot (Geniza = eine Art Depot für unbrauchbar gewordene religiöse Bücher und Gegenstände) entdeckt und ausgewertet wurden. Hieran haben Evelyn Friedlander, London, und ihre Stiftung "The Hidden Legacy Foundation" großen Anteil.

[4] Genaue Schreibweise sowie Etymologie des Namens sind umstritten. Einerseits werden sie mit Frau Holle in Zusammenhang gebracht, andererseits vom Französischen abgeleitet: "haut la crèche" = "hoch die Wiege!" Vgl. Grunwald, Art. Holekreisch, *Jüdisches Lexikon*, Bd. 2, 1653, sowie Navè Levinson, *Eva und ihre Schwestern*, 193-194.

wiederum ist ein Hinweis darauf, dass die in dieser Sprache überlieferte religiös-erbauliche Unterhaltungsliteratur gern von den des Hebräischen in der Regel nicht mächtigen Frauen konsumiert wurde, sozusagen als Ersatz für das sprachlich wie gesellschaftlich sehr hoch angesiedelte Tora- und Talmud-Studium.

Als Hauptwerk dieser Literatur ist die sogenannte "Zenne Urenne" zu nennen: eine für einfache Gemüter verfasste, in ungezählten Ausgaben und Variationen Generationen lang sehr verbreitete und äußerst populäre Sammlung von religiösen Texten, Erzählungen, Anweisungen, kurz: eine Frauenbibel.

Der leicht verständliche, einprägsame und in blumenreicher Sprache verfasste Inhalt der 'Zenne Urenne' ist – psychologisch und thematisch leicht durchschaubar – eindeutig auf die jüdische Frau zugeschnitten. In einer den Midraschim und Targumim entlehnten Sammlung von Legenden, Parabeln, Allegorien und anekdotenhaften Erzählungen werden die religiös begründeten Frauen- und Mutterpflichten und die weiblichen Tugenden zusammengefaßt und poetisch erläutert. So nimmt es nicht wunder, dass die in der mystischen Tradition des polnischen Judentums stehende 'Frauenbibel', nachdem sie bis 1622 zunächst nur im östlichen Raum Verbreitung gefunden hat, bis in das 19. Jahrhundert hinein mehrere hundert Neuauflagen erlebt hat und sich in jüdischen Kreisen Ost- und Westeuropas überaus großer Beliebtheit erfreute. Für die Zeit zwischen 1600 und 1850 kann die 'Zenne Urenne' mit Fug und Recht als das grundlegende Erziehungs- und Bildungsbuch der jüdischen Frau schlechthin angesehen werden. Als wöchentliche Sabbatlektüre dürfte sie in keiner jüdischen Familie gefehlt haben.[5]

Das Charakteristische dieser volkstümlich-theologischen Literatur war die Kombination von anregender Unterhaltung und erbaulicher Unterweisung. Als dann jüdische Druckereien zur Verfügung standen, führte dies zunächst zu regelrechter Massenproduktion jiddischer Druckerzeugnisse: Volksbücher, religiöse Unterhaltungsliteratur,[6] Sittenspiegel, Ethisch-Moralisches – ein reiches, blühendes Schrifttum, dessen große Zeit jedoch im aufgeklärten, akkulturierten Westjudentum des 19. Jahrhunderts zunächst einmal zu Ende gehen sollte. Zwar kam es später noch einmal zu einer gewissen

---

[5]  Helmut Dinse / Sol Liptzin, *Einführung in die jiddische Literatur* (Metzler: Stuttgart 1978), 31-32. Vgl. Ingedore Rüdlin, "Segen war in ihrem Teig. Eine Studie zur Religiosität frommer Jüdinnen", in: *Schlangenbrut* 49 (1995), 39-42.

[6]  Die bedeutendste solch religiöser Unterhaltungsschriften, die aus jüdischen (biblischen und talmudisch-hagadischen) ebenso wie aus orientalischen und abendländischen Erzählstoffen schöpfen, ist das um 1600 erstmals gedruckte Ma'assebuch.

Renaissance, ausgelöst vor allem durch die Begegnung mit orthodoxen, Jiddisch sprechenden 'Ostjuden', doch gelang es nicht mehr, der jetzt eher akademisch rezipierten jiddischen Kultur wieder den zentralen Stellenwert einzuräumen, den diese einst im religiösen Alltagsleben gerade der Frauen ganz selbstverständlich innegehabt hatte.

## Jiddische Frauengebete (Techinot)

Ein wichtiger Zweig dieser Literatur sind die sogenannten "Techinnes" (Techinot, Gebete speziell für Frauen): Entstanden gegen Ende des 16. Jahrhunderts, waren sie durch das gesamte 17. und 18., ja bis in das 19. Jahrhundert hinein äußerst populär und verbreitet unter den Jiddisch sprechenden Frauen, die sie – im Sinne des Wortes – in deren ureigenster Sprache anzusprechen vermochten: Ausgeschlossen von den Schauplätzen des öffentlichen religiösen Lebens, des Hebräischen in der Regel nicht kundig und an der Liturgie des Synagogengottesdienstes nicht aktiv beteiligt, fanden Jüdinnen hier Gebetstexte, die speziell *für* Frauen und oft auch *von* Frauen verfasst waren, und zwar nicht in der kultischen Hochsprache Hebräisch, sondern in ihrer eigenen Alltagssprache Jiddisch. Der ursprüngliche Sitz im Leben dieser frei formulierten, in volkstümlich-elementarem Stil verfassten Gebetstexte ist wohl in der Synagoge zu vermuten, genauer: auf der Frauenempore, und zwar in Gestalt und Amt der sogenannten "Vor-Sagerin", die als eine Art kultische Dolmetscherin simultan zum Ablauf des Synagogengottesdienstes den Frauen die einschlägigen Lesungstexte und Gebete in einer eigenen, schriftlich vorbereiteten und oft kunstvoll ausgearbeiteten jiddischen Version auf der Frauengalerie vortrug. Hierbei entwickelten sich neue, ganz eigene literarische Ansprüche, die über das simple Übersetzen der hebräischen Textvorlagen weit hinausgingen und schließlich einer spezifisch weiblichen Literaturgattung zur Blüte verhalfen. Die Mehrheit dieser Techinot-Dichterinnen blieb leider anonym, nur ein Name ist in der Überlieferung explizit benannt: Sara Bas-Tovim, bekannt für einen besonders lyrischen Stil.

Anlässe, Orte und Gelegenheiten zu solchen Gebeten waren jedoch nicht nur in der Synagoge angesiedelt, sondern vor allem auch im häuslich-familiären Aufgabenbereich der Frau: Familienfeiern, aber auch für Frauen spezifische religiöse Anlässe wie Neumond und die drei Frauengebote sowie 'biologisch' bedingte Themen wie Menstruation und rituelles Tauchbad (Mikwe), Schwangerschaft und Geburt. So hatten die Frauen in den Techinot eigene Gebetstexte nicht nur für offizielle, synagogale Anlässe wie Sabbat- und Festtagsgottesdienste, sondern vor allem für ihre diversen, sehr spezifischen

Bedürfnisse als jüdische Mütter und Ehefrauen: Allen voran die drei Frauen-mizwot Challa, Nidda und Hadlaka,[7] aber auch zahlreiche andere, dem volks-religiösen Brauchtum entstammende Rituale. Die Texte der Techinot, die bei solchen, oftmals in populären und folkloristischen Traditionen wurzelnden Bräuchen zur Anwendung kamen, zeichneten sich durch entsprechende Derb-heit und Direktheit – sowohl der Sprache als auch der Theologie – aus, die dann im Laufe des 19. Jahrhunderts als zunehmend unvereinbar mit dem Ver-bürgerlichungsstreben des deutschen Judentums empfunden wurde. Vor allem die im Themenzyklus: Fruchtbarkeit – Schwangerschaft – Geburt angesiedel-ten Texte wurden da als unsittlich angesehen und auf ein Minimum reduziert. Doch zeichneten sich die Texte der Techinot nicht nur durch volksreligiöses Brauchtum aus. Für ungebildete, des Hebräischen nicht mächtige Personen-kreise stellten sie auch eine Form von jüdischem Lernen dar. In dieser Funk-tion, jüdisches Wissen an ein breites Lesepublikum zu vermitteln, decken sich die Techinot mit dem übrigen jiddischen religiösen Schrifttum, in dessen Tra-dition sie stehen.

### Gebete für die Wöchnerin – vor und nach der Aufklärung

Im Folgenden gilt es, das Dargelegte an den Texten zu konkretisieren; Gebetsbeispiele aus dem angesprochenen Themenkreis sollen näher betrach-tet und miteinander verglichen werden: Gebete für die Frau und ihr neugebo-renes Kind, und zwar aus dem jeweiligem Literaturraum vor und nach der Aufklärung.

In einer alten *Techina*,[8] die beim ersten Synagogenbesuch nach der Ent-bindung zu sprechen ist, wird zunächst Bezug genommen auf das oben bereits genannte biblische Gebot für Wöchnerinnen im Tempel. Sodann wird eingeräumt, dass "wir gesündigt haben und keinen Tempel (bet hamiqdasch) mehr haben", weswegen die Beterin kein Opfer mehr darbrin-gen könne. Unter Berufung auf die Propheten wird jedoch postuliert, dass "die Lobgesänge unserer Lippen, die wir vor Gott sprechen, genauso akzep-tiert werden, wie wenn wir ein wirkliches Tempelopfer (qorban) darge-bracht hätten".

---

[7] D.h. Absondern des Teigs beim Brotbacken, Einhaltung der Reinheitsgesetze in der Ehe, Anzünden und Segnen der Sabbatlichter.

[8] Rivka Zakutinsky (Hg.), *Techinas. A Voice from the Heart. "As only a woman can pray"* (Aura Press: Brooklyn 1992), 382-389. Es handelt sich um eine zweisprachige (Jiddisch-Eng-lisch) Textausgabe. Ich übersetze direkt aus dem Jiddischen unter Beibehaltung mancher für das deutsche Sprachempfinden holpriger Wendungen.

Und ich sage [fährt die Beterin fort] "gelobt bist du, heiliger Gott, König von der Welt, du tust Gutes dem sündigen Mensch, du hast mir auch viel Gutes getan und mich gerettet von der großen Gefahr (sakkana), und hast mich gesegnet (gebentscht) mit Frucht von mein Bauch: a Kind auf lange Jahr. Und durch deine große Güte (chäsäd) will ich kommen in dein heiliges Haus und will ich niederknien und mich neigen in deinem heiligen Palast mit großer Furcht. Und ich bitt dich um Erbarmen (rachmanut), du sollst weiter nit abtun dein Güte (chäsad) von mir, und sollst mir und meinem Mann ein Tugendförderer (mesakkäh) sein, aufzuziehen das Kind ohne Sorge (za'ar) zu guter Jidischkeit und Ehrfurcht vor dem Himmel (jirat schamajim). Und möge es dein Wille sein, du sollst bauen den Tempel (bet hamiqdasch) in unserer Zeit. Dort wollen wir bringen vor dich die Tempelopfer (qorbanot), was du hast uns geboten in deine heilige Tora. Amen."

In dieser deutlich voraufklärerischen Techina wird kein Blatt vor den Mund genommen: Die Wöchnerin weiß, dass sie an dieser Stelle eigentlich in den Tempel kommen, sich dem Priester zeigen und ihr Tempelopfer darbringen müsste. Dies ist nun, durch Zerstörung des Tempels und Leben in der Zerstreuung, im Moment nicht möglich. Gott möge daher den Tempel baldmöglichst, noch zu Lebzeiten der Beterin, wieder erstehen lassen, so ihre Bitte, dann will sie auch wieder toragemäße Opfer darbringen. Das Gebet vertritt einen klar zionistisch-messianischen Standpunkt, nicht bereit, sich mit dem notdürftigen Provisorium einer Diasporaexistenz auf Dauer zufrieden zu geben.

Ganz anders steht es in einem *Frauengebet* von 1855: "Gebet einer Wöchnerin, die zum erstenmal wieder das Gotteshaus besucht" von Fanny Neuda.[9] Da sowohl die kultische Idee von Unreinheit und Sühnung als auch die eigentliche Handlung des Brandopferns an die Existenz eines intakten und funktionierenden Tempelbetriebs gebunden sind, entsteht hier für die moderne Gebetsverfasserin erst recht das Problem adäquater Übertragung in die Diaspora-Situation des 19. Jahrhunderts. Daher wird, wie einst der Tempel in Jerusalem, jetzt die Gemeindesynagoge am jeweiligen Wohnort in der Diaspora als "heilige Stätte des Herrn"[10] gepriesen, wo die Beterin in der Mitte der versammelten Gemeinde ihren Dank darbringen kann. Und wie wird nach der Aufklärung mit der – gesellschaftlich schwierig gewordenen – Opferthematik umgegangen? Sie wird allegoriserend umgedeutet:

---

[9] Fanny Neuda, *Stunden der Andacht. Ein Gebet- und Erbauungs-Buch für Israels Frauen und Jungfrauen zur öffentlichen und häuslichen Andacht, sowie für alle Verhältnisse des weiblichen Lebens* (Jakob B. Brandeis: Prag 1855) (mindestens 26 Auflagen!).

[10] A.a.O., 94.

Auf dem Altare meines Herzens will ich dir alle eitlen, sündigen Gelüste und Wünsche opfern, und hier in deinem heiligen Tempel... will ich dir... alle meine Lebenstage angeloben, will dir und mir selber angeloben, alle meine Kräfte und Fähigkeiten zu vereinen, um meine Pflichten als Mutter, als Gattin, als Mensch und Israelitin zu erfüllen, und ihnen Herz und Geist zu widmen und zu weihen mein Leben lang.[11]

Im Sinne der *Tempelopfer-Allegorie* versteht sich dies als "Gelöbnis", und es wird zugleich der göttliche Beistand bei der Pflichterfüllung erbeten:

Verleihe mir dazu deinen Segen, daß... die Erfüllung meiner Pflichten mir stets angenehm und herzbefriedigend bleibe und die Ausübung des Guten mir stets teurer und vozüglicher sei als alle Freuden und Reize der Welt. Verleihe mir Weisheit und Kraft, meine Kinder zu erziehen zu guten und edlen Menschen, zu redlichen und nützlichen Staatsbürgern, zu frommen, eifrigen Anhängern unseres Glaubens.[12]

Ebenso wie die Reihenfolge der hier aufgeführten weiblichen Identitäten – zunächst als Mutter und Gattin, dann als Mensch und erst zuletzt als Israelitin – bezeichnend ist für das Selbstverständnis der modernen Staatsbürgerin, so spricht auch die Prioritätenliste des Kindes eine klare Sprache: War es in der jiddischen Techina der größte Wunsch der Wöchnerin, ihr Kind ohne Sorgen zu guter Jüdischkeit und Gottesfurcht zu erziehen, so geht es beim deutschen Juden des 19. Jahrhunderts erst in zweiter Linie darum, ein 'frommer eifriger Anhänger unseres Glaubens' zu werden.

Was nun die arrivierte deutsch-jüdische Bürgerin für die Zukunft ihrer Kinder tatsächlich zu wünschen und anzustreben hatte, geht sehr viel deutlicher aus zwei Gebeten hervor, die Fanny Neuda speziell im Hinblick auf das neugeborene Kind verfasst hat. In ihrem Gebetbuch – ebenso wie in vielen weiteren Frauengebetbüchern jener Epoche[13] – gibt es neben dem "Gebet einer Mutter, wenn ihr Kind zur *Beschneidung* getragen wird" auch ein für das Mädchen-Ritual vorgesehenes "Gebet, wenn dem weiblichen Kinde der *Name* erteilt wird". Während hier beim Sohn wieder die staatsbürgerlichen

---

[11] A.a.O., 95.

[12] Ebd.

[13] Vgl. dazu meine Studie: *Für 'fromme Zionstöchter' und 'gebildete Frauenzimmer'. Andachtsliteratur für deutsch-jüdische Frauen im 19. und frühen 20. Jahrhundert* (HASKALA. Wissenschaftliche Abhandlungen hg. v. Moses Mendelssohn-Zentrum für europäisch-jüdische Studien und Salomon Ludwig Steinheim-Institut für deutsch-jüdische Geschichte, Bd.13; Olms: Hildesheim 1995).

Rechte und Pflichten im Vordergrund stehen, wird für die Tochter ein häuslich-familiäres Szenario entworfen.

Für ihren *Sohn* wünscht sich eine gute deutsch-jüdische Mutter, dass er als Staatsbürger wie auch als Israelit stark und aufrecht sein möge, bereit, die göttlichen "Wünsche und Gebote zu erfüllen":

> Und wie heute sein Blut vergossen wird auf dem Altare des Glaubens, er auch später freudig sein Teuerstes hinzugeben bereit sei für die Erinnerung des Edlen und Heiligen, für den Ruhm und das Heil seines *Volkes und Glaubens*, für das Wohl und Heil unseres *Vaterlandes* und zur Ehre und Verherrlichung deines gebenedeiten Namens. Amen.[14]

Für die *Tochter* hingegen ist eine bürgerliche Laufbahn als "biedere Gattin und Hausfrau" vorgesehen. Das Gebet benennt minutiös die einzelnen Stationen der damaligen weiblichen Normalbiographie mit den dazu gehörigen fraulichen Qualitäten:

> Möge sie gleich werden dem Bilde unserer frommen Mütter Sara, Rifka, Rahel und Lea, geschmückt, gesegnet und verherrlicht, mit allen Tugenden des Lebens und des Glaubens, mild und wohltätig, gläubig-fromm, sittsam, treu und ergeben, eine fromme *Tochter*, eine geist- und herzgewinnende *Jungfrau*, eine biedere *Gattin und Hausfrau*.[15]

Althergebrachte jüdische Rituale für neugeborene Kinder wurden hier im Zeitgeist der Epoche umgedeutet und in der Begrifflichkeit der im deutschen Bürgertum damals gerade aufkommenden "*Dissoziation der Geschlechtscharaktere*"[16] normativ umfunktioniert: Der große Wille zu Akkulturation, ja Assimilation des damaligen deutschen Judentums wird hier überdeutlich. Dass mit dieser Anpassung an den bürgerlichen Sittenkodex des 19. Jahrhunderts die angestammten, in der jiddischen Denk- und Sprachwelt tradierten *Frauen-Rituale* verloren gingen, ja systematisch abgeschafft wurden, wird von heutigen Jüdinnen bedauert. Sehr markant benannte dies Pnina Navè Levinson:

> Die heutigen Ausgaben [sc.: der Frauenbibel Zenne Urenne] sind gewissermaßen kastriert, denn im 19. Jahrhundert galten die offenherzigen, unbefangenen Darstellungen von Körperlichkeit und Sexualität als peinlich, anstößig, ja geradezu

---

[14] Neuda, *Stunden der Andacht*, 93.
[15] A.a.O., 94; Hervorhebungen von mir.
[16] Karin Hausen, "Die Polarisierung der 'Geschlechtscharaktere' – eine Spiegelung der Dissoziation von Erwerbs- und Familienleben", in: Werner Conze (Hg.), *Sozialgeschichte der Familie in der Neuzeit Europas* (Klett: Stuttgart 1976), 363-393.

obszön und sowohl für junge Mädchen wie für zartbesaitete Ehefrauen ungeeignet. Wieder einmal machte sich die Anpassung an die Umwelt bemerkbar.[17]

Von der *Reaktivierung* volksreligiöser Rituale würde sie sich denn auch eine positive Belebung weiblicher Spiritualität versprechen:

> Insgesamt führt die Wiederentdeckung der Volksreligion als Teil der psychischen Stärkung des Selbst in einer Gemeinschaft auch hier zu verbalen und nicht-verbalen Formen der Frömmigkeit, die gewiß für einen Teil der Akademikerinnen (das sind fast sämtliche Betroffene!) befreiend wirken.[18]

Die Reaktivierung, Weiterentwicklung und Neuschöpfung religiöser Rituale für Frauen in spezifischen Lebenssituationen stellt heute eine große Herausforderung dar. Auf jüdischer Seite wird diese gerade in letzter Zeit auf höchst kreative und produktive Art angegangen, indem Defizite ausgeglichen und einseitig männlich besetzte Themen aus spezifisch weiblicher Sicht ergänzt werden.

> Unser *Gebetbuch* hat für eine große Bandbreite von Lebenserfahrungen *keine Rituale*: keine Gebete für das Verlassen des elterlichen oder des ehelichen Hauses, keine für Organspenden oder gegen Depressionen, beim Verlust eines Kindes oder dem Eingeständnis der Unfruchtbarkeit, für die Menarche oder Menopause – die Liste ist endlos.[19]

So beschreibt Rabbinerin Sylvia Rothschild die Desiderate und fährt fort:

> Ich habe den Eindruck, daß Rabbinerinnen begonnen haben, vor allem Liturgien für die Erfahrungen von Frauen zu schreiben. Dies ist die wichtigste Erneuerung, die sowohl Männern als auch Frauen einen Anstoß für das Schreiben neuer Liturgien gibt, zumal wir uns gewahr werden, daß wir dies können und mehr noch, daß wir dies brauchen.[20]

Im Bereich des in Deutschland – inzwischen wieder in zweiter und dritter Generation – lebenden Judentums findet im Moment ein Aufbruch gerade jüngerer, theologisch kompetenter Frauen statt, der mit kraftvollen spirituel-

---

[17] Navé Levinson, *Eva und ihre Schwestern*, 176.

[18] A.a.O., 202-203.

[19] "Kreative Liturgie-Gestaltung", in: Lara Dämmig / Rachel Monika Herweg / Elisa Klapheck (Hg.), *Journal Bet Debora Berlin* Nr. 1 (2000), 24-25, hier 25. Es handelt sich um die Dokumentation einer "Tagung europäischer Rabbinerinnen, Kantorinnen, rabbinisch gelehrter und interessierter Jüdinnen und Juden", die erstmals im Mai 1999 im Berliner Centrum Judaicum statt fand.

[20] Ebd.

len Impulsen für die gesamte Gemeinde verbunden ist. Rachel Monika Herweg fasst die aktuelle Situation so zusammen:

> Wir Frauen bringen zur Zeit mit großem Nachdruck unsere religiösen und spirituellen Bedürfnisse an die Oberfläche. Von uns scheint eine größere Kraft auszugehen und ein größerer Wille zu Fort- und Neugestaltung als von Männern. Ich glaube, daß wir gerade dabei sind, Männer in ihrer traditionellen Rolle abzulösen. Dabei haben wir die Chance,… nach eigenen, unverstellten Ausdrucksformen zu suchen.[21]

Es herrscht also Aufbruchstimmung: Innerhalb des "Zentralrats der deutschen Juden", der gerade sein 50jähriges Bestehen in Deutschland begangen hat, scheint sich der weibliche Anteil neu zu orientieren. Wir dürfen gespannt sein, wohin die Reise unserer jüdischen Schwestern geht.

Judaism has a long tradition of specifically female rituals: for instance, for women who have recently given birth and for their babies. Prayers and magical practices were used in an attempt to prevent the death of the newborn baby caused by the "child eater" or other evil spirits which could besiege the place of lying in. The mother herself had to complete precisely prescribed rituals, sacrifices and prayers which varied according to whether she had given birth to a boy or a girl. These folklore practices, deeply anchored in women's every-day religious culture, increasingly became subject to a strong social criticism and, particularly as a result of the assimilation in the age of emancipation, were adapted to the cultural environment. This article shows first how this process of acculturation deprived women's ritual, rooted in popular religion, of substance and power. Secondly, it discusses attempts at the renewal and further development of religious ritual in modern Judaism. In this area, new impulses by theologically competent women can currently be observed; these are bound up with a strong impulse towards a new feminine spirituality.

Le judaïsme possède une vieille tradition de rites féminins effectués, par exemple, pour les femmes qui relevaient de couches et leurs nouveaux-nés. Ils servaient à combattre, avec des prières et des pratiques magiques, la mortalité du nourrisson personnifiée sous les traits de la "mangeuse d'enfants" ou autres esprits du mal, supposés assaillir la mère et l'enfant après l'accouchement. L'accouchée elle-même avait des rituels de prières et de sacrifices très précis selon qu'elle avait accouché d'une fille ou d'un garçon. Ces coutumes populaires, profondément ancrées dans la culture religieuse quotidienne des femmes, furent cependant

---

[21] Rachel Monika Herweg, "Beten Frauen anders?" in: *Journal Bet Debora Berlin* Nr. 1 (2000), 28-29, hier 29.

soumises, au fil du temps, à une censure sociale de plus en plus sévère, et adaptées aux nouvelles mœurs, notamment à l'époque de l'émancipation, où régnait l'esprit d'assimilation. L'article cherche à montrer d'une part que l'acculturation a privé de substance et de pouvoir un rituel de femmes profondément enraciné dans la religion du peuple, d'autre part que le judaïsme actuel tente, ici et là, de faire renaître les rituels religieux. Des femmes douées d'une compétence théologique s'éveillent, un éveil lié à de fortes impulsions pour une nouvelle spiritualité féminine.

***Bettina Kratz-Ritter*** studierte Evangelische Theologie, Klassische Philologie und Pädagogik in Frankfurt a.M., Heidelberg und Rom: 1. und 2. Staatsexamen 1982 und 1985, Dr. phil. 1988. Neben Schuldienst, Verlagslektorat und Wissenschaftsjournalismus hat sie sich auf das Forschungsgebiet Reformjudentum spezialisiert und zwei Monographien sowie zahlreiche Aufsätze veröffentlicht.

*Angela Berlis*

# Laienfrauen und Liturgie
## Acht Jahrzehnte "Frauensonntag" in der alt-katholischen Kirche in Deutschland[*]

Seit einundachtzig Jahren gibt es ihn im Katholischen Bistum der Alt-Katholiken in Deutschland: den "Frauensonntag". In der Regel wird er am ersten Sonntag im Advent gefeiert.

Wie ist er entstanden, wie hat er sich verändert, welche Bedeutung ist ihm in den unterschiedlichen Zeitabschnitten zugekommen, welche Rolle spielt er heute? Diesen Fragen soll im folgenden Beitrag nachgegangen werden. Nach einem Überblick über die Entstehung des alt-katholischen Bistums sowie einigen allgemeinen Bemerkungen zur Rolle der Laien in der Feier der Liturgie im deutschen alt-katholischen Bistum werden die Entwicklung und Wertschätzung des Frauensonntags skizzenhaft dargestellt.

Teresa Berger hat kürzlich festgestellt, daß die "gottesdienstlichen Lebenswirklichkeiten von Frauen" kein Thema traditioneller Liturgiegeschichtsschreibung seien.[1] Auch der Frauensonntag fand in bisherigen Darstellungen keine Beachtung. In ihm wird eine lebendige, wandlungsfähige Frauenliturgiekultur im deutschen Altkatholizismus sichtbar. Anhand des folgenden geschichtlichen Überblicks werden "gottesdienstliche[n] Inszenierungen der Geschlechterverhältnisse"[2] ausgemacht, und die Verwobenheit der liturgischen Rolle von Frauen mit dem jeweiligen gesellschaftlichen und kirchlichen Verständnis der Frauenrolle(n) verdeutlicht.

[*] Ich danke Erentrud Kraft, Charlotte Methuen, Katja Nickel, Mariette Kraus-Vobbe und den Teilnehmerinnen des Oberseminars bei Prof. Irmtraud Fischer für ihren Kommentar zu früheren Fassungen dieses Artikels.
[1] Teresa Berger, "'die weyber nach den mennern'? Interpretative Strategien zur Rekonstruktion einer Liturgiegeschichte (auch) von Frauen", in: *Berliner Theologische Zeitschrift* 17 (2000), 177-193, hier 178-179. S. auch: dies., *Women's Ways of Worship. Gender Analysis and Liturgical History* (Liturgical Press: Collegeville 1999).
[2] Berger, "'die weyber nach den mennern'?" 191.

## Die Entstehung des alt-katholischen Bistums

Die alt-katholische Bewegung ist als innerkatholische Reformbewegung entstanden. Nach dem Ersten Vatikanum bildeten sich im Deutschen Reich, in der Schweiz und in der Habsburger Monarchie Protestbewegungen gegen den Anspruch des Rechtsprimats und der Unfehlbarkeit des Papstes, die beim Ersten Vatikanum (1869-70) zum Dogma erhoben worden waren. Ein großer Teil dieses Protestes mündete in die alt-katholische Bewegung. Im Deutschen Reich entstand 1873 mit der Wahl und Weihe eines eigenen Bischofs das alt-katholische Bistum. Beim Protest gegen die neuen Dogmen sollte es nicht bleiben, die junge Bewegung strebte nach einer Erneuerung der Kirche nach altkirchlicher Maßgabe und führte in der Folgezeit verschiedene Reformen durch, wie etwa die Aufhebung des Pflichtzölibats der Geistlichen und die Abschaffung der obligatorischen Ohrenbeichte. Außerdem wurde eine kirchliche Rechtsordnung eingeführt, die – zunächst nur den männlichen! – Laien Mitverantwortungsrechte sicherte. Laien machen bis auf den heutigen Tag zwei Drittel der Mitglieder der Synode aus und sind außerdem in die 'Synodalvertretung' wählbar, ein Gremium, das dem Bischof bei der Leitung des Bistums zur Seite steht. In der Synode wählen Laien gemeinsam mit den Geistlichen den Bischof, in der Gemeindeversammlung wählen sie den Pfarrer bzw. die Pfarrerin.

## Die Beteiligung der Laien an der Liturgie

Auch im liturgischen Bereich wurden Reformen durchgeführt.[3] Die erste Synode stellte 1874 fest, daß es wünschenswert sei, beim Gottesdienst und bei der Spendung der Sakramente die Volkssprache als liturgische Sprache zu verwenden. In den Folgejahren wurde dieser Beschluß sukzessive für die Feier der Sakramente und für Teile der Messe umgesetzt. Schließlich gestattete die zehnte Synode 1887, daß die gesamte heilige Messe in deutscher Sprache gefeiert werden dürfe. Alt-Katholische Gemeinden konnten laut Synodenbeschluß selbst darüber beschließen, ob sie die deutsche Liturgie einführen oder die lateinische beibehalten wollten. Es dauerte nur wenige Jahre, bis alle alt-katholischen Gemeinden die deutsche Meßliturgie eingeführt hatten.

Bereits 1877 regte die vierte Synode die Feier von Laiengottesdiensten an. Die Synode erklärte, es sei wünschenschwert, daß an den Sonn- und

---

[3]  Vgl. dazu ausführlicher Sigisbert Kraft, "Die Erneuerung der Liturgie in den alt-katholischen und anglikanischen Kirchen", in: Karl Schlemmer (Hg.), *Gemeinsame Liturgie in getrennten Kirchen?* (Quaestiones Disputatae 132; Herder: Freiburg 1991), 11-28.

Festtagen, an denen in einer Gemeinde die Feier der Messe nicht möglich sei, ein anderer gemeinsamer Gottesdienst unter Leitung "eines von dem Vorstande mit Genehmigung des Bischofs bestellten Laien gehalten werde".[4] Die Synodalvertretung wurde damit beauftragt, "geeignete Formulare für einen solchen Gottesdienst zu entwerfen".[5] Bis auf den heutigen Tag ist im altkatholischen Gesangbuch 'Lobt Gott, ihr Christen' ein Formular für einen solchen "Gemeindegottesdienst ohne Priester" zu finden.[6]

Wer leitete diese Gottesdienste? Den Quellen aus dem 19. Jahrhundert zufolge waren es faktisch die Mitglieder des Kirchenvorstands, die die Leitung dieser Gottesdienste übernahmen. Da Frauen bis 1920 nicht Mitglied des Kirchenvorstands werden durften, kamen sie nicht als Laien-Liturginnen in den Blick. Daraus jedoch den Schluß zu ziehen, daß Frauen an den Entwicklungen der Liturgie keinen Anteil genommen haben, wäre weit gefehlt. So wurden in der Vierteljahrszeitschrift *Altkatholisches Frauen-Blatt*, die zwischen 1885 und 1899 erschien, die Leserinnen über kirchliche Feste und über die neuesten liturgischen Entwicklungen informiert. Eine musikalische Beilage enthielt – vor allem aus dem evangelischen Liedgut übernommene – deutsche liturgische Gesänge zum Jahreskreis. Auch die Anregung zum Abhalten "gemeinsamer Hausgottesdienste" – gemeint war die Feier von Morgen- und Abendlob – fehlte nicht.[7] Eine leitende Funktion im öffentlichen Gottesdienst der Gemeinde war allerdings auch hier nicht vorgesehen. Frauen wurden in erster Linie als "Priesterinnen des Hauses" bzw. als Teilnehmerinnen am öffentlichen Gottesdienst angesehen.

Eine Episode wie der "Freiburger Beichtstuhl-Streit" um die Wende zum 20. Jahrhundert macht jedoch deutlich, daß diese teilnehmende Rolle nicht gleichbedeutend mit Passivität war. Denn Laienfrauen fühlten sich sehr wohl

---

[4] *Beschlüsse der vierten Synode der Altkatholiken des deutschen Reiches, gehalten zu Bonn am 23., 24. und 25. Mai 1877. Amtliche Ausgabe* (P. Neusser: Bonn 1877), 9. 11.

[5] Ebd., 9.

[6] *Lobt Gott, ihr Christen. Gesangbuch des Katholischen Bistums der Alt-Katholiken für Christen heute* [Bonn 1986], 29-32.

[7] *Alt-Katholisches Frauen-Blatt* (1889), Nr. 20, 143-145. Die Herausgeberin des Blattes, Therese Freiin von Miltitz (1827-1912) interessierte sich sehr für die liturgische Erneuerung im alt-katholischen Bistum. Es ist davon auszugehen, daß die genannten Artikel im *Frauen-Blatt* von ihr initiiert worden sind. Vgl. zu ihr Angela Berlis, "Müßige Zuschauerinnen? Zur Partizipation von Frauen in der Anfangszeit der alt-katholischen Kirche (1870-1890)", in: Leonore Siegele-Wenschkewitz / Gury Schneider-Ludorff / Beate Hämel / Barbara Schoppenreich (Hg.), *Frauen Gestalten Geschichte: im Spannungsfeld von Religion und Geschlecht* (Lutherisches Verlagshaus: Hannover 1998), 137-160, hier 155-158.

auch für das geistlich-liturgische Leben mitverantwortlich. Anlaß dieser Auseinandersetzung zwischen dem dortigen Frauenverein und dem Pfarrer war,
daß der Pfarrer beim Kirchenvorstand durchgedrückt hatte, in der Kirche
einen Beichtstuhl aufstellen zu dürfen. Die Frauen des Frauenvereins machten
dem Pfarrer deutlich, daß sie sich von ihm nicht in den Beichtstuhl drängen
lassen wollten. Dazu beriefen sie sich auf eine Erklärung der ersten Synode
(1874), mit der die Verpflichtung zur regelmäßigen Ohrenbeichte aufgehoben
worden war. Die Freiburger Frauen bevorzugten an Stelle der Einzelbeichte
die gemeinschaftliche Bußfeier, die am Anfang der sonntäglichen Meßfeier
gehalten wurde.[8]

Nach diesem kurzen Überblick läßt sich folgendes feststellen: Das Wort
"Laie" ist bis ins 20. Jahrhundert hinein im alt-katholischen Bistum kein
geschlechtsneutraler Begriff. Laienmänner und Laienfrauen hatten im alt-
katholischen Bistum bis zur Einführung des Frauenwahlrechts im Jahr 1920
unterschiedliche Rechte und Pflichten.[9] Frauen wurden zudem im religiösen
Bereich andere Erwartungen entgegengebracht als Männern; so galten sie
entsprechend der zeitgenössischen Rollenerwartung auch in der alt-katholischen Kirche als 'religiöser' und als 'frömmer' als Männer.[10] Relativ viele
'selbständige', das heißt, unverheiratete oder verwitwete Frauen schlossen
sich nach dem Ersten Vatikanum aus Überzeugung der alt-katholischen
Bewegung an. In vielen alt-katholischen Gemeinden machten die Frauen
einen Großteil, wenn nicht sogar die Mehrheit der Gottesdienstgemeinde aus.
Obwohl es seit 1877 die Möglichkeit der Feier von Laiengottesdiensten gab,

---

[8] Die Bußfeier ist ein sakramentales Geschehen. – Ausführlicher zum Freiburger Beichtstuhl-
streit: Angela Berlis, *Frauen im Prozeß der Kirchwerdung. Eine historisch-theologische Studie zur Anfangsphase des deutschen Altkatholizismus (1850-1890)* (Beiträge zur Kirchen- und
Kulturgeschichte 6; Peter Lang: Frankfurt a.M. 1998), 335-352; Katja Nickel, "Als die
Frauen Verantwortung übernahmen…", in: Ruth Dombrowski / Katja Nickel / Edgar Nickel /
Siegfried J. Thuringer / Helen Rose Wilson (Red.), *125 Jahre altkatholische Gemeinde Freiburg. Eine Gemeinde auf ihrem Weg* (Selbstverlag: Freiburg 1998), 41-46.

[9] Ich benutze in diesem Beitrag den Begriff "Laienfrauen" oder "weibliche Laien" lieber als
das Wort "Laiinnen".

[10] Diese angenommene besondere Nähe von Frauen zur Religion war im 19. Jahrhundert Teil
der bürgerlichen Geschlechterkonstruktion (Stichwort 'Feminisierung der Religion') und ließe
sich anhand verschiedener Aussagen auch für den Altkatholizismus erhärten. Frömmigkeit
konnte dabei sowohl positiv als auch negativ gedeutet werden. Für das Negativbild der ultra-
montanen, klerusabhängigen Frau s. Berlis, *Frauen im Prozeß der Kirchwerdung*, 323-335.
Für ein positives Bild frommer alt-katholischer Frauen, s. Carl Jentsch, *Von ihm selbst, nach
seinen Werken. Eine Lese, zusammengestellt von Alois Mühlan und Anton Heinrich Rose*
(Wilhelm Grunow: Leipzig 1918), 77.

ist jedoch davon auszugehen, daß Frauen bis ins 20. Jahrhundert hinein nicht als Leiterinnen solcher Laiengottesdienste fungierten. Trotzdem wäre es falsch, ihnen aufgrund dieses Sachverhaltes lediglich eine Rolle im Privatbereich einer häuslichen Liturgie (Tagzeitengebet) zuzubilligen. Die Frauenvereine trugen dazu bei, bei den Frauen ein eigenständiges Bewußtsein ihrer Mitverantwortung als weibliche Laien zu schaffen, und diese auch für den geistlich-liturgischen Bereich wahrzunehmen. Aufgrund ihrer eingeschränkten rechtlichen Stellung taten sie dies jedoch re-agierend und nicht agierend.

### Die Anfänge des Frauensonntags

Am 8. September 1912 schlossen sich in Offenbach am Main dreißig alt-katholische Frauenvereine zum "Verband Altkatholischer Frauenvereine" zusammen. Die Offenbacher Pfarrersfrau Clothilde Erb geb. Bertele von Grenadenberg (1864-1963) wurde zur ersten Vorsitzenden gewählt. Die Pläne zur weiteren Vernetzung der Frauenarbeit konnten wegen des Erstes Weltkriegs nicht in der beabsichtigten Form ausgeführt werden, da die Frauen ihre Arbeitskraft anderweitig einbringen mußten. "Sechs schwere Jahre haben uns jede Arbeitsmöglichkeit genommen", klagte die Vorsitzende Anfang 1920.[11] Wo es ging, wurde caritative und diakonische Arbeit getan. Außerdem gab der Verband seit Dezember 1912 ein vierteljährlich erscheinendes Blatt für alt-katholische Kinder heraus. Die wohl bedeutsamste Aktivität zwischen 1913 und 1920 bestand im Engagement für das aktive und passive kirchliche Frauenwahlrecht, das Frauen schließlich durch Synodenbeschluß im Mai 1920 erhielten.[12]

Infolge des Krieges konnte die dritte Hauptversammlung des Verbandes erst sechs Jahre nach der zweiten Hauptversammlung im Juli 1920 in Freiburg i.Br. gehalten werden. Sie beschloß u.a. die Gründung von Landesverbänden als Unterabteilungen des Verbandes. Außerdem beauftragte die Versammlung ihren neu gewählten Vorstand, an Bischof und Synodalvertretung das Ersuchen zu richten,

> alljährlich für alle Gemeinden einen Frauentag einzuführen, an dem in Amt und Predigt der Frauenvereinsarbeit in unserer Kirche anregend und fördernd gedacht und der Ertrag der Opferbüchsen der Kasse des Verbands zugeführt werden soll.[13]

---

[11] *Alt-Katholisches Volksblatt* [= *AKVB* ] 34 (1920), 33.

[12] Vgl. dazu ausführlicher Berlis, *Frauen im Prozeß der Kirchwerdung*, 273-277. Zur Vorgeschichte des Verbandes und zur rechtlichen Stellung alt-katholischer Frauen im 19. Jahrhundert s. Berlis, "Müßige Zuschauerinnen?", 144-160.

[13] *AKVB* 34 (1920), 234. – Der eigentliche Beschlußtext war leider nicht auffindbar.

Die Motive, die dem Antrag zur Einführung eines kirchlichen Frauensonntags zugrunde lagen, sind aufgrund der mangelhaften Quellenlage – das Verbandsarchiv verbrannte 1944 bei einem Fliegerangriff – leider nicht mehr genau zu rekonstruieren. Ob der Gedanke eines Frauensonntags bereits früher unter den Mitgliedern lebendig war, kann nicht gesagt werden.

Möglicherweise spielte aber die Tatsache, daß es in der badischen Evangelischen Landeskirche seit 1916 einen Frauensonntag gab, bei der Einführung eine gewisse Rolle.[14] Die evangelische Frauenarbeit im Großherzogtum Baden, einem der Stammlande des Altkatholizismus, war den alt-katholischen Frauen mit Sicherheit bekannt. Der Frauensonntag in der evangelischen Kirche, der am zweiten Advent begangen wurde, war der landeskirchliche Kollektentag für die Frauenarbeit.[15] Er diente dem Kontakt der Frauen untereinander und der Frauenbildung durch – zumeist sozialpolitische, weniger theologische – Vorträge und Information. In seinem Ablauf – Vorträge mit musikalischer Umrahmung – war er den Bezirksfrauentagen vergleichbar. Er fand außerhalb der Gottesdienstzeit am Sonntagnachmittag oder -abend statt. Am Frauensonntag sollten "Frauen zu Frauen reden können", doch in der Praxis wurde dieser Plan schnell fallengelassen und auch männliche Redner eingeladen.[16] Erst seit der Anerkennung der Frauen im Predigtamt, die Frauen die Möglichkeit zur öffentlichen Wortverkündigung gegeben hat, wird der Frauensonntag auch liturgisch begangen und von Frauen gestaltet.[17]

---

[14] Am 12. Juli 1916 schlossen sich die evangelischen badischen Frauenvereine und –verbände zum 'Verband der evangelischen Frauenvereinigungen Badens' zusammen. Gleichzeitig wurde der Frauensonntag eingeführt. Vgl. Eva Loos, Wieso gibt es in der Badischen Landeskirche einen Frauensonntag?, vervielfältigtes Manuskript, [Karlsruhe 1992], 7 Seiten. Das Manuskript sowie weitere Literaturhinweise sind bei der Frauenarbeit der Evangelischen Landeskirche in Baden, ansässig in Karlsruhe, erhältlich. Anke Ruth-Klumbies bereitet im Rahmen ihres Pfarrvikariats eine Hausarbeit vor, in der sie die Geschichte der Aufnahme des Frauensonntags in Freiburg beschreibt.

[15] Heute wird der Frauensonntag gewöhnlich am 3. Sonntag im September gefeiert; alle zwei Jahre wird an diesem Sonntag nach der landeskirchlichen Kollektenordnung eine Kollekte für die Frauenarbeit der Landeskirche gehalten (vgl. Loos, *Frauensonntag*, 6).

[16] Vgl. ebd., 2.

[17] Vgl. ebd., 6. Pfarrerin Eva Loos hatte als theologische Mitarbeiterin und später als theologische Leiterin bei der Frauenarbeit in Baden seit 1977 wesentlichen Anteil an der Belebung des Frauensonntags, indem sie anfing, Vorschläge für die liturgische Gestaltung des Gottesdienstes am Frauensonntag zu erarbeiten und in einzelnen Kirchenbezirken Gottesdienstvorbereitungsveranstaltungen durchzuführen.

Dieser kleine Exkurs über Entstehung, Ziele und Feier des Frauensonntags in der badischen Evangelischen Landeskirche[18] liefert interessante Vergleichspunkte für den Frauensonntag in der alt-katholischen Kirche, der im folgenden näher beschrieben werden soll.

## Die Einführung des Frauensonntags im Jahr 1920

Bevor Bischof und Synodalvertretung in der Frage des Frauensonntags einen Beschluß gefaßt hatten, fand in Freiburg bereits am 17. Oktober 1920 auf Veranlassung des dortigen Frauenvereins ein Frauentag statt, der die Anregungen der dritten Hauptversammlung aufgriff. Im Gottesdienst predigte Stadtpfarrer Erwin Kreuzer (1878-1953) und wendete "das Evangelium von der Mutter der Zebedaiden auf die Frauenvereinsarbeit an".[19] Die Kollekte wurde für die Arbeit der neu gegründeten Landesverbände bestimmt. Am Nachmittag fand eine Versammlung des Frauenvereins statt, bei der der Ortspfarrer einen Vortrag über die Verfassung der alt-katholischen Kirche hielt. Darin ging er besonders auf die Konsequenzen des wenige Monate zuvor eingeführten kirchlichen Frauenwahlrechts für die Art der Mitarbeit der Frauen in der Kirche ein. Im Bericht über diesen 'Freiburger Frauentag', der im *Alt-Katholischen Volksblatt* veröffentlicht wurde, wurden die Frauenvereine an anderen Orten dazu aufgerufen, dem Freiburger Beispiel zu folgen.

Es war wohl kein Zufall, daß gerade in der Freiburger Gemeinde ein Frauentag stattfand, mit dem faktisch der – offensichtlich mit Ungeduld erwartete – Beschluß der Kirchenleitung vorweggenommen und gleichzeitig andere Gemeinden zur Nachahmung ermuntert wurden. Denn in Freiburg waren die drei Kernmitglieder des Verbandsvorstands ansässig, die Vorsitzende Wilhelmine Kreuzer (1867-1937), die den Verband von 1920 bis 1933 leitete, die Schriftführerin Emilie Betz (1884-1977), die gleichzeitig Vorsitzende des örtlichen Frauenvereins war, sowie die Rechnerin Anna Krieger (1874-1940).

Der offizielle Beschluß der Kirchenleitung zur Einführung einer gesamtkirchlichen Kollekte folgte schließlich im November. In ihrer Sitzung am 2. November 1920 beschlossen Bischof Dr. Georg Moog (1863-1934) und die Mitglieder der Synodalvertretung, dem Verband Altkatholischer Frauenvereine

---

[18] Zu weiteren "Frauensonntagen" in Evangelischen Landeskirchen vgl. Anm. 81. In der römisch-katholischen Kirche besteht kein offizieller Frauensonntag.
[19] *AKVB* 34 (1920), 234. Zum Evangelium s. Mt 20, 20-21. – Erwin Kreuzer, der 1935 zum Bischof gewählt und geweiht wurde, war der jüngere Bruder der 1920 gewählten neuen Verbandsvorsitzenden Wilhelmine Kreuzer.

"zur Förderung seiner Arbeiten eine jährliche Kirchensammlung auf den 1. Adventssonntag" zu bewilligen.[20] Der Beschluß wurde am 25. November 1920 im *Amtlichen Kirchblatt* veröffentlicht, drei Tage vor dem ersten Adventssonntag. Verschiedene Gemeinden hielten daraufhin am ersten Adventssonntag eine Kollekte für die Frauenarbeit. Für manche Gemeinden kam die Mitteilung vermutlich jedoch zu spät, um noch entsprechend zu reagieren. Einige überwiesen dem Verband die Kollekteneinnahmen, weiterreichende Aktivitäten konnten aber wahrscheinlich in der Regel nicht mehr organisiert werden. So war der erste Frauensonntag im alt-katholischen Bistum wohl in den meisten Fällen nicht mehr als ein Kollektensonntag für die Frauenarbeit.[21]

### Anliegen und Ziele des Frauensonntags

Welche Anliegen und Ziele verbanden die Frauen mit der Einführung des Frauensonntags? Wie bereits erwähnt, spielte die Kollekte dieses Sonntags eine wichtige Rolle. Sie war für die Frauenarbeit bestimmt und wurde an den Verband abgeführt. In der angespannten Nachkriegslage konnten die Frauenverbandsarbeit und die laufenden Projekte[22] durch die Kollekteneinnahmen aus dem Bistum finanziell mit abgesichert werden.[23] Bis dahin war die alt-katholische Frauenarbeit vor Ort aus den eigenen Mitteln und Aktivitäten der Frauen (Bazar, Einkünfte aus Mitgliedsbeiträgen und Geldsammelaktionen) finanziert worden, nun übernahm auch das alt-katholische Bistum eine gewisse Mitverantwortung für die Verbandsarbeit.

[20] *Amtliches Alt-Katholisches Kirchenblatt* VI (25. November 1920), Nr. 15/16, 87. Vgl. auch das Protokoll der Sitzung der Synodalvertretung am 2. November 1920 (Akten der Bischöflichen Kanzlei 1.37, Bischöfliches Archiv Bonn).

[21] Lediglich 26 Gemeinden überwiesen dem Verband 1920 ihre Kollekteneinnahmen vom ersten Advent, vgl. *AKVB* 34 (1920), 257-8; *AKVB* 35 (1921), 16. 21. 1921 kamen Überweisungen von etwa 35 Gemeinden, vgl. *AKVB* 36 (1922), 31. Fälschlich wurde in den letzten Jahrzehnten verschiedentlich das Jahr 1921 als Jahr der Einführung des Frauensonntags genannt, so auch in: *...nicht nur schweigend, ...nicht nur schön*, hg. vom Bund Altkatholischer Frauen Deutschlands (Selbstverlag: Bonn [1987]), 24.

[22] In der Anfangszeit des Frauensonntags wurden die Kollekten für die Arbeit der neu gegründeten Landesverbände verwendet, vgl. *AKVB* 34 (1920), 234. Möglicherweise war die Gründung der Landesverbände im Jahr 1920 ursprünglich sogar der äußere Anlaß zur Einführung der Kollekte, und damit des gesamten Frauensonntags. Für diese Vermutung spricht, daß das Thema Frauensonntag in den vorliegenden zeitgenössischen Berichten über die Hauptversammlung in Freiburg nicht als eigenständiges Thema auftaucht.

[23] Die finanzielle Lage des Verbandes war 1920 "geordnet, aber höchst knapp", vgl. *AKVB* 34 (1920), 183. 1922 mußte die geplante vierte Hauptversammlung des Verbandes "aus wirtschaftlichen Rücksichten" ausfallen, vgl. *AKVB* 54 (1923), 131.

Der finanzielle Aspekt war jedoch nicht alles. Den Frauen ging es bei der Einführung des Frauensonntags um mehr – dies macht bereits die genannte Initiative des 'Freiburger Frauentags' im Oktober 1920 deutlich. Die Frauen wollten einen Tag, an dem die Frauenarbeit in der Familie, in Gemeinde und Kirche, im Gottesdienst und im gemeinsamen Gedankenaustausch im Mittelpunkt stand. Den Frauen sollte dieser Tag Anregungen und Informationen für ihre Arbeit geben. Darüber hinaus bot er eine Gelegenheit, die Frauenarbeit in der Gemeinde deutlicher als bisher sichtbar zu machen. Dies wird aus dem Aufruf ersichtlich, den der Vorstand Anfang November 1921, einen Monat vor dem zweiten Frauensonntag, an die Frauenvereine richtete. Darin heißt es:

> Wir wollen ihn [sc. den ersten Adventssonntag] zu einem dauernden Frauensonntag in unserer Kirche ausgestalten, an dem nicht nur für unsere Kasse gesammelt, sondern auch in Amt und Predigt der Frauenarbeit gedacht werden und nachmittags oder abends Zusammenkünfte der Frauenvereine oder der Gemeinden stattfinden sollen, in denen durch Vorträge und Aussprachen das Verständnis für Frauenarbeit in Gemeinde und Kirche zu wecken und zu vertiefen gesucht wird. Dazu können uns Vorträge aus allen Lebensbereichen dienen. Haus und Familie mit allen Erziehungsfragen, Staaten- und Kirchengeschichte, Kunst und Wissenschaft, Volkswirtschaft und Wohlfahrtspflege bis in ihre letzten Einzelheiten, Werbearbeit und Organisationsfragen, innere kirchliche Unternehmungen und Bestrebungen, alles – alles kann den Blick weiten, Pflichtgefühl und Arbeitsfreude wecken, Lässige aufrütteln und Arbeitende zu höheren und weiteren Zielen führen.[24]

Warum wurde gerade der erste Adventssonntag gewählt – immerhin der erste Sonntag des Kirchenjahres? In den Texten der damaligen Zeit finden sich lediglich verdeckte Hinweise auf die Bedeutung des Adventssonntags in liturgischer und spiritueller Hinsicht. Die Adventszeit war "Frauenzeit".[25] Die biblische Marienfrömmigkeit, die Bezugnahme auf Maria als "Magd des Herrn", ihre Erwartung, ihre Geduld und ihr "in-guter-Hoffnung-Sein" – die Adventszeit bot genügend Anknüpfungspunkte für Frauenleben und für das damalige Selbstverständnis der Arbeit von Frauen.[26]

---

[24] *AKVB* 35 (1921), 163.
[25] Für den Hinweis auf die geschlechtsspezifische Prägung dieser Zeit (ein Begriff von Teresa Berger) in der Erfahrung früherer Frauengenerationen danke ich Erentrud Kraft (Kirrlach).
[26] Alt-katholische Christinnen und Christen stützen sich in der Marienverehrung auf das biblische Zeugnis und auf die Ehrentitel, die die ökumenischen Konzile der ersten Jahrhunderte Maria zugesprochen haben. Den römisch-katholischen Dogmen von der Unbefleckten Empfängnis (1854) und von der leiblichen Aufnahme Mariens in den Himmel (1950) kommt selbstver-

1923 etwa schreibt die Vorsitzende Wilhelmine Kreuzer anläßlich des bevorstehenden Frauensonntags über das Arbeitsethos der Frauenvereine und beschreibt es als "Liebe, die alles hofft und nicht das Ihre sucht".[27] "Alles hoffen" ist bei ihr eine Grundhaltung, aus der heraus die Frauenvereine handeln sollen. Eine solche – mehr oder weniger als "weiblich" qualifizierte – Grundhaltung konnte in der Adventszeit, in der die Hoffnung und Heilserwartung auf Ankunft und Wiederkunft im Mittelpunkt stehen, ihren liturgischen Ort erhalten.

### Frauen und Pfarrer

Die Feier des Frauensonntags bürgerte sich schnell ein. Von den 46 Vereinen, die 1937 dem Verband angehörten, feierten nach eigener Angabe 37 Vereine den Frauensonntag.[28] Die meisten Vereine begnügten sich mit der kirchlichen Feier des Frauensonntags, einige schlossen daran ein "weltliche Feier" an.[29] Insbesondere den kleinen Vereinen, die nicht so oft zusammenkamen, gab der Frauensonntag die Möglichkeit, die Mitglieder "in lebendige Fühlungnahme" miteinander zu bringen.[30]

Auch Pfarrer begrüßten die Einrichtung des Frauensonntags. Der Pfarrer von Karlsruhe, Josef Johne (1894-1950), nannte 1936 den Frauensonntag einen "segensreichen Ausgangsort" der Frauenarbeit in den Gemeinden.[31] Er sei "zu einer schönen Überlieferung geworden"[32] und kein Pfarrer werde ihn ungenutzt vorübergehen lassen,

> weil er ihm eine Gelegenheit gibt, der Frauenvereine und ihrer Arbeit für Kirche und Gemeinde dankbar zu gedenken. Er wird aber auch den Frauen als solchen

---

ständlich keine Verbindlichkeit zu, vgl. Christian Oeyen, "Alt-Katholizismus", in: Remigius Bäumer / Leo Scheffczyk (Hg.), *Marienlexikon* (Eos Verlag: St. Ottilien 1988), 116-118.

[27] *AKVB* 54 (1923), 146.

[28] Anfang der dreißiger Jahre scheint der Frauensonntag am zweiten Adventssonntag gefeiert worden zu sein, vgl. *Internationale Kirchliche Zeitschrift* [= *IKZ*] 21 (1931), 304-305. Auf Vorschlag des Weltbundes für internationale Freundschaftsarbeit der Kirchen wurde in vielen Kirchen am zweiten Adventssonntag des Weltfriedens gedacht (vgl. *IKZ* 22 [1932], 49-50). Auch die alt-katholischen Kirchen führten den Friedenssonntag ein. In diesem Zusammenhang ist davon die Rede, daß die deutsche alt-katholische Kirche den Frauensonntag vom zweiten Adventssonntag auf einen anderen Adventssonntag verlegen möge, da er "nur eine örtliche Bedeutung für das deutsche Bistum hat" (*IKZ* 21 [1931], 305). Genauere Belege fehlen jedoch.

[29] *AKVB* 69 (1938), 126.

[30] Ebd., 127.

[31] *AKVB* 67 (1936), 55.

[32] *AKVB* 68 (1937), 371.

einen Kranz winden, um ihrer Arbeit im Hause, in der Erziehung der Kinder und ihrer beruflichen Tätigkeit willen.[33]

Für die Pfarrer bot – dies wird aus J. Johnes Worten deutlich – insbesondere die Predigt beim Frauensonntag eine willkommene Gelegenheit, Frauen an ihre religiöse Verantwortung zu erinnern. Der Dank an die Frauen wurde damit gleichzeitig zum religiös-sozialen Platzanweiser.

Die Wichtigkeit der Zusammenarbeit des Frauenvereins mit dem Pfarrer wird auch auf der Seite der Frauen immer wieder hervorgehoben. Da Männer bis Anfang der sechziger Jahre als außerordentliches Mitglied dem Verband Altkatholischer Frauenvereine angehören konnten, besaßen Pfarrer die Möglichkeit, sich mit beratender Stimme in die Verbandsangelegenheiten einzubringen.[34] Die Funktion eines Geistlichen Beirats, wie andere konfessionelle Frauenverbände ihn kennen, gab es jedoch nie. Den Pfarrern brachten die Frauen ein gesundes Selbstbewußtsein entgegen, wie die Verbandsvorsitzende Wilhelmine Kreuzer in ihren Ausführungen zum Frauensonntag 1923 deutlich macht:

> Die Frauenvereinsarbeit soll (…) die Verkörperung der lebendigen Anteilnahme dieser [Laien-]Kreise in selbständiger Mitarbeit am Ausbau unserer Kirche sein. (…) Vorsitzende sollte stets eine warmherzige, arbeitsfrohe, mit allen örtlichen Verhältnissen genau vertraute, weitblickende Persönlichkeit sein, die auch den Mut hat, ihre eigene Auffassung der Frauenvereinsarbeit, *wenn nötig*, gegen die Auffassung des Pfarrers zu vertreten und durchzusetzen.[35]

## Der Frauensonntag in der Zeit des Dritten Reiches

Die Geschichte der alt-katholischen Kirche im Dritten Reich ist bisher noch nicht geschrieben.[36] Für eine kleine Kirche wie die alt-katholische war die Versuchung groß, das ekklesiologische Selbstverständnis als Ortskirche, die das gesamte Gebiet des Deutschen Reichs umfaßte, nationalistisch umzudeuten und sich dem politischen Regime als Alternative zum Rom-Katholizismus anzubieten. Man

---

[33] Ebd.

[34] Verschiedene Pfarrer waren den Quellen zufolge in die Arbeit des Verbandes involviert. Noch die Satzung vom 19. Mai 1959 sieht eine außerordentliche Mitgliedschaft von Männern in § 5b vor. Spätere Satzungen kennen nur Frauen als Mitglieder.

[35] *AKVB* 54 (1923), 146. W. Kreuzer spricht sich dagegen aus, daß Frauenvereine durch Pfarrersfrauen geleitet werden.

[36] Eine kurze Übersicht gibt Matthias Ring, "Versuchung und Irrtum. Die Alt-Katholische Kirche im Dritten Reich", in: *Christen heute. Zeitung der Alt-Katholiken* [= *CH*] 39 (1995), 72-74. Dieser Artikel ist auch im Internet abfragbar: http:www.alt-katholisch.de/info/historie/3reich.htm. Eine Dissertation von M. Ring ist in Vorbereitung.

verstand sich "als eine unpolitische und rein auf das Religiöse beschränkte Kirche",[37] was sich jedoch als naiver und gefährlicher Irrtum erwies.[38]

Die NS-Ideologie, die Frauen in den Bereich des Hauses verwies und sie auf die Mutterschaft zu beschränken suchte, machte sich auch in der alt-katholischen Kirche bemerkbar.[39] So versuchte der oben genannte Pfarrer Josef Johne in einem Artikel aus dem Jahr 1936, die Bedeutung des Frauensonntags im Rahmen der quasireligiösen nationalsozialistischen Ideologie zu interpretieren. Im gemeinsamen Empfang der Kommunion durch die Mitglieder des Frauenvereins am Frauensonntag fand seiner Ansicht nach "das Gelöbnis zu treuer Gemeinschaftsarbeit einen erhebenden Ausdruck" und in der weltlichen Feier solle "das Bewußtsein der kulturellen Verbundenheit mit den geistigen Gütern unseres Volkes lebendig werden".[40]

In der Zeit des Dritten Reichs veränderte sich die Tätigkeit der Vereine. Von der bis dahin üblichen Fürsorgearbeit wurden die kirchlichen Frauenvereine mehr und mehr zurückgedrängt und mußten sich auf eine rein innerkirchliche Tätigkeit beschränken. Zwischen 1934 und 1937 gingen die Einnahmen aus den Kollekten für den Frauensonntag um ein Viertel zurück, was vermutlich mit der allgemeinen finanziellen Lage vieler Gemeinden und ihrer Mitglieder zusammenhing.[41]

Mit dem Ausbruch des Zweiten Weltkriegs mußten viele Frauen, deren Männer zum Kriegsdienst eingezogen waren, daheim die volle Verantwortung für ihre Familie und deren Lebensunterhalt übernehmen. Diese Inanspruchnahme, dazu die allabendliche Verdunklung erschwerte das regelmäßige Zusammenkommen vieler Frauenvereine. Wenige Monate nach dem

---

[37] Ebd., 72.

[38] Bei der 54. Ordentlichen Bistumssynode im Oktober 2000 sprach Bischof Joachim Vobbe im Namen der deutschen alt-katholischen Kirche ein Schuldbekenntnis aus, das dem Zentralrat der Juden in Deutschland überreicht wurde, vgl. *CH* 44 (2000), 259.

[39] Über alt-katholische Frauen im Dritten Reich ist bisher nicht geforscht worden. Lediglich Monika Hinterberger hat über das Leben Margarete Biebers geschrieben. Margarete Bieber (geb. 1879) war die erste Professorin für klassische Archäologie in Deutschland und ließ sich 1920 in der alt-katholischen Kirche zu Bonn taufen. Ihre Entlassung aus dem Staatsdienst wegen "politischer Unzuverlässigkeit" und später aufgrund ihrer "nichtarischen Abstammung" erfolgte bereits am 1. Juli 1933. Sie wanderte in die USA aus, wo sie 1978 starb. Dort blieb sie – wie sie 1960 schrieb – ein *"Mitglied der Diaspora der Bonner alt-katholischen Gemeinde..."*. Monika Hinterberger, "Eine Archäologin in zwei Welten. Margarete Bieber", in: *CH* 43 (1999), 227-229. Der Beitrag ist im Internet nachzulesen unter: http://www.christen-heute.de/199910/bieber.htm.

[40] *AKVB* 67 (1936), 55.

[41] Vgl. *AKVB* 69 (1938), 132.

Beginn des Zweiten Weltkriegs wandte sich die Verbandsvorsitzende Elly Johne geb. Vermeulen (1894-1985)[42] mit der Bitte an die Vorsitzenden der Frauenvereine, wenigstens am Frauensonntag "eine bescheidene Zusammenkunft" zu organisieren.[43] Am Sonntagmorgen solle der Gottesdienst "im Zeichen des Frauensonntags stehen". In den Fürbitten solle die Arbeitsbelastung der Frauen besonders thematisiert werden und der Frauen gedacht werden, "die ihr Heim verlassen mußten und nun mit ihren Kindern oder alten Eltern in der Fremde voller Sehnsucht auf baldige Heimkehr, ihr hartes Los tragen müssen". Ein besonderes Anliegen sei es, "unsern Heiland zu bitten, daß er allen Frauen tapfere Herzen schenke und sie nicht müde werden lasse in der Erfüllung ihrer Aufgaben für Familie, Volk und Vaterland." Für den Nachmittag schlug Elly Johne eine "weltliche Feier" vor. Sie könne

> in einer geselligen und frohen Stunde bestehen und den Adventsgedanken dahingehend zum Ausdruck kommen lassen, daß mit der Erwartung des Friedensfürsten Jesus Christus, uns auch die Hoffnung erfülle, daß ein baldiger, siegreicher Friede uns wieder von den Sorgen des Krieges entlaste.[44]

Ein ähnlicher Aufruf Elly Johnes zum Frauensonntag erging auch ein Jahr später. Die Kriegszeit schränke das "Versammlungsleben" vieler Vereine stark ein – bei dieser Anspielung auf das tagespolitische Geschehen beließ Elly Johne es. Der Frauensonntag sei ein Tag, an dem alle Frauen sich "auf das engste miteinander verbunden wissen".[45] Betont wird der kirchliche Bezug des Frauensonntags; er sei "ein Tag der Besinnung und Einkehr, wie es sich für den beginnenden Advent geziemt".[46]

Der Zusammenhang zwischen den Vereinen wurde durch die immer ernster werdenden Kriegsereignisse mehr und mehr gelockert und nur noch durch Rundschreiben der Vorsitzenden notdürftig aufrecht erhalten. Ende Mai 1941 mußte das "Alt-Katholische Volksblatt" sein Erscheinen einstellen.[47] Die Mitteilungen über den Verband beschränkten sich in diesem Jahr auf eine Übersicht der eingegangenen Beiträge, Spenden und der Frauensonntagskollekten.[48]

---

[42] Elly Johne war die Ehefrau des bereits genannten Pfarrers Josef Johne. Sie war von 1936 bis 1949 Verbandsvorsitzende.

[43] *AKVB* 70 (1939), 321. Auch die folgenden Zitate stammen aus diesem Aufruf.

[44] Ebd.

[45] *AKVB* 71 (1940), 191 (535).

[46] Ebd.

[47] *AKVB* 72 (1941), 87. Grund: "Um Menschen und Material für andere kriegswichtige Zwecke freizumachen".

[48] *AKVB* 72 (1941), 24.

Hinsichtlich der Entwicklung des Frauensonntags in den ersten 25 Jahren seines Bestehens kann festgehalten werden, daß seine Einführung bei den Frauenvereinen und bei den Pfarrern Anklang fand. Die Frauenvereine sahen darin eine kirchenöffentliche Anerkennung ihrer Arbeit und nutzten den Frauensonntag als Tag der Zusammenkunft. Der erste Sonntag im Advent wie überhaupt die gesamte Adventszeit wurde augenscheinlich als geeignet für den Frauensonntag angenommen; der Grund dafür mag darin liegen, daß diese Zeit im Kirchenjahr als geschlechtsspezifisch geprägt erfahren wurde.[49] In den adventlichen gottesdienstlichen Themen von Hoffnung, Erwartung, Ausharren in Geduld fanden Frauen weibliche Lebenserfahrungen angesprochen, die freilich – dies sei kritisch angemerkt – in der Auslegung des Liturgen zwischen Frauenwirklichkeit und Frauenleitbild oszillieren konnten. Inwieweit die Frauen an der Gestaltung des Gottesdienstes beim Frauensonntag – zum Beispiel beim Aussuchen von Liedern – Anteil hatten oder nicht, konnte aufgrund der Quellenlage nicht festgestellt werden. In der ersten Hälfte des 20. Jahrhunderts war es in alt-katholischen Gemeinden von der liturgischen Ordnung her zwar möglich, aber in der Regel nicht üblich, daß alle Gemeindemitglieder allsonntäglich zur Kommunion gingen. An Frauensonntagen wie auch bei Hauptversammlungen des Verbandes empfingen die anwesenden Mitgliedsfrauen geschlossen die Kommunion. Die Verbundenheit der Mitglieder des Frauenvereins bzw. des Verbands fand so auch in der Mahlgemeinschaft einen Ausdruck. Vielfach wurde die Feier des Frauensonntags auch nach dem Ende der Eucharistiefeier fortgesetzt, sei es mit einem gemeinsamen Mittagessen, sei es mit einem geselligen Beisammensein, gestaltet mit Vorträgen, gelegentlich wohl auch mit musikalischer Umrahmung. Der Frauensonntag war damit ein Festtag, an dem Frauen ihrer haushaltlichen Verpflichtungen enthoben waren.[50] Auch die Pfarrer begrüßten die Einführung des Frauensonntags. Sie nahmen ihn zum Anlaß, über die Rolle von Frauen in der Gemeinde und in der Familie zu predigen und in den Fürbitten für sie zu beten. Dabei konnte der Dank an die Frauen auch als Gelegenheit dienen, Frauen auf die an sie gestellten Erwartungen hinzuweisen.

Wortschatz und Denkbilder aus der NS-Ideologie fanden in der Zeit des Dritten Reiches Eingang in Überlegungen zur Rolle und zum Dienst von

---

[49] Vgl. zu geschlechtsspezifisch geprägten Zeiten: Berger, "'die weyber nach den mennern'?" 189-190.

[50] Festtage bedeuteten für Frauen oft gerade eine Zunahme haushaltlicher Arbeit und keine Freistellung von ihr (vgl. Berger, *Women's Ways of Worship*, 18-19).

Frauen in der alt-katholischen Kirche; so findet sich in dieser Zeit eine stärkere Betonung der Mutterschaft von Frauen als in früherer Zeit.[51] Die Arbeit der Vereine und des Verbandes wurde in den innerkirchlichen Bereich zurückgedrängt.

## Der Frauensonntag nach 1945

Nach dem Zweiten Weltkrieg standen zunächst die Sorge für Heimatvertriebene und Flüchtlinge und der Wiederaufbau im Vordergrund. Auch die Verbandsarbeit kam wieder in Gang. Aus dieser Zeit sind die Informationen über die Feier des Frauensonntags spärlich. Wo es sie gibt, wird vor allem die kirchliche Dimension des Frauensonntags hervorgehoben. So in einem Rundbrief aus dem Jahr 1965. Für Dr. Ilse Brinkhues (geb. 1923), die zwischen 1965 und 1987 Vorsitzende des Verbandes war, kommt in der Feier des Frauensonntags die Anerkennung der Arbeit von Frauen zum Ausdruck. Deren Tätigkeit ist – dem Denken der damaligen Zeit entsprechend – vor allem auf das Wohl von Kirche und Gemeinde bezogen. Die Erfahrung der Gemeinschaft, die in den Texten der dreißiger Jahre relativ stark hervortritt, wird dagegen kaum hervorgehoben. Die Geselligkeit der Zusammenkünfte erscheint als schöne Beigabe, aber nicht als Hauptzweck der Feier. Die Hauptaufgabe der Frauen liege in Gottesdienst und Gebet, sie sollen "als treue Beterinnen dem Pfarrer zur Seite" stehen.[52]

Dreizehn Jahre später hat sich die Aussagerichtung geändert. In ihrem Adventsrundbrief des Jahres 1978 ruft die Vorsitzende Dr. Brinkhues dazu auf, das Thema des Weltgebetstags von 1979, "Geistlich wachsen", bei der Feier des Frauensonntags aufzugreifen. Die Frauen könnten sich zum Beispiel fragen:

> Hat das, was wir im vergangenen Jahr unternommen haben, uns geholfen, geistlich zu wachsen?[53]

Frauen werden nun nicht mehr in erster Linie wahrgenommen in dem, was sie für andere tun oder was ihre Arbeit für die Gemeinde und Kirche bedeutet, sondern wer sie selbst als individuelle Frauen und als gläubige Christinnen sind.

---

[51] So erschienen etwa 1940 und 1941 Betrachtungen zweier Pfarrer zum Muttertag, vgl. *AKVB* 71 (1940), 73-4; *AKVB* 72 (1941), 73-4.

[52] Rundbrief der Vorsitzenden Dr. Ilse Brinkhues, Advent 1966 (Archiv des Frauenbundes, Bonn).

[53] Rundbrief der Vorsitzenden Dr. Ilse Brinkhues, Advent 1978 (Archiv des Frauenbundes, Bonn).

Diese Veränderung hängt mit dem Einfluß der neuen Frauenbewegung in Deutschland zusammen. Auch bei den alt-katholischen Frauen fand ab Mitte der sechziger Jahre ein Bewußtseinswandel statt. Damals begann die Auseinandersetzung mit der Rolle der Frauen in Familie, Staat und Kirche. Erstmals wurde bei den mehrtägigen Jahrestagungen, die sich ab den siebziger Jahren zu einer festen Institution entwickelten, eine neue Art der Bibelarbeit angewendet, die biblische Frauen in den Mittelpunkt stellte und Interpretationen aus weiblicher Sicht zuließ.[54]

**Neue Anliegen: Frauen zur Verkündigung anregen**
In den siebziger Jahren wurde die Gleichberechtigung in der Kirche mehr und mehr Thema des "Bundes Altkatholischer Frauen Deutschlands", wie sich der Verband seit 1962 nannte. Bei den alljährlichen Jahrestagungen des Bundes stand u.a. die Schulung der Frauen zur Mündigkeit im Vordergrund.[55] Sie lernten zum Beispiel, wie sie sich in einer Kirchenvorstandssitzung behaupten und durchsetzen können. Der Bund forderte damals, daß Frauen in kirchlichen Leitungsgremien in größerer Zahl als bisher vertreten sein müßten; außerdem gab er wesentliche Anstöße zur Diskussion um die Frauenordination. Auch die Rolle der Frauenvereine in den Gemeinden wurde neu überdacht. 1976 stellte die Vorsitzende fest, daß es

> eigentlich kaum 'typische' Frauenkreisaufgaben [gibt], sondern in erster Linie allgemeine Aufgaben, die der Frauenkreis stellvertretend für die Gesamtheit der Gemeindemitglieder übernimmt. Sollten wir in diesem Zusammenhang den Standort unseres Frauenkreises in der Gemeinde nicht einmal neu überdenken?[56]

Diese Neubesinnung warf auch im Hinblick auf den Frauensonntag seine Früchte ab. War es bis in die sechziger Jahre hinein üblich, daß am Frauensonntag im Gemeindegottesdienst mit dem darin meist vollzählig versammelten Frauenverein durch den Pfarrer über die Frauen gepredigt und gebetet

---

[54] Der Bund Alt-Katholischer Frauen war es, der in den achtziger Jahren die "afrikanische Methode der Bibelarbeit", das sog. Bibelteilen, im alt-katholischen Bistum einführte (Vorstandssitzung 6.-7. Mai 1990, Archiv des Frauenbundes, Bonn). Inzwischen wird diese Methode regelmäßig benutzt, zuletzt bei der 54. Ordentlichen Bistumssynode im Oktober 2000.

[55] Diese Jahrestagungen fanden mit unterschiedlicher Zielsetzung und Namensgebung ab 1953 statt. Anfangs "Freizeiten" genannt, wurden sie seit Anfang der siebziger Jahre mehr und mehr zu thematisch ausgerichteten "Tagungen".

[56] Dr. Ilse Brinkhues an die Mitglieder des Bundes Altkatholischer Frauen am 5. August 1976 (Archiv des Frauenbundes, Bonn).

wurde, so änderte sich dies nun grundlegend.[57] Frauen fingen seit Anfang der siebziger Jahre in verschiedenen Gemeinden an, den Gottesdienst selbst zu gestalten oder mitzugestalten, indem sie die Lesung und die Fürbitten übernahmen. In Einzelfällen predigten sie auch.

Die Verselbständigung der Frauen hatte nicht nur Auswirkungen auf die Teilhabe der Frauen an der Gestaltung der Gottesdienste, sondern auch auf deren thematische und spirituelle Ausrichtung. Als Arbeitshilfen zur Vorbereitung des Frauensonntags gibt der Bundesvorstand seit 1988 einen "Materialdienst" heraus. Diese Anregungen zur Gestaltung eines Gottesdienstes sollten "in besonderem Maße Frauen in der Kirche ansprechen und zur Verkündigung anregen".[58] Die Vorlagen für den Frauensonntagsgottesdienst stützen sich dabei auf die Texte des bei der Jahrestagung gefeierten Gottesdienstes. Auch Symbole spielen in diesen Gottesdiensten eine wichtige Rolle; sie sind oft Mitbringsel aus Alltag und Natur, die symbolhaft auf die Lebenswirklichkeit von Frauen gedeutet und vor Gott gebracht werden. Die Frauen nehmen die Erfahrungen des Gottesdienstes bei der Jahrestagung als Anregung mit nach Hause. Wichtig ist, daß die kreativen Elemente, an denen die Liturgie der jeweiligen Jahrestagung reich ist, zuerst im sicheren Raum ausprobiert worden sind, bevor sie zur Gestaltung des Gottesdienstes am Frauensonntag eingebracht werden.

Bei allen Gottesdiensten wird auf eine frauenfreundliche Sprache geachtet.[59] Gebete und Lieder sind häufig aus der ökumenischen Frauengebetskultur, regelmäßig werden aber auch von alt-katholischen Teilnehmerinnen bei der Jahrestagung selbst formulierte Gebete und Gebetsmeditationen als Bausteine angeboten. Für den Predigtteil gibt es im Materialdienst Anregungen zu einer Predigtmeditation oder einer zu spielenden Szene für mehrere Sprecherinnen. In den letzten Jahren finden sich im Materialdienst auch Hinweise, welches der zahlreichen Eucharistiegebete als besonders geeignet erscheint. Eine Vorliebe

---

[57] Auch die Feier des Weltgebetstages, der in den sechziger Jahren zunehmend von Alt-Katholikinnen mitgefeiert wurde (vgl. *AKKZ* NF 9 [1965], 68), dürfte bei dieser Entwicklung eine Rolle gespielt haben.

[58] Bericht der Vorsitzenden Katja Nickel für die Synode 1991 (Archiv des Frauenbundes, Bonn).

[59] Ich verstehe hier 'frauenfreundlich' und weiter unten auch 'frauengerecht' als Allgemeinbegriff. Für eine Unterscheidung zwischen nicht-sexistischer, inklusiver und emanzipativer Sprache s. Marjorie Procter-Smith, *In Her Own Rite. Constructing Feminist Liturgical Tradition* (Abingdon Press: Nashville 1990), 59-84; vgl. auch Denise J.J. Dijk, *Een beeld van een liturgie. Verkenningen in vrouwenstudies liturgiek, met bijzondere aandacht voor het werk van Marjorie Procter-Smith* (Narratio: Gorinchem 1999), 131-154.

besteht dabei für das zwölfte Eucharistiegebet im alt-katholischen Eucharistie-
buch, in dem Maria von Magdala als Apostolin und andere Frauen als Zeugin-
nen des Gottesreiches namentlich genannt werden. Es handelt sich um ein Rollen transzendierendes, die Unterschiedlichkeit von Menschen betonendes
Eucharistiegebet.[60] Nach dieser Darstellung muß nicht eigens betont werden,
daß der Gottesdienst am Frauensonntag kein Gottesdienst für Frauen allein,
sondern die Feier der ganzen Gemeinde ist. Vielfach werden diese Gottesdienste als eine Bereicherung für das Gemeindeleben erfahren.

Im letzten Jahrzehnt wurden verschiedene Themen behandelt, die Frau-
eninteresen und die Lebenswirklichkeit von Frauen besonders berühren. Biblische Frauengestalten wie Hanna, Schiphra und Pua oder Hagar[61] standen im
Mittelpunkt, oft wurde dabei das Thema der Jahrestagung aufgegriffen. Des
öfteren werden die Themen dabei zu aktuellen politischen Geschehnissen in
Beziehung gesetzt; so rief 1992 die damalige Vorsitzende Katja Nickel (geb.
1934) folgendermaßen zum Frauensonntag auf:

> Nehmen wir Hagars Schicksal zum Anlaß, darüber nachzudenken, wo wir Frauen
> in der Fremde zum Brunnen ihres Lebens verhelfen können.[62]

Seit 1999 wählt der Bundesvorstand ein Jahresthema, das mit der Jahrestagung im Herbst anfängt und die Arbeit des ganzen Folgejahres begleitet. Für
das Jahr 1999-2000 wurde das Thema "Aufbruch" und als jahresbegleitendes
Motto "Schlagt die Trommel, tanzt und fürchtet euch nicht"[63] gewählt, für
2000-2001 das Thema "Ich rette dich, laß los", das eine Geschichte von Anthony de Mello aufgreift.[64] Im Materialdienst für den Frauensonntag am ersten
Advent 2000 werden Bausteine angeboten, um dieses Thema in Gebeten,
Gesängen, Fürbitten und in einem Sprechspiel im Rahmen einer Eucharistiefeier zu entfalten. Die Lesungen, die Präfation sowie mehrere Lieder sind der

---

[60] Vgl. *Die Feier der Eucharistie im Katholischen Bistum der Alt-Katholiken in Deutschland.
Für den gottesdienstlichen Gebrauch erarbeitet durch die liturgische Kommission und herausgegeben durch Bischof und Synodalvertretung* (Bistumsverlag: Bonn 1995), 198-9.

[61] Zu Hanna s. 1 Sam 1-2, 11; zu Schiphra und Pua s. Ex 1, 15-21; zu Hagar s. Gen 21, 8-21.

[62] Brief der Vorsitzenden Katja Nickel zum Ersten Adventssonntag 1992 (Archiv des Frauenbundes, Bonn).

[63] Nach dem gleichnamigen Titel eines Artikels von Elisabeth Lüneburg über das Tanzlied
Miriams (Ex 15, 20-21), in: Eva Renate Schmidt / Mieke Korenhof / Renate Jost (Hg.), *Femi-
nistisch gelesen. 32 ausgewählte Bibeltexte für Gruppen, Gemeinden und Gottesdienste*, Bd. 1
(Kreuz Verlag: Stuttgart 1988), 45-52.

[64] Die Geschichte ist zu finden in: Anthony de Mello, *Warum der Schäfer jedes Wetter liebt*
(Herder: Freiburg ⁴1999), 57.

Kirchenjahreszeit entsprechend gewählt. In den zur Auswahl vorgeschlagenen Eucharistiegebeten wird Bezug genommen auf Jesus Christus als Gottes "helfende Hand" bzw. Gottes "rettendes Wort".[65] Einige Psalmverse, die das Thema des Abgrunds und des von Gott Getragen-Werdens aufgreifen, sowie das Tagesgebet stammen von der anglikanischen Gottespoetin Janet Morley.[66] Die zum Teil selbst formulierten Texte und Gebete handeln vom bewußten Aufgeben von Sicherheiten und vom Vertrauen, aufgefangen zu werden, vom Loslassen, von Lösung und Erlösung. Konkret kann es dabei auch darum gehen, sich aus festgefahrenen, einengenden eigenen Rollenvorstellungen von der "idealen Frau" zu lösen. Im Schlußgebet heißt es u.a.:

> Erlöse mich mit dem Sturmwind deiner Weisheit
> mit dem Feuer deiner Liebe
> dann werde ich fallen, schweben, fliegen
> in ein neues Leben
> das du immer schon
> für mich bereit gehalten hast.[67]

Als Ergebnis ist festzuhalten, daß der Frauensonntag nach dem Zweiten Weltkrieg einige gewichtige Akzentverschiebungen erfahren hat. Diese sind im Zusammenhang mit den veränderten Rollen von Frauen in Kirche und Gesellschaft sowie ihrem wachsenden liturgisch-spirituellen Selbstbewußtsein zu sehen. Frauen haben die Gestaltung der gottesdienstlichen Feier am Frauensonntag an vielen Orten selbst in die Hand genommen und machen darin mit Hilfe von Gebeten, Symbolen, Handlungen sowie durch die Auslegung biblischer Texte die Lebenswirklichkeiten von Frauen zum Bestandteil des gottesdienstlichen Geschehens. Frauen denken sich dabei nicht nur Neues aus, sondern holen auch Altes aus dem Schatz der Kirche hervor und verschaffen ihm neue Wertschätzung (etwa Segensrituale, aber auch alte Symbole wie Wasser, Licht oder Öl).

Die aktive oder "tätige Teilnahme" der Mitfeiernden – das Zweite Vatikanum spricht von *participatio actuosa* – ist konstitutiv für jede gottesdienstliche

---

[65] *Die Feier der Eucharistie im Katholischen Bistum der Alt-Katholiken in Deutschland*, 196. 208. Es handelt sich um die Eucharistiegebete XI bzw. XVII.

[66] Janet Morley, *Preisen will ich Gott, meine Geliebte. Psalmen und Gebete* (Herder: Freiburg 1989), 12-13; Gebet zum 5. Sonntag vor Weihnachten, vgl. ebd., 23.

[67] Heidi Herborn (Hg.), *Materialdienst Frauensonntag, 1. Advent 2000* (Archiv des Frauenbundes, Bonn). Das Gebet stammt von Eva Repits, Wien; im Materialdienst ist nur ein Teil des ursprünglich längeren Gebets wiedergegeben.

Feier.[68] "Die Gemeinde als ganze gilt demnach als Subjekt der Feier".[69] In den von Frauen gestalteten Liturgien kommt zum Ausdruck: Frauen sind *"volle[n] Subjekte[n] der Feier der Liturgie"*.[70] Dies verwirklicht sich in der aktiven Mitwirkung an der Gestaltung von Formen und Inhalten der gottesdienstlichen Feier. Der Schwerpunkt des Frauensonntags liegt nach dem Zweiten Weltkrieg auf der gottesdienstlichen Feier. In manchen – etwa in südbadischen – Gemeinden wird der Frauensonntag oft verbunden mit einem gemeinsamen Mittagessen oder einem Bazar, an manchen Orten auch mit einem Einkehrtag.

## Abschließende Überlegungen

Der Gottesdienst am Frauensonntag hat sich in den einundachtzig Jahren seines Bestehens von einem Gottesdienst über Frauen zu einem Gottesdienst von Frauen für die ganze Gemeinde gewandelt. Aus den Anfängen, in denen die Geistlichen mit Gebeten und manchmal auch mit Predigten der Arbeit der Frauen besonders gedacht haben, entwickelte sich die Beteiligung der Frauen an Liturgie und Verkündigung. Die Darstellung zeigt die Verwobenheit der liturgischen Rolle von Frauen mit dem gesellschaftlichen und kirchlichen Verständnis der Frauenrolle(n).

Die Gestaltung der Frauensonntagsgottesdienste hat in den letzten Jahrzehnten von der gediegenen Vorbereitung bei den Jahrestagungen des Frauenbundes profitiert. Dies gilt in thematischer, aber auch in gestalterischer Hinsicht. Viele Frauen erfahren die Gottesdienste bei den Jahrestagungen als Zurüstung für ihre eigene liturgische Tätigkeit beim Frauensonntag. Außerdem ist es ihnen auf diese Weise möglich, etwas von dem, was bei diesen Tagungen geschieht, in die alt-katholischen Gemeinden hineinzutragen.

Der Bund Altkatholischer Frauen Deutschlands hat sich die Mitverantwortung für das geistliche Leben in der altkatholischen Kirche zur Aufgabe gemacht.[71] Von ihm sind in den letzten Jahrzehnten wichtige spirituelle Impulse für die alt-katholische Kirche ausgegangen. Der Bund hat wesentlich dazu beigetragen, Frauen zu ermutigen und zu befähigen, Aufgaben in der

---

[68] *AKVB* 33 (1919), 296.

[69] Hans Bernhard Meyer, *Eucharistie. Geschichte, Theologie, Pastoral* (Handbuch der Liturgiewissenschaft 4; Pustet Verlag: Regensburg 1989), 488.

[70] Teresa Berger, *Sei gesegnet, meine Schwester. Frauen feiern Liturgie. Geschichtliche Rückfragen – Praktische Impulse – Theologische Vergewisserungen* (Echter: Würzburg 1999), 21. Kursivierung von mir.

[71] Diese Aufgabe wurde als §1 in die Satzung vom 19. Mai 1959 aufge- und in alle späteren Ausgaben der Satzung übernommen.

Liturgie zu übernehmen. Damit wird die bereits im 19. Jahrhundert zutage
tretende Mitverantwortung der weiblichen Laien auch auf geistlich-liturgische
Fragen ausgedehnt und im 20. Jahrhundert in einer (mit-)gestaltenden Beteiligung an der Verkündigung im Gottesdienst konkretisiert. Dieses Engagement
für die Laienfrauen hat folgerichtig zum Eintreten für die Einbeziehung von
Frauen in das kirchliche Amt geführt, an dessen Einführung in der alt-katholischen Kirche der Frauenbund maßgeblich Anteil hatte.[72] Mit seinen Frauen-
Liturgien kann der Bund Altkatholischer Frauen zur ökumenischen Liturgischen Aufbruchbewegung der Frauen in der zweiten Hälfte des 20.
Jahrhunderts gezählt werden, die Teresa Berger kürzlich als "eigentlichen
gottesdienstlichen Meilenstein des 20. Jahrhunderts" bezeichnet hat.[73]

Eine Umfrage unter den Gemeinden im Jahr 1999 hat ergeben, daß von den
heute bestehenden 44 Frauengruppen 34 den Frauensonntag feiern. In sieb-
zehn Gemeinden findet kein spezieller Frauensonntagsgottesdienst statt;
dabei spielt auch deren extreme Diasporasituation und/oder das Nicht-Vor-
handensein eines Frauenkreises eine Rolle. Von den 34 Frauenkreisen, die
den Frauensonntag feiern, tun dies 23 am ersten Adventssonntag. Die anderen
elf Frauenkreise feiern ihn an einem anderen Sonntag im Advent oder zu
einem für die betreffende Gemeinde geeigneten Datum.

Der Frauensonntag bietet immer wieder Anlaß zur Diskussion, wie etwa:
Ist der Erste Adventssonntag nicht liturgisch zu sehr festgelegt, so daß ein
anderes Thema nur schwerlich dazu paßt? Andere wiederum finden den Zeit-
raum zwischen den Jahrestagungen, die im Herbst stattfinden, und dem Frauensonntag zu kurz für eine gute Verarbeitung der Themenvorschläge in Vorbereitung auf den Gottesdienst am Ersten Advent. In der Vergangenheit waren
ab und zu Stimmen zu hören, die sich fragten, ob der Name 'Frauensonntag'

---

[72] 1988 wurde die erste Frau zur Diakonin, 1996 die ersten Priesterinnen geweiht. – An dieser
Stelle soll auf einen Unterschied zum Frauensonntag in der Evangelischen Landeskirche in
Baden hingewiesen werden. Der evangelische Frauensonntag wurde erst nach der Einbeziehung von Frauen in das Predigtamt auch zu einem in der Liturgie gefeierten Geschehen: "Die
volle Anerkennung der Frau im Predigtamt in unserer Kirche hat allen Frauen die Möglichkeit
der Beteiligung an der öffentlichen Wortverkündigung gegeben. Ich denke, daß daraus bald
(…) der Wunsch entstanden ist, in dem Gottesdienst, in dem für sie [sc. die Frauen] und ihre
Arbeit gesammelt wird, zu Wort zu kommen" (Loos, *Frauensonntag*, 6). Im alt-katholischen
Bistum wurde der Frauensonntag lange vor der Einbeziehung von Frauen in das kirchliche
Amt innerhalb der Liturgie gefeiert. Hier waren es eher die Laienfrauen, die den Frauen im
Amt den Weg gebahnt haben.

[73] Berger, "'die weyber nach den mennern'?" 185. Eine Analyse dieser Liturgischen Aufbruchbewegung ist zu finden in: Berger, *Sei gesegnet, meine Schwester*.

nicht irreführend sei, da Männer gelegentlich meinten, der Gottesdienst am Frauensonntag sei eine "reine Frauenangelegenheit".[74] Die gleichen Stimmen fragten sich damals auch, ob eine "solche isolierte Hervorhebung der Frauen", verstanden als eine Art "Muttertag im Advent" notwendig sei.[75] In der heutigen Diskussion spielen die beiden letztgenannten Fragen in der so gestellten Weise keine Rolle mehr. Denn sie spiegeln ein Rollenverständnis und ein Selbstbild von Frauen, das heute weitgehend überholt ist. Die Frage, ob ein solcher spezifischer Frauengottesdienst notwendig ist, lautet im 21. Jahrhundert in veränderter Form: Brauchen die Frauen den Frauensonntag heute noch – in einer Zeit, in der die Gleichberechtigung von Frauen und Männern als Laien und im Amt auch rechtlich festgelegt ist und inklusive und frauengerechte Sprache so weit wie möglich über das offizielle Missale prak-tiziert wird?[76] Meine Antwort: ja.

Drei Gründe seien dafür genannt. Der geschichtliche Überblick über die Entwicklung des Frauensonntags zeigt, erstens, daß der Frauensonntag in sei-ner Anfangszeit die Bedeutung einer 'Frauenzeit' hatte; nicht nur die Adventszeit selbst, sondern auch der von Haushaltspflichten entlastete Frau-ensonntag wurde als Zeit der Frauen erfahren. Für jüngere Frauen ist diese Erfahrung in der Regel wohl nicht mehr ohne weiteres nachvollziehbar. Aber unter verändertem Vorzeichen kann der Gedanke einer 'Frauenzeit' und eines 'Freiraums' für Frauen durchaus weiterhin von Bedeutung sein. Denn das Bemühen um Frauengerechtigkeit ist ein Prozeß, der noch lange nicht abge-schlossen ist. Deshalb braucht es Frei-Räume und Frei-Zeit, um frauenge-rechte Liturgie zu erproben und zu feiern. 'Frauengerecht' heißt dabei nicht nur das Sprechen einer inklusiven und emanzipatorischen Sprache, sondern auch das Einbeziehen der Lebenswirklichkeiten von Frauen in die Feier der Liturgie. Eine frauengerechte Liturgie hat das Ziel, den Erfahrungen von Frauen im gottesdienstlichen Zeit-Raum gerecht zu werden.

---

[74] *CH* 28 (1985), Nr. 11, 8.

[75] So der Heidelberger Frauenverein im Jahr 1985, vgl. *CH* 28 (1985), Nr. 11, 8.

[76] Zur Entwicklung zu frauengerechter Sprache und Liturgie in der alt-katholischen Kirche vgl. Joachim Vobbe, "Solidarität der Kirchen mit den Frauen – Hat die Ökumenische Dekade die christlichen Kirchen verändert?", in: Christine Busch / Brigitte Vielhaus (Hg.), *Kirche wird anders. Unterwegs zu einer Reform der Kirchen. Ökumenische Dekade 'Solidarität der Kir-chen mit den Frauen' 1988-1998. Erfahrungen und Perspektiven* (Klens Verlag – Evangeli-scher Presseverband der Evangelischen Kirche im Rheinland: Düsseldorf 1998), 79-85, hier 81.

Damit haben – zweitens – derartige Liturgien von Frauen automatisch immer auch eine kritische Funktion anderen, herkömmlichen Gottesdienstfeiern gegenüber.[77] Dies gilt auch für den Gottesdienst am Frauensonntag, der *nolens volens* mit seinen Texten und Ritualen eine Anfrage an anderntags geübte Gottesdienstpraxis darstellt und gleichzeitig eine Herausforderung an die Gemeinden ist, die Stimmen und die Wirklichkeiten von Frauen auch an Sonntagen, an denen nicht der Frauensonntag gefeiert wird, stärker wahrzunehmen und einzubeziehen. Aber auch für die Frauen, die den Gottesdienst am Frauensonntag gestalten, ist es oft eine Herausforderung, ihre Erfahrungen und ihre Spiritualität zu gottesdienstlichem Wort werden zu lassen und diese preiszugeben auch an solche Teilnehmende im Gottesdienst, die wenig oder kein Verständnis für solche ungewohnten Auslegungen und andere Perspektiven aufbringen.[78] Der Frauensonntagsgottesdienst ist so – heute sicher mehr als in seiner Anfangszeit – ein Zeit-Raum der Herausforderung, über Gottes Gerechtigkeit und Liebe in einer Sprache zu reden, die Ungehörtes ausspricht, nachdenklich macht, aufrüttelt, ohne zu entzweien, und neue Wege sucht und öffnet – zur Begegnung mit dem Gott des Lebens und für das Miteinander von Frauen und Männern in der Gemeinde.

Drittens bringt die Feier des Frauensonntags Mitverantwortung in zwei Richtungen zum Ausdruck: Einerseits geht es um die geistlich-liturgische Mitverantwortung der Frauen, die in der Feier des Frauensonntags einen sichtbaren (aber hoffentlich nicht den einzigen!) Ausdruck findet.[79] Andererseits geht es auch um die solidarische Mitverantwortung der Kirche für die Frauen, deren Arbeit und Lebenswirklichkeiten am Frauensonntag innerhalb der einzelnen Ortsgemeinde ausdrücklich thematisiert, danksagend gefeiert und durch die Kollekte unterstützt werden.

---

[77] Auf diese Funktion von Frauenliturgien hat Mary Collins, "Principles of Feminist Liturgy", in: Marjorie Procter-Smith / Janet R. Walton (eds), *Women at Worship: Interpretations of North American Diversity* (Westminster John Knox Press: Louisville 1993) 9-26, hier 11-13 hingewiesen.

[78] Einen ähnlichen Gedanken, allerdings bezogen auf die Sakramente, fand ich bei: Susan A. Ross, *Extravagant Affections. A Feminist Sacramental Theology* (Continuum: New York 1998), 229.

[79] Diese Mitverantwortung der Frauen erstreckt sich auch darauf, daß die Gemeinde bei solchen Gottesdiensten nicht nur Zuschauerin bei einem – überspitzt formuliert – "Theaterstück" sein darf, das von den Frauen aufgeführt wird. Die Liturgie an Frauensonntagen darf nicht nur etwas für Eingeweihte sein, sondern soll mitvollziehbar sein, damit das Prinzip der *participatio actuosa* gewährleistet bleibt.

Die Mitverantwortung der Kirche, die bei der Feier des Frauensonntags in der alt-katholischen Kirche von Anfang an im Bewußtsein war, könnte in Zukunft ausdrücklicher als bisher unter dem Aspekt der gerechten Gemeinschaft von Frauen und Männern und der Solidarität der Kirche mit den Frauen gedeutet werden. Damit würden die Anliegen der "Ökumenischen Dekade Kirchen in Solidarität mit den Frauen" (1988-1998) programmatisch in den Frauensonntag einbezogen. In verschiedenen evangelischen Landeskirchen hat sich während der Dekade die Feier eines einmal im Jahr gefeierten Dekadegottesdienstes eingebürgert. Nach dem Ende der Dekade setzten einige Landeskirchen diese Praxis fort, um so die Ziele der Dekade im Bewußtsein zu halten und auch im Liturgischen Kalender zu verankern.[80] Diese neuen Frauensonntage werden in den evangelischen Landeskirchen zusätzlich zu den traditionellen Frauensonntagen gefeiert.[81] Für das alt-katholische Bistum ist nicht zu erwarten, daß ein weiterer bistumsweiter Frauensonntag eingeführt wird. Statt dessen bietet der althergebrachte Frauensonntag genug Möglichkeiten zur weiteren Entfaltung. In den acht Jahrzehnten seines Bestehens hat der Frauensonntag ja bereits bewiesen, eine eigene, wandlungsfähige Tradi-

---

[80] So feiert die Evangelische Kirche im Rheinland seit 1998 und die Evangelische Kirche in Westfalen seit 1999 jeweils am 14. Sonntag nach Trinitatis den "Mirjam-Sonntag" bzw. den Sonntag "gerechte Gemeinschaft von Frauen und Männern". Auch die Landeskirche von Hannover kennt einen "Sonntag der Solidarität mit den Frauen", der in der Regel am 1. Sonntag nach Trinitatis gefeiert wird. Jedes Jahr wird dazu von einem Kirchenkreis bzw. von einer Gruppe ehrenamtlich arbeitender Frauen in Zusammenarbeit mit einer Theologin und einer Diakonin eine Arbeitshilfe zu einem ausgewählten biblischen Text erarbeitet und über die Frauenhilfe bzw. das Frauenwerk verbreitet. Themen waren bisher in der rheinischen Kirche "Schlage die Trommel und fürchte dich nicht" (1998), "Vashtis Nein" (1999) und "Schifra und Pua – Frauen die sich trauen" (2000), in Hannover "Rebekka" (2000). Welche anderen evangelischen Landeskirchen einen derartigen Frauensonntag kennen, konnte nicht erfaßt werden. Die Synode der EKD hat allen Landeskirchen empfohlen, solche Gottesdienste zur Geschlechtergerechtigkeit zu organisieren (mit Dank an Mieke Korenhof, Stephanie Lüders und Kirsten Schönewolf für ihre Auskünfte; vgl. auch Elvira Finkeldey, *Die Ökumenische Dekade "Solidarität der Kirchen mit den Frauen" 1988-1998 in der Evangelisch-lutherischen Landeskirche Hannovers. Eine Dokumentation der Gottesdienste*, hg. vom Amt für Gemeindedienst in Zusammenarbeit mit dem Frauenwerk im Auftrag des Landeskirchenamtes [Selbstverlag: Hannover 1999]).

[81] So etwa in der rheinischen Landeskirche, wo außer dem "Mirjamssonntag" am ersten Advent der Frauensonntag gefeiert wird. Er besteht in der rheinischen Landeskirche (wie in anderen Landeskirchen auch) schon seit längerem als Kollektensonntag; seit etwa zwanzig Jahren gibt die evangelische Frauenhilfe im Rheinland dazu auch Materialhefte und Gottesdienstentwürfe heraus (mit Dank an Heidemarie Theis für ihre Auskunft).

tion zu sein. Den Wunsch, daß dies auch in Zukunft so bleiben möge, sprach vor einigen Jahren Heidi Herborn (geb. 1943) aus, seit 1996 Vorsitzende des Bundes:

> Seit 75 Jahren wird in unserer Kirche der Frauensonntag am Ersten Advent gefeiert. Das ist ein Grund zur Freude und zur Hoffnung, daß wir die Kraft haben, immer wieder Neues hervorzubringen, Veränderungen wahrzunehmen und Visionen wachzuhalten.[82]

Since 1920 the Old Catholic Church in Germany has marked a "women's Sunday", generally the first Sunday in Advent. In the eighty-one years of its existence, the "women's Sunday" service has changed its character from a service about women to a service organised by women. Originally, the clergy generally made special mention of the work of women in the congregation in the intercessions, and sometimes also in the sermon. Later an active involvement of women in the shaping of liturgy and proclamation developed. This article demonstrates the way in which the liturgical role of women is bound up with socio-cultural and ecclesiastical images of women. Moreover, it shows the extent to which the "Bund Altkatholischer Frauen Deutschands" (League of Old Catholic Women in Germany) has encouraged women to involve themselves liturgically and has equipped them to do so.

L'Église vieille-catholique d'Allemagne célèbre chaque premier avent le "Dimanche des femmes". Institué en 1920, l'office évolua en quatre-vingt-une années d'existence d'un office sur les femmes en un office célébré par elles. Les premières années, le prêtre remerciait ce jour-là les femmes de la paroisse pour leur dévouement en les évoquant dans ses prières et parfois dans son sermon. Plus tard, les femmes prirent une part de plus en plus active à la liturgie et à la prédication. Le dimanche des femmes devint peu à peu un office célébré par les femmes. Cet article montre la relation entre le rôle liturgique des femmes et l'image de la femme dans l'Église et la société. Il évoque, en outre, le rôle capital que joua la Ligue des Femmes Vieille-Catholiques d'Allemagne (Bund Altkatholischer Frauen Deutschlands) en encourageant ses membres à servir comme liturgistes et en les préparant à cette tâche.

***Angela Berlis*** arbeitet an einem Forschungsprojekt des Dominikanischen Studienzentrums in Nijmegen (Niederlande) mit und ist Dozentin am Alt-Katholischen Seminar in Utrecht. Sie ist Vorstandsmitglied der deutschen Sektion der ESWTR und seit 1999 reviews editor des Jahrbuchs der ESWTR.

---

[82] Heidi Herborn (Hg.), Materialdienst November 1997 (Archiv des Frauenbundes, Bonn).

*Charlotte Methuen*

# Women priests have real presence reflections on liturgy and presidency[*]

"Women priests have real presence" proclaims a badge produced by England's Movement for the Ordination of Women in the 1980s. The real presence that we are talking about here is not to be related only to the elements of bread and wine, but to the whole community. The reformers suggested that the real presence must be manifested in the body of Christ as incarnated in the presence of the community, so that the change in substance – the transubstantiation – wrought by faith is the transubstantiation of the whole community, and not of the elements.[1] The question of the real presence in the Eucharist is thus intimately bound up with another: what does it mean for the Holy Spirit to be present in a celebration of the liturgy, for God or for Christ to be a real presence in the Eucharist? And this in turn is bound up with yet another: what does it mean for me, a priest and a woman, to preside at a celebration of the Eucharist?

For me as an Anglican, these questions are inevitably and deeply connected with reflections about our use of liturgy. The liturgical tradition has been vitally important to the Anglican church since its inception during the Reformation, although it is only in the last seventy years that emphasis has come to be laid upon regular, in the sense of weekly, celebrations of the Eucharist as the main Sunday service. At the same time, another shift has taken place to a focus on the importance of the community:

---

[*] An earlier version of this article appeared in Dutch as "Gedeelde macht als kracht. De rol van vrouwelijke priesters in de liturgie," in: *Fier* 3/1 (Jan/Feb 2000), 4-5.

[1] See especially Martin Luther, "Ein Sermon von den hochwirdigen Sacrament des Heiligen Waren Leichnams Christi," in: Martin Luthers Werke (Böhlau: Weimar 1884), 2, 742-758, esp. 749, and Huldrych Zwingli, "Vorschlag wegen der Bilder und der Messe," in: Zwinglis sämtliche Werke (Heinsius Nachfolger: Leipzig 1914), 3, 124-126. Compare also Bucer's emphasis on the congregation as the body of Christ: Von der waren Seelsorge, in: Bucers Deutsche Schriften (Gütersloher Verlagshaus Mohn: Gütersloh 1964), 103-107.

we have lived for centuries with a presumption that the liturgy in whatever tradition is the domain of the ordained clergy, and in recent decades we have had the first tentative beginnings of a recovery of the theological principle that liturgical actions are the work of the whole people of God (*leitourgia*).[2]

In my understanding of our tradition, liturgy, whether eucharistic or not, should offer a space in which we, as a community, can focus our individual lives upon God, experience the love of God for each of us, and be touched and inspired[3] to live our lives in relationship with God. Liturgy should be a place in which we encounter ourselves and one another in love, as gifted but broken children of God, in which we can indeed encounter the *praesentia realis* of Christ in the community of faith.

There are good reasons why many people – men as well as women – have begun to ask whether such an experience can be possible within traditional forms of the liturgy. In seeking to answer that question, I want here to address two central, albeit interrelated, issues. One is the words, form and intention of the liturgy, and the other is the role of the priest.

In much of the Anglican Communion, which includes the Church of England, the Eucharist is celebrated (sometimes reluctantly) in a modern language version. There is now a great breadth of authorised liturgical forms, most of which can trace their ancestry back to the sixteenth century *Book of Common Prayer*.[4] "Modern language" has not necessarily meant inclusive language, and despite a great deal of improvement, parts of many of these liturgies remain exclusive of women. Thus, in the form of the Nicene Creed authorised for use in the new *Common Worship* of the Church of England, we are still supposed to affirm that in Christ God was "made man" rather than "made human"; this seems to me both a bad translation of the original Greek and highly inappropriate, given the use of Christ's maleness as an argument for the exclusion of women from the priesthood of the Church of England.[5] On the other hand, the newly authorised liturgies introduce a far broader spectrum of

---

[2] Louis Weil, "Community: The Heart of Worship," in: *Anglican Theological Review* (*ATR*) 82 (2000), 129-147, here 132. This principle is at the heart of Orthodox understandings of liturgy; compare Katerina Karkala-Zorba in this volume, p. 23

[3] In the sense also of being filled with the breath/spirit of God.

[4] In the Church of England, ordained and accredited lay ministers agree to conduct services only in accordance with the wording and structure of authorised forms, agreed by centrally by General Synod.

[5] On the grounds that a woman cannot "represent" the male Christ.

biblical imagery when speaking of God, moving away from predominantly male, triumphalist terminology and helping us to explore the possibilities of realising, as Janet Morley has put it, "that to examine how and why the feminine has been omitted from our ways of addressing God is to discover also what else has been left out."[6] It is still too soon to see how these new liturgies will enrich the life of the community,[7] but the expansion of possibilities means that it will be easier to introduce new images while remaining within the range of what is authorised.

Preserving this balance, or practising what Elizabeth J. Smith has called the "Art of Accountability"[8] is in my view an important consideration precisely because liturgy is an expression not only of the local but also of the wider community. As a local congregation we pray the liturgy together with the wider church. This means that the question of recognising what is a good, valid expression of faith, is not local, and nor is it mine alone. As a priest, it is essential, and not optional, to "acknowledge that the community's spiritual identity is larger than my own."[9] This is especially true because familiarity with word and form can be vital if liturgy is to act as an effective structure for and springboard into prayer. Those who are ordained need to recognise that they have "enormous power to enable or disallow liturgical speech,"[10] and to realise too that they have enormous power to facilitate or to block the prayers of those who are present. The priest who changes too much can cause just as much exclusion and pain as do those who do nothing to shape the liturgy in accordance with the changes within the celebrating community. If the liturgy is to live, it must change, but not arbitrarily, for, as Elizabeth J. Smith comments:

> A very important thing for liturgically creative spirits to remember is that my delight in innovation may far outstrip your desire to have novelty inflicted upon you in the course of your worship, and my individual expressions of piety may not be conducive to your "Amen." Especially important for the unadventurous worshiper to remember is the fact that every old favourite hymn or prayer was once an innovation. Somewhere in this tension between innovation and continuity, between individuals' gifts and communities' needs, lies the fertile ground for growing new

---

[6]  Janet Morley, *All Desires Known* (SPCK: London ²1992), xi.

[7]  *Common Worship* was authorised for use from the beginning of Advent 2000; at the time of writing, we are only just beginning to explore its possibilities.

[8]  Elizabeth J. Smith, "Women, Word, and Worship," in: *ATR* 82 (2000), 113-128, here 124, but cf. 124-126.

[9]  Ibid., 125.

[10]  Ibid.

words, new visual images and new body language to take Anglican worship into its next stage of its evolution.[11]

This is a process in which the whole church must be engaged, on the level of the particular community and of the wider church. Within this process, there is a danger that if a priest chooses to reorder the liturgy simply to suit her own preferences, she/he may be abusing her/his authority. As priests, we are ordained to a complicated relationship of authority and service; we need to reflect on our responsibilities as well as our rights, not only pastorally but liturgically. As a priest I may certainly indicate, but should not impose, my own preferences. Individual style is inevitable and enriching. Individual domination is not. This balance is both delicate and paradoxical; I shall return to it later in the article.

Before doing so, I want to raise another issue linked to the question of inclusive language: the complex relationship between words and meaning, and thus between terminology and practice. While the use of inclusive language is important, it is also important not to be naïve. An inclusive language by no means presupposes an inclusive praxis. There is a danger that an over-emphasis on the words can obscure the fact that much of what shapes and makes liturgy is not its words but the act of its "doing," for "the liturgy is something *done* not *said*."[12] An particularly appropriate example of this is the sixteenth-century Anglican prayer of preparation for the Eucharist, the so-called "prayer of humble access," which asserts that "we are not worthy even to gather up the crumbs under the table." This is clearly an articulation of a theology which believed, not only that human beings had no right to demand anything of God, but that they were not worthy to be given anything. As such it has been much criticised in the twentieth century. But for me, the prayer of humble access is a reminder always of the story of the Syro-Phoenician woman who came to Jesus asking for healing for her daughter, and was refused:

> [Jesus] said to her, "Let the children [the people of Israel] be fed first, for it is not fair to take the children's food and throw it to the dogs." But she answered him, "Sir, even the dogs under the table eat the children's crumbs." [Mk 7.24-30; Mt 15.21-28]

Even as I say that "we are not worthy even to gather up the crumbs under the table," the Syro-Phoenician woman's voice rings in my ears, arguing with

---

[11] Ibid., 122-123.
[12] John F. Baldovin, "The Changing World of Liturgy," in: *ATR* 82 (2000), 65-81, here 71 (citing Gregory Dix).

Jesus and asserting the right of the dogs to the crumbs. This creative tension between humility and assertion, emptying and filling seems deeply appropriate as an approach to the Eucharist. Others will not find it so, but it is an example of how meaning can break through the literal. As Elizabeth Smith puts it, drawing on the imagery of 1 Corinthians 15:

> What dies is not identical with what is raised, instead it is changed. It is sown a Prayer Book; it will be raised a liturgy. It is sown patriarchal; it will be raised for liberation.[13]

Lived and living liturgy transcends the written words to become something larger and deeper.

The non-verbal is of crucial importance in our worship because we are people who gather together, bringing our own cares and concerns, experience and knowledge. Michael Aune writes speakingly of the way in which observations and thoughts and distractions come together when we participate in liturgy, and concludes:

> What kind of theology is embodied by furtive questions, wandering thoughts, and "the great poetry of Bread and Wine"? Whatever we think liturgy is, it is always an embodied practice, regardless of what theologians or pastors intend or claim is the "the real meaning."[14]

Indeed, the "real meaning" of the liturgy may be precisely that it allows these "furtive questions [and] wandering thoughts" to be incorporated into "the great poetry of Bread and Wine," affirming that God's presence is to be experienced, not only in focused, theologically precise thinking, but in the minutiae of daily life: wondering whether the roast is burning in the oven may not be an especially elevating spiritual response to the liturgy, and should probably not be the central response, but it may nonetheless represent deep care for family and guests, and the liturgy should enable the recognition that this is so.

In theological terms, perhaps this is to say that "gathering right"[15] means allowing

---

[13] Smith, "Women, Word, and Worship," 132.

[14] Michael B. Aune, "The Changing World of Liturgy: A Response to John F. Baldovin," in: *ATR* 82 (2000), 83-92, here 84-85.

[15] Stephen Cottrell suggests that the gathering rite of the Eucharist (or any worship) is about "gathering right": paper at the Affirming Catholicism Conference, Durham, 14-17 September 2000. The papers from this conference will be published by DLT later in 2001.

an approach to the sacrament based on the conviction that "the world is permeated by the grace of God. In this model, the sacrament is no longer an isolated encounter with God, but rather the manifestation of God's grace that quietly but effectively permeates the world.[16]

If the sacrament is about the way in which God's grace permeates the world, "quietly and effectively," but also radically and painfully, then this needs to be made clear, and the liturgy needs to become a space where the community learn to recognise the kingdom of God in their lives. That means that within the Eucharistic liturgy, the Ministry of the Word should be taken seriously, so that our preaching "models and teaches interpretative strategies that equip those who hear sermons to be confident and critical users of the Bible in their turn."[17] This inevitably means filtering the scriptures through the personal to reach the universal: "I bring a very personal approach to preaching," notes Joanna Anderson, "concerned always to connect scripture with ordinary people's lives and experience."[18] And if this is to be an authentic experience, then it has to be our experience as well. We preach, as Rowan Williams has put it, "in and as a witness that conversion is possible."[19] Barbara Brown Taylor speaks of the need for preachers to

> speak in their own voices out of their own experience, addressing God on the congregation's behalf and – with great care and humility – the congregation on God's behalf. ... When the holy vision speaks, it is my own heart that is pierced. While I may struggle to make sure that my response is true to those whom I represent, I cannot stay out. Every word I choose, every image, every rise in my voice reveals my own involvement in the message.[20]

At the same time, "those of us who preach ... speak as members of a body and not for ourselves alone, which means that we may not dominate the sermon any more than we may be absent from it."[21] The community is not there

---

[16] Aune, "Response to John F. Baldovin," 86; quote from Karl Rahner, "Considerations on the Active Role of the Person in the Sacramental Event," in: *Theological Investigations* XIV (Seabury: New York 1976), 166.

[17] Smith, "Women, Word, and Worship," 121.

[18] Joanna Anderson, "Paths are made by those who walk in them," in: Lesley Orr MacDonald (ed.), *In Good Company: Women in the Ministry* (Wild Goose Publications: Glasgow 1999), 135-142. here 141.

[19] Rowan Williams, paper on Homiletics at the Affirming Catholicism Conference, Durham, 14-17 September 2000.

[20] Barbara Brown Taylor, *The Preaching Life*, Cowley: New York 1993, 78.

[21] Ibid., 79.

for the preacher, but for the gospel, for God: "Ordinary, sane people are in love with the gospel ... 'much as one might be in love with a person.'" notes Kathleen Norris. "And they are there to find him, not me."[22] As a preacher and a priest, I am in the sermon, I am in the liturgy, but I am not doing it for myself.

Writing for (male) ordinands of the 1960s and '70s, Michael Ramsey, then Archbishop of Canterbury, emphasises that being a priest should never be a self-conscious (or, perhaps better, self-centred) act of being:

> "As servants of God we commend ourselves in every way" if our consciousness is not of our own status but of Christ whose commission we hold and of the people we serve in [Christ's] name. ... O Sacerdos, quid es tu? Non es te, quia de nihilo, Non es ad te, quia mediator ad Deum, Non es tibi, quia sponsus ecclesiae, Non es tui, quia servus omnium, Non es tu, quia Dei minister, Quid es ergo? Nihil et omnia, O Sacerdos."[23]

"You are nothing and everything, O priest." This is the paradox of ministry, the paradox of priesthood, the paradox of the liturgy. Every minister, every preacher, every priest is faced with this paradox. I do not minister, preach, celebrate for myself, for I am doing it to enable myself and others to encounter God. And yet I can only minister, preach, celebrate as myself, if that encounter with God is to be possible. Celebrating the liturgy, just like any other aspect of living as a Christian, is nothing about selflessness in the sense of denying the self, but all about selflessness in the sense of aligning myself to God, of knowing myself, but seeking not to impose myself.

It is tremendously important for us as (women) priests to grapple with the challenge of knowing ourselves, especially of knowing ourselves as active agents who hold authority. Reflecting on her experience as a priest, Barbara Baisley recounts the difficulties she encountered in defining her self out of the mixed messages about "woman" she received from her up-bringing.[24] In a

---

[22] Kathleen Norris, *Amazing Grace. A Vocabulary of Faith* (Riverhead: New York 1999), 187.

[23] Michael Ramsey, *The Christian Priest Today* (SPCK: London 1972), 10-11. The Latin may be translated: "O priest, who are you? You are not from yourself, because you are from nothing; you are not to yourself, because you are the mediator for God; you are not for yourself, because you are the bridegroom of the church; you are not of yourself, for you are the servant of all; You are not yourself, because you are the minister of God. Who are you? Nothing and everything, O priest."

[24] Barbara Baisley, "Being realistic about feminism," in: Hilary Wakeman (ed.), *Women Priests. The First Years* (DLT: London 1996), 97-116.

discussion of priesthood amongst a group of Anglican women priests a number claimed that "For me priesthood does not mean power." This claim borders on the naïve; whether we like it or not, the Anglican church still has a pretty high view of its priests. Although the woman who prayed for the clergy (including me) in the intercessions at the parish Eucharist as "those who are in authority over us" may be a minority in her articulation of this thought, it still exists. All priests, and especially those whose vision is a different kind of church, must grapple with the relationship between priesthood, presidency and power.

It is possible, and desirable, to use presidency to share power because it is possible to use leadership to share power. We can learn from the experience of the St Hilda community in London, which developed eucharistic forms of service involving the whole congregation and offering forms of mutual absolution and blessing.[25] Sharing even in simple liturgical acts can be both powerful and empowering: we finished a chaplaincy study day with a service including a renewal of baptism vows in which each person made a cross with water on their neighbour's forehead. "Will they feel manoeuvred into this?" I wondered whilst planning the liturgy; "We were allowed to…" reported a woman the next day. Part of sharing power is moving away from the understanding that only the leader is "allowed" to do things, away from liturgy as a place where only the president or leader feels enabled, to an understanding that the liturgy as the work of the people means ensuring that the people are involved, and welcome.

This may sometimes mean letting go of expectations, as Kathleen Norris found, as she fled over-planned liturgy in search of

> worship with room for the Holy Spirit, worship hospitable enough to welcome a confused soul such as myself. And there, among strangers, I found it: living worship, slightly out of control, and not terribly educational. Orthodox in the ancient sense, as "right worship," joyful enough to briefly house a living God.[26]

This is a reminder, above all else, that celebrating the Eucharist (or indeed any liturgy, or preaching a sermon, or living any part of our Christian lives) is about taking what we do seriously, about being open to God, but not primarily about "getting it right". Liturgy is not about presenting ourselves

---

[25] Described and collected in: *Women Included: A Book of Services and Prayers* (SPCK: London 1991).

[26] Norris, *Amazing Grace*, 250.

through play-acting but about setting the stage for the real presence, for the encounter with "the uncomfortable, even frightening closeness of the difficult God who is not made in our image."[27]

For that should be our aim: that each Eucharist, every liturgy bring spiritual sustenance, an encounter with God, to all those present. "I go out uplifted and strengthened for the week to come," says someone. "You could feel the Holy Spirit in that silence," comments another. Surely that is real presence – brought about by community and priest turning together to God.

La liturgie de l'Église anglicane est un havre où nous venons nous recueillir et nous rencontrer devant Dieu dans l'amour, comme des enfants de Dieu tout ensemble comblés et brisés. Cet article considère que le rôle du ministre du culte, femme et homme, est de faire tout ce qui est en son pouvoir pour que cet idéal soit vraiment vécu. Il est certain qu'un usage scrupuleux de la langue évite que la liturgie, en étant exclusive, choque certains. De même que notre conception de Dieu s'enrichit extrêmement lorsque nous faisons usage d'un large éventail de représentations du théologien. Il est néanmoins important de comprendre que la liturgie permet de trouver le sens caché des mots. En outre, quand elle découvre un changement à faire et l'introduit, la femme revêtue de la charge de ministre du culte doit être consciente de sa responsabilité face à tous les groupes qu'elle dessert au sein d'une communauté ecclésiastique. Un paradoxe de son sacerdoce est qu'elle ne peut être prêtre qu'en restant elle-même – et ne devrait l'être qu'à cette condition. D'un autre côté, elle ne doit pas imposer sa personne à la paroisse, mais lui ouvrir la voie vers Dieu.

Die Liturgie der anglikanischen Kirche bietet einen Ort, an dem wir uns selbst und einander vor Gott als beschenkte und zugleich als gebrochene Kinder Gottes in Liebe begegnen. Dieser Artikel geht auf die Rolle des/der Priester/in ein: er/sie soll ermöglichen, daß dieses Ideal zu einer wirklichen Erfahrung wird. Es steht außer Frage, daß ein sorgfältiger Gebrauch der Sprache die Liturgie weniger exklusiv für manche Menschen machen kann; es kann auch nicht geleugnet werden, daß unser Verständnis von Gott durch eine Vielfalt an Bildern für das Göttliche bereichert werden kann. Es ist jedoch wichtig zu verstehen, daß die liturgische Handlung auch eine Bedeutung außerhalb der buchstäblichen Worte eines Texts ermöglichen kann. Umso mehr muß der/die Priester/in sich seiner/ihrer Verantwortung bewußt sein, für verschiedene Gruppen innerhalb der kirchlichen Gemeinschaft zuständig zu sein. Dies ist ein Beispiel des Paradoxes dieses Amtes: Um Priesterin sein zu können, muß ein Mensch ganz er (sie!) selbst sein; gleichzeitig darf dieser

---

[27] Morley, xii.

Mensch aber nicht seine eigenen Bedürfnisse und Meinungen in den Vordergrund stellen, sondern soll der Gemeinde helfen, ihren Weg zu Gott zu finden.

***Charlotte Methuen*** studied Mathematics at Cambridge and Theology at Edinburgh, where she was awarded her PhD in 1995 [thesis published as *Kepler's Tübingen: Stimulus to a theological Mathematics* (Ashgate: Aldershot 1998)]. Her publications include a number of articles discussing women and authority in the early church. Since 1995 she has been *Assistentin* for Church History (Reformation and Modern) at the Ruhr-Universität, Bochum, Germany. She has served on the Board of ESWTR and as co-ordinating editor of ESWTR's Yearbook since 1997. She was ordained Priest in the Church of England at Pentecost 1999.

# I. BIBLIOGRAPHIE – BIBLIOGRAPHY – BIBLIOGRAPHIE[1]

*Zusammengestellt von Angela Berlis*

## I.1 Exegese (Erstes Testament, Neues Testament, nicht kanonisierte jüdische und frühchristliche Schriften) und Hermeneutik

Regina Bärthel, **Inspiration zum Töten. Ein etwas anderer Aspekt der Judith-Ikonographie**, Mikrofiche-Ausgabe, Tectum-Verlag: Marburg 1997, 2 Mikrofiches (Edition Wissenschaft: Reihe Kunstgeschichte; 2), ISBN 3-89608-682-0, DM 68,00

*Gerlinde Baumann, **Liebe und Gewalt. Die Ehe als Metapher für das Verhältnis JHWH – Israel in den Prophetenbüchern**, (Stuttgarter Bibelstudien; 185), Katholisches Bibelwerk: Stuttgart 2000, 261 S., ISBN 3-460-04851-4

Eleonore Beck (Hg.) **Was wäre, wenn Eva den Apfel nicht gegessen hätte? Die Bibel anders gelesen**, Schwabenverlag: Ostfildern 2000, 198 S., ISBN 3-7966-0979-1, DM 29,80

Phyllis A. Bird, **Missing Persons and Mistaken Identities: Women and Gender in Ancient Israel, Overtures to Biblical Theology**, Augsburg Fortress Press: Minneapolis 1998, 320pp., ISBN 0800631285, £12.99

Fiona C. Black / Roland Boer / Erin Runions (eds), **The Labour of Reading: Desire, Alienation, and Biblical Interpretation**, Society of Biblical Literature: Williston 1999, 336pp., ISBN 0-88414-011-3

Annette Böckler, **Gott als Vater im Alten Testament. Traditionsgeschichtliche Untersuchungen zur Entstehung und Entwicklung eines Gottesbildes**, Chr. Kaiser – Gütersloher Verlagshaus: Gütersloh 2000, 464 S., ISBN 3-579-02664-X

*Athalya Brenner (ed.), **Genesis**, (FCB II/1), Sheffield Academic Press: Sheffield 1998, 276pp., ISBN 1-85075-838-7, £16.95

---

[1]  Zu Büchern mit * siehe unter "Rezensionen" – Books marked * are reviewed below – Pour les livres avec * voire sous "Critique des livres".

*Athalya Brenner / Carole Fontaine (ed.), **Wisdom and Psalms**, (FCB II/2), Sheffield Academic Press: Sheffield 1998, 332pp., ISBN 1-85075-917-0, £16.95

Claudia V. Camp, **Wise, Strange and Holy: The Strange Woman and the Making of the Bible**, (Gender, Culture, Theory 9), Sheffield Academic Press: Sheffield 2000, 372pp., ISBN 1-844127-167-5

Joan E. Cook, **Hannah's Desire, God's Design: Early Interpretations of the Story of Hannah. A Literary, Theological, and Historical Analysis of Hannah in 1 Samuel 1-2, Pseudo-Philo's Biblical Antiquities, Targum of the Prophets, and the Infancy Narrative in Luke 1-2**, (JSOT.S 282), Sheffield Academic Press: Sheffield 1999, 136pp., ISBN 1-85075-909-X, $46.50

Irmtraud Fischer, **Gottesstreiterinnen**, Kohlhammer: Stuttgart 2000 (2., überarbeitete Auflage), 208 S., ISBN 3-17-016647-6, DM 34,00 / ATS 234

Ellen Frankel, **The Five Books of Miriam. A Woman's Commentary on the Torah**, Harper Collins Publications: San Francisco 1998, 355pp., ISBN 0-06-0630337-X, $16.00

Esther Fuchs, **Sexual Politics in the Biblical Narrative: Reading the Hebrew Bible as a Woman**, (JSOT.S 310), Sheffield Academic Press: Sheffield 2000, 244pp., ISBN 1-84127-138-1

Elisabeth Gierlinger-Czerny, **Judits Tat – Die Aufkündigung des Geschlechtervertrages**, Promedia: Wien 2000, 208 S., ISBN 3-85371-166-9

Elyse Goldstein, **Revisions: Seeing Torah through a Feminist Lens**, Jewish Lights Publishing: Woodstock/VT 1999, ISBN 1-58023-147-4, $19.95

Elyse Goldstein (ed.), **A Women's Torah Commentary: New Insights from Women Rabbis on the 54 Weekly Torah Portions**, Jewish Lights Publishing: Woodstock/VT 2000, 320pp., 1-58023-076-8, $34.95 / £17.82

Marianne Grohmann, **Aneignung der Schrift. Wege einer christlichen Rezeption jüdischer Hermeneutik**, Neukirchener: Neukirchen-Vluyn 2000, 280 S., ISBN 3-7887-1801-3, DM 78,00

Judith M. Hadley, **The Cult of Asherah in Ancient Israel and Juda. The Evidence for a Hebrew Goddess**, (University of Cambridge Oriental Publications 57), Cambridge University Press: Cambridge 2000, ISBN 0521662354, $64.95

*Maria Halmer / Barbara Heyse-Schäfer / Barbara Rauchwarter (Hg.), **Anspruch und Widerspruch. Evi Krobath zum 70. Geburtstag,** Mohorjeva Verlag: Klagenfurt – Ljubljana – Wien 1999, 231 S., ISBN 3-85013-723-6

Betsy Halpern-Amaru, **The Empowerment of Women in the *Book of Jubilees*,** (Supplements to the Journal for the Study of Judaism 60), Brill: Leiden 1999, 182pp., ISBN 90 04 11414 9, £34.64

Judith Hartenstein, **Die zweite Lehre. Erscheinungen des Auferstandenen als Rahmenerzählungen frühchristlicher Dialoge,** (TU 146), Akademie Verlag: Berlin 2000, 362 S., ISBN 3-05-003534-X

Judith Hauptman, **Rereading the Rabbis. A Women's Voice,** Westview Press: Oxford 1998, 304pp., ISBN 0-8133-3406-3, $29.00

Claudia Janssen / Luise Schottroff / Beate Wehn (Hg.), **Paulus. Umstrittene Traditionen – lebendige Theologie. Eine feministische Lektüre,** Chr. Kaiser – Gütersloher Verlagshaus: Gütersloh 2001, 208 S., ISBN 3-579-05318-3

Rainer Keßler / Eva Loos (Hg.), **Eigentum: Freiheit und Fluch. Ökonomische und biblische Einwürfe,** Chr. Kaiser – Gütersloher Verlagshaus: Gütersloh 2000, 197 S., ISBN 3-579-05175-X, DM 29,80

Anna Kiesow, **Löwinnen von Juda, Frauen als Subjekte politischer Macht in der judäischen Königszeit,** (Theologische Frauenforschung in Europa 4), Lit: Münster 2000, 224 S., ISBN 3-8258-4653-9, DM 39,80

Ingrid Rosa Kitzberger (Hg.), **Transformative Encounters. Jesus and Women Reviewed,** (BIS 43), Brill: Leiden 2000, 418pp., ISBN 90-04-11311-8

Ruth Kossmann, **Die Esthernovelle – Vom Erzählten zur Erzählung. Studien zur Traditions- und Redaktionsgeschichte des Estherbuches,** (VTS 79), Brill: Leiden 2000, 400 S., ISBN 90 04 15556-0, DM 185,00

Ross Shepard Kraemer / Mary Rose D'Angelo, **Women and Christian Origins,** Oxford University Press: Oxford 1999, ISBN 0-19-510396-3, £15.99

Ulrike Metternich, **"Sie sagte ihm die ganze Wahrheit". Die Erzählung von der "Blutflüssigen" – feministisch gedeutet,** Grünewald: Mainz 2000, ca. 256 S., ISBN 3-7867-2234-X, DM 48,00

Susan Niditch, **A Prelude to Biblical Folklore: Underdogs and Tricksters,** University of Illinois Press: Illinois 2000, 208pp., ISBN 0-252-06883-1, $15.00 / £10.71

Helen C. Orchard, **Courting Betrayal. Jesus as Victim in the Gospel of John**, (Gender, Culture, Theory 5), Sheffield Academic Press: Sheffield 1998, ISBN 1-85075-884-0, £16.95

*Silke Petersen, **'Zerstört die Werke der Weiblichkeit!' Maria Magdalena, Salome und andere Jüngerinnen Jesu in christlich-gnostischen Schriften**, (Nag Hammadi and Manichean Studies 48), Brill: Leiden – Boston – Köln 1999, 383 S., ISBN 90-04-11449-1, $124.00

*Tina Pippin, **Apocalyptic Bodies: the Biblical End of the World in Text and Image**, Routledge: New York – London 1999, 224pp., ISBN 0415182492, £14.99

Sharon H. Ringe, **Wisdom's Friends. Community and Christology in the Fourth Gospel**, Westminster John Knox Press: Louisville 1999, 176pp., ISBN 0-664-25714-3, $15.95

*Susanne Scholz, **Rape Plots. A Feminist Cultural Study of Genesis 34**, (Studies in Biblical Literature 13), P.Lang: New York 2000, 232pp., ISBN 0-8204-4154-6

*Luise Schottroff / Marie-Therese Wacker (Hg.), unter Mitarbeit von Claudia Janssen and Beate Wehn, **Kompendium Feministische Bibelauslegung**, Chr. Kaiser / Gütersloher Verlagshaus: Gütersloh [2]1999, 852 S., ISBN 3-579-00391-7, DM 125,00

Elisabeth Schüssler Fiorenza, **Gerecht ist das Wort der Weisheit. Feministische Bibelinterpretation im Kontext**, Exodus: Luzern 2001, 250 S., ISBN 3-905577-43-7, DM 48,00

Elisabeth Schüssler Fiorenza, **Jesus and the politics of interpretation**, Continuum: New York 2000, 180 pp., ISBN 0826412734

Helen Schüngel-Straumann, **Die Frau am Anfang. Eva und die Folgen**, (Kontextuelle Bibelinterpretationen 6), Lit: Münster [3]2000, 160 S., ISBN 3-8285-3525-1

Dorothee Sölle / Luise Schottroff, **Jesus von Nazareth**, Deutscher Taschenbuchverlag: München 2000, 160 S., ISBN 3-423-31026-X, DM 16,50 / EUR 8,44

Hanna Stenström, **The Book of Revelation: A Vision of the Ultimate Liberation or the Ultimate Backlash? A Study in 20th Century Interpretations of Rev 14:1-5, with Special Emphasis on Feminist Exegesis**, (Diss. Univ. Uppsala), Uppsala 1999, 355pp. *(This book can be ordered from: Dr. Hanna Stenström, Uppsala University, Box 1604, 75146 Uppsala, Sweden)*

Sonja Angelika Strube, **"Wegen dieses Wortes...".** **Feministische und nichtfeministische Exegese im Vergleich am Beispiel der Auslegungen zu Mk 7, 24-30**, (Theologische Frauenforschung in Europa 3), Lit: Münster 2000, 368 S., ISBN 3-8258-4521-4, DM 49,80

Rut Törnkvist, **The Use and Abuse of Female Sexual Imagery in the Book of Hosea. A Feminist Critical Approach to Hos 1-3**, (Acta Universitatis Uppsaliensis. Uppsala Women's Studies, A. Women in Religion 7), Uppsala 1998, ISBN 91-554-4135-1, $47.50

Anja Wißkirchen, **Identität gewinnen an Maria Magdalena. Eine Untersuchung der mythologischen Erzählstrukturen in den biblischen Texten und deren Rezeption in "Jesus Christ Superstar" und "Die letzte Versuchung Christi"**, (Pontes 6), Lit: Münster – Hamburg – London 2000, 141 S., ISBN 3-8258-4976-7, DM 29,80

## I.2. Kirchen- und Religionsgeschichte

Ulrike Altherr, **Sachwalterinnen des Vormodernen oder Förderinnen der Mündigkeit von Frauen? Katholische Frauenorganisationen der Diözese Rottenburg-Stuttgart vom Kriegsende bis zur Würzburger Synode**, P.Lang: Frankfurt/M. u.a. 2000, (EHS.T 694), 624 S., ISBN 3-631-36005-3, DM 148,00

Gail Ashton, **The Generation of Identity in Late Medieval Hagiography: Speaking the Saint**, Routledge: London – New York 1999, 184pp., ISBN 0-415-18210-7

Angela Berlis / Charlotte Methuen (eds), **Feminist Perspectives on History and Religion / Feministische Zugänge zu Geschichte und Religion / Approches féministes de l'histoire et de la religion**, (Jahrbuch der Europäischen Gesellschaft für Theologische Forschung von Frauen 8), Peeters: Leuven 2000, 318pp., ISBN 90-429-0903-X, BEF 900 / EUR 23,00

Wolfgang Beutin, **Anima. Untersuchungen zur Frauenmystik des Mittelalters**, 3 Bde., P.Lang: Frankfurt am Main u.a. 1997-1999 (Bd. 1: Probleme der Mystikforschung – Mystikforschung als Problem, 1997, 200 S., ISBN 3-631-31488-4, DM 59,00; Bd. 2: Ideengeschichte, Theologie und Ästhetik, 1998, 235 S., ISBN 3-631-31489-2, DM 59,00; Bd. 3: Tiefenpsychologie – Mystikerinnen, 1999, 261 S., ISBN 3-631-31490-6, DM 59,00)

Gisela Bock, **Frauen in der Europäischen Geschichte. Vom Mittelalter bis zur Gegenwart**, C.H. Beck: München 2000, 400 S., ISBN 3-406-46167-0, DM 49,80

Catherine A. Brekus, **Strangers and Pilgrims: Female Preaching in America, 1740-1845**, University of North Carolina Press: Chapel Hill 1998, 480pp., ISBN 0-8078-4745-3

Marie A. Conn, **Noble Daughters: Unheralded Women in Western Christianity, 13th to 18th Centuries**, (Contributions to the Studies of Religion 60), Greenwood Press: London 1999, 144pp., ISBN 0-313-30669-9, £39.95

Doris Brodbeck, **Hunger nach Gerechtigkeit. Helene von Mülinen (1850-1924), eine Wegbereiterin der Frauenemanzipation**, Chronos Verlag: Zürich 2000, 252 S., ISBN 3-905313-53-7, CHF 38,00 / DM 44,00 / ATS 300

*Christiane Burbach, **Frauen Erinnern. Frauen in der Gedächtniskultur der Kirche**, Lutherisches Verlagshaus: Hannover 2000, 170 S., ISBN 3-7859-0812-1, DM 19,80 / EUR 10,12

*Christiane Burbach / Susanne Wendorf-von Blumröder (Hg.), **Frauen gestalten Frauengestalten**, Katalog zur Ausstellung, Ronnenberg 1996 – Hannover ⁶2000, 72 Seiten, ISBN 3-932011-25-2, DM 12,00

*__Frauen gestalten Frauengestalten__, 12 Doppelkarten mit den Frauenfiguren dieser Ausstellung, Inszenierung und Fotografie von Charlotte Ilse Kik, Hanna Strack Verlag: Pinnow 2000, DM 22,- *(Zu bestellen bei: Kuckucksallee 9, 19065 Pinnow, Deutschland; Tel./Fax +49-3860-8685)*

Carol K. Coburn / Martha Smith, **Spirited Lives. How Nuns Shaped Catholic Culture and American Life, 1836-1920**, University of North Carolina Press: Chapel Hill 1999, 400pp., ISBN 0-8078-4774-7

Trude Dehn (Hg.), **Ein brauchbares Wesen. Die Frau im Pfarrhaus. Lebensgeschichten aus sechs Jahrzehnten**, Wichern: Berlin 2000, 226 S., ISBN 3-88981-076-4

Jule DeJager Ward, **La Leche League, At the Crossroads of Medicine, Feminism, and Religion**, University of North Carolina Press: Chapel Hill 2000, 272pp., ISBN 0-8078-4791-7

Hermann Düringer / Karin Weintz (Hg.), **Leonore Siegele-Wenschkewitz. Persönlichkeit und Wirksamkeit**, Haag und Herchen Verlag: Frankfurt/M. 2000, 371 S., ISBN 3-89846-23-1, DM 64,00

Ute Eisen, **Women Officeholders in Early Christianity: Epigraphical and Literary Studies**, The Liturgical Press: Collegeville 2000, 312pp., ISBN 0814659500

Esther Fuchs (Hg.), **Women and the Holocaust. Narrative and Representation**, (Studies in the Shoah 22), University Press of America: Lanham/Md. 1999, 168pp., ISBN 0-7618-1344-6, $29.50

Elisabeth Guggenheim, **Zwischen Fürsorge und Politik: Geschichte des Bundes Schweizerischer Jüdischer Frauenorganisationen**, hrsg. vom Bund Schweizerischer Jüdischer Frauenorganisationen BSJF, Limmat-Verlag: Zürich 1999, 219 S., ISBN 3-85791-329-0

Gulnar Eleanor Francis-Dehqani, **Religious Feminism in an Age of Empire. CMS Women Missionaries in Iran, 1869-1934**, (CCSRG Monograph Series 4), University of Bristol: Bristol 2000, ISBN 0-86292-489-8

*Irene Gysel / Barbara Helbling (Hg.), **Zürichs letzte Äbtissin Katharina von Zimmern (1478-1547)**, Verlag Neue Zürcher Zeitung: Zürich 1999 (2. Aufl. 2000), 216 Seiten, ISBN 3-85823-782-5, CHF 38,00 / DM 48,00 / ATS 350

Barbara Heller (Hg.), **Starke fromme Frauen? Eine Zwischenbilanz konfessioneller Frauenforschung heute**, (Hofgeismarer Protokolle 320), Evangelische Akademie: Hofgeismar 2000, 200 S., ISBN 3-89281-229-2, DM 25,00

Cornelia Helfrich, **Die Rezeption von Gestalt und Werk der hl. Therese von Avila in der französischen Literatur des 19./20. Jahrhunderts**, P.Lang: Frankfurt/M. 2000, 216 S., ISBN 3-631-35989-6, DM 65,00

Dagmar Herbrecht, **Emanzipation oder Anpassung. Argumentationswege der Theologinnen im Streit um die Frauenordination in der Bekennenden Kirche**, Neukirchener: Neukirchen-Vluyn 2000, 159 S., ISBN 3-7887-1785-8

Christel Hildebrand (Hg.), **Wie im Himmel so auf Erden. Festschrift zum 75-jährigen Bestehen des Konvents Evangelischer Theologinnen in der Bundesrepublik Deutschland e.V.**, TVT Medienverlag: Tübingen 2000, ISBN 3-929128-24-1

Paula E. Hyman / Deborah Dash Moore (eds), **Jewish Women in America. An Historical Encyclopedia**, Routledge: London – New York 1999, ISBN 0-415-91935

Gerda Hoffer, **Zeit der Heldinnen. Lebensbilder außergewöhnlicher jüdischer Frauen**, dtv: München 1999, 238 S., ISBN 3-423-30701-3, DM 24,90

Tanja Hommen, **Sittlichkeitsverbrechen. Sexuelle Gewalt im Kaiserreich**, (Reihe Geschichte und Geschlechter 28), (= Diss., Univ. Bielefeld, 1998), Campus: Frankfurt – New York 1999, 305 S., ISBN 3-593-36309-7, DM 68,00 / EUR 39,88

Hildegard König / Irene Leicht (Hg.), **Heilige Unruh. Bewegende Frauen in den Zeiten der Kirche**, Don Bosco: München 2000, 196 S., ISBN 3-7698-1252-2, DM 24,80 / ATS 181

Martina Kreidler-Kos, **Klara von Assisi. Schattenfrau und Lichtgestalt**, (Tübinger Studien zur Theologie und Philosophie 17), Francke: Tübingen 2000, 350 S., ISBN 3-7720-2585-4, DM 98,00

Sophie Lafont, **Femme, Droit et Justice dans l'Antiquité orientale. Contribution à l'étude du droit pénal au Proche-Orient ancien**, (OBO 165), Ed. Univ.: Fribourg 1999, 562 S., ISBN 3-525-53339-X, DM 218,00

*Relinde Meiwes, **"Arbeiterinnen des Herrn". Katholische Frauenkongregationen im 19. Jahrhundert**, Campus-Verlag: Frankfurt – New York 2000, 341 S., ISBN 3-593-36460-3

Aurora G. Morcillo, **True Catholic Womanhood. Gender Ideology in Franco's Spain**, Northern Illinois University Press: DeKalb/IN 2000, 220pp., ISBN 0-87580-256-7, $36.00 / £28.95

Lesley Orr MacDonald, **A Unique and Glorious Mission: Women and Presbyterianism in Scotland 1830-1930**, John Donald: Edinburgh 2000, 300pp., ISBN 0859764788

Sue Morgan, **A Passion for Purity: Ellice Hopkins and the politics of gender in the late-Victorian church**, (CCSRG Monograph Series 2), University of Bristol: Bristol 1999, ISBN 0-86292-478-2

Susan Signe Morrison, **Women Pilgrims in Late Medieval England**, Routledge: London – New York 2000, 240pp., ISBN 0-415-22180-3

Claudia Opitz / Ulrike Weckel / Elke Kleinau (Hg.), **Tugend, Vernunft und Gefühl. Geschlechterdiskurse der Aufklärung und weibliche Lebenswelten**, Schwabe: Basel 2000, 284 S., ISBN 3-7965-1432-4, DM 68,00

Patricia Ranft, **Women and Spiritual Equality in Christian Tradition**, MacMillan: Houndmills – London 2000, 307pp., ISBN 0-333-92990-X

Esther Röhr (Hg.), **Ich bin was ich bin. Frauen neben großen Theologen und Religionsphilosophen des 20. Jahrhunderts**, (Gekürzte Taschenbuchausgabe), 272 S., Chr. Kaiser – Gütersloher Verlagshaus: Gütersloh 2001, ISBN 3-579-00549-9, DM 29,80

Lucetta Scaraffia / Gabriella Zarri (eds), **Women and Faith. Catholic Religious Life in Italy from Late Antiquity to the Present**, Harvard University Press: Harvard 1999, 432pp., ISBN 0-674-95478-5

Nina Schröder: **Hitlers unbeugsame Gegnerinnen. Der Frauenaufstand in der Rosenstrasse**, Heyne: München 1998, ISBN 3-453-13181-9, DM 16,90

Regine Schweizer-Vüllers, **Die Heilige am Kreuz. Studien zum weiblichen Gottesbild im späten Mittelalter und in der Barockzeit**, P.Lang: Frankfurt/M. u.a. [2]1999, 302 S., ISBN 3-906761-92-4, DM 65,00

Heidemarie Wawrzyn, **Vaterland statt Menschenrecht. Formen der Judenfeindschaft in den Frauenbewegungen des Deutschen Kaiserreiches**, (Religionswissenschaftliche Reihe 11), Diagonal-Verlag: Marburg 1999, 275 S., ISBN 3-927165-60-3, DM 48,00

Marilyn J. Westerkamp, **Women in Early American Religion, 1600-1850. The Puritan and Evangelical Traditions**, Routledge: London – New York 1999, 240pp., ISBN 0-415-19448-2

## I.3 Systematische Theologie, Ökumene und Interreligiöser Dialog

Marcella Althaus-Reid, **Indecent Theology**, Routledge: London – New York 2000, 240pp., ISBN 0-415-23604-5

Sue Barton, **Scripture as Empowerment for Liberation and Justice: The Experience of Christian and Muslim Women in Bangladesh**, (CCSRG Monograph Series 1), University of Bristol: Bristol 1999, ISBN 0-86292-477-4

Tina Beattie, **God's Mother, Eve's Advocate: A Gynocentric Refiguration of Marian Symbolism in Engagement with Luce Irigaray**, (CCSRG Monograph Series 3), University of Bristol: Bristol 1999, ISBN 0-86292-488-X

Sybille Becker / Gesine Kleinschmit / Ilona Nord / Gury Schneider-Ludorff (Hg.), **Das Geschlecht der Zukunft. Frauenemanzipation und Geschlechtervielfalt**, Kohlhammer: Stuttgart – Berlin – Köln 2000, 182 S., ISBN 3-17-016612-3, DM 37,95

Mary Farrell Bednarowski, **The Religious Imagination of American Women**, Indiana University Press: Bloomington – Indianapolis 1999, 241pp., ISBN 0-253-21338-X

*Frans van der Beek, **Het Jezus Mysterie. Kunstenaars en visies over de man die tweeduizend jaar de westerse beschaving een gezicht gaf**, De Bookmakers: Diemen 1999, 98pp., ISBN 90-804045-4-3, NLG 39,50 (full-colour)

Sarah Boss, **Empress and Handmaid. On Nature and Gender in the Cult of the Virgin Mary**, Continuum: New York 2000, 264pp., ISBN 0-304-70781-3, $24.95

Christina von Braun / Inge Stephan (Hg.), **Genderstudien. Eine Einführung**, J.B. Metzler: Stuttgart – Weimar 2000, ISBN 3-476-01636-6

Lavinia Byrne, **Woman at the Altar: The Ordination of Women in the Roman Catholic Church**, Continuum: New York 1999, £12.10

Anne Cranny-Francis / Johan Kirkby / Wendy Waring, **Gender Studies: Terms and Debates**, Macmillan: London 2000, 272pp., ISBN 0-333-77612-7, £14.99

Gavin D'Costa, **Sexing the Trinity: Gender, Culture and the Divine**, SCM Press: London, 304pp., ISBN 0334 02810 8

**"De wijsheid doordringt alles". Reflecties vanuit vrouwenstudies theologie**, met bijdragen van M. De Haardt, G. Dresen, H. Meyer-Wilmes, L. Troch, Themenheft von: Tijdschrift voor Theologie 40 (2000), Nr. 1

Eleanor Abdella Doumato, **Getting God's Ear: Women, Islam, and Healing in Saudi Arabia and the Gulf**, Columbia University Press: New York 2000, 498pp., ISBN 0231116675, $18.50

Margaret A. Farley / Serene Jones (eds), **Liberating Eschatology: Essays in Honor of Letty M. Russell**, Westminster John Knox Press: Louisville 2000, 261pp., ISBN 0 664 25788 7

**Feministische Rechtfertigungslehre**, Themenheft von: Evangelische Theologie 60 (2000), Heft 5 (mit Beiträgen von Luise Schottrof, Elisabeth Moltmann-Wendel und Bärbel Wartenberg-Potter)

Julika Funk / Cornelia Brück (Hg.), **Körper-Konzepte**, (Literatur und Anthropologie 5), Narr: Tübingen 1999, 246 S., ISBN 3-8233-5704-2, DM 76,00

Kyriaki Fitzgerald (ed.), **Orthodox Women Speak. Discerning the "Signs of the Times"**, WCC Publications: Geneva 2000 – Holy Cross Orthodox Press: Brookline/MA 2000, 212pp., ISBN 2-8254-1317-8

Majella Franzmann, **Women and Religion**, Oxford University Press: New York – Oxford 2000, 192pp., ISBN 0-19-510773-X

Ivone Gebara, **Die dunkle Seite Gottes. Wie Frauen das Böse erfahren**, (Theologie der Dritten Welt 27), Herder: Freiburg i. B. – Basel – Wien 2000, ISBN 3-451-27243-1, 230 S., DM 39,80

Carmen Gransee, **Grenz-Bestimmungen. Zum Problem identitätslogischer Konstruktionen von "Natur" und "Geschlecht"**, (Perspektiven 13), Ed. diskord: Tübingen 1999, 224 S., ISBN 3-89295-664-2, DM 28,00

Mary Grey, **The Outrageous Pursuit of Hope: Prophetic Dreams for the 21st Century**, DLT: London 2000, 128pp., ISBN 0-232-52319-3, £9.95

Andrea Günter, **Die weibliche Hoffnung der Welt. Die Bedeutung des Geborenseins und der Sinn der Geschlechterdifferenz**, Chr. Kaiser – Gütersloher Verlagshaus: Gütersloh 2000, 128 S., ISBN 3-579-02667-4, DM 36 / ATS 263 / CHF 34,00

Ruth Hagengruber (Hg.), **Klassische philosophische Texte von Frauen**, dtv: München 1998, 224 S., ISBN 3-423-30652-1, DM 24,90

Mary Hancock, **Womanhood in the Making: Domestic Ritual and Public Culture in Urban South India**, Westview Press: Oxford 1999, 304pp., ISBN 0-8133-3583-3, $75.00

Susanne Heine, **Frauenbilder – Menschenrechte. Theologische Beiträge zur feministischen Anthropologie**, (Mensch – Natur – Technik 11), LVH: Hannover 2000, ISBN 3-7859-0795-8, DM 38,00

Birgit Heller, **Heilige Mutter und Gottesbraut. Frauenemanzipation im modernen Hinduismus**, (Reihe Frauenforschung), MILENA: Wien 1999, ca. 360 S., ISBN: 3-85286-074-1, DM 50,00

Susanne Hennecke, **Der vergessene Schleier. Ein theologisches Gespräch zwischen Luce Irigaray und Karl Barth**, ( = Diss. Universität von Amsterdam 2000), Chr. Kaiser – Gütersloher Verlagshaus: Gütersloh 2001, ISBN 3-579-05319-1, 320 S., DM 78,00

Carter Heyward, **A Priest Forever: One Woman's Controversial Ordination in the Episcopal Church**, Pilgrim Press: Cleveland/OH 1999, ISBN 0-8298-1315-2, $15.95 / £11.39

Carter Heyward, **When Boundaries Betray Us**, Pilgrim Press: Cleveland/OH 1999, 206pp., ISBN 0-8298-1347-0

Lisa Isherwood, **Liberating Christ: Exploring the Christologies of Contemporary Liberation Movements**, Pilgrim Press: Cleveland 1999, ISBN 0-8298-1350-0, £12.99

Alision M. Jaggar / Iris Marion Young, **Companion to Feminist Philosophy**, Blackwell: Oxford 1999, 724pp., ISBN 0-631-22067-4, £75.00

Doris Janshen (Hg.), **Blickwechsel. Der neue Dialog zwischen Frauen- und Männerforschung**, Campus: Frankfurt/M. – New York 2000, 213 S., ISBN 3-593-36442-5, DM 38,00

Claudia Janssen u.a. (Hg.), **Erinnern und aufstehen – antworten auf Kreuzestheologien**, Matthias-Grünewald-Verlag: Mainz 2000, 162 S., ISBN 3-7867-2272-2, DM 42,00

*Ann-Cathrin Jarl, **Women and Economic Justice: Ethics in Feminist Liberation Theology and Feminist Economics**, (Uppsala Studies in Social Ethics 25), (= Diss. 2000), Uppsala University Press: Uppsala 2000, 212pp. ISBN 91-554-4759-7,

Anne Jensen / Maximilian Liebmann (Hg.), **Was verändert Feministische Theologie?**, Interdisziplinäres Symposium zur Frauenforschung in Graz 1999, (Theologische Frauenforschung in Europa 2), Lit: Münster 2000, 256 S., ISBN 3/8258-44616-4, DM 39,80

*Serene Jones, **Feminist Theory and Christian Theology: Cartographies of Grace**, (Guides to Theological Inquiry), Fortress Press: Minneapolis (USA) 2000, 214pp ISBN 0-8006-2694-X, US $ 17.00.

Manuela Kalsky, **Christaphanien. Die Re-Vision der Christologie aus der Sicht von Frauen in unterschiedlichen Kulturen**, Chr. Kaiser – Gütersloher Verlagshaus: Gütersloh 2000, 368 S., ISBN 3-579-05317-5, DM 54

Christina Kayales, **Gottesbilder von Frauen auf den Philippinen. Die Bedeutung der Subjektivität für eine Interkulturelle Hermeneutik**, Lit: Münster 1998, 376 S., ISBN 3-8285-3700-9

Katharina von Kellenbach / Susanne Scholz (Hg.), **Zwischen-Räume. Deutsche feministische Theologinnen im Ausland**. Mit Beiträgen von Teresa Berger, Elisabeth

Gössmann, Elisabeth Schüssler Fiorenza u.a., (Theologische Frauenforschung in Europa 1), Lit: Münster 2000, 163 S., ISBN 3-8258-4289-4

Jenny Kien, **Reinstating the Divine Woman in Judaism**, Universal Publishers: Parkland/Florida 2000, 273pp., ISBN: 1-58112-763-4

*Elisa Klapheck (Hg.), **Fräulein Rabbiner Jonas: Kann die Frau das rabbinische Amt bekleiden? Eine Streitschrift von Regina Jonas**, Hentrich & Hentrich: Teetz 1999 (2., korrigierte Auflage 2000), 325 S, ISBN 3-933471-17-6

Ruth Klein-Hessling (Hg.), **Der neue Islam der Frauen. Weibliche Lebenspraxis in der globalisierten Moderne. Fallstudien aus Afrika, Asien und Europa**, Transcript: Bielefeld 1999, 315 S., ISBN 3-933127-42-4, DM 48,00

Gritt Klinkhammer, **Moderne Formen islamischer Lebensführung. Eine qualitativ-empirische Untersuchung zur Religiosität sunnitisch geprägter Türkinnen der zweiten Generation in Deutschland**, (Religionswissenschaftliche Reihe 14), diagonal-Verlag: Marburg 2000, 316 S., ISBN 3-927165-69-7, DM 48,00 / ATS 350

Anne-Marie Korte, **Gods geslacht. Gender en verwantschap in vrouwenstudies theologie**, Rede uitgesproken bij de aanvaarding van het ambt van bijzonder hoogleraar Vrouwenstudies Theologie op 27 januari 2000, (Utrechtse Theologische Reeks 42), Universiteit Utrecht: Utrecht 2000, 46pp., ISBN 90 72235436

Hamid Rez Kusha, **The Sacred Law of Islam: A case study of women's treatment in the Islamic Republic of Iran's justice system**, Ashgate: Aldershot 2000, 300pp., ISBN 1-84014-729-6, £40.00

*Rosine A. Lambin, **Le voile des femmes. Un inventaire historique, social et psychologique**, (Studia Religiosa Helvetica), P.Lang: Bern 1999, 270 S., ISBN 3-906762-87-4, DM 63,00 / BEF 1250

Sung-Hee Lee-Linke (Hg.), **Ein Hauch der Kraft Gottes. Weibliche Weisheit in den Weltreligionen**, Lembeck: Frankfurt/M. 1999, 170 S., ISBN: 3-87476-346-3, DM 29,80

Marie-Thérès Van Lunen-Chenu, **Femme et hommes. Propos recueillis par Bénédicte Dubois**, Édition du Cerf: Paris 1998, ISBN 2-204-05800-9, FRF 45,00

*Cettina Militello, **Maria con occhi di donna**, Edizioni Piemme: Casale Monferrato 1999, 318 S., ISBN 88-384-4313-0, LIT 28.000

*Cettina Militello, **Nostra Donna coronata di dodici stelle**, (Con Maria verso il duemila 3), Edizioni Monfortane: Roma 1999, 143 S., ISBN 88-87103-15-1, LIT 23.000

Elisabeth Moltmann-Wendel, **Wach auf, meine Freundin. Die Wiederkehr der Gottesfreundschaft**, Kreuz Verlag: Stuttgart 2000, 158 S., ISBN 3-7831-1800-X, DM 24,90 / EUR 12,73

Elisabeth Moltmann-Wendel, **Rediscovering Friendship**, SCM Press: London 2000, 144pp., ISBN 0334 02818 3

Anne-Claire Mulder, **Divine Flesh, Embodied Word: Incarnation as a hermeneutical key to a feminist theologian's reading of Luce Irigaray's work**, (= Diss. University of Amsterdam), privately published: Amsterdam 2000, 389pp., ISBN 90-9013830-7 *(This book can be ordered for NLG 50,00 from the author: Bouwstraat 16, 3572 SR Utrecht, The Netherlands)*

Mechtild M. Jansen / Ingeborg Nordmann (Hg.), **Lektüren und Brüche. Jüdische Frauen in Kultur, Politik und Wissenschaft**, Ulrike Helmer Verlag: Königstein 2000, 273 S., ISBN 3-89741-036-2

Joan M. Martin, **More than Chains and Toil: A Christian Work Ethic of Enslaved Women**, Westminster John Knox: Louisville 2000, 220 S., ISBN 0-664-25800-X, $24.95

Kathleen O'Grady / Anne L. Gilroy / Janette Patricia Gray (eds): **Bodies, Lives, Voices: Gender in Theology**, Sheffield Academic Press: Sheffield 1998, ISBN 1-85075-854-9, £16.95

Gabriele Peetz, **Grenzen überwinden. Das Frauenreferat im Lutherischen Weltbund – Geschichte und Analyse**, Lit: Münster 1999, 320 S., ISBN 3-8285-4314-9

Eva Pelker, **Gott, Gene, Gebärmütter. Anthropologie und Frauenbild in der evangelischen Ethik zur Fortpflanzungsmedizin**, Gütersloher Verlagshaus: Gütersloh 2000, 304 S., ISBN 3-579-02657-7, DM 78,00

Ina Praetorius, **Zum Ende des Patriarchats. Theologisch-politische Texte im Übergang**, Matthias-Grünewald-Verlag: Mainz 2000, 157 S., ISBN 3-7867-2230-7, DM 32,00

Anne Primavesi, **Sacred Gaia. Holistic theology and earth system science**, Routledge: London – New York 2000, 196pp., ISBN 0-415-18834-2

Kelley A. Raab, **When Women become Priests: The Catholic Women's Ordination Debate**, Columbia University Press: New York 2000, 320pp., ISBN 0-231-11335-8

Heinrich Reinhardt, **Herz und Auge. Eine christliche Wahrnehmung der Frau in der Kirche**, (EHS.T 690), P.Lang: Bern u.a. 2000, 233 S., ISBN 3-906764-62-1, DM 72,00

*Rosemary Radford Ruether, **Women and Redemption: A Theological History**, SCM Press: London 1998, 366pp., ISBN 0 334 02734 9

Deborah F. Sawyer / Diane M. Collier (eds), **Is There a Future for Feminist Theology?**, Sheffield Academic Press: Sheffield 1999, 210pp., ISBN 1-85075-979-0

Annemarie Schimmel, **My Soul Is a Woman: The Feminine in Islam**, Continuum: New York 1999, ISBN 0-8264-1014-6

*Christa Schnabl, **Das Moralische im Politischen. Hannah Arendts Theorie des Handelns im Horizont der theologischen Ethik**, (Interdisziplinäre Ethik 23), P.Lang: Frankfurt – Berlin 1999, 399 S., ISBN 3-631-34066-4

Susan Sered, **Women of the Sacred Groves: Divine Priestesses of Okinawa**, Oxford University Press: Oxford 2000, 320pp., ISBN 0195124871

Arvind Sharma / Katherine K. Young, **Through Her Eyes: Women's Perspectives on World Religions**, Westview Press: Oxford 2000, 256 S., ISBN 0-8133-6906-1, $24.00

Helen Thorne, **Journey to Priesthood: An In-depth Study of the First Women Priests in the Church of England**, (CCSRG Monograph Series 5), University of Bristol: Bristol 2000, 213pp., ISBN 0-86292-499-5

Karma Lekshe Tsomo (Hg.), **Innovative Buddhist Women: Swimming against the Stream**, (Curzon Critical Studies in Buddhism 15), Curzon: Richmond 1999, 350p., ISBN 0-7007-1253-4

Karin Ulrich-Eschemann, **Vom Geborenwerden des Menschen. Theologische und philosophische Erkundungen**, LIT: Münster 2000, 264 S., ISBN: 3-8258-5098-6, DM 39,80

Angelika Vauti / Margot Sulzbacher (Hg.), **Frauen in islamischen Welten. Eine Debatte zur Rolle der Frau in Gesellschaft, Politik und Religion**, Brandes und

Apsel: Frankfurt a.M. – Südwind: Wien 1999, 155 S., ISBN 3-86099-186-8, DM 29,80

Paula-Irene Villa, **Sexy Bodies. Eine soziologische Reise durch den Geschlechtskörper**, (Geschlecht und Gesellschaft 23), Leske und Budrich: Opladen 2000, 275 S., ISBN 3-8100-2452-X, DM 29,00

Matthieu Wagemann, **Two Trains Running: The Reception of the Understanding of Authority by ARCIC I. Related to the Debates on the Ordination of Women**, P. Lang: Bern – Berlin. 1999, (European University Studies 23, 676), 507 pp., ISBN 3-906763-57-9, DM 120,00

Marianne Wallach-Faller, **Die Frau im Tallit. Judentum feministisch gelesen**, herausgegeben von Doris Brodbeck und Yvonne Domhardt, mit einem Vorwort von Eveline Goodman-Thau und Marie-Theres Wacker, Chronos-Verlag: Zürich 2000, 272 S., ISBN 3-905313-65-0, CHF 34,00 / DM 39,00 / ATS 270

Mary-Paula Walsh, **Feminism and Christian Tradition. An Annotated Bibliography and Critical Introduction to the Literature**, Greenwood Press: Westport/ Conn. 1999, 480pp., ISBN 0-313-26419-8, £67.95

Sylvia Wetzel, **Das Herz des Lotos. Frauen und Freiheit**, Fischer: Frankfurt/M. 1999, 205 S., ISBN 3-596-14254-7, DM 18,90

## I.4 Praktische Theologie, Spiritualität, Liturgiewissenschaft, Religionspädagogik, Homiletik

Gudrun Althausen u.a., **Kinder, Kirche und Karriere. Von der berufstätigen Mutter im Dienst des Herrn. Erfahrungsberichte**, Wichern: Berlin 2000, 208 S., ISBN 3-88981-119-1

Christel Anton, **Religionspädagogische Annäherung an eine "feministische Theologie der Beziehung" (Carter Heyward)**, Lit: Münster 1999 (Theologie und Praxis: Abt. B, 2), ISBN 3-8258-4149-9, DM 24,80

Maria Pilar Aquino / Elisabeth Schüssler Fiorenza (Hg.), **Die Macht der Weisheit. Feministische Spiritualität**, Matthias-Grünewald-Verlag: Mainz 2000, ca. 125 S., ISSN 0588-9804 (Themenheft der Zeitschrift Concilium 5/2000, erschienen in sieben Sprachen)

Kristina Augst, **Religion in der Lebenswelt junger Frauen aus sozialen Unterschichten**, Kohlhammer: Stuttgart 2000, 332 S., ISBN 3-17-016297-7

Michael Bangert / Claudia Fuchs-von Brachel (Hg.), **Konnte mein Glaube nicht Euer Glaube werden? Frauen erzählen Geschichten ihres Glaubens**, Aschendorff: Münster 1999, 128 S., ISBN 3-402-03420-4, DM 19,80

Christine Bauhardt / Angelika von Wahl, **Gender and Potitics. "Geschlecht" in der feministischen Politikwissenschaft**, (Politik und Geschlecht 1), Leske + Budrich: Opladen 1999, ISBN 3-8100-2240-3, 216 S., DM 39,00

Heidrun Baumann (Hg.), **"Frauen-Bilder" in den Medien. Zur Rezeption von Geschlechterdifferenzen**, Daedalus-Verlag: Münster 2000, 213 S., ISBN 3-89126-073-3, DM 38,00

Britta L. Behm / Gesa Heinrichs / Holger Tiedemann (Hg.), **Das Geschlecht der Bildung – Die Bildung der Geschlechter**, Leske + Budrich: Opladen 1999, 300 S., ISBN 3-8100-2458-9, DM 48,00

*Teresa Berger, **Women's Ways of Worship: Gender Analysis and Liturgical History**, Pueblo Books: Collegeville 1999, 180pp., ISBN 0-8146-6173-4, $21.95

Sandra Billington / Miranda Green (eds), **The Concept of the Goddess**, Routledge: London – New York 1998, ISBN 0-415-19789-9

Sabine Bobert-Stützel, **Frömmigkeit und Symbolspiel. Ein pastoraltheologischer Beitrag zu einer evangelischen Frömmigkeitstheorie**, (Arbeiten zur Pastoraltheologie 37), Vandenhoeck & Ruprecht: Göttingen 2000, 424 S., ISBN 3-525-62360-7

Elizabeth Bounds / Pamela K. Brubaker / Mary E. Hobgood (eds), **Welfare Policy: Feminist Critiques**, Pilgrim Press: Cleveland/OH 1999, ISBN 0-8298-1305-5, $21.95

Carol Christ, **Rebirth of the Goddess: Finding Meaning in Feminist Spirituality**, Routledge: London – New York 1998, ISBN 0-415-92186-4

Gary David Comstock / Susan E. Henking (eds), **Que(e)rying Religion. A Critical Anthology**, Continuum: New York 1999, 560pp., ISBN 0-8264-0924-5, $29.95

Karin Derichs-Kunstmann / Susanne Auszra / Brigitte Müthing, **Von der Inszenierung des Geschlechterverhältnisses zur geschlechtsgerechten Didaktik. Konstitution und Reproduktion des Geschlechterverhältnisses in der Erwachsenenbildung**, (Wissenschaftliche Reihe 111), Kleine: Bielefeld 1999, 216 S., ISBN 3-89370-297-0, DM 36,90

Bettina Eltrop / Anneliese Hecht (Hg.), **Frauendinge**, (FrauenBibelArbeit 4), Verlag Katholisches Bibelwerk: Stuttgart 2000 – Klens: Düsseldorf 2000, 88 S., ISBN 3-460-25284-7, DM 17,90 / CHF 17,90 / ATS 131

Bettina Eltrop / Anneliese Hecht (Hrsg.), **Frauengefühle**, (FrauenBibelArbeit 5), Verlag Katholisches Bibelwerk: Stuttgart 2000 – Klens: Düsseldorf 2000, 94 S., ISBN 3-460-25285-5, DM 17,90 / CHF 17,90 / ATS 131

Brigitte Enzner-Probst / Irene Löffler / Hanna Strack (Hg.), **FrauenKirchenKalender 2001**, Hanna Strack Verlag: Pinnow 2000, ISBN 3-929813-18-1

Brigitte Enzner-Probst / Hanna Strack (Hg.), **Mädchenkalender 2001. Ich bin ich,** Hanna Strack Verlag: Pinnow 2000, ISBN 3-929813-21-1, DM/CHF 12,00 / ATS 90

Christine Färber, **Frauenförderung an Hochschulen. Neue Steuerungsinstrumente zur Gleichstellung**, (Politik der Geschlechterverhältnisse 15), ( = Diss. Freie Univ. Berlin 1999), Campus: Frankfurt – New York 2000, 306 S., ISBN 3-593-36467-0, DM 68.00 / EUR 34.77

**Gewalt gegen Frauen – Theologische Aspekte I + II**, Gelnhausen 1997 *(Zu bestellen für DM 12,00 bei: Ev. Pressedienst, Emil-von-Bering-Str. 3, 60439 Frankfurt, Deutschland; Tel. 069-58098-0)*

Helga Barbara Gundlach Sonnemann, **Religiöser Tanz. Formen – Funktionen – aktuelle Beispiele**, (Religionswissenschaftliche Reihe 13), diagonal-Verlag: Marburg 2000, 160 S., ISBN 3-927165-68-9, 38,00 DM / 277 ÖS / CHF 35,00

Carol Hagemann-White, **Sozialisation: weiblich – männlich**, Leske + Budrich: Opladen 1999, 2. völlig überarb. Auflage, 280 S., ISBN 3-8100-1900-3, DM 36,00

Marianne Horstkemper / Margret Kraul, **Koedukation. Erbe und Chancen**, Deutscher Studienverlag: Weinheim 1999, 265 S., ISBN 3-89271-871-7, DM 44,00

Birgit Hoyer, **Gottesmütter. Lebensbilder kinderloser Frauen als fruchtbare Dialogräume für Pastoral und Pastoraltheologie**, Lit: Münster 1999, (Tübinger Perspektiven zur Pastoraltheologie und Religionspädagogik 2), 352 S., ISBN 3-8258-4329-7, DM 49,80

Wendy Hunter Roberts, **Celebrating Her: Feminist Ritualizing Comes of Age**, The Pilgrim Press: Ohio 1998, 162pp., ISBN 0-8298-1258-X

Lynda Katsuno / Edna Orteza (eds), **Of Rolling Waters and Roaring Wind: A Celebration of the Woman Song**, WCC Publications: Geneva 2000, 152pp., ISBN 2-8254-1287-2

Ans Kits, **De pastor is een vrouw**, Narratio: Gorinchem 2000, 176pp., ISBN 90 5263 235 9

Stephanie Klein, **Gottesbilder von Mädchen. Bilder und Gespräche als Zugänge zur kindlichen religiösen Vorstellungswelt**, Kohlhammer: Stuttgart – Berlin – Köln 2000, 208 S., ISBN 3-17-016303-5, DM 39,90

Elmar Klinger / Stephanie Böhm / Theodor Seidl (Hg.), **Der Körper und die Religion. Das Problem der Konstruktion von Geschlechterrollen**, Würzburg: Echter, 2000, 230 S., ISBN 3-429-02215-0, DM 39,00

Anneliese Knippenkötter / Marie-Luise Langwald (Hg.), **FrauenGottesDienste. Thema: Gemeinschaft**, Schwabenverlag: Ostfildern – Klens Verlag Düsseldorf 2000, 88 S., ISBN 3-7966-0993-7, CHF/DM 14,50 / ATS 106

Hanne Köhler / Arbeitsgruppe Abendmahl, **Brot des Lebens – Kelch des Heils**, (Materialhefte 85), Frankfurt 1999 *(Zu bestellen bei: Beratungstelle für Gestaltung von Gottesdiensten und anderen Gemeindeveranstalungen, Eschersheimer Landstraße 565, 60431 Frankfurt, Deutschland)*

Eleonore Kostjuk / Hanna Strack (Hg.), **Christlicher Kalender für Frauen 2001**, Deutsch-russische Sonderausgabe, Hanna Strack Verlag: Pinnow 2000, ISBN 3-929813-49-1, DM/CHF 19,80 / ATS 150

Beate Krais (Hg.), **Wissenschaftskultur und Geschlechterordnung. Über die verborgenen Mechanismen männlicher Dominanz in der akademischen Welt**, (Campus Sozialwissenschaften), Campus: Frankfurt – New York 2000, ISBN 3-593-36230-9, 225 S., DM 48,00 / CHF 46,00 / ATS 350

Ingeborg Kruse, **Mirjams Lied. Frauen und Mädchen in den Geschichten der Bibel**, Gabriel: Wien 2000, 228 S., ISBN 3-7072-6622-2

Judith Lorber, **Gender-Paradoxien**, Leske + Budrich: Opladen 1999, 230 S., ISBN 3-8100-2223-3, DM 44,00

Ingrid Lukatis / Regine Sommer / Christof Wolf (Hg.), **Religion und Geschlechterverhältnisse**, Leske und Budrich: Opladen 2000, (Veröffentlichungen der Sektion Religionssoziologie in der DGS 4), 300 S., ISBN 3-8100-2546-1, DM 64,00

*Carola Moosbach, **Lobet die Eine. Schweige- und Schreigebete**, Mathias-Grünewald-Verlag: Mainz 2000, 117 S., ISBN 3-7867-2244-7

Mechtild Oechsle / Birgit Geissler (Hg.), **Die gleiche Ungleichheit. Junge Frauen und der Wandel im Geschlechterverhältnis**, Leske + Budrich: Opladen 1998, 282 S., ISBN 3-8100-2156-3, DM 39,00

Mechtild Oechsle / Karin Wetterau (Hg.), **Politische Bildung und Geschlechterverhältnis**, Leske + Budrich: Opladen 1999, 240 S., ISBN 3-8100-2476-7, DM 33,00

Eva Pelkner, **Gott, Gene, Gebärmütter. Anthropologie und Frauenbild in der evangelischen Ethik zur Fortpflanzungsmedizin**, Chr. Kaiser – Gütersloher Verlagshaus: Gütersloh 2000, 304 S., ISBN 3-579-02657-7

Nancy Werking Poling (Hg.), **Victim to Survivor: Women Recovering from Clergy Sexual Abuse**, Pilgrim Press: Cleveland 1999, ISBN 0-8298-1323-3, $15.95

**"Religionspädagogik feministisch – jenseits der Trivialisierung"**, Religionspädagogische Beiträge 43/1999 *(Zu bestellen für DM 25,00 bei Birgit Menzel, Universität Gesamthochschule Kassel, Fachbereich 1, Erziehungswissenschaft / Humanwissenschaften, Fachgruppe Theologie, Diagonale 9, 34127 Kassel, Deutschland)*

*Susan A. Ross, **Extravagant Affections: A Feminist Sacramental Theology**, Continuum: New York 1998, 240pp., ISBN 0-8264-1083-9, $24.95.

Sylvia Rothschild / Sybil Sheridan (eds), **Taking up the Timbrel: The Challenge of Creating Ritual for Jewish Women Today**, SCM Press: London 2000, 144pp., ISBN 0-334-02806-X

Renate Semier, **Frauen und Gender in der öffentlichen EZA und in der Entwicklungszusammenarbeit der Katholischen Kirche Österreichs. Institutionenvergleich und Fallstudien**, hg. v. Österreichische Forschungsstiftung für Entwicklungshilfe, Südwind: Wien 1999, 129 S., ISBN 3-900592- 55-1

*Sozialwissenschaftliche Forschung & Praxis für Frauen e.V. (Hg.), **Lesbenleben quer gelesen**, (beiträge zur feministischen theorie und praxis 52), Verlag des Vereins Beiträge zur feministischen Theorie und Praxis e.V.: Köln 1999, 152 S., ISSN 0722-0189, DM 23,00

Marlene Stein-Hilbers, **Sexuell werden. Sexuelle Sozialisation und Geschlechterverhältnisse**, Leske + Budrich: Opladen 1999, 230 S., ISBN 3-8100-2221-7, DM 29,00

Silvia Stoller / Eva Waniek u.a. (Hg.), **Verhandlungen des Geschlechts. Zeitgenössische Reflexionen zur Gender-Forschung**, Turia & Kant: Wien 2000

Hanna Strack, **Reise zu den Quellen. Ein Meditationsbuch**, Hanna Strack Verlag: Pinnow/Schwerin 2000, ISBN 3-929813-36-X, 80 S., DM/CHF 16,80

*Hanna Strack, **Segen strömt aus der Mitte. Neue Segenstexte von Hanna Strack mit Mandalas zum Ausmalen von Sigrid Kaußler-Spaeter**, Hanna Strack Verlag: Pinnow/Schwerin ²2000, ISBN 3-929813-05-X, 104 S., DM/CHF 16,80 / ATS 140

*Segen – Herberge in unwirtlicher Zeit**. Texte und Schreibwerkstatt von Hanna Strack, Scherenschnitte von Adelheid Strack-Richter, Hanna Strack Verlag: Pinnow 1993 (4. Auflage 1998), 72 Seiten, ISBN 3-929813-01-7, DM/CHF 14,80 / ATS 120

*Hanna Strack / Christiane Freking (Hg.), **Segen ist nicht nur ein Wort. Tänze, Gesten, Meditationen, Rituale, Ikebana**, Hanna Strack Verlag: Pinnow 1996 (2. Auflage 1996), 64 Seiten, ISBN 3-929813-19-X, DM/CHF 14,80 / ATS 120

Anke Spies, **"Wer war ich eigentlich?". Erinnerung und Verarbeitung sexueller Gewalt**, (Campus Forschung 813), ( = Diss. Univ. Münster 1999), Campus: Frankfurt/M. – New York 2000, ISBN 3-593-36473-5, 239 S., DM 58,00 / EUR 29,65

*Julia Strecker, **Der Sehnsucht Sprache geben. Liturgische Texte für den Gottesdienst**, Gütersloher Verlagsaus: Gütersloh 2000, 128 S., ISBN 3-579-03194-5

Lore Toman, **Abschied vom Patriarchat. Entlarvte Strategien der Zurichtung des starken Geschlechts**, P.Lang: Frankfurt/M. u.a. 2000, 224 S., ISBN 3-631-36010-X, DM 65,00

Janet R. Walton, **Feminist Liturgy: A Matter of Justice**, Liturgical Press: Collegeville/Minn. 2000, 93 pp., ISBN 0814625967

Chava Weissler, **Voices of the Matriarchs: Listening to the Prayers of Early Modern Jewish Women**, Beacon Press: Boston 1999, 304 S., $28.50

Elizabeth A. Wilson, **Neural Geographies: Feminism and the Microstructure of Cognition**, Routledge: London – New York 1998, 256pp., ISBN 0-415-91600-3, £12.99

Laurie Zoloth, **Health Care and the Ethics of Encounter: A Jewish Discussion of Social Justice**, University of North Carolina Press: Chapel Hill 1998, 384pp., ISBN 0-8078-4828-X

## II. Rezensionen – Book Reviews – Critique des Livres

### II.1 Exegese (Erstes Testament, Neues Testament, nicht kanonisierte jüdische und frühchristliche Schriften) und Hermeneutik

Gerlinde Baumann, *Liebe und Gewalt. Die Ehe als Metapher für das Verhältnis JHWH – Israel in den Prophetenbüchern*, (Stuttgarter Bibelstudien 185), Katholisches Bibelwerk: Stuttgart 2000, 261 Seiten, ISBN 3-460-04851-4

Die Ehe als Metapher für das Verhältnis zwischen Gott und Israel ist ein wohlbekanntes Motiv in mehreren Prophetenbüchern. JHWH und Israel bzw. Jerusalem werden metaphorisch als 'Ehemann' und 'Ehefrau' dargestellt. Der Bund Gottes mit seinem Volk wird mit der Liebe zwischen Mann und Frau verglichen. Es ist jedoch fraglich, ob der Aspekt des 'liebenden Ehemannes' wirklich der zentrale Punkt in der Metaphorik ist. Der Wortwahl der Texte zufolge steht vielmehr die 'Bestrafung Israels bzw. Jerusalems' im Vordergrund. Damit wird das mit dieser Metapher vermittelte Gottesbild problematisch; denn die männliche Hauptperson, der 'Er' in der Metapher, wird als sexueller Gewalttäter dargestellt. In den bisherigen theologischen Kommentaren hat dies kaum Beachtung gefunden. Auch feministische Autorinnen haben zwar die (weibliche) Rolle Jerusalems und Israels untersucht, sich aber kaum mit der Problematik des in diesen Texten vorzufindenden Gottesbildes befaßt.

Inwiefern ist der Aspekt der sexuellen Gewalt untrennbar verbunden mit der prophetischen Ehemetaphorik? Diese Frage ist der Ausgangspunkt der Überlegungen Gerlinde Baumanns, die mit ihrem Buch eine tiefgehende und sorgfältig aufgebaute Untersuchung über die Ehemetaphorik der verschiedenen prophetischen Texte erarbeitet hat. Ihre hermeneutische Leitlinie ist dabei, daß Gewalt nicht nur das prägende Thema der behandelten Texte ist, sondern daß unterschiedliche Formen von Gewalt, insbesondere Gewalt gegen Frauen, auch in unserer heutigen gesellschaftlichen Wirklichkeit potentiell oder aktuell anwesend sind. Deshalb steht im Hintergrund der Studie die Überlegung, wie heutzutage mit der Problematik dieser biblischen Metapher umzugehen ist.

Im ersten Teil des Buches bietet die Autorin einen Forschungsüberblick und diskutiert die Sprachbilder der prophetischen Ehemetaphorik und die hermeneutischen Probleme, die damit zusammenhängen. In einer ausführlichen Beschreibung grenzt sie das Wortfeld der prophetischen Ehemetaphorik und damit den Bereich der zu behandelnden Texte ab. Besondere Aufmerksamkeit widmet sie dem Verhältnis der Ehemetaphorik zur – damit verwandten – Vorstellung von Gottes Bund mit Israel.

Im zweiten Teil legt G. Baumann sorgfältig exegetisierte Textuntersuchungen aus den verschiedenen Prophetenbüchern vor; besonders hebt sie die Kontextbezogenheit von Metaphern hervor. Die Autorin unterscheidet dabei zwischen 'Erklärung' und 'Interpretation'. Die Erklärung befaßt sich mit der alttestamentlichen Bedeutung der Metapher, insofern diese aus dem damaligen Sprach- und Lebenskontext zu erheben ist; die Interpretation ist auf die heutige Auslegung in unserem eigenen Kontext zugespitzt.

Im dritten Teil werden die Resultate der Forschung zusammengebracht und ausgewertet. Die Autorin kommt zu dem Schluß, daß "die strafende Gewalt JHWHs tatsächlich notwendiger Bestandteil der prophetischen Ehemetaphorik ist" (234). Damit tritt das hermeneutische Problem dieser Texte klar in den Vordergrund: Wie ist mit der Gewalttätigkeit im biblischen Gottesbild heutzutage umzugehen? Diese spannende Frage muß im Rahmen dieser exegetischen Untersuchung leider offen bleiben. Sie bleibt am Ende des Buches stehen als Aufgabe, als unumgängliche Herausforderung an Exegeten und Exegetinnen, weitere Forschungen zu dieser Problematik zu betreiben. Baumanns imposante Exegese bietet dazu ein wertvolles Fundament.

*Jopie Siebert-Hommes (Amsterdam / Niederlande)*

Athalya Brenner (ed.), *Genesis*, (FCB II/1), Sheffield Academic Press: Sheffield 1998, 276 Seiten, ISBN 1-85075-838-7, £16.95

Athalya Brenner / Carole Fontaine (ed.), *Wisdom and Psalms*, (FCB II/2), Sheffield Academic Press: Sheffield 1998, 332 Seiten, ISBN 1-85075-917-0, £16.95

Die beiden ersten Sammelbände der zweiten Serie des *Feminist Companion to the Bible* (FCB) dokumentieren methodische Vielfalt und sind gleichzeitig Spiegelbild aktueller Forschungsschwerpunkte. Die Bände versammeln

Einzeluntersuchungen mit verschiedenen methodischen Ansätzen, die häufig auf sehr gelungene Weise miteinander ins Gespräch gebracht werden.

So stehen sich zum Beispiel im Genesisband mit *Ronald A. Simkins'* kulturhistorischer Untersuchung des Körper- und Sexualitätsverständnisses in Gen 2-3 und der strukturalistisch, v.a. an V. Propp orientierten narrativen Analyse *Diane M. Sharons* zwei Untersuchungen zum gleichen Textkorpus gegenüber, die zu entgegengesetzten Ergebnissen kommen. Während Simkins ein Verständnis der sexuellen Differenz und der sexuellen Reproduktion eruiert, das in Begriffen der Agrarkultur metaphorisiert wird (der Mann als Farmer, die Frau als Land), erarbeitet Sharon für die narrative Ebene des Textes ein Egalitätsmodell der Geschlechter.

Der zweite mit dem Wortspiel "Mal[e] Practices" überschriebene Teil wendet sich biblischen Männergestalten, ihren patriarchalen Verhaltensmustern sowie männlicher Gewalt zu. Noahs sexuelle Exponierung in Gen 9,18-29 und Lots inzestuöses Verhalten auf dem Hintergrund Freudscher Theorie (*Ilona N. Rashkow*), Abrahams Kommunikationsunfähigkeit in Gen 21,12 (*Mayer I. Gruber*) und die 'Bindung Isaaks' in Gen 22 (*Carol Delaney*), deren Lesart von Gen 22 als patriarchales Gründungsmodell der drei monotheistischen Religionen meines Erachtens in gefährliches Fahrwasser gerät, sind Beleg dafür, daß feministische Exegese sich längst nicht mehr auf Frauengestalten beschränkt. Daß dabei nicht nur Sexismus, sondern das gesamte Geflecht patriarchaler Unterdrückungsstrukturen in feministische Analysen einbezogen wird, zeigt *Lyn Bechtels* Untersuchung von Gen 19,1-11, in der der Text als Diskurs über Fremdenfeindlichkeit vs. Offenheit gegenüber Fremden gelesen wird. Wie interdisziplinäre Orientierung Exegese bereichern kann, dokumentiert auch *Susanne Scholz'* Artikel zur Vergewaltigung Dinas. Ihre Untersuchung medizinischer Bücher und exegetischer Auslegungen von Gen 34 aus dem 19. Jahrhundert zeigt, daß Vergewaltigung nur aus der Perspektive der Täter gesehen wurde. Demgegenüber legt sie eine feministische Interpretation aus der Perspektive des Opfers vor.

Im dritten Teil finden die Frauengestalten der Genesis Aufmerksamkeit. Die ansonsten starke Konzentration der Beiträge auf die Figur der Hagar wird durch *Phyllis Silverman Kramers* Beitrag etwas relativiert, der dem bisher wenig beachteten Thema von Frauenpaaren in biblischen Erzählungen nachgeht.

Der zweite Band des FCB II zu *Psalmen und Weisheit* ist durch eine auffallend hohe Präsenz übersetzter Beiträge deutschsprachiger Exegetinnen gekennzeichnet: ein positives Zeichen für die zunehmende Vernetzung zwischen deutschsprachiger, englischer und amerikanischer feministischer Exegese. Er wird mit dem erstmals 1984 erschienenen Beitrag von *Roland E. Murphy* zum Verhältnis von Weisheit und Schöpfung als Paradigma für eine "mainstream"-Exegese ohne jede genderspezifische Fragestellung eröffnet. Damit verbinden die Herausgeberinnen die Hoffnung, feministische Bibelkritik möge von den guten wie den schlechten Lektionen traditioneller Forschung lernen (24). Die Beiträge zur Weisheitsliteratur aus feministischer Perspektive zeigen, wie dies vonstatten gehen kann: so zum Beispiel *Gerlinde Baumann*s Interpretation von Spr 1-9, die den Text als literarischen Ausdruck didaktisch-pädagogischer Familienunterweisung liest.

F(emale) oder M(ale) voice – das ist die Frage, wenn *Alice Ogden Bellis'* Untersuchung von Spr 7 und *Christl Maiers* Beitrag zur 'fremden Frau' in Spr 1-9 nebeneinander zu stehen kommen – ein weiteres Beispiel für die dialogische Konzeption der Beiträge. Maier weist das Konstrukt der als sexuell unersättlich stilisierten 'fremden Frau' als einen "M interests" dienenden Diskurs aus. Daß er einer Sprecherin in den Mund gelegt wird, ändere daran nichts. Dagegen behauptet Bellis, wenn eine Mutter in Spr 7 ihre Söhne mahnt, sich nicht mit Prostituierten einzulassen, sei dies weibliche Kritik an einer männlichen Doppelmoral und damit als F voice zu charakterisieren. Daß das Konzept der F voice hier gegen sich selbst gewendet wird, ein misogyner Text mit weiblich-mütterlichen Argumenten zur F voice stilisiert werden kann, stellt meines Erachtens nicht das Konzept selbst in Frage. Es zeigt vielmehr, daß nicht nur im Text, sondern auch in seiner Interpretation M voice aus Frauenmund möglich ist.

Einen weiteren Schwerpunkt in diesem Band bildet Kohelet. Die seit Lohfink die Koheletforschung bewegende Frage, ob Kohelet ein Frauenfeind war oder nicht, greift *Eric S. Christianson* in einem pointierten Forschungsüberblick auf. Dabei steht nicht mehr Kohelet, sondern sein Exeget im Blickpunkt: Exegeten der 'Old boy'- wie der 'New Man-School' wird nachgewiesen, daß sie in Kohelet lediglich ihre eigenen Vorannahmen spiegeln. Der Blick in die Rezeptionsgeschichte, wie ihn *Carole Fontaine* und *Brian B. Noonan* vornehmen, widmet u.a. der christlichen Rezeption von Koh 7,25-8,1a im Malleus Maleficarum besondere Aufmerksamkeit. Gelungene intertextuell orientierte feministische Exegese wird nicht nur hier vorgeführt, sondern auch in *Sidnie White Crawfords* Beitrag zu weisheitlichen Texten in Qumran und *Ross Kraemers* Beitrag zu Asenets Entwicklung 'Joseph und Aseneth', die als Transformation von der Frau Torheit bzw. der fremden Frau zur Frau Weisheit gelesen wird.

Daß feministische Exegese nun auch die Psalmen für sich entdeckt, scheint deutlich mit der "Karriere" der Intertextualität in den vergangenen Jahren zusammenzuhängen. Sowohl *Ulrike Bails* Interpretation von Ps 55 als Klage einer Beterin, die ihre sexuelle Gewalterfahrung zur Sprache bringt, als auch *Beth LaNeel Tanners* Lesart von Ps 109 als Gebet Rahels und Leas aufgrund des väterlichen Zwangs zur Heirat, greifen auf einen leserinnenorientierten intertextuellen Ansatz zurück. Daß der Band insgesamt nur drei Beiträge zu den Psalmen enthält, zeigt, wie viel Potential es hier noch zu heben gilt.

Nicht alle Beiträge der beiden Bände sind von gleicher, herausragender Qualität. Dennoch wird, wer exegetisch forscht, so manchen hier veröffentlichten Artikel zur Kenntnis nehmen müssen.

*Claudia Rakel (Bonn / Deutschland)*

(Gekürzte Fassung der in der ThLZ veröffentlichten Rezension)


Silke Petersen, *'Zerstört die Werke der Weiblichkeit!' Maria Magdalena, Salome und andere Jüngerinnen Jesu in christlich-gnostischen Schriften*, (Nag Hammadi and Manichean Studies 48), Brill: Leiden – Boston – Köln 1999, 383 Seiten, ISBN 90 04 11449 1, $124

This book, Silke Petersen's dissertation, is a most welcome study of the women disciples of Jesus in Christian Gnostic documents: Mary Magdalene, Salome, Martha, Arsinoe, several unnamed women disciples (among them Jesus' seven women disciples) and Mary, the mother of Jesus. The fact that so many female disciples have a role in Christian Gnostic literature might lead one to conclude that they – or perhaps even that women in general – were quite important in Christian Gnostic circles. However, Petersen's research, which focuses on the particular significance of women disciples in Christian Gnostic texts, casts doubt on this assumption. She is concerned with how and why the New Testament tradition of women disciples became part of these texts and what kind of Gnostic theology lies behind the process.

In the central part of her book Petersen presents a detailed examination of the representation of women disciples in the Nag Hammadi documents (the Gospel of Thomas, the Gospel of Philip, the Sophia of Jesus Christ, the Dialogue of the Saviour and the first Apocalypse of James) and other early Gnostic sources (the Gospel of Mary and Pistis Sophia), as well as in Patristic anti-Gnostic documents and Manichean Psalms (94-294). This is preceded by a comprehensive introduction to these texts and a critical re-examination of the genre of the Gnostic dialogue (35-93).

In the final part of the book the author focuses on the single aspect which appears to be common to all Christian Gnostic texts in which women disciples have a role: their comments on femininity and masculinity (295-334). Petersen places these in the broader context of the treatment of this subject in the literature of late antiquity. In her view, the Christian texts of antiquity show a fatal alternative: either women must become men or, as women, they are to be submissive to men. Petersen argues that women entered the Christian Gnostic community on condition that they put aside their feminine nature. She concludes that the superiority of mind (asexual and masculine) to body (sexual and feminine), which in her definition is fundamental to Gnostic thinking, is at the root of the Gnostic Christian discipleship of women.

Although I think this conclusion is too general (does the Gospel of Mary, for instance, not take a different stand?) Silke Petersen's study makes a major contribution to this field. Her book is the first to open up the wealth of sources pertaining to women's discipleship in Christian Gnostic texts and to place them in a broader context. Her research is thorough, stimulating, and challenging.

*Esther A. de Boer (Ouderkerk aan de Amstel / The Netherlands)*


Tina Pippin, *Apocalyptic Bodies. The Biblical End of the World in Text and Image*, Routledge: London – New York, 1999, 160 pages, ISBN O-415-18248-4 (hbk); 0-415-18249-2 (pbk), $ 24.99 / £14.99

In *Apocalyptic Bodies*, Pippin explores a number of texts from both the Hebrew Bible and the New Testament, which can be described as 'apocalyptic' in the broad sense of the word. The main biblical texts and topics under discussion are Mark 13 (discussed in chapter 2); Jezebel (chapter 3); Babel (chapter 4) and the abyss, apocalyptic horror and apocalyptic fear in the book of Revelation (chapters 5-7). Rather than focusing on the meaning of these biblical texts *per se*, Pippin chooses to interpret their presence in Western, and more specifically American, culture. She does so from a decidedly cultural critical and postmodern perspective, using a number of different analytical tools, including semiotics; Marxist feminist critical theories; deconstruction; horror and fantasy theories. This approach is very much in line with her earlier work, especially her book *Death and Desire. The Rhetoric of Gender in the Apocalypse of John* (1992).

Pippin's readings in this book are both engaging and engaged. She brings together a wealth of material and offers refreshing new insights and challenging interpretations. She makes no secret of her position as a resisting reader, but instead of opting for a "counter-apocalypse" as Catherine Keller does, Pippin goes for an "anti-apocalypse". The closing words of her book therefore hardly sound surprising: "In the Apocalypse, the Kingdom of God is a kingdom of perversity" (125). This statement characterises her position in more than one sense. For Pippin the Apocalypse is a male space, made perverse by the male gaze; a pornoapocalypse in which female bodies are featured as objects of male desire (94). Her negative evaluation is ethically motivated: "If hope is a moral action, we must be moral about the way we hope" (8). I like this statement, but it is also here that her own analysis falls short, for she does not sufficiently criticise and deconstruct the moral dualism inherent in this and other apocalypses. Another problem is that the hermeneutical choices she makes are not sufficiently explicated and can therefore give the impression of being eclectic or arbitrary. Nevertheless, Pippin's work merits attention not only from exegetes or theologians, but from anyone interested in the influence of the Bible on Western culture and in The End.

*Caroline Vander Stichele (Amsterdam / The Netherlands)*

Susanne Scholz, *Rape Plots. A Feminist Cultural Study of Genesis 34*, (Studies in Biblical Literature 13), P.Lang: New York 2000, 232 pages, ISBN 0-8204-4154-6

Les exégètes prétendent que la Bible et les sciences bibliques ont formé et pétri la culture occidentale. L'auteur examine la relation qu'il y a entre un phénomène social comme le viol au XIXe siècle, tel qu'on le trouve rapporté dans les dossiers médicaux de la justice de l'époque, et ce même phénomène analysé dans les commentaires théologiques sur le viol, à l'exemple de "La violence faite à Dina par Sichem" (Gn 34). Elle utilise d'anciens commentaires, des interprétations bibliques actuelles et des commentaires féministes. Ses conclusions confirment les thèses scientifiques féministes à ce sujet, à savoir que face au viol, il y a toujours marginalisation et accusation de la victime, condamnation des allié(e)s, identification avec le coupable (dans l'interprétation du récit de la Genèse cité, les exégètes excusent même Sichem en disant qu'il aime Dina) et minimisation de l'acte (Dina est une femme adulte et sait ce qu'elle fait).

Au cœur de ce livre on trouve une confrontation entre une lecture féministe de la violence faite à Dina dans le récit de la Genèse (Gn 34) par la méthode de la critique rhétorique (Ph.Trible), et une analyse littéraire de ce passage de la Bible par R.Alter. Dans une analyse syntaxique détaillée, Scholz fait le portrait de tous les participants au débat sur le viol de Dina – un débat causant d'énormes tensions au sein de la maison de Jacob–; le père de Dina et ses frères, Sichem et son père Hamor. Elle expose leurs raisonnements et démasque leurs stratégies, pour autant que le texte le permette. La décision de Sichem après le viol – il est rapporté dans le verset 3 que son cœur s'attacha à Dina (דבק נפש), qu'il eut de l'amour pour la jeune fille (אהב) et qu'il parla à son cœur (דבר) – est généralement expliquée par les exégètes comme de la solidarité et de la tendresse. Scholz au contraire pense que par sa conduite Sichem dissimule son acte de violence: il garde Dina (comme sa propriété), il la désire et essaye de la calmer après l'avoir violée.

Contrairement à R.Alter, Scholz voit dans "La violence faite à Dina" (Gn 34) une scène de fiançailles. Comme Ruth (2,22), Dina sort (יצא); comme Rebecca (Gn 24,14; 16), Dina est appelée "jeune femme" (נערה); et comme dans l'histoire de Samson (Jg 14,5-6) il n'y a pas ici de rencontre près du puits. Au lieu de flirter près du puits, Sichem viole Dina. Le viol empêche l'histoire de bien se terminer. Le rituel d'hospitalité devient un rituel d'hostilité.

Pour l'auteur, la violence faite à Dina est fondamentale dans cette histoire. Tous les évènements suivants sont la conséquence de cet acte. Ce récit montre que le débat sur le viol ne doit pas cesser. Selon Scholz, le viol ne se comprend que de la perspective de la victime qui y a survécu, ce qui veut dire que le récit de la violence faite à Dina dans la Genèse doit être interprété du point de vue de Dina, du point de vue de la jeune femme violée et prisonnière. Bien que Dina ne dise rien, elle est centrale dans l'histoire, constate Scholz. Elle n'accorde pas une importance excessive au discours sur le viol des femmes tenu par des hommes (chaque homme pouvant, théoriquement, être un coupable). Mais la voix de Dina, est-elle vraiment représentée et entendue dans la société? Et le débat sur le viol en tient-il compte?

Cette étude se lit facilement et engage les lecteurs et les lectrices de la Bible à réfléchir au problème.

*Barbara Leijnse (Arnhem / Pays-Bas)*

Luise Schottroff / Marie-Therese Wacker (eds), with the assistance of Claudia Janssen and Beate Wehn, *Kompendium Feministische Bibelauslegung*, Chr. Kaiser / Gütersloher Verlagshaus: Gütersloh ²1999 (¹1998), 852 pages, ISBN 3-579-00391-7, DM 125,00

The *Kompendium Feministische Bibelauslegung* is a manifestation of German feminist biblical scholarship. 74 articles by 60 female exegetes present feminist readings of all the biblical books (the broadest definition of the Christian canon) and some non-canonical writings. It is an impressive achievement.

Each article includes a bibliography of feminist works and of non-feminist works used by the author, predominantly in German or English. Many bibliographies are more substantial than in the *Women's Bible Commentary* (*WBC*) or *Searching the Scriptures (SSc)*, although these also include works not mentioned in the *Kompendium*. Much of the German material could prove difficult for non-Germans to find: works originally written in another language are cited in the German translation. Brief presentations of the authors and three indices – of modern authors, of female names and a substantial subject index – complete the volume.

The primary intention is to provide German readers, especially those with theological education who are working in churches or teaching at any level, with an introduction to feminist interpretation of the Bible in their own language. The *Kompendium* may also serve as a resource for students and biblical scholars. It thus shares the popular audience of the *WBC* but most of the articles are, in their length and the detailed analyses they present, similar to those in *SSc*. Like *SSc*, the *Kompendium* seeks to offer critical feminist analyses of the writings as a whole, and not simply to focus on texts about, or of specific relevance for, women. Examples of feminist criticism understood as more than reading "women texts" can be found in critiques of the understandings of society and of God found in Exodus and of the dualistic thinking of 2 Cor.

Most of the authors are German, with a number from other European countries, and a handful from North American, Asian, and Latin America. They represent the whole range from postgraduates to internationally known professors. The oldest was born in the 1920s and nearly half in the 1960s. Thus, a broad spectrum of scholars – well-known and unknown, senior and junior – is given the opportunity to share their findings with a wider audience.

As a work shaped by and for its German context, it is marked by Germany's pattern of confessional theological faculties. Moreover, although the bibliographies often include works by Jewish authors and/or about Jewish interpretations and works from other parts of the world than Europe and North America, the range of authors reflects the situation in European universities in that only one contributor is Jewish and only a very few are women of colour.

The *Kompendium* shows the rest of the world what German-speaking feminist biblical scholars are doing and have done. Some authors identify themselves as (white) Europeans, not as a confession of guilt (or the lack of it), but as a matter-of-fact description of their identity and context. Many relate their work to the European context on the threshold of the twenty-first century. But although it is certainly important that we speak as Europeans in a feminist theological conversation which is often dominated by North Americans of all colours, as a Swede, I sometimes felt myself protesting against this formulation of "European". Is this really my context? Is it really possible to include us all in this European identity? Am I, is my country, part of this Europe? And do I – we – really want to be?

It is difficult to review such a work. The value of a volume which presents feminist scholarship, and in doing so provides university teachers with teaching material and students and scholars with new research ideas and includes bibliographies into the bargain, is beyond discussion. But the work is too big and too diverse to allow a fair presentation and discussion in this limited space, especially since, as in the *WBC* and *SSc*, the articles differ widely in their understanding of "feminism", in their choice of theoretical and methodological tools and in quality.

A number of articles, including that on Mark, provide, however briefly, an introduction to earlier feminist readings of the biblical writing in question. However, some articles do not fulfil their promise to give such an introduction. Thus, the article on Gen 1-11 states that the author intended Gen 1:27 to affirm that woman shares in the image of God, but that this meaning has often been hidden in the interpretation of the text. This is to make a complicated issue too easy: I would have liked to have seen a presentation of the arguments against this description of both original intent and history, together with Trible's reading of Gen 2-3 and criticisms of her reading. Similarly, the article on 1 Cor mentions alternative feminist readings (even of such contested texts as 1 Cor 7 and 14:34-35) only in passing or simply presupposes a knowledge of them. I also missed references to the work of Tina Pippin and (recently) of Elisabeth Schüssler Fiorenza in the article on Rev and in its bibliography.

Taken as a whole, the *Kompendium* shows the decisive influence on German feminist biblical scholarship of Elisabeth Schüssler Fiorenza and – at least for New Testament scholars – of Luise Schottroff. To some extent, therefore, an evaluation of the work is dependent on whether you are willing to make the positions of Schüssler Fiorenza and Schottroff your own. Personally, I would have liked to see more consistent analysis with gender as analytical tool and less general liberation theology or finding traces of women and our history even where we are obviously absent. Nonetheless, as a work of the late nineteen-nineties, the *Kompendium* generally recognises the androcentrism of the texts and only very seldom offers facile solutions.

The *Kompendium* documents, as well as forming a part of, a process which continues not only in and among its contributors but also, I think, with the reader. She is, explicitly and implicitly, invited to learn new things, to agree or disagree, to protest, to nod approvingly, or to formulate her own questions, as well as to continue reflecting about problems that are mentioned in the articles, and to pick up on issues that are not made explicit but ought to be thought through. Taken as a whole, the *Kompendium* is a useful work, to be read selectively together with other works, including *SSc*, the *WBC*, and the *Feminist Companion* series.

*Hanna Stenström (Uppsala / Sweden)*

Maria Halmer / Barbara Heyse-Schäfer / Barbara Rauchwarter (Hg.), *Anspruch und Widerspruch. Evi Krobath zum 70. Geburtstag*, Mohorjeva Verlag: Klagenfurt – Ljubljana – Wien 1999, 231 pages, ISBN 3-85013-723-6

This collection of essays and poems honors Evi Krobath, a prominent activist and teacher of the feminist theological movement in Austria. The *Festschrift* gives tribute to her relentless, courageous, and inspiring efforts to disseminate feminist theological theory and practice in Protestant and ecumenical circles in Austria and Europe since the early days of feminism. Her career as a high school teacher of religious studies and her numerous workshops on feminist theologies have inspired a generation of Protestant women who are devoted to eradicating sexism and patriarchal hierarchies in Austrian church life.

Besides a biography and bibliography of publications by Evi Krobath, the volume contains twenty-eight articles, which express gratitude and admiration for Krobath's supportive influence in feminist church activism. For instance, Inge Schintlmeister from the "Evangelische Frauenarbeit in Österreich"

(Protestant Women's Committee of Austria) emphasizes that from the beginning Krobath worked with the committee and shaped its theological outlook. Christa Esterházy remembers her first encounter with Krobath during a conference of the "Ökumenisches Forum Christlicher Frauen in Europa" (Ecumenical Forum of Christian Women in Europe). In her view, "women like Evi Krobath whose long term commitment, lasting educational interests, personal courage, wholehearted engagement and impressive abilities" (154; my translation) helped to transform religious institutions. Michael Bünker recalls Krobath's abilities as a comedian who challenged patriarchal church praxis with humor and wit. He praises her talent to make church audiences laugh about women's realities in Austrian churches and by doing so to create opportunities for change. The *Festschrift* thus illustrates Krobath's grassroots involvement with the Protestant churches in Austria. As such, the book is a historical document of the feminist theological movement in Austria during the 1970s and 1980s.

The volume also contains articles from prominent feminist theological scholars of German-speaking countries, including Irmtraud Fischer, Eveline Goodman-Thau, Elisabeth Moltmann-Wendel, Ina Praetorius, Luise Schottroff, Helen Schüngel-Straumann, and Dorothee Sölle. All refer warmly to Krobath; they honor her with articles on redemption in the Jewish tradition, Miriam, Huldah, the resurrection, salvation, and reconciliation.

Krobath's commitment to ecumenical work finds particular expression in articles by Christa Esterházy, Sumaya Farhat-Naser, Eveline Goodman-Thau, Magret Moers Wenig, and Birgit Lesjak. Whereas most of the twenty-eight articles relate to Protestant church praxis in Austria, these five authors honor Krobath's ecumenical activities. Writing from the Jewish-Israeli, Jewish-American, Roman Catholic-Austrian, and Christian-Palestinian settings, they testify to Krobath's ecumenical ambitions and contacts. Krobath aimed to dialogue with women from other cultures and religions, which sometimes placed her in a mediating position. She embraced both Israeli and Palestinian women, and so the *Festschrift* includes articles by Jewish-Israeli Eveline Goodman-Thau and Christian-Palestinian Sumaya Farhat-Naser. Krobath's ability to reach beyond established boundaries, and her commitment to doing so, may be rooted in her own experience as a child when she was classified by the Nazis as a "Mischling ersten Grades" ("half breed of the first degree"; 221).

This potpourri of articles provides a colorful and vibrant picture of Austrian feminist church praxis in recent decades. The *Festschrift* offers hope that the engagement of religious institutions, such as the Protestant churches of Austria,

Austria in the marathon for "women's rights as human rights" is worthwhile. However, the insults and injustice experienced by women like Krobath in the struggle to gain equal voice and space in their religious institutions are unacceptable. How many generations of women must face the exclusionary practices and theories exemplified in the article by Gerhilde Merz? In an interview presented by Johanna Dohnal, the former women's minister Monika Salzer suggests that women have "to break the brothers together" (167). But how do we avoid being broken ourselves? The balance between being co-opted by institutional power and preserving one's integrity is indeed a difficult one. The contributors of *Anspruch und Widerspruch* concur that Evi Krobath succeeded in this balancing act. Her life-long efforts to eradicate injustice against women within the Austrian Protestant churches shine through every page.

*Susanne Scholz (Wooster,* OH /USA)

## II.2 Kirchen- und Religionsgeschichte

Christiane Burbach / Susanne Wendorf-von Blumröder (Hg.), *Frauen gestalten Frauengestalten,* Katalog zur Ausstellung, Ronnenberg 1996 – Hannover [6]2000, 72 Seiten, ISBN 3-932011-25-2, DM 12,00

Christiane Burbach, *Frauen erinnern. Frauen in der Gedächtniskultur der Kirche,* Lutherisches Verlagshaus: Hannover 2000, ISBN 3-7859-0812-1, 167 Seiten

*Frauen gestalten Frauengestalten,* 12 Doppelkarten mit den Frauenfiguren dieser Ausstellung, Inszenierung und Fotografie von Charlotte Ilse Kik, Hanna Strack Verlag: Pinnow 2000, DM 22,00 *(zu bestellen bei: Kuckucksallee 9, 19065 Pinnow, Tel./Fax +49-3860-8685)*

Wo geschieht es beim Eintritt in einen Raum, daß wir gleichzeitig Frauen aus verschiedenen Epochen, näherhin dem 12./13. Jahrhundert, der Moderne und der Zeit um 1900 begegnen? Wie gelingt es in unserer Zeit, bei einem Gang durch eine Kirche Glaubenspraxis und -erfahrung mit (feministischer) Theologie zu verbinden?

Als ich Thekla, Hildegard, Héloise, den Beginen, Klara von Assisi, Katharina von Siena, Jeanne d'Arc, Katharina Zell, Elizabeth Fry, Maria Montessori, Katharina Staritz und Louise Sophie Freifrau Knigge bei ihrem Aufenthalt in der Melanchthonkirche in Hannover begegnete, fragte ich mich, was mich an diesen Gestalten anzog, die stehend, sitzend oder liegend in der Kirche anwesend waren. Während ich durch die Kirche ging, stand ich immer wieder vor einer anderen Frau und schaute mal Thekla, mal Katharina Staritz in die Augen. Als ich mich in eine Kirchenbank setzte, saßen neben mir drei Beginen. Es war, als hätten sie mich erwartet. Mir wurde bei dieser Ausstellung bewußt, daß nicht ich die Stimmen dieser Frauen hörbar machte – nein, die Frauen selbst waren es, die mich durch ihre Anwesenheit zum Teil einer lebendigen Geschichte und Gemeinschaft werden ließen, einer, wie Christiane Burbach es in ihrem Buch nennt, *Ecclesia Matrix* oder *Ecclesia Nutrix* durch die Zeiten hindurch.

Im Katalog ist der Entstehungsprozeß dieser Ausstellung beschrieben. Fünfzehn Frauen haben unter Leitung von Christiane Burbach, Professorin an der theologischen Fachhochschule in Hannover, und Susanne Wendorf-von Blumröder, Pastorin in der Johanniskirche in Empelde, zwölf historische Frauen gestaltet. Die Eindrücke von Kirchenbesuchern und ihre Erfahrungen mit diesen Frauengestalten sind im Katalog ebenfalls nachzulesen. Manche fühlte durch die Frauen "Kämpferisches in mir" (*Katalog*, 70) geweckt, andere waren durch die Figuren in den Bänken eher irritiert und empfanden Texte und Figuren gleichzeitig als eindrucksvoll und gewöhnungsbedürftig. Ein/e BesucherIn fühlte sich ergriffen von der "weiblichen Kraft in der Stille des Raumes" (*Katalog*, 71).

In ihrem Buch über *Frauen in der Gedächtniskultur der Kirche* geht Christiane Burbach auf die theologischen Voraussetzungen und Konsequenzen des Projekts ein. Das Buch besteht aus vier Teilen. Zuerst wird das Projekt *Frauen gestalten Frauengestalten* näher beschrieben. Danach setzt sich die Autorin mit den Erfahrungen der Teilnehmerinnen sowie der BesucherInnen während der Entstehung bzw. bei den Ausstellungen an verschiedenen Orten auseinander. Bei den Ausstellungen kam es gelegentlich auch zu Diskussionen mit dem Publikum.

Drittens behandelt Christiane Burbach die Frage der Repräsentanz von Frauen in der Kirche, und zwar sowohl als Personen (ihre vielfältige Anwesenheit im Gottesdienst) als auch ihre symbolische Repräsentanz. Im letztgenannten Bereich machen nach Frauen benannte Kirchenpatrozinien sowie Perikopen im Gottesdienst, in denen Frauen im Mittelpunkt stehen, nur einen kleinen Teil aus; die Repräsentanz der Männer steht dazu in Kontrast. Die männliche Überrepräsentanz an der Spitze der Hierarchie und im symbolischen Bereich erweist sich als "so effektiv, daß die personale Repräsentanz vernachlässigt werden kann" (115). Die Autorin zieht daraus den Schluß, daß die Solidarität der Kirchen, die in der Haltung und der Handlungsweise gegenüber Frauen zum Ausdruck kommt, unzulänglich ist (127).

Im vierten Kapitel sucht Christiane Burbach nach Lösungen für die Unterrepräsentanz von Frauen, indem sie die Methode der Systemaufstellung von Bert Hellinger benutzt. Seine Aufstellungen machen in der Familientherapie Kräfteverhältnisse, Familienbande, Rollen, Abhängigkeiten und Verstrickungen sichtbar. Mit Hilfe dieser Systemaufstellung untersucht die Autorin, wie Machtverhältnisse in Kirche und Kirchengeschichte aufgedeckt werden können. Dazu hat sie elf Personen (Frauen und Männer), die an verschiedenen Stellen und auf verschiedenen Hierarchiestufen in der Kirche arbeiten, als Repräsentanz für elf Positionen aufgestellt, u.a. für Geborgenheit, männliche Dominanz, mangelnde weibliche Solidarität, lebendige Balance und weibliches Potential. Sie vertritt die Ansicht, daß in der Bewegung der Positionen sichtbar werden kann, wo Geborgenheit, weibliches Potential oder mangelnde weibliche Solidarität am besten positioniert werden können, um das Ziel, die gegenseitige Anerkennung von Frauen und Männern, zu erreichen.

Beim Lesen kam mir eine solche Systemaufstellung sehr theoretisch vor. Aber wer seine/ihre eigene Position durch den Raum verschoben und dabei das Gesamtgefüge der eingenommenen Positionen mit beeinflußt hat, wird feststellen, daß dabei die Wahrnehmung für die eigene Position und für die der anderen geschärft werden kann. Die Autorin nennt dies "repräsentierende Wahrnehmung" (128). Nach ihrem Urteil könnte aus dieser Art der Wahrnehmung eine neue Bewertung sowohl der persönlichen als auch der kirchenpolitischen Situation entstehen, die nicht ohne Konsequenzen bleiben würde, etwa hinsichtlich der Aufarbeitung der lokalen Kirchen- und Diakoniegeschichte unter dem Gesichtspunkt der Frauen oder im Hinblick auf die Überarbeitung von Kirchengeschichte, Perikopenbüchern und Ikonographie in Kirchenräumen. Außerdem sollten – dies in Ergänzung zu Burbachs Schlußfolgerung – meines Erachtens auch Konsequenzen gezogen werden für die Würdigung der verschiedenen Positionen von Frauen in der Kirche.

Im Buch *Frauen erinnern* sind Schwarz-Weiss-Fotos abgebildet. Im Hanna-Strack-Verlag sind die Abbildungen jetzt auch auf zwölf Karten, die jeweils mit einem Text versehen sind, in Farbe erschienen. Die Karten können einzeln oder im 12er-Pack bezogen werden und sind zur Dekoration oder zum Verschicken geeignet. Aber es hätte noch mehr daraus gemacht werden können, zum Beispiel eine katechetische Handreichung zu den Karten oder die Mitlieferung einer sogenannten "Sehhilfe". Dabei handelt es sich um

Fragen, mit deren Hilfe der gewonnene Eindruck über die jeweilige Abbildung und den zugehörigen Text erspürt werden kann. Mit Hilfe solcher Sehhilfen könnten Frauen und Männer in Gruppen anhand der Bilder und Texte ihren eigenen Glaubensraum erschließen und neu gestalten.

Die Ausstellung, die noch an verschiedenen Orten in Deutschland zu sehen sein wird, macht auf überzeugende Weise deutlich, wie das Problem der Frauenrepräsentanz im Glaubensraum durch Denken, Handeln und Erfahrungen mitten im modernen Leben sichtbar gemacht werden kann.

*Felicia Dekkers (Driebergen / Niederlande)*

Irene Gysel / Barbara Helbling (Hg.), *Zürichs letzte Äbtissin Katharina von Zimmern (1478-1547)*, Verlag Neue Zürcher Zeitung: Zürich 1999 (2. Aufl. 2000), 216 Seiten, ISBN 3-85823-782-5, CHF 38,00 / DM 48,00 / ATS 350

Katharina von Zimmern gehört zu jenen Frauen, die zwar in ihrer Zeit eine herausragende Stellung innehatten, jedoch von der Geschichtsschreibung bislang kaum wahrgenommen wurden. Als letzte Fürstäbtissin des Fraumünsters, des bedeutendsten Frauenkonvents Zürichs, war sie an den Umbrüchen, die die reformatorische Bewegung mit sich brachte, unmittelbar beteiligt. Formell war das Fraumünster eine Benediktinerinnenabtei, deren Äbtissin herrschaftliche Rechte in der Stadt ausübte, faktisch lebten die Nonnen jedoch Anfang des 16. Jahrhunderts mit den Freiheiten von Stiftsdamen, und die Abtei stand weitgehend unter der Verwaltung des städtischen Rats. Katharina von Zimmern pflegte als Äbtissin ein gutes Verhältnis zum Rat, wahrte aber auch in vieler Hinsicht, etwa beim Ausbau der Abtei, ihre Eigenständigkeit. Schon früh setzte sie sich mit der reformatorischen Theologie auseinander. Zwingli predigte regelmäßig am Fraumünster, und dessen Mitarbeiter Oswald Myconius wurde zum Leiter der wieder errichteten Abteischule berufen. Als 1523/24 die Reformation in Zürich durchgesetzt und die Klöster säkularisiert wurden, erklärte Katharina von Zimmern den Verzicht auf ihre Rechte und übergab die Abtei an die Stadt, die ihr als Ersatz ihren Lebensunterhalt zusicherte. Wie weit dies auf Druck des Rats und der reformatorischen Öffentlichkeit geschah, oder wie weit die Fürstäbtissin dabei ihrer inneren Überzeugung folgte, läßt sich aus den Quellen nicht sicher erschließen. Die unspektakuläre Übergabe der Abtei, die Heirat Katharina von Zimmerns wenige Monate später und das Einvernehmen, in dem sie in den späteren Jahren in und mit der Stadt Zürich lebte, sprechen allerdings für ihre Sympathie mit der reformatorischen Bewegung.

Die einzelnen Beiträge des Bandes nähern sich der Persönlichkeit Katharina von Zimmerns auf unterschiedlichen Wegen. *Roswith Günter* untersucht in zwei Beiträgen ("Herkunft und Jugend", "Ein Leben als Bürgerin") mit großer biographischer Detailgenauigkeit die Familiengeschichte Katharinas. *Barbara Helbling* ("Katharina im Fraumünster") beschreibt ihren Werdegang als Nonne und Äbtissin. Mit "Ausbau und Ausstattung der Fraumünsterabtei unter Katharina von Zimmern" befassen sich *Regine Abegg* und *Christine Barraud Wiener* und geben damit Einblick in die kunsthistorisch interessanten Aktivitäten der Äbtissin. Die rechtshistorische Untersuchung *Eduard Rübels* ("Die Übergabe des Stifts an die Stadt – rechtlich gesehen") bietet wichtige Hintergrundinformationen für die Frage nach den Motiven der Äbtissin bei der Übergabe der Abtei. *Christine Christ-von Wedel* fragt schließlich aus der Perspektive der historischen Frauenforschung genauer nach dem Selbstverständnis Katharina von Zimmerns. Sie verbindet dabei die genaue Analyse der bekannten Quellen mit einer Interpretation von Inschriften, die auf Veranlassung Katharinas im Empfangsraum der Abtei sowie auf einer Glocke angebracht wurden. Katharina von Zimmern erscheint dabei als eine selbstbewußte und gebildete Frau, die das überkommene christlich-klösterliche Traditionsgut mit einer neuen humanistischen Weltoffenheit zu verbinden suchte.

Im Anhang des Buches findet sich neben dem Anmerkungsapparat, einem ausführlichen Quellen- und Literaturverzeichnis und einer Zeittafel zur Biographie der Abdruck der zwei wichtigsten schriftlichen Quellen: Katharina von Zimmerns Verzichterklärung vom 30. November 1524 und die Übergabeurkunde vom 8. Dezember 1524. Insgesamt zeigt der durchweg sehr lesenswerte und gut lesbare Band, daß sich trotz einer auf den ersten Blick schwierigen Quellenlage mit wissenschaftlicher Akribie und den Ansätzen der Frauen- und Geschlechtergeschichte ein lebendiges und eindrucksvolles Bild der Persönlichkeit Katharina von Zimmerns und ihrer Rolle in den theologischen und politischen Kontroversen ihrer Zeit rekonstruieren läßt.

*Anne Conrad (Hamburg-Köln / Deutschland)*

Elisa Klapheck (Hg.), *Fräulein Rabbiner Jonas. Kann die Frau das rabbinische Amt bekleiden?* Eine Streitschrift von Regina Jonas, ediert – kommentiert – eingeleitet von Elisa Klapheck, Hentrich & Hentrich: Teetz 1999 (2. Auflage 2000), 325 Seiten, ISBN 3-933471-17-6, DM 39,80

Regina Jonas ist weltweit die erste Frau, die 1935 zur Rabbinerin ordiniert wurde. Wenige Jahre später, im Oktober 1944, wurde die 42-Jährige in Auschwitz ermordet. Danach hat es lange gedauert, bis wieder Rabbinerinnen ordiniert wurden: 1972 in Cincinnati (USA), 1976 in London. Und es hat noch länger gedauert, bis Leben und Werk von Regina Jonas dem Vergessen entrissen und dem öffentlichen Bewusstsein zurückgegeben wurden. Daran hat das vorliegende Buch großen Anteil. In minutiöser Genauigkeit hat die Berliner Journalistin Elisa Klapheck den Weg rekonstruiert, den Regina Jonas, aus ärmlichen Verhältnissen im frommen Berliner Scheunenviertel stammend, gegangen ist, um ihren früh gefassten Vorsatz zu realisieren. "Ich werde Rabbinerin", soll die 13-Jährige ihren Mitschülerinnen erklärt haben. Heute noch exotisch, war dies damals, 1915, fast absurd.

Regina Jonas gilt auch heutigen Jüdinnen als Mut machendes, Identität stiftendes Vorbild: "Etwa 40 Rabbinerinnen aus Europa wurden inzwischen ordiniert… Jede dieser Frauen hat um ihre Anerkennung ringen müssen. Jede Rabbinerin kann sich in Regina Jonas wiedererkennen. In jeder von ihnen lebt ihr Mythos fort" (86). Ihr langer Weg ins Rabbinat, auf dem es an Vorurteilen, Widerständen und Verboten nicht mangelte, ist aufschlussreich: Regina Jonas hat – stets mit Unterstützung und Vermittlung von Seiten väterlicher Freunde und Lehrer – eine beharrliche Politik der kleinen Schritte betrieben und so die direkte Konfrontation mit dem Patriarchat konsequent zu vermeiden gewusst.

Darüber hinaus hat sie aber auch eine theoretische Auseinandersetzung mit dem eigentlichen Problem geleistet und als Dokument hinterlassen: "Kann die Frau das rabbinische Amt bekleiden?", so der Titel ihrer halachischen Abschlussarbeit von 1930 an der Berliner Hochschule für die Wissenschaft des Judentums. Nicht nur das Ergebnis ist interessant: "Ausser Vorurteil und Ungewohntsein steht halachisch fast nichts dem Bekleiden des rabbinischen Amtes seitens der Frau entgegen" (301). Auch die Argumentationsweise ist ungewöhnlich: Jonas argumentiert in erster Linie gerade nicht damit, dass den Anforderungen einer neuen Zeit – damals gab es ja bereits Frauen in anderen akademischen Berufen – eben auch im Judentum mit Neuerungen und Liberalisierungen entgegenzukommen sei. Auch stellt sie sich nicht in das Lager des Reformjudentums, das sich damals bereits gesellschaftlich etabliert hatte. Im Gegenteil: Als traditionelle Jüdin bedient sich Jonas ausschließlich theologischer Argumente und leitet ihre Überzeugung aus den ältesten Quellen des Judentums ab. In den biblischen, nachbiblischen und talmudischen Texten belegt sie anhand zahlreicher Beispiele, dass, "soweit die

Frauen in alten Zeiten hervortreten wollten und konnten, ihnen nichts hindernd in den Weg gelegt wurde, wenn sie Wertvolles und Gediegenes leisteten" (121). Oberstes Kriterium für die Zulässigkeit öffentlichen Wirkens von Frauen sei die Einhaltung der *Z'niuth*: ein für Jonas zentraler talmudischer Begriff, der sich etwa mit Zurückhaltung im Sinne von Demut, Keuschheit, Sittsamkeit übersetzen lässt. Allerdings gelte dies nicht nur dem weiblichen Geschlecht: Jonas verlangt von jüdischen Frauen und Männern strengste Einhaltung des "Prinzips der Heiligkeit" (293).

Herausgeberin wie Verlag gebühren Dank für die äusserst informative, sauber dokumentierte und kenntnisreich kommentierte Edition. Abgesehen von wenigen Druckfehlern, typographischen Ungereimtheiten und dem eher ungünstigen Kleinformat ein schönes, wichtiges und empfehlenswertes Buch.

*Bettina Kratz-Ritter (Göttingen / Deutschland)*

Relinde Meiwes, *"Arbeiterinnen des Herrn". Katholische Frauenkongregationen im 19. Jahrhundert*, Campus-Verlag: Frankfurt – New York 2000, 341 Seiten, ISBN 3-593-36460-3

Wie Pilze schossen im 19. Jahrhundert in der römisch-katholischen Kirche neue Frauenkongregationen aus dem Boden, mit deren Wachstum weder die kontemplativen Frauenorden noch die Männerorden Schritt halten konnten. Die Autorin möchte den gängigen Begriff "Ordensfrühling" vermeiden, da er die Initiative zur Gründung von Kongregationen durch Frauen und ihre Arbeit verschleiert. Untersucht wird die Frage, wie es zu diesem "Frauenkongregationsfrühling" kam und was diese traditionelle Form religiöser Vergemeinschaftung für Frauen so attraktiv machte. Dazu stellt die aus der Bielefelder Schule stammende Historikerin im ersten Teil die Entwicklung der 23 Kongregationen dar, die in Preußen zwischen 1803 und 1872/73 – die meisten davon im Zeitraum von 1840 bis 1860 – neu gegründet wurden. In sechzehn Fällen ging die Initiative zur Gründung von Frauen aus. Die zumeist aus bürgerlichen Verhältnissen stammenden Frauen konnten so ihre Vorstellungen religiösen Frauenlebens in die Tat umsetzen und brachten dabei eigene materielle Ressourcen ein. Exemplarisch beschreibt Relinde Meiwes den Prozeß der Gründung der "Schwestern vom armen Kinde Jesu" in Aachen.

Im zweiten Teil beschreibt sie das Innenleben der Kongregationen: die Aufnahmebedingungen, die Lebensführung und die Arbeitsfelder der Kongregationen. Es zeigt sich, daß diese Lebens- und Arbeitsgemeinschaften zwar grundsätzlich von der Gleichheit aller Angehörigen ausgingen, der klösterliche Alltag jedoch gleichzeitig von einem "feinstrukturierte[n] System von Ungleichheit und Hierarchie" (144) bestimmt war. Da die Kongregationen jedoch gesellschaftliche Unterschiede nicht einfach reproduzierten, boten sie auch Frauen aus nicht-bürgerlichen Schichten ungekannte Aufstiegschancen in leitende Positionen.

Die Frauenkongregationen haben für die Entwicklung der Krankenpflege und für die Herausbildung von Frauenberufen wegweisende Arbeit geleistet (181). Die Kongregation bot Frauen Handlungsräume, die sie in der bürgerlichen Gesellschaft nicht gehabt hätten: Schwestern betätigten sich als Krankenschwestern und Lehrerinnen, aber auch als Bauleiterinnen, Verwalterinnen, Buchhalterinnen, Künstlerinnen, ohne als Frauen in einem "Männerberuf" schief angeschaut zu werden. R. Meiwes zufolge war es die Symbiose von religiösen und weltlichen Elementen, von (Berufs-)Handeln und Kontemplation im genossenschaftlichen Frauenleben, die die Anziehungskraft der Kongregationen für Frauen ausmachte.

Im dritten Teil analysiert die Autorin die Beziehungen der Frauenkongregationen zur bürgerlichen Gesellschaft. Ohne die Umbrüche des 19. Jahrhunderts hätte es keinen Frauenkongregationsfrühling gegeben. Frauen haben sich aktiv an der "Vitalisierung der Religiosität" (W. Schieder) beteiligt, die ihren Ausdruck im Ultramontanismus fand. Sie empfanden sich als "fromme Mitstreiterinnen der streitenden Kirche", wie eine Regel formuliert (247). Die Frauenkongregationen sind nicht als Randerscheinung bei der Bildung des katholischen Milieus zu behandeln, wie eine Forschung ohne Einbeziehung der Kategorie Geschlecht annehmen konnte. Gegen Positionen, die vor allem Kleriker als "Milieumanager" und als Repräsentanten der (römisch-)katholischen Kirche ansehen, kommt R. Meiwes zu dem Schluß, daß "Schwestern bald zu den respektiertesten Vertreterinnen der katholischen Kirche avancierten" (217). Nüchtern widerlegt R. Meiwes hier und da auch heute noch vorfindliche kirchliche Kulturkampfrhetorik, indem sie zeigt, daß der Kulturkampf und seine Gesetzgebung für die Frauenkongregationen nicht eine vollständige, sondern eine selektive Beeinträchtigung ihrer Tätigkeitsfelder zur Folge hatte; während ihnen vom Staat der Elementarschulunterricht aus den Händen genommen wurde, geschah im Bereich der Armen- und Krankenpflege hingegen eine beträchtliche Ausweitung ihres Tätigkeitsbereichs.

R. Meiwes wertet Frauenkongregationen als "Übergangsphänomen auf dem Weg katholischer Frauen vom Ancien régime in die Moderne" (314), deren Attraktivität in der zweiten Hälfte des 20. Jahrhunderts infolge verschiedener gesellschaftlicher Entwicklungen abnahm. Das empfehlenswerte und gut lesbare Buch füllt eine Forschungslücke im Hinblick auf Frauenkongregationen in Deutschland (Preußen) und bietet Vergleichsmaterial zu ähnlichen Veröffentlichungen in anderen Ländern.

*Angela Berlis (Arnhem / Niederlande)*


## II.3 Systematische Theologie, Ökumene und Interreligiöser Dialog

Frans van der Beek, *Het Jezus Mysterie. Kunstenaars en visies over de man die tweeduizend jaar de westerse beschaving een gezicht gaf*, De Bookmakers: Diemen (The Netherlands) 1999, 98 pages, ISBN 90-804045-4-3, NLG 39,50 (full-colour).

Art and Christian religion mostly relate to each other as art and kitsch. Taken as a whole, this criticism cannot be levelled at this catalogue, even though some artists have (deliberately) visualised Christianity as kitsch, in the sense of shining but empty. Some works of art in this catalogue do indeed belong to this category.

Fifty artists were invited to visualise their vision of Jesus, and to exhibit their works in a (Roman Catholic) church in The Hague. This is the catalogue of that exhibition; it contains fifty-two full colour images, including some really wonderful pieces of art, well worth looking at and enjoying. Almost half of the works were created by women artists, which makes the catalogue a small treasury for feminist theologians. And we may be thankful that it exists, for otherwise we would probably never have seen two intriguing works of art.

Just before the opening of the exhibition two paintings were excluded from the exhibition as "irreverent". It is surely no coincidence that both subjects were nude women: a female Christ (Jenny Collot d'Escury: Het Lichaam / The Body) and a seductive nun (Raymond Lobato: Sweet Jesus!). The inclusion of a nude male Christ was, on the other hand, no problem at all, although he is shown being flagellated and pictured with his naked bottom (Maurice Heerdink: The Flagellation). Whenever nudity, women and Christianity come together, blasphemy and sin seem to be in the mind of churchmen.

The artists offer a postmodern mixture of visions on Christianity and Christ. Some simply reproduce well-known themes: the crucifixion, the pieta, and the last supper. Adding a slight touch of personal interpretation, they stay within the tradition. Others de- and reconstruct Christianity and Christ. Christ seems to be a particularly inspiring figure when it comes to the question of suffering. In spite of, or perhaps thanks to, the high degree of secularisation in the Netherlands, artists frequently visualise the question of human suffering in connection with the suffering Jesus had to endure. Another striking topic is the focus on the world's being destroyed by war and or by an over-consuming society. But what amazed me was the lack of conceptualisation of redemption and resurrection. It seems that there is not much hope left, unless it can be found in the refusal of one soldier to fight in a war (Suzette Born: Stranger in Hell).

Human suffering is seen in the face of Jesus, but except for the one (excluded) painting by Jenny Collot d'Escury, this is the face of a man. To understand Jesus as a woman is clearly not the done thing. Jesus may be represented as an ordinary guy, the boy next-door, but he has always an aesthetically correct body and face. Jesus is thus presented not only as the ideal lover for women but also for men, as the (hu)man par excellence.

That the text of the catalogue is written in Dutch does not really matter, since the articles do not offer an inspiring view of Christ; nor (which is worse) do they comment on the exhibition. In spite (or perhaps because) of this, the catalogue is something of a revelation in comparison to books on art and religion that mostly write about art instead of letting art speak for itself. The art in this catalogue has the power to speak about the Christian message and its contemporary interpretation to anyone who wants to listen.

*Sylvia Grevel (Arnhem / The Netherlands)*

Ann-Cathrin Jarl, *Women and Economic Justice: Ethics in Feminist Liberation Theology and Feminist Economics*, (Uppsala Studies in Social Ethics 25), (= Diss. 2000), Uppsala University Press: Uppsala 2000, ISBN 91-554-4759-7, 212 pages

Die Feministische Ökonomie hat in den Neunziger Jahren einen bedeutenden Aufschwung erlebt. In zahlreichen Publikationen haben Feministinnen und Gendertheoretikerinnen die Denkmodelle, Methoden und Fokussierungen der marxistischen, der instuitutionellen und insbesondere der heute dominanten neoklassischen Denkschulen kritisiert und alternative Möglichkeiten etabliert, das Ökonomische zu denken. Dadurch hat sich das Verständnis der ökonomischen Wissenschaft schon heute signifikant verändert: Eine auf geldvermittelte Tauschakte und idealtypische Märkte eingeschränkte mechanistische bzw. mathematisierte Sichtweise weicht einer Ökonomie, die sich als empirische Kulturtheorie versteht, in der – u.a. durch die Aufhebung der unsachgemässen Trennung zwischen Geldmarkt und Haushalt – die Komplexität menschlichen Produzierens, Tauschens und Verbrauchens sichtbar wird und die die genuin ökonomische Frage nach der Erfüllung grundlegender Bedürfnisse für alle wieder in den Mittelpunkt des Interesses rückt.

Die schwedische Theologin Ann-Cathrin Jarl leistet mit ihrer Dissertation zu dieser lebhaften Debatte einen Beitrag, indem sie feministische Befreiungstheologie, Ethik und Ökonomie in ein Gespräch bringt. Anhand von sechs ausgewählten, aus dem angelsächsischen Sprachraum und Indien stammenden Entwürfen stellt sie die Frage, wie ethische Kategorien – Gerechtigkeit, Gleichheit, Macht, Erfüllung von Grundbedürfnissen u.a. – die femi-nistische Ökonomie(kritik) leiten bzw. präzisieren (könnten). Ihr Ausgangspunkt ist dabei die Betroffenheit über die existenzielle Not eines grossen Teils der Weltbevölkerung, der, allen wissenschaftlich-ökonomischen Heilsversprechen zum Trotz, das Lebensnotwendige entbehrt. Ihr Ziel ist eine ethisch fundierte ökonomische Theorie, die Fragen der Gerechtigkeit und des guten Lebens für alle nicht an die Politik oder die Moral der einzelnen delegiert, sondern zu ihrer eigenen Aufgabe macht.

In einem ersten Teil untersucht Jarl, nach einer allgemeinen Einführung in die feministische Kritik der Neoklassik, die ethischen Grundlagen, die in den Untersuchungen von Julie Nelson, Nancy Folbre, Bina Agarval und Gita Sen expliziert bzw. impliziert sind – mit dem Ergebnis, dass zwar alle von ethischen Positionen ihren Ausgang nehmen, diese aber im allgemeinen unbefragt als gültig voraussetzen, statt sie zu begründen und zu explizieren.

Der zweite Teil fragt konsequenterweise nach den Begründungsgängen für die von den Ökonominnen fraglos vorausgesetzen normativen Grundlagen, wie sie von den befreiungstheologisch inspirierten Ethikerinnen Beverly Wildung Harrison und Karen Lebacqz geleistet werden. Dabei erweist sich die Gerechtigkeit als tragendes Prinzip, das von der Gottesebenbildlichkeit der Menschen hergeleitet wird und sich an der jesuanischen Zuwendung zu den Ausgestossenen misst. Was Gerechtigkeit konkret bedeutet, lässt sich nach Harrison und Lebacqz nicht berechnen oder mittels exakter Methoden entscheiden. Gerechtigkeit zu verstehen, setzt vielmehr voraus, dass ich – nach jesuanischem Vorbild – den Geschichten Gehör schenke, in denen die Entrechteten ihren Unrechtserfahrungen Ausdruck geben.

Auch Ann-Cathrin Jarl gelingt es nicht, das bisher unerreichte Kunststück einer argumentativ schlüssigen Vermittlung zwischen dem androzentrischen

Ideal einer "wertfreien" ökonomischen Theorie und den ethisch oder kulturell orientierten Denkansätzen zu vollbringen. Am Ende plädiert sie für eine erneuerte ökonomische Theorie, deren organisierende Mitte die Frage nach der Erfüllung grundlegender Bedürfnisse nach Nahrung, Kleidung, Bildung und Gesundheitsvorsorge bildet – ein Modell, dem frau nur wünschen kann, dass es die Herzen auch der Hardliner von Davos erreichen möge.

*Ina Praetorius (Krinau / Schweiz)*

Serene Jones, *Feminist Theory and Christian Theology: Cartographies of Grace*, (Guides to Theological Inquiry), Fortress Press: Minneapolis (USA) 2000, 214 pages, ISBN 0-8006-2694-X, US $ 17.00

This book fittingly appears in the series "Guides to Theological Inquiry" which has been at the forefront of bringing new intellectual disciplines to bear on theological reflection. The author, who teaches theology at Yale Divinity School, makes room for a sustained conversation between feminist theory and theology, or, more specifically, constructive systematic theology in the Reformation tradition. As an aid to understanding the relationship between feminist theory and theology, Jones uses the image of cartography: she sees herself as "mapping," that is, as laying feminist theory over the terrain of Christian doctrine. Feminist theory thus reorients the conceptual markers of Christian theology. The structure of the book follows this image. In the six main chapters, the author "remaps" by pairing three feminist theoretical concepts with three theological themes: feminist debates about "women's nature" with the doctrines of justification and sanctification, feminist theorizing about women's oppressions with the doctrine of sin, and feminist notions of community with the doctrine of the church. Interwoven in Jones's text are her own experiences, and those of other women, especially women in her local church. This narrative quality makes the book particularly appealing and engaging to read. Such a way of writing is also paradigmatic of a theology that values daily life, particularly that of women, and finds ways to foreground its revelatory potential.

After an introductory chapter, chapter 2 sketches feminist theories of "women's nature," focusing on the essentialist, constructivist, and strategic essentialist sides of the debate. In chapter 3, Jones takes the insights of feminist debates about "women's nature" as a map, and lays them over the landscape of the theological doctrines of justification and sanctification. Jones appropriates the strategic essentialist position (in a move she terms "eschatological essentialism") to develop the contours of a feminist theological anthropology. Chapter 4 sketches feminist theorizing about women's oppression; chapter 5 uses these theories of women's oppression to remap a conventional account of sin, more particularly, of Calvin's doctrine of sin. Jones' feminist remapping of sin shifts both feminist theorizing – to where women's oppressions can be named "sin", and women's flourishing seen as God-sustained – and traditional doctrine- to where women can inhabit its landscape more meaningfully . Chapter 6 describes feminist theorizing of community (with a focus on political philosophy). Chapter 7 sketches a feminist ecclesiology, in conversation with feminist theory and Reformation images of the church.

Kathryn Tanner, one of the editors of "Guides to Theological Inquiry," has recently challenged feminist theologians to "remain traditional", that is, not to abdicate "tradition" as a site of struggle for meaning today. Jones' book is one way of rising to this challenge. The fact that questions linger speaks to the difficulty of the task Jones envisions: can feminist theory be laid over the terrain of Christian doctrine in the way she suggests? Or are there insurmountable inconsistencies between these two maps? And which one is privileged at any given point, and why? Jones' book is not least a wonderful invitation to continue probing these questions.

*Teresa Berger (Durham, NC / USA)*


Rosine A. Lambin, *Le voile des femmes. Un inventaire historique, social et psychologique*, (Studia Religiosa Helvetica), P.Lang: Bern 1999, 270 S., ISBN 3-906762-87-4, DM 63,00 / BEF 1250

L'auteure de cet essai propose des thèses claires et tranchées au sujet du voile féminin. Primo, ce voile est un héritage païen, et en soi n'a donc rien de juif, chrétien ou musulman. Secundo, le port du voile féminin version "intégriste», appelé foulard islamique, doit être proscrit dans les espaces communs des états démocratiques, en particulier à l'école publique.

Bien entendu, cette double thèse est étoffée de développements et précédée d'une recherche minutieuse. Rosine Lambin a en effet rassemblé les fruits d'une longue enquête portant notamment sur l'assimilation du voile et des rites liés à celui-ci dans le christianisme primitif. "Les liens, à ce sujet, entre les usages de la religion romaine et la volonté du christianisme de se forger une bonne réputation morale auprès des païens, sont clairs et incroyablement forts.» (43). Le judaïsme mérite une attention toute particulière: en des lieux et à des moments précis de son histoire, il accepte la coutume de la chevelure recouverte, mais il ne justifie pas cela de manière théologique: "Le seul voile lié à la foi en Israël n'est pas celui des femmes mais celui de Dieu» (62). La christianisation du voile fait l'objet d'un chapitre d'histoire et d'anthropologie sociale regorgeant de détails insolites et fort bien documentés. La troisième partie de ce livre, "Signification profonde du voile des femmes» est sans doute la plus risquée, puisque l'auteure fait siennes des interprétations symboliques issues de la psychanalyse. Cette partie – même si on salue le courage intellectuel qu'elle manifeste – est finalement la moins convaincante. Ainsi, il est loin d'être évident, comme l'affirme Rosine Lambin, que "La chevelure fait partie des représentations symboliques du pubis» (220); or ce serait le principal ressort de l'ambiguïté perverse du voile qui souligne ce qu'il prétend cacher.

La conclusion est un plaidoyer pour une attitude ferme de la part des autorités politiques en Occident pour préserver la neutralité de l'*agora*. Si on ne peut contester le droit de l'auteure d'avoir des avis aussi nets, on pourrait en revanche lui tenir grief de n'avoir pas laissé s'exprimer des opinions (y compris de femmes musulmanes) favorables au foulard islamique; en effet, même si on adhère à l'analyse de Rosine Lambin, on a le sentiment de ne pas recevoir les informations qui permettraient, pour le moins, de comprendre de l'intérieur ce phénomène remarquable, le retour en force d'un attribut religieux porté avec défi.

Il est regrettable que l'ouvrage n'ait pas été relu et corrigé scrupuleusement: quelques fautes de grammaire et barbarismes (p. 244 "réluctantes») le défigurent inutilement.

Ces réserves ne doivent pas faire oublier le mérite de ce livre passionnant, état de la question et réflexion engagée sur le voile des femmes.

*Anne Marie Reijnen (Bruxelles / Belgique)*

Cettina Militello, *Maria con occhi di donna*, Edizioni Piemme: Casale Monferrato 1999, 318 Seiten, ISBN 88-384-4313-0, LIT 28.000

Cettina Militello, *Nostra Donna coronata di dodici stelle*, (= Con Maria verso il duemila 3), Edizioni Monfortane: Roma 1999, 143 Seiten, ISBN 88-87103-15-1, LIT 23.000

In ihrem Buch *Maria con occhi di donna* (Maria aus weiblicher Sicht) entwirft Cettina Militello eine Mariologie im Kontext der feministischen Theologie italienischer Prägung, der "Teologia al femminile" – ein Begriff, den sie selbst in den achtziger Jahren eingeführt und fortgeschrieben hat. Der bislang männlich bestimmten, Frauen ausschließenden Theologie wird eine "weiblich deklinierte Theologie" gegenübergestellt, die auf Gegenseitigkeit und Reziprozität gründet und damit eine inklusive und zweistimmige Theologie ("Teologia a due voci") sein will (*Maria* 15). Ganz auf dieser Linie entfaltet Militello in zehn Kapiteln ihre "Mariologia al femminile". Sie ordnet diese zunächst in den Kontext der feministischen Debatte ein und zeigt ihre Entwicklung für den Zeitraum vom Zweiten Vatikanum bis in die neunziger Jahre hinein auf. Ausgehend vom anthropologischen Konzept der Gegenseitigkeit ist für Militello gerade Maria Prototyp und Modell eines reziproken Handelns in der Kirche. Kirche soll ein Ort sein, an dem Frauen und Männer als Subjekte in gegenseitiger Anerkennung ihren Platz finden können. Ein schwieriger Themenkreis in der weiblichen Reflexion ist die Suche nach einem Verständnis von Jungfräulichkeit, zu dem auch heutige Frauen Zugang finden können. Ohne fertige Lösungen anzubieten, legt Militello die verschiedenen Positionen dar, wobei sie manche männlichen Theologien kritisiert, die mit ihren zum Teil biologistischen Ansätzen erst recht die Integrität der Frau und somit die der *Maria Vergine* verletzen. Das Ideal der Jungfrau und Mutter muss nicht notwendigerweise als ein unvereinbarer Anspruch verstanden werden, wenn darin ein Ausdruck von Autonomie und Beziehungsfähigkeit, von Stärke und Zärtlichkeit zugleich und von der Kooperation von Gottes Macht und menschlichem Handeln gesehen wird (*Maria* 101). Auch wenn Militello unterschiedliche Themenkreise berührt, verfolgt sie vor allem ihr Anliegen, eine Mariologie unter anthropologischer und ekklesiologischer Perspektive zu entwickeln, die aber auch auf Spiritualität und auf die *via pulchritudinis* Wert legt. "Eine von Frauen entwickelte Mariologie wird in diesen Bereichen eigene Akzente setzen. Frauen werden ihr (Selbst-)Verständnis und ihre Auffassung von Weiblichkeit, von Maria, von Kirche, von Schönheit als theologischer Kategorie, und von Spiritualität als Kategorie der theologischen Erfahrung einbringen" (*Maria* 31), und daraus Konsequenzen für die Kirche ziehen: "Maria der Kirche und Maria den Frauen zurückzugeben, bedeutet im eigentlichen Sinn, sich die Kirche wieder in der Ganzheit ihres gemeinschaftlichen Mysteriums aneignen zu können" (*Maria* 32; eigene Übersetzung).

Ein weiterer Gedanke, den Militello auch in ihrem mehr meditativ gestalteten Buch *Nostra Donna coronata di dodici stelle* (Unsere Frau, mit zwölf Sternen gekrönt) aufgreift, ist die bereits in der Patristik belegte Vorstellung, dass Maria das Wort zunächst im Geist und erst danach im Schoß empfangen habe. Damit sind für Militello Wort und weiblicher Leib unzertrennlich verbunden. Dies bedeutet für Frauen eine Aufforderung, sich wieder des Wortes zu bemächtigen: "Frauen sind aufs engste mit dem Geheimnis des göttlichen Wortes ver-

bunden. Auch sie müssen davon zehren können, es empfangen und in sich
wachsen lassen, um es immer wieder neu auf und in die Welt zu bringen"
(*Nostra Donna* 45; eigene Übersetzung). Für Militello ist die Bedingung für
eine vollkommene Jüngerschaft, dass Frauen und Männer zusammen, und nicht
die einen ohne die anderen, die göttliche Botschaft in die Welt bringen. Damit
entwirft Militello ihre Vision einer partnerschaftlichen Kirche. Hiesse dies dann
aber nicht, dass Maria als Modell und Prototyp der Kirche auch entsprechend
durch Frauen in allen kirchlichen Bereichen repräsentiert werden müsste?

*Valeria Ferrari Schiefer (Bobingen / Deutschland)*

Anne Marie Reijnen, *L'Ange obstiné. Ténacité de L'imaginaire spirituel*,
Labor et Fides: Genève 2000, 126 pages, ISBN 2-8309-0932-1

Dès le début du livre, *L'Ange obstiné* d'Anne Marie Reijnen, on découvre que
le véritable acteur de l'essai est l'imaginaire symbolique. Quant à l'ange, il
est plutôt la figure de proue permettant à l'auteur de conduire son argumentation: la réhabilitation de la thématique angélique pourrait rendre à tout discours formel, surtout théologique, la sève indispensable à son accueil. Or,
parce que l'ange est un signifiant privilégié des aspirations religieuses univer-
selles, il est important que lui soit reconnu de nouveau le rôle qui est proprement le sien, à savoir de médiatiser la distance entre la raison et l'imaginaire.

Grâce à son double caractère sémantique humano-divin, l'ange se donne
comme signe, d'une part, de la rupture moderne entre le rationnel et le symbolique, et d'autre part, de leur nécessaire réconciliation. Il renvoie au besoin
d'insuffler une vitalité nouvelle aux vérités chrétiennes trop appauvries par un
rationalisme minimaliste, par une épuration dommageable de tout ce qui rele-
vait du symbolisme ou de l'étonnement mystique. En effet, le refus obstiné de
l'ange de disparaître de l'imaginaire populaire et de la piété religieuse est un
argument puissant pour le remettre en valeur. Le merveilleux, interdit de
séjour par la théologie contemporaine à la suite des Lumières, revient en force
là où on l'attendait le moins: dans les médias. Or, contre toute attente, c'est
l'ange qui exprime le mieux pour la culture séculière sa perception du merveilleux. La théologie peut-elle rester indifférente devant un phénomène qui
touche de si près ses propres traditions scripturaires et historiques?

Cette question, omniprésente dans le livre d'Anne Marie Reijnen, déter-
mine largement sa plaidoirie en faveur de la figure angélique pour réduire les
excès du rationalisme actuel dans le christianisme. La première partie du livre

est largement consacrée à la place que l'ange occupe depuis toujours dans la littérature sacrée et profane de l'humanité, plus particulièrement dans celle héritée des traditions monothéistes. De nombreux exemples précisent bien l'importance de l'ange dans la Bible, dans les arts plastiques et dans les usages populaires. En cela, l'"ange déchu" n'est pas oublié, même si l'auteure pense que son importance réside surtout dans sa capacité sémantique de signifier la condition ambivalente de l'humanité: depuis toujours, elle est tiraillée entre son élan vers Dieu et son désir d'affranchissement de ce même Dieu perçu comme obstacle à son propre progrès.

La deuxième partie du livre fait appel au regard critique du lecteur lui demandant d'éviter un jugement trop hâtif. Qu'il réfléchisse surtout sur l'une des causes profondes de la mise à l'écart de l'ange de la théologie, à savoir une certaine méfiance du protestantisme vis-à-vis du surnaturel. Cependant, sur le rôle de l'ange dans ce processus, il faudrait apporter des nuances car il n'a pas entièrement perdu sa place honorable dans les écrits des réformateurs comme Luther et Calvin.

L'attention du lecteur sera surtout attirée par la beauté des dernières pages où est orchestré le point culminant du livre: signe de la gratuité du cosmos, l'ange rappelle aussi la gratuité de la foi: que le croyant "convertisse son regard" quant à sa véritable place au sein de l'univers. Ainsi "l'attente de l'inespéré" à laquelle la gratuité de l'ange le renvoie, rejoindra-t-elle l'attente de la création tout entière.

La démonstration du livre est convaincante. Elle est clairement annoncée et largement justifiée. Il est légitime de penser que les lecteurs et les lectrices de ce beau livre ne s'obstineront pas dans leur hésitation à y adhérer.

*Donna Singles (Lyon / France)*


Rosemary Radford Ruether, *Women and Redemption. A Theological History*, SCM Press: London 1998, 366 pages, ISBN 0 334 02734 9

In this book, Rosemary Radford Ruether presents her attempt to "trace historically the changing paradigms of gender, male and female, in relation to the Christian claim of a universal and inclusive redemption in Christ" (1). She follows the theme of redemption through history, beginning with questions of gender and redemption in the New Testament and ending with three chapters on today's feminist theological thinking in Western Europe, Northern America, and Latin America, Africa and Asia. On this journey through history Ruether highlights the work and thinking of important female theologians and mystics, discusses competing theological paradigms of subordination and equality throughout the centuries, and presents the work of many contemporary theologians from all over the world.

As a reference work this book may be useful, offering a quick look at the thinking of certain theologians or particular periods. Nevertheless Ruether's book may also be misleading. Because it claims to offer an overview of theological thinking on redemption throughout history, and because it refers to the names of a good many theologians, it also renders some important contemporary thinking invisible. The overview of the European situation, given in one of the last three main chapters, is rather oddly structured and very limited. Is this an indication of language restraints? I was strangely surprised to find only one brief reference to Elizabeth Schüssler Fiorenza, placing her in the field of Biblical Studies and as such made irrelevant for the subject at issue.

Ruether's definition of the term "redemption" sometimes takes it in a broad sense while in other cases it functions only as an gateway to a presentation of a theologian's thought. Some of these presentations are somewhat superficial and the description of the theology of several women is not very adequate. But these problems may reflect the (over?-)ambitious character of this book. Most probably it is simply no longer possible to give a thorough overview of what is going on in the field of theological thinking on redemption in just one book.

*Lieve Troch (Breda / The Netherlands)*

Christa Schnabl, *Das Moralische im Politischen. Hannah Arendts Theorie des Handelns im Horizont der theologischen Ethik*, (Interdisziplinäre Ethik 23), P.Lang: Frankfurt – Berlin 1999, 399 Seiten, ISBN 3-631-34066-4, DM 98,00

Die katholische Theologin Christa Schnabl legt mit ihrer Dissertation (Universität Wien) eine Abhandlung vor, die in hervorragender Weise aufmerksam macht auf die Dimension des Moralischen im politischen Handeln – eine Dimension beziehungsweise ein Problem, das unbestreitbar aktuell ist. Gehört die Moral in den Bereich der Politik oder nicht? Die Verfasserin findet Orientierung bei Hannah Arendt, die selbst moralkritisch denkt, sich deshalb ausschließlich der Politik zuwendet. Die Ethik liegt für Arendt ganz im Bereich des Politischen. Sie lehnt eine moralische Fundierung des Politischen ab, denn das Moralische ist immer selbstbezüglich. Schnabl führt diese Position Arendts kritisch weiter.

Die fundierte Darstellung der politischen Theorie Hannah Arendts, insbesondere deren anthropologische Grundlagen, nimmt Bezug auf Arendts Gesamtwerk. Insofern erfüllt die Dissertation auch die Funktion einer guten Einführung in das Werk und das Denken der Philosophin. Der Zugang zu Hannah Arendt ist zudem – zumindest in den ersten Kapiteln – biographisch orientiert und dadurch narrativ-anschaulich. Die Verfasserin verknüpft die Theorie Arendts mit dem derzeitigen ethischen Diskurs. Zunächst geht es ihr darum, die Politische Theorie der Philosophin als eine Theorie des Handelns darzustellen und ihr Denken zuerst von seinen eigenen Voraussetzungen her zu verstehen, bevor dann später die Handlungstheorie in ein Gespräch mit der theologischen Ethik gebracht wird. Christa Schnabl versteht die Theorie des Handelns von Hannah Arendt, wiewohl sie deren "quasi-religiöse" Überhöhung kritisiert, als eine Herausforderung für die theologische Ethik, insbesondere der katholischen Moraltheologie und Sozialethik, die sich entweder als normenorientiert oder subjektiv-situationsethisch versteht. Arendts Theorie des Handelns kann eine Brückenfunktion ausüben.

Die politische Theorie ist eine personal und anthropologisch ausgerichtete Theorie des Handelns: "Das Politische konstituiert sich durch ein auf der Anerkennung von Personalität und Pluralität basierendem Handeln" (327). Der einzelne Mensch erfährt sich selbst als Subjekt und Person erst und nur im gemeinsamen Handeln und miteinander Sprechen. Menschen in ihrer Verschiedenheit handeln gemeinsam miteinander in der Öffentlichkeit. Im gemeinsamen Handeln sind sie 'mächtig'. Die für die Philosophin grundlegende Unterscheidung von Macht und Herrschaft kommt hier zum Zuge. Das Politische ist ausgerichtet auf das Personale. Zum Handeln kommt das reflexive Denken hinzu, zwischen beiden (Handeln und Denken) steht als Bindeglied die Fähigkeit des ethischen Urteilens; Arendt spricht von der Urteilskraft.

Die Konzentration der Ethik Arendts auf das Miteinander von Menschen verlässt die ausschließliche Orientierung am autonomen Subjekt, das für sich selbst oder am anderen Subjekt moralisch handelt. Der/die andere kommt ins Spiel, nicht nur personal-dialogisch im Sinne Martin Bubers, sondern als 'TrägerIn von ethischen Ansprüchen', "als eigenständige Quelle der Moralität" (367). Dieses Alteritätsdenken kann wegführen von der Vorstellung des autonomen moralischen Selbst, das sich aus sich selbst heraus konstituiert. Der Vergleich der Ethik Hannah Arendts mit Emmanuel Lévinas' Denken

(Die Konstitution der moralischen Person vom Anspruch des anderen/der anderen her) ist aufschlussreich. Die Forderung der Autorin nach einer neuen Diskussion über das Autonomieverständnis kann ich nur unterstützen. Schade, dass die Autorin nicht an einem Beispiel vorführt, was die Theorie des Handelns für die ethische Orientierung und in ethischen Konfliktsituationen leisten kann. Darauf kommt es jetzt an.

Ein nicht nur lesenswertes und gut lesbares Buch einer belesenen Autorin, sondern auch ein notwendiges Buch für die philosophische und theologische Ethik – über die Beschäftigung mit Hannah Arendt hinaus!

*Karin Ulrich-Eschemann (Erlangen / Deutschland)*

## II.4 Praktische Theologie, Spiritualität, Liturgiewissenschaft, Religionspädagogik, Homiletik

Teresa Berger, *Women's Ways of Worship. Gender Analysis and Liturgical History*, Pueblo Books: Collegeville 1999, 180 pages, ISBN 0-8146-6173-4, $21.95

The author describes this book as a modest attempt to write a history of women at worship. In the past Berger has shown herself to be concerned to establish women's liturgical studies as a distinct field of research, and she has already contributed a number of elaborate bibliographies, several studies and an anthology on women and worship. However, until now, there has been no study that assembles so much scholarly work on women and worship.

Berger's historical roots are clear in the structure of the book. The first chapter, on methodological principles, is indebted to research on women's history. Modifying and applying these principles to research on women and worship, she chooses two periods as "examples" of women's history in worship. Thus, the second chapter considers women at worship in the early church (from 30 to approximately 500 CE), while the third and fourth chapters discuss women and worship in the twentieth century. The author explains this focus on early Christianity and the twentieth century as being periods which are crucial in the history of women and worship. However, it is surely no coincidence that – so far – these are also the periods upon which most research has focussed.

The chapter on women's worship in the early church provides a treasure-trove of information for anyone who wants a introduction to these topics. It sketches the development from Christian communities in the private space of the household, to a public church based on a strong gender differentiation, considering issues such as the patronage of women, women's ministries, feminine imagery, menstrual taboos, the veneration of Mary, women's religious communities, and sermons on women.

The next chapter deals with the contribution of women to the Liturgical Movement in the Roman Catholic Church in the first half of the twentieth century. This, the third, chapter is based on Berger's own research and is very different from the second. Berger demonstrates how women have been rendered invisible in the "traditional" historiography of the Liturgical Movement, but offers a fascinating reconstruction which makes it clear how many women were in fact writing, studying and teaching at different levels of liturgical research.

The fourth chapter deals with the Women's Liturgical Movement of the second half of the twentieth century. This description is not the first (and certainly will not be the last) but its approach is original. Berger stresses the continuity between women's role in the history of worship (as described in the previous chapters) and the efforts of the new feminist liturgical movement in the second half of the twentieth century. She claims to give a description of women's liturgies world-wide, but unfortunately she does not place the different movements in their own contexts.

Berger succeeds in describing present-day women's activities in worship and the study of worship as part of an ongoing history of women with worship. With this book she has indeed made in important contribution towards the recognition of women's liturgical studies as a distinct discipline.

*Marian Geurtsen (Utrecht / The Netherlands)*


Susan A. Ross, *Extravagant Affections. A Feminist Sacramental Theology*, Continuum: New York 1998, 240 pages, ISBN 0-8264-1083-9, $24.95.


The power of sacraments is the leading theme throughout the seven (!) chapters. Important and characteristic for this work is the emphasis on the ambiguity of that power: although Ross strongly believes in the positive potential of the sacraments and shows what this means for humankind, she never forgets their many negative, repressive effects, especially for women. Both traditional and modern sacramental theology have failed to consider either embodiment or gender. On the other hand, until now feminist theology has not given much attention to the area of sacraments.

This book seeks to explore "the difference that gender makes in relation to the sacraments, and to sacramental and liturgical theology" (p. 23) in the hope that this will help to make sacraments more what they are: gifts of God's "extravagant affections". Ross draws upon a number of insights from feminist theologies and feminist secular theories; she also discusses traditional Roman Catholic and Vatican standpoints and makes use of modern sacramental theology. By combining these discussions and considering arguments on different levels, she is able to take seriously the complexity of the theme, to analyse deeply rooted presuppositions and to make visible blind spots within traditional, modern, and feminist theology.

In the first part Ross sets out her approach to and presuppositions about sacramental theology and proposes many important and refreshing questions. She begins with an number of examples which make clear the need for a feminist perspective, bringing together feminist and sacramental theology to form her starting point: "sacramentality". The relation between women, the sacraments and ambiguity is worked out thoroughly in a separate chapter. The ambiguities surrounding both sacramentality and women's relation to the sacraments can offer critical and transformative resources for sacramental theology. It is, therefore, necessary to say more than that ambiguity is a part of life, and Ross distinguishes between metaphysical, expressive and moral ambiguity.

In the second part, the accent is on family as "the embodied context for sacramentality." Both the possibilities and the difficulties of this theme are discussed. The understanding of human embodiment in sacramental theology (Vatican and modern theologies) is compared with the role of the body in (especially) feminist (including womanist and mujerista) theologies. Psychoanalytic and feminist psycholinguistic theories throw a different light upon women and sacraments. Ethics forms a third, and for Ross central, focus for the issue. The book ends with a consideration of worship in parish structures and in women's groups in the light of the theories she has considered.

*Extravagant Affections* broaches many subjects (from ordination to care and from dualism to language), and will stimulate further constructive and critical thinking. It offers a committed and reflected contribution to this interesting and central, but very complex and broad, issue. There is much work still to be done but a good start has (finally) been made.

*Marianne Merkx (Drunen / The Netherlands)*

Sozialwissenschaftliche Forschung & Praxis für Frauen e.V. (Hg.), *Lesbenleben quer gelesen*, (beiträge zur feministischen theorie und praxis 52), Verlag des Vereins Beiträge zur feministischen Theorie und Praxis e.v.: Köln 1999, 152 Seiten, ISSN 0722-0189, DM 23,00

Theologisch-feministischen Beiträgen mangelt es meiner Ansicht nach noch immer an einem sozialwissenschaftlichen Dialog. Dieser hilft jedoch beim Focussieren abgehobener Diskurse auf "irdische" Probleme, und er nötigt zu neuer Klärung oder auch Korrektur. Insofern empfiehlt es sich, die Reihe "beiträge zur feministischen theorie und praxis" zur Kenntnis zu nehmen. Der Band "Lesbenleben quer gelesen" wird besonders interessant sein für Theologinnen, die in die Queer-Diskussion einsteigen wollen. Bei der Queer-Theory handelt es sich um vielfältige politische und theoretische Ansätze zu einer grundlegenden Neubestimmung von Geschlecht und Sexualität. Dabei sollen problematisch gewordene Identitätspolitiken (zwischen Körper, sozialem Geschlecht und sexueller Identität), wie sie auch in der Frauen- und Lesbenbewegung vertreten wurden, u.a. durch Dekonstruktion überwunden werden. Zudem bearbeitet der Band einen "blinden Fleck im Feminismus" (*Lising Pagenstecher*), der auch insofern für den theologischen Feminismus gilt, als auch hier weitgehend die heterosexuelle Perspektive auf Frauenanliegen universalisiert wird. Diesen blinden Fleck weiter bestehen zu lassen, würde jedoch einen Erkenntnisverlust bedeuten: denn Lesben thematisieren als doppelt marginalisierte Frauen noch klarer gesellschaftliche Grenzlinien des "Weiblichen" als heterosexuelle Frauen.

*Stefanie Soine* führt in ihrem Artikel "Queer als Herausforderung" (9-26) relativ verständlich in Judith Butlers Theorie ein und konzentriert sich dabei auf deren Heterosexismus-Kritik – diese kam in der bundesdeutschen Butler-Rezeption kaum zur Geltung. Ferner arbeitet sie Probleme in der Butler-Rezeption durch die queer-Bewegung heraus. Butlers radikale Kritik am Essentialismus von Geschlecht, Sexualität und Begehren (ihre Deontologisierung) wird in der queeren Praxis aufgenommen als Lob der Uneindeutigkeit und Parodieren von Geschlechtsidentitäten, ferner als Idealisierung "polymorph-perverser Sexualität" (es wird egal, "wer wen auf welcher Grundlage warum und wie liebt", 17). Soine verweist aus sozialwissenschaftlicher Sicht auf die Grenzen dieser "revolutionären Praktiken": Das Konzept ästhetischer Subversion geht von einem omnipotenten, autonomen Handlungsakteur aus, ohne materielle Einschränkungen durch Status, Klasse oder Geschlecht, Alter, Gesundheit, Bildung, größere soziale Zusammenhänge zu bedenken. Ferner wird kurzschlüssig von der Erkenntnis auf die Veränderbarkeit geschlossen: "Hegemoniale Konstrukte wie Geschlecht und Sexualität sind (...) nicht schon durch das Wissen um die Konstruiertheit aus der Welt zu schaffen und sicherlich auch nicht mit Hilfe parodistischer Geschlechterinszenierungen oder durch sexuell uneindeutiges Verhalten" (23). Selbst entschleierte Konstruktionen sind in Fleisch und Seele übergegangen.

*María del Mar Castro Varela* illustriert abstrakte Theoreme von Butler an bundesrepublikanischer Rechtsprechung asylsuchenden Lesben gegenüber ("Queer the Queer. Queer Theory und politische Praxis am Beispiel Lesben im Exil", 29-40). Für eine queer informierte feministische Seelsorge werden – neben dem bodenständigen Einspruch von Soine – die Beiträge über eher tabuisierte Themen wie Lesben und Armut (73-84) sowie Lesben und Altwerden (61-70) von Interesse sein. Wen eher das kulturelle Symbolsystem der Medien interessiert, die kann sich über präsente Nichtpräsenz von Lesben in Talkshows, Erotikmagazinen und Soaps informieren ("Lesben im Fernsehen", 87-91).

*Sabine Bobert-Stützel (Berlin / Deutschland)*


*Segen – Herberge in unwirtlicher Zeit.* Texte und Schreibwerkstatt von Hanna Strack, Scherenschnitte von Adelheid Strack-Richter, Hanna Strack Verlag: Pinnow 1993 (4. Auflage 1998), 72 Seiten, ISBN 3-929813-01-7, DM/CHF 14,80 / ATS 120

*Segen ist nicht nur ein Wort.* Tänze, Gesten, Meditationen, Rituale, Ikebana, herausgegeben von Hanna Strack und Christiane Freking, Hanna Strack Verlag: Pinnow 1996 (2. Auflage 1996), 64 Seiten, ISBN 3-929813-19-X, DM/CHF 14,80 / ATS 120

*Segen strömt aus der Mitte.* Texte von Hanna Strack, Mandalas von Sigrid Kaußler-Spaeter, Hanna Strack Verlag: Pinnow 1998 (2. Auflage 2000), 104 Seiten, ISBN 3-929813-05-X, DM/SF 16,80 / ATS 140

Bestelladresse: Hanna Strack Verlag, Kuckucksallee 9, 19065 Pinnow / Schwerin, Tel./Fax: 03860/8685, E-Mail: Hanna.Strack@t-online.de, http://home.t-online.de/home/Hanna.Strack/

"Mut machen, eigene Lebenserfahrungen mit Gott zusammenzusehen, besser: Gottes Gegenwart mit ihnen in Verbindung zu bringen" (1993, 9) – so beschreibt die evangelische Pfarrerin und Verlagsleiterin Hanna Strack ihre Motivation, eigene Segensworte zu schreiben und andere Frauen als Mitautorinnen in ihre *"Schreibwerkstatt: Segen"* (67-71) einzuladen. Angeregt durch biblische Segensmotive und -geschichten und angestoßen durch die inzwischen zum Klassiker gewordene Segenstheologie ihres Lehrers Claus Westermann (Der Segen in der Bibel und im Handeln der Kirche, München 1968, 2. Auflage 1992) begegnet Hanna Strack einer kirchlichen Segenspraxis, die den Segen hinter Kirchenmauern verbannt und neben dem Sonntagsgottesdienst auf wenige Amtshandlungen (Sakramente und Kasualien) eingeschränkt hat. Die lebendige Fülle biblischer Segenstraditionen ist dabei ebenso verkümmert wie vertraute Erfahrungen des Segnens und Gesegnetwerdens im alltäglichen, vor allem familiären Lebenszusammenhang fremd, ja befremdlich geworden sind. H. Stracks Segenstexte holen den Segen und das Segnen aus dem geschützten und geordneten Binnenraum der Kirche in die bedrohten und zunehmend unüberschaubaren Lebensräume unseres Alltags zurück. Ihre "Schreibwerkstatt: Segen" hat so Anteil an der Wiederentdeckung des Segnens als Gottesdienst im Alltag der Welt. In ihr wird das PriesterInnentum aller Glaubenden praktisch: Segnen ist kein Privileg ordinierter AmtsträgerInnen. Wer sich als gesegnet wahrnimmt, kann selber segnen, wird anderen zum Segen werden.

Der ebenso einladende wie programmatische Titel ihrer ersten Sammlung von Segenstexten *Segen – Herberge in unwirtlicher Zeit* dokumentiert, dass Hanna Strack dem wachsenden Bedürfnis nach jenem guten Wort auf der Spur ist, das die Gegenwart Gottes ermutigend und bestärkend, bergend und schützend, aufrichtend und heilend, wegweisend und zukunftsorientierend zuspricht. Es sind vor allem die Schwellensituationen des Lebens, in denen Menschen der Vergewisserung der freundlichen und erhellenden Nähe Gottes bedürfen. Dass das Segnen Inbegriff der *rites de passage*, das Übergangsritual schlechthin, ist, spricht aus vielen der Segenstexte H. Stracks, die den Segen in konkrete Lebenssituationen einschreiben. Im Überschreiten der Schwelle bieten sie Herberge. So gibt es in diesem ersten Band, dessen Texte gebündelt sind unter den Themen "Segen in Raum und Zeit" (11-31), "Segen für Menschen auf dem Weg" (33-57) und "Ich segne dich!" (59-65), den "Segen über dem Neugeborenen" (37) wie den "Segen über einer alten Frau" (53), den "Segen für einen Führerscheinneuling" (44) wie den "Segen am Ende einer Familientherapie" (51). Die Segenstexte H. Stracks sind geprägt von der Einsicht, dass der Segen Gottes unserem Mangel, den Erfahrungen von Scheitern und Mißlingen abhelfen will. Dem Fehlen von Gesundheit und Glück, von Schönheit und Sinn, von Anerkennung und Liebe... gelten so zum Beispiel der "Segen für eine junge Diabetikerin" (45), der "Segen für Aschenputtel" (46) oder der "Segen für eine Verwirrte" (54).

Ist der Segen die sinnlich wahrnehmbare, die leibhaft spürbare Präsenz Gottes in seiner Schöpfung, dann reichen Worte nicht aus, um Segen zum Ausdruck zu bringen und weiterzugeben. In *Segen – Herberge in unwirtlicher Zeit* illustrieren die Scherenschnitte von Adelheid Strack-Richter die Segenstexte H. Stracks nicht nur. Sie setzen sie so eindrücklich ins Bild, dass sie ihrerseits zum Segen fürs Auge werden. Ein besonders ansprechendes Beispiel dafür ist der "Metamorphose-Segen", der den Wandel von der Raupe über die Puppe zum Schmetterling zu*mut*et (42f.).

*Segen ist nicht nur ein Wort* – der Titel des zweiten Bandes, in dem Segenstänze (11-19) und -gesten (21-30), Segensmeditationen (31-40) und -rituale (41-52) verschiedener Autorinnen gesammelt sind und Segensworte mit den kunstvoll-natürlichen "Ikebana"-Gestecken von Maria Freking korrespondieren (61), unterstreicht, dass "Segen mit dem Leib gespendet und aufgenommen wird" (6). Die leibhafte Erfahrung, gesegnet zu sein und zur Segensträgerin zu werden, macht nicht nur singen; im Segenstanz, dem "Beten mit den Füßen" (8), schafft sich der Segen einen sozialen, kommunikativen Raum, der Menschen zueinander in Bewegung bringt und gegenseitige Bejahung und Anerkennung ermöglicht. Die Segensgesten und -gebärden üben ein in die Bewegung des Segensflusses: in das dankbare und staunende Empfangen der Segensgaben, in das bestärkende Wahrnehmen des eigenen Gesegnetseins, in das solidarische Teilen und Weitergeben des Segens. In den Segensmeditationen vermischen sich sinnliche, sättigende Segenserfahrungen (etwa beim "Segen mit wohlriechendem Öl", 32f., oder beim "Brotsegen", 34-36) mit symbolischen Veranschaulichungen und Deutungen des Segens (so bei der "Segensmeditation mit Schalen", 38f.). Am Beispiel eines "Heilrituals für eine vergewaltigte Frau" (46f.) und "Anregungen für ein Menstruationsritual" (48-50) wird gezeigt, wie liturgisch einfühlsam ausgestaltete Segensworte und -gebärden ihre heilende Kraft entfalten können. Segnen ist mehr als ein Hand-Werk.

Kommen in *Segen ist nicht nur ein Wort* vor allem Segenshandlungen in Frauengruppen in den Blick, die den Segen mit allen Sinnen erfahrbar machen, geht es dort also um die Kommunikation und die Sozialität des Segens, so knüpft der dritte Band, *Segen strömt aus der Mitte* wieder an *Segen – Herberge in unwirtlicher Zeit* an, indem er die Segensbedürftigkeit von Einzelnen (und Paaren) in Schwellensituationen in den Vordergrund rückt. Dem entspricht nicht nur die Gliederung der Texte in "Segen im Laufe des Jahres" (9-27), "Segen im Laufe des Lebens" (29-55), "Segen für innere Zeiten" (57-75), ergänzt um den Abschnitt "Segen zu biblischen Texten" (77-97). Der Eindruck der Individualisierung stellt sich hier vor allem durch die 50 Mandalas von Sigrid Kaußler-Spaeter ein, die als "Bilder der Seele" (unter diese Überschrift stellt die Malerin ihre Betrachtungen zur Bedeutung der Mandalas, 99-102) zum Gang in die eigene Mitte einladen sollen. Es sind die energetischen Dimensionen des Segens, die Texte und Mandalas miteinander verbinden: Während die Segenstexte die dynamische Lebenskraft des Segens aus göttlicher Quelle schöpfen und austeilen, leiten die Mandalas den Segensstrom ins Innere der BetrachterInnen, lassen ihn unter die Haut gehen, damit er von dort wieder nach außen strömt und zu anderen überfließt. Zwar hat H. Strack in ihrer Einleitung "Segen – Quelle der Kraft" (5-7) auf das biblische Motiv, Gott zu segnen, das im Zentrum jüdischer Segenspraxis steht, hingewiesen. Doch findet diese Erinnerung in ihren Texten keine Entsprechung. Es gibt kein Segenswort, das den von Gott empfangenen und untereinander weitergegebenen Segen zu Gott, der Quelle des Segens, zurückbringt.

Mit wenigen Ausnahmen thematisieren die Segenstexte H. Stracks die affirmative Funktion des Segens. So wichtig und not-wendig gerade für viele Frauen die Bejahung und Anerkennung, die Ermutigung und Ermächtigung ist, die der Segen ihnen schenkt – ohne die Berücksichtigung seiner kritischen Funktion kann das Segnen aber zum bloßen Absegnen gerade nicht lebensförderlicher Verhältnisse verkommen. Der Segen bietet nicht nur schützende Herberge und Heimat, sondern kann auch zur Heimsuchung werden. Er ist nicht nur Zuspruch der heilenden Nähe Gottes, er beansprucht auch die Gesegneten; D. Bonhoeffer hat ihn "die Inanspruchnahme des irdischen Lebens für Gott" genannt. Es bleibt zu fragen, ob die eigene Mitte, in die vor allem die dritte Sammlung mit den Mandalas einweisen möchte, nicht nur außerhalb meiner selbst zu finden ist. Ein "So wie du bist, bist du gut" kann ebenso heilvoll wie unbarmherzig sein.

Dass der verpflichtende Charakter des Segens zu kurz kommt, mag mit der fast völligen Ausblendung des Fluchens und mit der starken Betonung der weisheitlichen Traditionen des Segnens zusammenhängen. Die prophetischen Dimensionen und der Zusammenhang von Segen und Tora bleiben dabei unterbestimmt.

Die Segensbücher von Hanna Strack bieten Gebrauchstexte – zunächst in dem Sinne, dass sie geschrieben worden sind, um benutzt zu werden. Sie sollen angenommen und weitergegeben, wiederholt und fortgeschrieben, - gesungen, -getanzt und -gefeiert werden. Die ausdrückliche Aufforderung zum Kopieren (für nicht kommerzielle Zwecke) gilt auch für die Scherenschnitte, die eindrückliche Motive etwa für Segensgrußkarten abgeben, und für die Mandalas, die ausgemalt werden können (dem Band ist ein Malbogen mit vergrößertem Motiv beigefügt). Gebrauchstexte sind die Segensworte H. Stracks aber auch, weil sie aus dem Bedürfnis nach Segen und aus den Erfahrungen von Gesegnetwerden und Segnen unter Frauen erwachsen sind und zu einem je *eigenen* kreativen Nehmen und Geben des Segens anregen wollen. Dem dienen die *Schreibwerkstatt: Segen* im ersten Band, in der H. Strack Wege zur Entstehung ihrer Segenstexte beschreibt, und die vielen Gestaltungshinweise in *Segen ist nicht nur ein Wort.*

Nicht wenige der neueren Segenstexte sind von einer unerträglichen Geschwätzigkeit; sie nutzen sich ab im Gebrauch, werden beliebig und belanglos. Hanna Strack dagegen überzeugt durch die klare thematische Konzentration ihrer Texte, durch deren präzise Zuschreibung auf ein "Datum", durch die Sparsamkeit der Worte, durch die geordnete, oft trinitarisch gegliederte Form und durch die theologische Reflexion, die nicht nur aus ihren instruktiven Einleitungen in allen drei Bänden, sondern auch aus den Segensworten selbst spricht. In diese Gebrauchstexte ist die gegenwärtige wissenschaftliche Erörterung des Segensthemas eingeflossen, ohne dass auf diese ausdrücklich verwiesen würde. Segenstheologie und Segenspraxis werden hier nicht gegeneinander ausgespielt. Der Erfahrungsbezug ersetzt das theologische Nach- und Mitdenken nicht. So verhelfen die Segensbücher Hanna Stracks und ihrer Mitarbeiterinnen zu einem ver*antwort*lichen Segnen. Sie werden gebraucht.

*Magdalene L. Frettlöh (Bochum / Deutschland)*


Julia Strecker, *Der Sehnsucht Sprache geben. Liturgische Texte für den Gottesdienst*, Gütersloher Verlagshaus: Gütersloh 2000, 128 Seiten, ISBN 3579-03194-5, DM 25,80

Carola Moosbach, *Lobet die Eine. Schweige- und Schreigebete*, Mathias-Grünewald-Verlag: Mainz 2000, 117 Seiten, ISBN 3-7867-2244-7, DM 24,80

Beide "Gebetbücher" sprengen das Korsett der traditionellen Gebets- und Gottesdienstsprache, wobei Julia Strecker der Sehnsucht eine Sprache und

Carola Moosbach Angst und Verwundung einen Namen gibt. Beide Bücher bestechen durch die Intensität und Intimität der Sprache, was diese für eine "öffentliche" Verwendung gleichzeitig herausfordernd und irritierend erscheinen läßt. Herausfordernd sind sie da, wo sie aufrütteln, konfrontieren (Strecker, 16, 20, 21; Moosbach 61-62), hinweisen auf die Passion für das Transzendente (Strecker 11, 145; Moosbach 39, 42). Irritierend sind sie dort, wo die Intimität ihrer Erfahrung sich nicht so einfach in öffentliche Räume transportieren läßt (z.B. Moosbach 58, 117 und Strecker 43, 48, 53-54). Die Schweige- und Schreigebete erzählen uns kraftvoll von bitteren Wahrheiten, unaufgebbaren Hoffnungen und der anwesenden Abwesenheit Gottes. Das macht diese Gebete "betenswert" für Gottsuchende und Gläubige. Die liturgischen Gebete (bei Strecker) lösen diese Spannung auf, vielleicht auch als Zugeständnis an ihren gottesdienstlichen Charakter. Daß es sich hier um liturgische Texte handelt, wird oftmals nur an der Überschrift deutlich, Form und Inhalt widersprechen dem Altvertrauten (Strecker, 57, 69-70). Beide Bücher zeugen von der besonderen Gabe, Nähe zum/r LeserIn und Nähe zu Gott durch erlebte Sprache herzustellen, ob es sich nun um Streckers "Liebesgedicht" Du (27-28) oder um Moosbachs "Vatergebete" (56, 71, 73) handelt. Dorothee Sölle hat einmal gesagt, Dichten sei eine Form von Beten. Die Verdichtung des spirituellen Wortes ist den beiden Autorinnen in vollendeter Weise gelungen. Für alle in liturgischen Zusammenhängen Tätige sind diese Bücher eine reichhaltige Fundgrube und für spirituell Suchende klare, persönliche Wegweiser.

*Hedwig Meyer-Wilmes (Nijmegen / Niederlande)*

# EUROPEAN SOCIETY OF WOMEN IN THEOLOGICAL RESEARCH

# EUROPÄISCHE GESELLSCHAFT FÜR THEOLOGISCHE FORSCHUNG VON FRAUEN

# L'ASSOCIATION EUROPÉENNE DES FEMMES POUR LA RECHERCHE THÉOLOGIQUE

**President – Präsidentin – Président:**
*Prof. Dr. Hedwig Meyer-Wilmes,*
*University of Nijmegen, The Netherlands*

**Vice-President – Vize-Präsidentin – Vice-Président:**
*Eleni Kasselouri, Thessaloniki, Greece*

**Secretary – Sekretärin- Secrétaire:**
*Dr. Caroline Vander Stichele,*
*University of Amsterdam, The Netherlands*

**Vice-Secretary – Vize-Sekretärin – Vice-Serétaire:**
*Prof. Dr. Lieve Troch, University of Nijmegen, The Netherlands /*
*São Paulo, Brazil*

**Treasurer – Schatzmeisterin – Trésorière:**
*Regula Strobel, Fribourg, Switzerland*

**Vice-Treasurer – Vize-Schatzmeisterin – Vice-Trésorière**
*Dr. Charlotte Methuen, University of Bochum, Germany*

*Elżbietha Adamiak, Poznan, Poland*

**Contact for Bulletin of the ESWTR:**
*Dr. Caroline Vander Stichele,*
*University of Amsterdam, The Netherlands*

# Yearbook of the European Society of Women in Theological research

1 **Luise Schottroff, Annette Esser**, *Feministische Theologie im europäischen Kontext - Feminist Theology in a European Context - Théologie féministe dans un contexte européen*, 1993, 255 p., ISBN: 90-390-0047-6
810 BEF / 21 EURO

2 **Mary Grey, Elisabeth Green**, *Ecofeminism and Theology - Ökofeminismus und Theologie - Ecoféminisme et Théologie*, 1994, 145 p., ISBN: 90-390-0204-5
900 BEF / 23 EURO

3 **Angela Berlis, Julie Hopkins, Hedwig Meyer-Wilmes, Caroline Vander Stichele**, *Women Churches: Networking and Reflection in the European Context - Frauenkirchen: Vernetzung und Reflexion im europäischen Kontext - Eglises de femmes: réseaux et réflections dans le contexte européen*, 1995, 215 p., ISBN: 90-390-0213-4
900 BEF / 23 EURO

4 **Ulrike Wagener, Andrea Günter**, *What Does it Mean Today to Be a Feminist Theologian? - Was bedeutet es Heute, feministische Theologin zu sein? - Etre théologienne féministe aujourd'hui: Qu'est-ce que cela veut dire?*, 1996, 192 p., ISBN: 90-390-0262-2 900 BEF / 23 EURO

5 **Elisabeth Hartlieb, Charlotte Methuen**, *Sources and Resources of Feminist Theologies*, 1997, 286 p., ISBN: 90-390-0215-0900 BEF / 23 EURO

6 **Hedwig Meyer-Wilmes, Lieve Troch, Riet Bons-Storm**, *Feminist Pespectives in Pastoral Theology - Feministische Perspektive in Pastoraltheologie - Des perspectives féministes en théologie pastorale*, 1998, 161 p., ISBN: 90-429-0675-8 900 BEF / 23 EURO

7 **Charlotte Methuen**, *Time - Utopia - Eschatology. Zeit - Utopie - Eschatologie. Temps - Utopie - Eschatologie*, 1999, 177 p., ISBN: 90-429-0775-4 900 BEF / 23 EURO

8 **Angela Berlis, Charlotte Methuen**, *Feminist Perspectives on History and Religion - Feministische Zugänge zu Geschichte und Religion - Approches féministes de l'histoire et de la religion*, 2000, 318 p., ISBN: 90-429-0903-X
900 BEF / 23 EURO

All ESWTR-Yearbooks can be ordered from Peeters Publishers,
Bondgenotenlaan 153, B-3000 Leuven
Fax: +32 16 22 85 00; e-mail: order@peeters.be

PRINTED ON PERMANENT PAPER • IMPRIME SUR PAPIER PERMANENT • GEDRUKT OP DUURZAAM PAPIER - ISO 9706

N.V. PEETERS S.A., KLEIN DALENSTRAAT 42, B-3020 HERENT